THE CENTRE FOR ENVIRONMENTAL STUDIES SERIES, Volume 2
General Editor: David Donnison

LONDON: URBAN PATTERNS, PROBLEMS, AND POLICIES

This book is the second volume in a series edited at the Centre for Environmental Studies and published on its behalf by Sage Publications Inc. The series will present work in the fields of planning, and urban and regional studies. The Centre is an independent research foundation charged with the furtherance and dissemination of research in these fields. Further information about this series and the Centre's work can be obtained from the General Editor.

Authors

DAVID DONNISON, *Director, Centre for Environmental Studies*

DAVID EVERSLEY, *Centre for Environmental Studies: formerly Chief Strategic Planner, Greater London Council*

BARBARA ADAMS, *Department of the Environment and Centre for Environmental Studies*

NICHOLAS DEAKIN, *Head of Social Research, Department of Planning and Transportation, Greater London Council, formerly University of Sussex*

CHRISTOPHER FOSTER, *Director, Centre for Urban Economics, London School of Economics*

RUTH GLASS, *Director, Centre for Urban Studies, University College, London*

MICHAEL HARLOE, *Centre for Environmental Studies*

MARGARET HARRIS, *Department of Planning and Transportation, Greater London Council*

RUTH ISSACHAROFF, *Joint Unit for Planning Research, University College, London*

RICHARD KIRWAN, *Centre for Environmental Studies*

ALAN LITTLE, *Community Relations Commission, formerly Director of Research, Inner London Education Authority*

GRAHAM LOMAS, *General Secretary, London Council for Social Service, formerly Greater London Council*

CHRISTINE MABEY, *Research and Statistics Group, Inner London Education Authority*

RICHARD MINNS, *Centre for Environmental Studies*

JOHN PARKER, *Department of Planning and Transportation, Greater London Council*

RAY RICHARDSON, *Centre for Urban Economics, London School of Economics*

CLARE UNGERSON, *Centre for Environmental Studies*

PETER WILLMOTT, *Co-Director, Institute of Community Studies, London, and Visiting Professor, University College, London*

MICHAEL YOUNG, *Director, Institute of Community Studies, London*

London: Urban Patterns, Problems, and Policies

Centre for Environmental Studies Series
Volume 2

Edited by
DAVID DONNISON
and
DAVID EVERSLEY

SAGE PUBLICATIONS
Beverly Hills, California

For Information Address:
SAGE PUBLICATIONS, INC.
275 South Beverly Drive
Beverly Hills, California 90212

Printed in Great Britain

International Standard Book Number 0-8039-0270-0

Library of Congress Catalog Card No. No. 73-80440

First Printing

Preface

It was the preparation of the Development Plan for Greater London and the debate it provoked which prompted the Greater London Council's Chief Strategic Planner and the Director of the Centre for Environmental Studies to convene at the Centre the series of seminars which produced the papers in this book. The group they assembled came from the Greater London Council, the Inner London Education Authority, the London School of Economics, the Centre for Urban Studies, the Institute of Community Studies and CES. Others, from community action groups, from Bedford College, Brunel University and the National Institute for Social Work Training, came to some of their meetings. John Parker, one of the GLC's research staff who was spending a year at the Centre as a CES Fellow, acted as secretary to the seminar and played a major part in editing this book.

Participants in the seminar were not asked to formulate general policies for London: many of them were already contributing elsewhere in various ways to the preparation, discussion, or amendment of the Development Plan. Neither were they asked to do new research: most were already doing as much as they could handle. They aimed instead to draw on past research and on work already in hand to examine various aspects of London's development, to gain a clearer understanding of the policy makers' problems, and to learn from each other. At an interim stage, some of their work was discussed in the sociology section at the British Association meeting in 1971. In July 1972, all but one of the papers in this book were discussed at a conference of research workers, planners, administrators, community workers and politicians organized by CES.

These papers do not attempt to cover the whole range of urban problems and policies. Little or nothing is said about transport and communications, the market for land, health and medical care, or the redistribution of income through taxes and social security schemes. Too little is said, because too little is known, about the interactions between those aspects of urban structure which have been studied, and about the relationships between the development of London and the development of the rest of the country. Results of the 1971 Census, not yet available when these papers went to press, will soon throw fresh light on many of the problems they discuss.

In an opening chapter David Eversley sets the scene by posing many of the problems which confront those planning for London. In discussing these problems he shows that planners and policy makers are extending their functions and seeking new relationships with the public in their attempts to adopt a more comprehensive approach to their work.

Although the chapters that follow were not intended to reach general conclusions about policy, their arguments and findings have many practical implications. The slow but massive evolution of the industrial structure of London and the consequent changes in workers' opportunities are examined by Lomas, Foster and Richardson who show how perceptive and cautious planners should be about modifying these trends. Only by understanding them and turning them to our advantage can we solve some of the problems which arise in the housing market, the schools and elsewhere. Kirwan shows how the financial procedures and powers of government may exacerbate inequities between inner and outer parts of the city and distort the allocation of resources between different government programmes. Harris shows that we should distinguish more clearly between the different meanings of terms such as 'social polarization', often used in a loose and alarmist way, and monitor the the evolution of London's social structure more carefully. Willmott's and Young's analysis of the economic and geographical basis of this social structure suggests that the massive redevelopment of dockland now envisaged offers the biggest opportunity London has ever had for modifying it. Deakin and Ungerson examine the meaning of 'ghetto', another term often used in loose and alarmist ways, and go on to consider whether ethnic ghettos are forming in London: their discussion has many implications for policies in housing, race relations and other fields. Parker summarizes some of the lessons to be learnt from studies of slum clearance and rehousing. Little and Mabey suggest that the social composition of pupils in London primary schools has less effect on their attainment than many people have hoped or feared—less effect than the social composition and character of the neighbourhoods in which they live. Two chapters on housing follow where Harloe, Issacharoff, Minns and Adams explore the steps taken to help people now confined to poorer parts of Inner London, and show why these policies have often had limited success. They imply that many more of those who are crowded into inner areas should be enabled to move out. Donnison argues that we should find better ways of combining 'micropolitical' and administrative initiatives if we are to do justice to deprived groups, and suggests how that might be achieved. In a concluding chapter, prepared after the conference which was held on the other papers, Ruth Glass reflects on some of London's problems and considers the contribution which research can make to their clarification.

The book deals with four more general themes. The first is the economic and social structure of London—its basic industries and its incomes, its communications and housing, the educational, retailing and other services which must be located within reach of people's homes—and hence with important but ill-defined notions of 'social mix', 'equilibrium' and 'polarization'. The authors were well aware that their research, derived from different disciplines and directed to different problems, throws too little light on the interaction between different elements of this structure.

Central to the second theme were the opportunities which London's economy affords people: the jobs, earnings, housing standards, educational levels and living conditions they attain. That led to consideration of who exactly constitutes the population of London—those who live, or work, or come for holidays there? those there now, or in future?—and to critical analysis of concepts such as 'opportunity' and 'choice'. Judgements about economic and social structures depend upon the impact they make on people. Considered in isolation, terms like 'social mix' are neutral: they acquire values as their effects on human relations, political rights, housing opportunities, educational attainment and so on begin to be understood.

Although no more than a start is made upon it, the third theme of this book is government—planning and decision making procedures, politics and power. The organization, boundaries, resources and functions of governments determine the ways in which urban problems are formulated, and the criteria for their solution. If planning institutions and procedures are not treated as being themselves researchable and plannable, students of urban problems would become mere servants of the regimes in which they operate.

A fourth theme running through the book is its concern, not only with totals, averages and rates of growth, but always with distributions—distributions of jobs, incomes, living conditions, opportunities and rights among different kinds of people: rich and poor, old and young, black and white, men and women, Inner and Outer London residents and so on. The authors concentrated particularly on those at the bottom of these distributions. If that concern sometimes led them to underemphasize the extent to which the opportunities of the poor depend on the behaviour of middle and upper income groups, it is at least no mere idiosyncracy of research workers. Whether by personal choice or simply from electoral necessity, politicians of all parties who try to cope with urban problems recognize that they are dealing essentially with poverty, inequality and injustice.

Some of the essential chapters in this book, and much of the evidence used in all of them, came from staff of the GLC and the ILEA who were allowed to publish their findings and engage in controversy (even with each other) as freely as the academics—subject to the usual warning that the authors, not their employers, are responsible for the views expressed. If other research groups in central and local government follow this example, it will help them to secure good research workers, to test their findings more thoroughly before policies are based upon them, and to give university research workers a keener interest in the policy makers' problems and a better grasp of the issues at stake. The Centre for Environmental Studies hopes to bring academic and official research workers together for similar seminars in future.

If such collaboration is to be fruitful, policy makers and research workers each need a clearer understanding of the others' work and the world in which it is done.

Research workers have to define their problems ever more precisely if they are to find conclusive solutions to them. They are as concerned with questions of value as with matters of fact, but they must distinguish very clearly between fact and value. They cannot be sure about their findings till they have been published and exposed to the sharpest criticisms their colleagues can focus upon them. Although research workers may extend our general understanding of urban problems in many directions, they can present firm conclusions about very few things—most of which tend to be negative.

Policy makers, by contrast, have to decide what to do and how to get it done. Thus they must constantly reach firm conclusions about all sorts of things, based on guesswork about many ill-defined or unknown factors. Value judgements, the stuff of politics, pervade their work. They are cautious about publishing the evidence and arguments for their actions and usually do their best to achieve consensus and avoid criticism.

The different demands of scholarship and policy making must be understood if people trained in these divergent traditions are to collaborate productively. If research workers are to present authoritative conclusions they must confine themselves to carefully specified questions which may seem frustratingly narrow or abstract to policy makers. Some of the chapters in this book make that sort of contribution. But policy makers are also entitled to ask research workers what should be done. That question, calling for an assertion of value judgements and guesses about many unknown factors, is not strictly a researchable one. If they are willing to answer such questions (and some chapters in this book attempt to do so), research workers are not presenting authoritative conclusions but drawing on their general experience as scholars or scientists and mixing it with their values, just like others who participate in debates about policy. The outcome is not conclusive or scientifically authoritative, but it may nevertheless be interesting.

1973   *David Donnison*

Contents

Chapter One

Problems of Social Planning in Inner London

DAVID EVERSLEY[1]

Introduction

This volume largely presents the findings of research workers who, in one capacity or another, have contributed to the large task of helping us to understand the nature of the big city and its problems. This introductory chapter is not a piece of research, though it must draw heavily on the findings of others. It is intended rather as a scene-setting exercise. It tries to place the individual problems treated in this volume in the totality of the London environment. It starts with some definitions which may in themselves help to show what social planning is about. It tries to show examples of the inter-dependence of various forms of governmental activity in shaping the lives of people as well as the quality of the environmental framework, in the widest sense, in which these lives are lived. It shows the limitations which governmental activities necessarily recognize, especially the need to leave as much as possible to the free choice of individuals. The object of government is not to create

[1] The author is indebted to many friends for helpful suggestions during the writing of this chapter. The main debt is to David Donnison, not only for arranging the seminar, but for his pertinent criticism of the earlier drafts. Thanks are also due to Susan L. Garrett for her help in the early stages.

an ideal society according to some theoretical notions, but to interfere with individual choices only where the unrestricted licence to do as one pleases limits the choices and enjoyment of life of others. This much has at least been common ground among reformers and legislators for a long time; the fourth chapter of John Stuart Mill's *On Liberty* said it all, more than a century ago.

The chapter is designed also to show that, apart from this general constraint (which we need not consider much further), there is also the limit of action for any government, which is the result of adopting a mixed economy: that is, where authority reserves to itself only a part of the community's investment decisions, and controls a good deal less than half of all expenditure. Private enterprise, from giant industrial complexes to the operations of a one-man business, while subject to regulation, plays a decisive part in determining the nature of our society and the living standards of individuals. And the individual himself, in making choices in the composition of expenditure, helps to determine the nature of the market for goods and services, though not totally freely where competition is limited, and in making choices about where and how he will live, what he will buy, and what he will do with his free time, he is contributing to the total activity within the community which must, by any definition of objectives in a free society, determine the actions of government.

We shall show many, though not all, of the imperfections from which our urban society suffers, drawing particularly on the experience of London. We shall examine the remedies which have been proposed (and in many cases operated for a quarter of a century) and demonstrate that none of them is perfect: not only is there no single and simple solution to any or all of our problems, but each of the remedies advocated, or tried in practice, is seen to have adverse effects for some while helping others. Nor can such a conflict nowadays be resolved by a simple appeal to Bentham's felicific calculus. We recognize today that we have long passed out of those crude ages when thousands might be sacrificed so that millions might live. We are not at war. We pretend, at least, that ours is a civilized society. Therefore we cannot appeal to the advantage gained by a hundred thousand motorists from a new road when it can only be built by destroying a community, even if it consists only of a few hundred people. Nor, on the other hand, can we allow the aesthetic prejudices of a tiny minority stand in the way of improvement which will benefit a great many disadvantaged people. Again all this is not new: Henry Steele Commager's *Majority Rule and Minority Rights* was published nearly thirty years ago, in time of war, and we have not escaped from the basic dilemma that a democracy presents: no rights are absolute, no veto is absolute, the sovereignty of the people has little meaning at the decision making level in a complex society. Therefore today the answers to the problems of big cities are not magnificent and easily understood gestures: government is a question of compromise,[1] of compensation for those injured in the process of change. It is a question of consultation, of involving communities even at street level in the process of government. 'Consensus politics' is a dirty word: it is a way of keeping the majority of the community content because they have got what they wanted, while the weakest suffer, no party espousing their cause.

Thus the task of the urban planner in the widest sense is less grandiose than that of the builders of Florence or Haussmann in Paris under Napoleon III: it needs more understanding, more patience, more research. He will suffer and be defeated, he will not have the freedom to right wrongs at a stroke.

Thus this chapter will offer no clear solutions. It will show both the limitations of simple political prescriptions, and the even greater limitations of academic research as a royal road to Utopia. The author, having spent most of his life as an academic teacher and researcher in the field of urban history, population and regional planning, was plunged, three years before this chapter was written, into the task of helping to devise strategic planning policies for London. In a way, the introduction is an admission that the academic in his arrogance and ignorance tends to dismiss the needs of the administrator in government: to get on with the job, not to wait for ever until the social scientists reach a consensus about the needs of

---

[1] For a good assessment of this kind of necessary compromise, see LOMAS, G. M., 'Urban planning and social welfare,' in ed. LOMAS, *Social Aspects of Urban Development* (London: National Council for Social Service, 1966, p. 76), where he expresses great pessimism about the outcome of such planning.

urban communities or the best way to deal with ghettos and de-segregation. On the other hand, we can also show that research has shed a great deal of light on the problems of government: and this volume has arisen out of a concentrated attempt to bring together those with academic research experience and those with the day-to-day responsibility to make the city work. If there is any message from the seminar which gave rise to these papers, it is that such collaboration must increase: to bend the mind of the 'pure' social scientist more effectively towards a practical solution to the real world's problems, and to induce the administrator to listen more carefully to what the researcher has to say.

It will be obvious that the author of this introduction some-times disagrees with the research findings of his colleagues. He has often advised his political masters to act on intuitions and hunches, to introduce policies as prophylactics against dangers as yet only dimly seen. For this he naturally earned the op-probium of the intellectual purists. But when the last 'hard' facts are ten years out of date, one cannot risk possible disasters in the ten years ahead simply because not every assertion in a policy document is historically proven. Equally of course he incurs the censure of those whose main urge is to do something, preferably before the next election, and who are unwilling to wait until the next leisurely (and probably inconclusive) re-search project is presented in the form of a report only partly intelligible to a layman.

Thus there are huge gaps to be bridged in all directions. This first chapter seeks to identify just some of the difficulties, not to draw conclusions or to take issue with the research papers in the main body of the volume.

What is Social Planning?

Social planning,[1] in this essay, means the total effort by all

---

[1] There are so many definitions of 'social planning' in American and British literature that it is impossible to give even an abbreviated account here. It will be obvious that I have drawn on many of these without adopting any one of them. Among useful British examples are:
CHERRY, G. E., *Town Planning in its Social Context* (London: Hill, 1970) ch. 4, especially pp. 122, ff. and
BROADY, MAURICE, *Planning for People* (London: Bedford Square

agencies to achieve changes in the physical environment, and in the economic and social structure which exists within that environment, in pursuit of improvements in the living standards of an urban population. This form of planning is an entirely different activity from traditional physical planning which was mainly concerned with the tangible shortcomings of the urban environment, consisting of such activities as slum clearance, road improvements and the creation of open spaces. Social planning is still concerned with the quality of the housing stock, with safety and amenity and with environmental quality in the form of the control of air and water pollution. But it is also concerned with health and education in the wider sense, with community relations, with real incomes and with problems of disadvantaged groups in society. In other words, social planning also covers not only the whole range of services which local authorities provide within their area but also the many aspects of public and private activity which are not directly under the control of local government at all. Inasmuch as it concerns itself with employment structure, the quality of social services and benefits and the actions of individuals outside the framework of statutory services, to cite just a few examples, social planning becomes a matter of attempting to influence events rather than to control them. Often it is a matter of advice, advocacy or example rather than of executive action.[1]

The term has, as yet, no accepted definition in British

Press, 1968) especially ch. 5, pp. 70 ff. (but neither of these really go beyond the idea that 'social planning' is planning with social problems, social services, human needs, participation, etc. in mind).

Among American authorities are:

MAYER, ROBERT, *Social Planning and Social Change* (New York: Prentice-Hall, 1972), KAHN, A. J., *Theory and Practice of Social Planning* (New York: Russell Sage Foundation 1969) and

GANS, H. J., *People and Plans* (New York: Basic Books, 1968) especially ch. 7 'Memorandum on Social Planning', p. 103 ff.

For an authoritative British view of what social planning means in official terms, see Wilfred Burns, 'Social Planning', paper presented to an SSRC Seminar on 'Social Research and Planning', 5 May 1971.

See also 'Action Research in Social Planning', Patrick Quinn, Elliott Stern, Tavistock Institute, 1971 ref. HRC 572, paper presented to same SSRC Seminar on 5 May 1971.

[1] cf. *Greater London Development Plan: Statement Revisions*, February 1972, especially Section 2, pp. 3–8.

administrative language. No authority sets out to undertake social planning as such.[1] As an art, it is being developed pragmatically in a situation in which the limitations of purely physical re-arrangements of the environment are seen to be insufficient for the attainment of objectives which are themselves not yet clearly formulated. In the absence of any definition of what constitutes a desirable form of society, social planning tends to express its aims principally in terms of the identification of a range of manifestations of adverse social and economic conditions: poverty, community friction, delinquency, physical and mental ill-health, loneliness and so on. Beyond this therapeutic approach, social planning also tries to understand the cause of these conditions and, if possible, to prevent them arising. This often involves attempts to redistribute income, or, by means of physical planning of communities, to create a framework in which better relationships can develop. Social planning also involves the design of monitoring systems which measure the health of a society, i.e. the development of social indicators which are not themselves immediately connected with the executive content of planning. Thus, the number of houses built in a year is a measure of planning performance, but the number of homeless, of people evicted from their tenancies, and the proportion of households sharing a dwelling, are indicators of inadequacy.

In other words, social planning is really a form of urban management. Its objectives are social, its methods avowedly political (i.e. it aims at redistributing goods, services and amenities, that is, real incomes, between different sections of society).

It does not replace executive action: it precedes it. Social planning is strategic planning: long-term forward thinking about the nature of the city and the society it contains. Social planning neither prophesies nor lays down long-term rigid prescriptions for executive management. Instead, it identifies problems, researches into their causes, puts forward possible options to be chosen by those who are democratically elected to

---

[1] One of the recommendations of the Seebohm Committee was for the provision of social research and planning, within the reorganized Social Services Departments. cf. *Report of the Committee on Local Authority and Allied Personal Social Services* (London: H.M.S.O.) especially Chapter XV, 'Research', pp. 142–6, and para. 152, pp. 47–8.

exercise control over policies, and, once an option is chosen, helps the executive machinery to devise actions to attain the objective. Where there is no direct control over the executive agency, social planning presents a case to those who have it in their power to contribute to these objectives: be it central government, lower-tier local authorities or private agencies.

Social planning, by definition, does not recognize administrative boundaries or statutory divisions of functions: therefore it deals with the London problem in a regional, national and international context, and it is less concerned with the question of which government or local authority department regards itself as being responsible for a particular activity: to adjust such demarcation lines in the interests of the attainment of policy objectives is the task of the administrator.

Social planning is an activity which involves many forms of skill: it is not the prerogative of one type of specialist, or any specialist at all. There are no schools of social planning. A great deal of the work therefore consists in identifying the expertise required to help solve a particular problem: to bring together practitioners from many fields; to mobilize existing information; to commission research in fields where it may yield usable results within the time available before decisions must be taken; and to evaluate such research in terms of policy making (often only to rule out certain courses of action as impracticable). Such work is not a substitute for policy making as such: this remains the prerogative of elected politicians. But these politicians themselves are also social planners, in the sense that the decisions they make to allocate resources, to enforce prohibitions and to encourage activities by subsidies, are themselves a part of the total process. If there is such a recognizable person as a social planner, a professional in the service of the authority, whether in a planning department or elsewhere in the corporate management process, it is as principal adviser to the elected representatives on such matters as have a bearing on the future of the city. But a moment's reflection shows that there is very little that is not a part of such a comprehensive activity. One might say that there are certain routine functions of government which can be done well or badly, but which are only marginally concerned with the city and its environment. However, they are essential to its good functioning: the public health services, the supply of water and the disposal of waste, the fire and ambulance services, the maintenance of roads and parks, the collection of rates and keeping of accounts and many others. That these activities must be brought into the total picture of corporate management is indisputable. If this chapter is mostly concerned with crucial questions like housing, employment, incomes and social structure, it is because it is in these fields that the greatest urban failures lie, that the greatest political decisions will have to be taken, that most of the new capital investment must go, and where the complex process of social planning is best demonstrated as an interaction between central and local governments, private agencies and the community itself.

To a large extent, such confident assertions belie the real state of affairs. Though a good deal of progress has been made in London towards identifying the social planning process, and towards corporate management, the obstacles are still formidable. Departmental jealousies survive in central as well as in local government, whatever administrative amalgamations take place. There are inter-professional rivalries. There is natural antagonism between the experienced official and the academic researcher. In the social sciences in general, and in urban sociology in particular apart from the recent origins of the subjects, their lack of agreed scientific methods, and their susceptibility to value judgements and distortions by political ideology, there is the additional disadvantage that in-fighting between different schools of thought is an almost obligatory activity. To agree with another researcher working in the same field is almost proof of lack of originality; to work for a practical policy objective is considered second-class work, and to be asked to prove or disprove a hypothesis on which existing policies are based is beneath anyone's dignity.

And yet the scope is there. Tentative as our beginnings in London are, the contents of the chapters which follow must be seen as demonstrating that there is a contribution to social planning which the social scientist can make. As so often happens in our British system of pragmatism, far-reaching decisions are taken long before any systematic foundations have been laid. Thus the political consensus that London shall not be 'a city only of the rich and the poor', was arrived at long before any statistician had defined what was meant by rich and poor, before anybody had thought of finding six definitions of 'social polarization' and long before anybody had started any empirical investigations into the possible disadvantages that might result if large tracts of a metropolitan area were inhabited solely by people dependent on public subsidies for their survival —if indeed such tracts existed. The chapters on social polarization and educational policies illustrate the difficulties.

Similarly, the alarm about London incomes dropping as compared with the rest of the region was raised before the existence of the phenomenon was proved. Warnings were uttered against the over-rapid run-down of both population and manufacturing industry (and to some extent acted upon) before any researcher had recognized that there might be problems, let alone produced results to show whether or not such fears might be justified.

Thus, social planning is a new concept, ill-defined, not yet recognized administratively or professionally. In the present state of organization and professional activities, including research, it may never come about. The reader must make up his mind whether the London Seminar proved the viability of such a concept, or not.

The Scope of Social Planning

This chapter will attempt to identify some of the issues which have been observed in London at the beginning of the 1970s. In 1969, a first version of the Greater London Development Plan was published, which was still largely oriented towards the physical planning solutions which stemmed from the post-war traditions of urban improvement. By 1972, a new version of the Plan incorporated an explicit set of socio-economic objectives and recognized that a programme of housing, roads, open spaces and shopping centres had no justification in itself without a clear-cut set of objectives in terms of the well-being of individuals, and that a whole range of policies not primarily dependent on land use planning and construction was needed to supplement the basic investment in the built environment.[1]

We shall attempt to illustrate the kind of approaches which are needed to achieve a corporate form of government, in part

---

[1] *G.L.D.P.: Statement Revisions*, February 1972.

by showing the limitations of a purely sectional approach to the problems of urban populations, to what is in effect a situation of multiple deprivation and disadvantage. At the same time, it can be shown that the social planning approach to the problems of London, even if it is taken in a very broad sweep, can only make sense if it is seen as part of a much wider national concern with the distribution of incomes and wealth and with those policies of central and local government which effectively counteract market forces. These tend to perpetuate some of the most distressing aspects of modern urban life; yet they can, with proper guidance, be harnessed to play a significant part in the improvement of urban conditions. The Greater London Council's office location and floorspace allocation policies are designed to achieve this sort of objective.[1] In a mixed economy the harnessing of market forces (especially in terms of private investment decisions) to the social needs of the community is an essential ingredient of urban survival, let alone improvement.

Inner London

The term 'Inner London' is used loosely in this chapter and is not to be taken as being synonymous with the old LCC area, nor with the GLC 'Group A' Boroughs (those which were built up mainly before 1920), though the latter definition is closer to a working concept. The problem is that we need a more sophisticated social typology than any so far developed before we can use any single set of indices to produce a more clear-cut definition. 'Inner London' sometimes has connotations of high-density settlement, low rateable values, high proportions of people in rented accommodation and so on. But the point is that there are also many areas *outside* this old (physical) core which show all the characteristics of decline, obsolescence and clustering of disadvantaged people, and there are also many parts *inside* the core where incomes are high and the environment is continuously improving.

Constraints

Since this chapter is concerned not merely with an analysis of social conditions, but with practical planning policies, it is as

---

[1] cf. GLC, *Council Minutes*, 8 February 1972, pp. 75–80.

well to describe clearly the assumptions which underlie social planning, or, for that matter, any effective form of national or local government. We may take some of these for granted: efficiency, honesty, openness, technical competence. But there are constraints, less well understood, which narrow down the efficacy of government and the social planning process in particular. The clear recognition of these limitations is an essential part of the task of the planner. He must be able to say where the objectives of policies can still be obtained within the existing framework, and where more radical legislation or administrative practice may be needed. It is the awareness of the existence of constraints which one hopes will lead to a consideration of the whole socio-political framework of planning today as well as of particular problems and their solutions. The planner in the public service cannot identify his critical issues unless he does so within this framework, and not as if he were operating in an ideal world where information and good intentions are enough to produce viable solutions.

The Planner in his Institutional Framework

What follows here is written about the planner in the widest sense. Most of what is said is probably true of all other specialists in the total field of social planning, which includes, as later chapters indicate, not only others concerned with the physical environment in one form or another, but also educationists, treasurers and others. But we may well use the example of the professional officer who is, at present, usually located in a planning or transportation department, in a city engineer's and surveyor's office, in a housing department, or with a city architect, to illustrate the constraints which face so many engaged in the total process of government.

The planner is, in theory, a professional worker qualified usually in one of the skills which traditionally figure largely in what might loosely be termed environmental improvement, ranging from architecture and civil engineering to landscape design and surveying. In other words, the planner is the person trained to provide technically feasible solutions to defined problems. He is not trained to be concerned with the question of whether any particular solution is the one which is preferred by those for whom it is designed, nor with the social consequences of his activities. He is not even trained to analyse the situation in terms of individual needs or preferences, but in terms of accepted canons for norms of collective welfare.

Social planning and indeed the whole process of government, should involve the participation of those for whom the city is designed as a place to live in and work in, to ensure that there is some identity between the aspirations of the community and the planner's objective. However, for this there is not only little training for any public servant, but the institutional framework virtually excludes the possibility of anything but the most perfunctory publicity and consultations with organized groups.

Participation is yet to be defined. We know that it does not mean holding long public enquiries; it does not mean listening only to the submissions of self-appointed interest groups of one sort or another; it does not mean opinion surveys or referenda. All these are involved, yet they do not make planning a popular process.[1]

The problem of participation is therefore extremely complex. Do we merely provide the opportunities for people to voice their opinions, and hope that the process will encourage more people to become actively involved, or do we run the risk of perpetuating a situation where the greatest opportunities are given to the people who are already activists in their own cause? In other words, we begin the consideration of the problem in a climate where the identification of needs, and the choices of options to deal with these needs, is still constrained by a very limited system of popular involvement.

The Administrator's Ideology

The administrator's own ideology is only partially tempered by the dictates of the political system within which he operates. In so far as the pressures which are brought on him proceed so clearly from identifiable lobbies, he will be forced to rely on

---

[1] For a refreshingly practical American definition of what is involved in popular participation in real planning situations, see 'Citizen participation as a positive force', in United States, Department of Transportation, Environment and Urban Systems, *Metropolitan Transportation Seminars*, Washington D.C., 1971.

his own inner resources—firstly his technical competence which in itself constitutes an ideology (in that it creates a belief that there is, given the will and the resources, a technical solution to every problem); secondly, in so far as he has ideal social concepts, these themselves will be heavily influenced by his professional training, which leads him towards a preference for orderliness, cleanliness, speed, for light and for smooth functioning.[1] Whether or not such ideologies represent the value and aspirations of the community at large, the planner is not required to investigate. Therefore the planning process necessarily acquires its own internal momentum, which, the more complex and efficient it becomes in a technical sense, will tend to widen the gap between those whose problems we are concerned with, and those who are charged with the execution of the urban improvement and renewal process.[1]

One additional great difficulty is that those activities which we subsume under the heading of social planning by and large do not figure in any system of popular ideology. On a large number of subjects, many people, even those with little education, have strong opinions which collectively may be termed ideologies. Sometimes they overlap with our own preoccupations, e.g., bad housing, poor educational facilities, danger on the roads. Sometimes they are merely negative manifestations of something they do not understand but dislike because of the immediate consequence for them (a new road scheme, redevelopment, the siting of an airport). But over a large range of topics which we must discuss here, people do not form opinions, not even of the kind which are based not on facts but on prejudice. 'Planning', by and large, is a dirty word, and the planner in the popular image is a bowler-hatted chap with a briefcase who tells old people to get out of their life-long homes, or a man sitting on a bulldozer, or a bow-tied architect dreaming of mile-high towers.

The questions we are concerned with here certainly touch on the lives of individuals, and may come up against resentment and prejudice, but they usually do not form part of a consistent

---

[1] For a discussion of planning ideologies, cf. EVERSLEY, D. E. C., 'New horizons for planners', Town and Country Planning Summer School, Southampton, 1971.

system. Blacks are all right but we don't want them in our block. We don't want unemployment but some of these dockers are only getting what they deserve. People should be taxed so that they couldn't live in big houses and drive Rolls-Royces, but I like my neighbourhood to have a bit of 'class' myself. Everyone should have a decent house, but I don't suppose there is much you can do about dossers and meths drinkers and tinkers and such like.

If, therefore, we are to have a system of participation where the planner or administrator is in constant touch with those whom his planning most concerns, education will have to affect both sides. We are a long way from an identity between planner and planned, or even effective collaboration.

London Government

It is not the purpose of this introductory chapter to describe in detail the constraints which are imposed by the anomalies of the 1963 London Government Act. This has been done elsewhere.[1] However, it needs to be said straight away that, although the Greater London Council is in theory the Strategic Planning Authority, the provisions of the Act are such that the London Boroughs can to a large extent defeat the intentions of the GLC. At the time when these proposals were passed into law, strategic planning still meant overall land use allocation, a road system, and a few specific features like strategic shopping centres, the designation of conservation or action areas (the distinction is artificial) and other two-dimensional features of the 'Metropolitan Structure Map'. The kind of problems raised here were not then thought of, and it is no wonder that the present division of duties and powers scarcely meets modern requirements.

Hence the frequent demands for a new system of government, perhaps of the kind which the 1972 Act introduced for the country as a whole. But apart from the shortcomings of that piece of legislation, especially in respect of the problems

---

[1] See SELF, PETER, *Metropolitan Planning*, Greater London Papers, no. 14, 1971 and ROBSON, WILLIAM A., *The Heart of Greater London*, Greater London Papers, no. 9, 1965. (London School of Economics and Political Science.)

discussed here, it is useless to blame the GLC/Borough division of responsibility for the fact that we have no system of social planning. As has already been said, social planning would result from an overall view which could not recognize geographical or administrative boundaries, or divisions of functions between agencies. The first task is therefore to put forward a viable procedure designed to attain identified objectives: when this has been done (and it can only be done by the quasi-regional, strategic authority), powers to implement such planning should not be too difficult to obtain. It is lack of ideas, rather than powers, that form the most formidable set of constraints in this field.

In addition to the Boroughs, the role of the central government is crucial. But quite apart from the question of capital and revenue, it is the social policies of the central governments which play a decisive part in ensuring (or failing to ensure) minimal living standards for people in London. The whole range of services and cash benefits which we describe loosely as the Welfare State, however inadequate in some respects, still provides the basis of all effective redistribution of incomes and furnishes a floor of personal standards below which no individual or household should fall. How far the present system accomplishes this aim is beyond the scope of this paper. What is certain is that if the apparatus of pensions and allowances, supplementary benefits and rebates, health and educational services which makes up such a large part of the real incomes of the lowest income groups is to play an adequate part in social planning, then the local authority can only act as a pressure group on behalf of its residents: it cannot of itself remedy the deficiencies of the system.[1]

A special case is provided by education. It need hardly be stressed that the education services play a major role in the achievement of social objectives within the community. The Inner London Education Authority is not even theoretically under the control of the Greater London Council, and thus its objectives may still in some cases differ from those of the corporate management process which undertakes the overall planning

---

[1] EVERSLEY, D. E. C., 'Urban problems in Britain today', *GLC: Quarterly Bulletin of the Intelligence Unit*, no. 19, June 1972.

of London. Outside Inner London, the education committees of individual boroughs are not even at one remove under the control of the metropolitan planning body, and any identity of objectives with those of the central authority would be the result of central government pressures rather than purposeful and co-ordinated planning.

Then there is the whole range of urban provision furnished by the statutory undertakers, public corporations and quasi-public agencies, on whom a great deal of responsibility rests for maintaining a high standard of service, amenity and environmental improvement but who, legally, are not susceptible to the influence of the planning authority. They include gas and electricity undertakings, the railways, the Port of London Authority, the hospital boards, the Department of the Environment in its role as custodian of parks and public buildings and many others. It may be surmised that on the whole such bodies conduct themselves in a responsible manner, according to the objectives which they themselves have been set by the statutes under which they operate: but of course such objectives may be concerned with profit maximization, with the provision of services for the rest of the country, or for groups in society to which planning authority would not wish to accord the greatest priority. Thus there are potential sources of conflict here which in practice often make rational resource and land use planning, let alone social planning, extremely difficult.

The Source of Finance for Investment and Revenue

For the public sector to undertake a much larger share of the total investment in the environment needed to renew the outworn social capital of London would probably mean not only very much higher rates of national and local taxation but also the concentration on Inner London of a much larger share of the total amount available for investment in the country as a whole, and a diversion away from other sectors of public enterprise of funds for the purpose of helping London.[1]

As has been argued elsewhere[2] it is unlikely that in future our

---

[1] For a fuller discussion of this whole question, see ch. 4, pp. 119–155.
[2] EVERSLEY, D. E. C., 'Old cities, falling populations and rising costs', *Quarterly Bulletin of the Intelligence Unit, GLC*, no. 18, March 1972.

large cities will be able to bear, from their own financial resources as represented by property values, the larger portion of
the burdens which arise from maintaining even minimal
standards of public service. Even if the basis of local taxation
were changed to the incomes of residents rather than rates on
houses, or to the turnover of enterprises, or non-residents were
made to contribute, it is unlikely that any great improvements
could come about, given the tendency of some of these alternative bases to decline relative to the costs incurred. (Residents'
incomes, output of manufacturing industry.)

It follows that social planning within the urban framework
has to take place on the basis of massive subventions, whether
on a regional or national basis, to maintain and improve the
infrastructure. So far, the proportion of personal incomes of
London residents which are furnished by central government in
the form of social benefits, is still very low (6.8 per cent in 1971,
compared with a national average of 8.8 per cent)[1] but the
proportion in Inner London is much higher and it will rise over
time if current trends continue. Much clearer, however, is the
reliance of the large urban areas on central government funds
for meeting the deficit on their housing accounts, the cost of
roads and railways or rapid transit systems, and other large
engineering works required to keep the urban economy functioning. We shall have to tackle growing poverty in the inner
cities in any case, but the financing of necessary expenditure in
those areas is a separate question.

Technical Constraints: the Problem of Time-scale

All planning in an urban context is exposed to an inescapable
dilemma of time-scale. At the beginning of the planning process lies the inadequacy of the existing social fabric, often created a century ago. This inadequacy is measured in terms of the
needs of the present-day population. Now the more affluent
part of this population does not, by and large, suffer from the
inadequacies of the environment: it can make sure that it
chooses homes, workplaces and amenities which conform to its

---

[1] Department of Employment, *Family Expenditure Survey 1971*, (London:
H.M.S.O., 1972) p. 115, Table 57.

own expectations. To this extent the public effort is quite largely geared to the need to bring the most disadvantaged part of the population up to standards which became accepted some years back. It follows that, if standards and aspirations continue to rise, much of what is created today will shortly be inadequate again for very large parts of the population.

That much has been commonplace for two decades. However, what happens when owing to a combination of general economic stagnation and an inability to promote progressive redistributions of income, the standards of public investment effort fail to measure up to the requirements of future populations? Economic growth generally means that the progressive redistribution of current incomes (in terms of benefits paid from taxes) and of future incomes (in terms of higher standards applied to the public infrastructure) can take place reasonably painlessly. This process can end, and even go into reverse, in a stagnating economy.

The choice then is between justice to the present deprived populations and a prudent eye on future standards. Past builders had no such scruples to contend with. We owe almost everything that we now cherish as a national heritage to the gross inequalities of income and wealth in the past. In 1972, a house costing five times the average of a local authority dwelling is described as a 'luxury residence' fit for a millionaire. Only a hundred years ago, such people normally built themselves mansions costing one hundred times more than a labourer's cottage. Today we regard cathedrals, palaces or even colonnaded piazzas as frivolous extravagances when we need hundreds of thousands of houses for ordinary people.

It has been suggested that the fairly expensive new office buildings, universities, airports and air terminals, hotels and so on are the equivalent of the extravagances of the past. But this is scarcely true. First of all, they generally serve great masses of people; secondly they are not, by and large, monuments to the feudal lords who built or financed them and thirdly they are much more egalitarian than past buildings: accommodation for managing directors, bishops and vice-chancellors differs only marginally from that provided for the ordinary customer or official. Even the difference between first and second class accommodation on railways is now very small.

If, in the next twenty five years, *per capita* real incomes double as they did between 1945 and 1970, some of our housing efforts of today will be seen as attempts to create new slums. But if we build today with an eye to the future, we shall condemn to-day's people to a longer life of squalor.

Thus both inflation and stagnation, growth and notions of equality, all place the planner in the role of an arbiter allocating benefits between sections of the population, and between generations.

There is a special angle to this problem for London, a city already threatened by adverse movements in population and economy. On the face of it, it is one of the richest cities on earth, with a veneer of opulence, permanence and glamorous extravagance which is envied by lesser towns. What is the planner to achieve by way of additions to this wealth? The very rich and the tourists will look after themselves, but what of the middle income groups? Can we add to our social equipment at the standards they expect? And if we cannot do so, will they stay? The famous 'housing yardstick' against which local authorities operate, is almost calculated to accentuate social divisions and to accelerate the transformation of new housing schemes into twilight areas.

Thus we face a double difficulty: we must, from today's resources, create durable items for the infrastructure which will meet the needs of people in the future who have higher real incomes; at the same time we must also be prepared for the possibility that even though the *average* may rise, the levels of real incomes of very sizeable parts of London's population will still be quite inadequate to meet the costs of living in an improved environment. It is not just a matter of making up one's mind about priorities: if we were to cater, from misplaced idealism or out of short-term political necessity, only for the lower 20 per cent of income groups, the resultant increased disparity between expectation and achievement for the other 80 per cent would probably result in an accelerated outflow of this majority from an area where their needs were not being met.

What is quite clear is that we cannot trade solely on the assets created by our forebears, though the conservation of these assets has a specific social as well as aesthetic or sentimental connotation.

Environmental Planning and People

There are other fundamental dilemmas facing the planner in present day society. There are choices to be made between rival contenders for priorities.

On one hand, the aesthetes, the conservationists, the historians, generally the 'haves', are determined to avoid rapid change, intrusion, modern contraptions that vitiate the older townscape and landscape. They may be few, but they are noisy. They will, if they can, stop airports, reservoirs, motorways, new cities, mining operations. They have a strong hold on the media.

But there are others, not so vocal, probably more numerous, and generally ill-organized: they are those who two generations ago could not have dreamt of a daily bath, or a dozen electric appliances in the house, to whom a package tour holiday in Majorca was an unattainable Utopia; a car, something to use on one's wedding day, perhaps. These are the people who need a possible extra one hundred million gallons of water a day[1] and an extra 6000 megawatts of power. They are the ones to whom the motor car is the means of liberation: the first chance to get out of their neighbourhood at a price they can afford. This is perhaps one of the greatest unsolved problems: how to balance the legitimate demands of the preservationists who feel that a beautiful and tranquil environment is the essence of civilized life in London and its surroundings, against the equally legitimate aspirations of many of the millions who live there, and to whom water, power and movement are experiences which have been dearly bought and not to be easily given up for some academic theory about what constitutes an acceptable environment.

On one hand, if London does not maintain its present attractiveness, both in the physical sense in its beauty, cleanliness and great oases of tranquillity, and in the larger sense of affording security, variety, stimulation and intellectual

---

[1] There is evidence in this connection that the need for extra water has been exaggerated, thus further raising the fears of environmentalists about drowned valleys and vitiated streams. See J. and R. REES 'Water demand forecasting and planning margins in South-East England', *Regional Studies*, **6**, no. 1, March 1972, pp. 37–48.

resources, it will cease to attract many of those who now come to visit or even live there because they prefer London to New York or Sydney. On the other hand, if all else is sacrificed for the sake of maintaining this traditional London which is such a magnet for the wealthy, and even the impecunious but aesthetic, the social problem will grow. Visitors and rich immigrants cause many other problems apart from displacing residents, they are not an unmixed blessing. And the same applies to the lush pastures of south-eastern England, the coasts and islands, and the mountain and lake scenery of the north and west.

The Failure of Traditional Policies

The Inadequacy of the Traditional Approaches

One purpose in outlining some of the problems facing us today is to demonstrate that some of the traditional approaches to social and economic questions are beginning to look inadequate. We are witnessing, in the 1970s, a reappraisal of the long accepted weapons in the armoury of legislation. We are also facing the fact that many of the simple relationships in which we believed, like that between growth and full employment, public expenditure and unemployment, no longer obtain.

Post-war planning

This, in a sense, is all the more surprising because British planning since the war has been commonly regarded as being extremely successful. We have introduced an effective system of land use planning, the Green Belts have been held, the outflow from the cities has been made an object of policy and forms part of comprehensive regional plans complete with investment proposals for housing, industry and population; five of the seven conurbations have shown net population losses between 1951 and 1971; inter-regional policies have been moderately successful, and net outflows from the development and 'grey' areas have slowed down, with investment shifting decisively away from the prosperous and congested areas in the late 1960s. There has also been a large-scale unorganized movement to planned urban growth zones around our large conurbations. The South East no longer gains by migration, but shows net losses over the past few years. 'New' new towns have been founded and old ones are flourishing. Public expenditure on goods and services and grants to persons have risen from under £6000 million (1951) to about £23 000 million at present: this means a rise from under 35 per cent of the G.N.P. to well over 40 per cent, whilst the G.N.P. itself, at constant prices, has risen by 80 per cent. Given the decline of spending on defence, expenditure in real terms on the social and environmental services has more than doubled since 1951.[1]

In 1950 there were about 50 million people in the country, and over 14 million dwellings. By 1971 there were 56 million people and about 19 million dwellings—a net gain of 6 million people and nearly 5 million dwellings. On average over 300 000 new dwellings have been constructed annually for the last twenty years. The growth of population has slowed down since the early 1960s. It is now down to less than one half of one per cent. Housing stocks are rising by $1\frac{1}{2}$ per cent per annum. There is net emigration from Britain now, and fertility is still falling. Housing subsidies in 1971–2 are running in real terms, at more than twice the rate of the early 1960s.

There may be argument about whether the distribution of wealth and income, and the incidence of taxation and social benefit on various groups, have always moved in the direction desired by egalitarian legislators. Possibly they have not, but it is not true to say that there has been *no* redistribution of real incomes through taxes and social services.[2] Even so, the fact remains that a large proportion of British people still live under housing conditions, and at living standards, well below those generally considered acceptable, and without much hope that they, or their children, will ever break out of these conditions.

Failure or Short-fall?

In 1951, nobody would have predicted, given this sort of performance, that there would still be an acute housing prob-

---

[1] cf. EVERSLEY, D. E. C., 'Urban problems in Britain today', *op. cit.* The figures are derived from the *National Income and Expenditure Blue Book* (London: H.M.S.O., 1971).

[2] cf. 'Redistribution of income through taxes and benefits in 1969', *Social Trends*, no. 3 (London: H.M.S.O., 1972) p. 96, Table 46.

lem in 1972, and that between 15 and 30 per cent of the people of this country would still be living in poverty (as defined now, not in 1951). One does not need to have more accurate figures than those currently available to prove that there is a widespread problem of delinquency, violence, bad housing, real poverty, friction within the community and educational failure. The problem, however, is not so much to find out why the existing policies have failed but rather why it is that the end results seem to have fallen so far short of what was intended, given the relative magnitude of the total effort. Has the total been inadequate, or is it that the wrong people have benefited, as has been shown to be the case in health and education?

The Search for policies

What then are we to do? London is more than a collection of manifestations of social pathology: it is also, at least potentially, a thriving economic unit performing tasks without which the national, let alone the local economy, would be impoverished beyond the stage where mere redistributive measures would provide remedies. We have pointed out that the traditional cures for urban ills have latterly shown signs of being inadequate, if not futile. It remains now to characterize in greater detail some of the problems which arise in this situation, and to see how they may be dealt with in the future.

London—Role and Problems

London's Role

We must now turn from the consideration of the framework in which the planner operates to the actual tasks which confront him in London. What is said here applies mainly in Inner London, but problems are not confined to that area, and many of the problems mentioned also occur in our other large cities.

We have to consider the significance of the regional, national and international role of London. Inner London serves, apart from its (problematical) two or two and a half million inhabitants, twenty million regional shoppers, a nation of fifty-five or sixty million people, and by the middle seventies, ten or twelve million overseas visitors. The situation is rapidly approaching where during the summer months there will, at any one time, be almost as many non-Londoners in Inner London during the day as Londoners, not to speak of the daily working population, amounting to half a million people or more in the Central area alone, travelling in from outside London.

Obviously the needs of this working and visiting population cannot simply be ignored. But a great many of the policies which have been advocated as remedies for the problems of obsolescence and poverty in Inner London do ignore the fact, problematical though it may be in many ways, that a great, and increasing, proportion of Londoners earn a living through the services which are provided for non-residents, or in undertakings in which the commuting labour force plays a leading role. Consequently, if owing to excessively parochial attitudes, conditions for visitors and non-resident workers are allowed to become very much worse, the circumstances of the residents are also likely to be aggravated.

The financial complications of this situation are great. Under existing arrangements, a large part of the corporate and individual income of London depends on the maintenance of commercial and administrative activities. Any reduction in such activities (e.g. for the sake of regional policies) will have consequences for London's economy and for the incomes of its individuals. This has already come about in the case of manufacturing industry. The complications arise because on one hand much of the income earned in the activities of the tertiary and quaternary sectors[1] accrues to people who live outside London, and profits from London-based enterprises may be paid to individuals and firms elsewhere, including other countries. Yet a reduction in activity, with its attendant reduction in investment and direct and indirect employment, can seriously weaken the economic and social fabric of a city. It is this aspect of the 'economic base' of our large cities which has so far received too little attention and has led to some rather crude prescriptions for our urban ills.

---

[1] Tertiary means services performed for individuals or firms in the area ranging from running buses to hairdressing; quarternary means services performed largely for people or institutions other than local residents: banking, finance, insurance, brokerage, etc.

Of these, the crudest of all is simply to allow an unchecked and even accelerated outflow of population and jobs from London, without regard to any of the consequences which follow for those who are left behind in the general outward rush, in the naïve hope that because in this way more 'space' is created, notably that improvements in environmental standards will accrue to the remaining population.[1]

Low Incomes

In some ways the problem of low incomes is easiest to define and identify. Although adequate statistics are still rather scarce and are not likely to be available on a comparative basis for some time, nevertheless, at least we know what we mean by low incomes, partly because a fairly uniform code of practice is developing with respect to supplementary benefits and rent rebates. We define 'low incomes' as those of households which are eligible for (though do not necessarily receive) supplementary benefits apart from their normal National Insurance entitlements, and/or rent rebates from the local authority.[2]

There are inadequacies of legislation, and certainly not all those who are entitled to allowances and concessions ask for them, or receive them. There are also households which for one reason or another are still living in sub-standard conditions

---

[1] cf. the publications of the Town and Country Planning Association, e.g. David Hall's review of the revised Greater London Development Plan, in *Town and Country Planning*, **40**, no. 4, April 1972.

[2] For the purposes of most enquiries into poverty levels, including those instigated by successive governments, the National Assistance/Supplementary Benefit eligibility rate has been habitually taken as the definitive, indeed, the 'official', dividing line. However, two studies, in particular, were based on the assumption that it is justifiable to draw the poverty line at 40 per cent above the basic scale rates, as the National Assistance Board/Supplementary Benefits Commission has always had in its power to make certain discretionary payments, and been permitted to overlook certain amounts of capital or savings. cf. ABEL-SMITH, B. and TOWNSEND, P., *The Poor and the Poorest*, Occasional Papers on Social Administration, no. 17, December 1965; and COATES, K. and SILBURN, R., *Poverty: The Forgotten Englishmen* (Harmondsworth: Penguin, 1970).

(i.e. have low *real* incomes), even though they receive a higher income than the minimum required to qualify for benefits. This may be, for example, because their housing, though cheap, is of poor standard, or adequate and beyond their means, or both inadequate and expensive. Because we still have no reliable indices of local London living costs, the figures we have are confined to money incomes. The Family Expenditure Survey only tells us that Londoners spend more on housing and fares than people elsewhere, but this information is not enough to construct a local cost of living index. Some work done at the Greater London Council,[1] however, suggests that any possible calculation of real incomes would reinforce the conclusions arrived at in this section.

The problem is quite simply this: how does one keep four people alive in London on £25.00 per week? In 1972, 27.9 per cent of all male earners in London had gross earnings of less than £30.00 per week or slightly over £25.00 net.[2] (Of all households in 1971, 25 per cent had less than £24.00 a week from all sources.)[3] It is not, therefore, a problem confined to old age pensioners. The average for all London households was much higher, nearly £40.00 per week, but the distribution of incomes is such that the average is unduly weighted by the very high salaried and self-employed incomes which are also characteristic of London, and a good deal more than half of all households had less than this average income (i.e. the median lay under the mean).

The Low-paid Workers

Why should this be so? London has, as we have said, the highest average earnings in the country, taking all earners together.

---

[1] 'Some aspects of the polarisation issue', *G.L.D.P. Inquiry Support Paper S11/113*, June 1971; and 'The development of personal incomes within the GLC area compared with the rest of the South-East region in the light of the publication of the 1970 Family Expenditure Survey figures', *G.L.D.P. Inquiry Support Paper S11/153*, November 1971.

[2] 'New Earnings Survey 1972, Part II, Analyses by region and other results', *DOE Gazette*, December 1972, p. 1156, Table 65.

[3] Department of Employment, *Family Expenditure Survey Report* 1971 p. 86, Table 35.

It is noticeable,[1] however, (a) that London's advantage has had a tendency to shrink in the last few years, (b) that the advantage is confined to the salaried groups among the men, who form a higher proportion of the workforce in London, (c) that women have a noticeably greater advantage than men, (d) that the earnings of manual men earners in Central London are actually lower than those in the rest of the region, and that the earnings of all London manual workers lie below those of the peak earnings areas of the Midlands.

London, therefore, not only has a greater than average concentration of wealthy people, but also, compared with the rest of the South East, a relatively greater concentration of people in low income groups. This is related partly to the concentration of personal service workers, and those in the employment of public authorities, including transport undertakings, and the relative immobility of these lower paid groups. Two forces are at work: as London becomes a city which is increasingly devoted to the provision of services (regionally, nationally and internationally), so the number of people in manual, unskilled and semi-skilled jobs with no prospects and containing a large seasonal element is bound to rise proportionally if not absolutely. But whereas those in the better paid service jobs, especially in the City and in Westminster, the managers and professional workers, have a high propensity to live outside London, those in the lower echelons (cleaners, porters, waiters, drivers) usually live in Inner London, if only, in many cases, because their hours of work make it impossible to live far from their work, and because their wages are insufficient to allow for commuting over long distances. London is rapidly losing its former mainstay of steady incomes for manual workers: manufacturing industry is declining rapidly and looks like continuing to do so. For the skilled industrial worker, a move to an area of industrial growth is generally possible. But, for the semi-skilled and unskilled, despite the Industrial Selection Scheme for new and expanded towns, the prospects are much worse; for these people the service trades are probably the main alternative, but offer much lower earnings

---

[1] cf. footnote on p. 17. Also, 'New Earnings Survey 1971', *DE Gazette*, November 1971, **80**. no. 11; December 1971, **80**. no. 12.

levels. Distributive trades employment, another former main-stay of the un- and semi-skilled, especially women, is also de-clining very rapidly indeed. The demand for office workers is rising slowly, but, of course, the big problem is that even in areas where demand is rising, labour may not be sufficiently adaptable to move from one market to another. These people are not normally recruited from former factory, shop or dock workers. The danger in all this is quite clearly that London will have one relatively flourishing labour market for the young, well-educated, and professionally skilled, and one relatively declining market for the older, less skilled and less well educated worker. The situation in these two markets may soon be quite different.

Selective Migration

The second factor in this situation is migration. It is precisely those who have always found it easiest to survive in the urban battle who also find it easiest to get away. Out-migration is highly selective. The greatest demand in the Outer Metro-politan, South Eastern, South Western and East Anglian growth zones is for those with qualifications. It is true, of course, that the London schools system provides the market with in-creasing numbers of leavers with the minimal educational qualifications which leaves them with the choice of a fair range of jobs both inside and outside London. But on balance opportunities are shrinking, at least for those with no special skills, as the traditional apprenticeships become scarcer, and as mechanization and automation reduce the demand for those who have nothing but the strength of their hands to offer. Some recent labour demand projections undertaken by the Greater London Council make gloomy reading from this point of view.[1] Under these circumstances there is considerable likelihood of steadily more selective migration.

The Less Skilled and the Old

Therefore, if we have a continuation of the change of London's economic character towards a heavier dependence on tourism,

---

[1] *G.L.D.P. Inquiry Background Paper B452*, May 1971, p. 34, Table III.2.

catering and similar trades, and no reduction in the number of people depending on public transport, utilities, local authority employment and the usual metropolitan range of porters, caretakers, jobbing gardeners, window-cleaners, and others affected by seasonal variations or the uncertainties of the unskilled labour market, we may expect the proportion of those with inadequate incomes to rise. The same applies to the old: even without further differential migration, the proportion of pensioner households in London may well rise to 30 per cent or more. (Already in 1971, 23 per cent of all households contained no workers, and over 25 per cent of all heads of households were described as 'retired and unoccupied'.)[1] Again, the young have more mobility: the old who move to the south west or the south coast are the relatively better off, the poorer ones stay behind.

Inner London's Share

These, the common urban phenomena of our time, have been well described in America,[2] but only recently identified here. Although the problems apply to London as a whole, we would like to know how much worse they are in Inner London. However, until we have worked on the detailed results of the 1971 Census, we can only base our assertions on the analysis of the 1966 Census, which had no income data so that we cannot assess the situation with any great certainty. The 1966 Census does, however, confirm that there is a concentration of adverse indices in the 'inner ring' which are now more extensively concentrated in the inner north, south and west as well as in the traditionally poor areas in the east where much rebuilding has been done;[3] and even without any breakdown between areas in London of up-to-date income and employment figures, it is a safe guess that the characteristics which have been

---

[1] Department of Employment, *Family Expenditure Survey Report 1971*, p. 117–8, Tables 61 and 63.
[2] For a good collection of recent essays, cf. MOYNIHAN, DANIEL (ed.), *Toward a National Urban Policy* (New York: Basic Book Inc., 1970).
[3] cf. ch. 5 and 6.

mentioned are more strongly present in Inner London than in the suburbs. Service workers and public employees must be near their work. We know that the recent poor arrivals (immigrants who arrived before 1962), with few exceptions, are concentrated in the Inner Boroughs,[1] though the 1971 Census will probably show more outward movement. The 1967 Housing Survey also confirms the picture.[2] It would indeed be surprising if it were otherwise in view of the large concentration of unfit but relatively more readily available housing in Inner London. The results of the 1972 1 per cent income census are not yet available, but it is possible that other recent surveys (e.g. the London Transportation Study up-date exercise, also in 1971) will throw further light on the territorial distribution of poverty.

The Poverty Trap—A Permanent Proletariat?

Recent enquiries have drawn attention to the special problems posed where a system of multifarious means-tested benefits creates a relatively large group of the population which apparently cannot better their conditions, because the more they earn, the less benefit they receive, so that their marginal rate of taxation may effectively be from 50 to 100 per cent.[3]

While such a system may be regarded as an effective way of

---

[1] ROSE, E. J. B., et al., Colour and Citizenship: a report on British race relations, (Oxford University Press, 1969).

[2] cf. Greater London Council, Department of Planning and Transportation, Intelligence Unit, The Condition of London's Housing—A Survey; Research Report no. 4, August 1970. The Characteristics of London's Households, Research Report, no. 5, August 1970.

[3] MEACHER, MICHAEL, 'The poverty wage trap', The Guardian, 20 March 1972. The factors at work that devalue many gains by lower-paid workers (in this instance, the coal miners) are discussed. See also idem, 'The malaise of the low-paid worker' in A Special Case? (Harmondsworth: Penguin, 1972) edited for the N.U.M. by John Hughes and Roy Moore) written as evidence for the Wilberforce Committee and Inquiry.

allocating aid to those with the lowest incomes (and in principle no different from any progressive system of income tax or any of the traditional means-tested benefits), the total effect is to create a large bottom layer of society which is disadvantaged in a peculiar way. If we take the bottom point of the 'adequate' incomes, for a man with a wife and two children, the point where rent rebates no longer apply (where rents are £6 a week or less), we arrive at a threshold income of £2080 a year, or £40 a week. This in fact is somewhat above the *average* London household income, which in 1971 was just over £43.80 per week,[1] and therefore we can say that, given the skewed distribution of incomes which is shown by the fact that the mean lies considerably above the median, only something like 40 per cent of all households were definitely not in poverty by any definition. But we know too little about special factors (house ownership, savings and other positive factors on one hand, special responsibilities to dependants, sickness, etc. on the other hand) to be sure that these divisions are meaningful. What one cannot doubt is the existence of a large, and very likely increasing, mass of people with incomes which are increasingly insufficient in comparison with the average for London, let alone the rest of the region.[2] The median personal income lay at about £23·50 in 1971, compared with over £25 in many counties around London.

Are Countervailing Employment Policies Feasible?

The employment situation is changing because, although the number of residents has been falling, the actual supply of labour has declined much less rapidly, partly because of the high activity rates of the remaining residents and partly because of maintained or increased commuting levels. Meanwhile demand has declined dramatically in manufacturing industry and distribution, and slightly so in other areas where productivity is rising fast or outward movement is proceeding. Equilibrium of supply and demand has been passed for some

---

1 Department of Employment, *Family Expenditure Survey* 1971, p. 114, Table 56.
2 Abstract of Regional Statistics, no. 8, 1972, (London: H.M.S.O., 1972) p. 84, Table 65.

classes of workers and in some London sectors and in other areas it is probably not far away.

For some time the GLC has attempted to control the level of employment by means of its floorspace policies.[1] Essentially, this involves rationing the amount of additional floorspace created in industry and commerce, according to factors such as type of enterprise and location as well as total size. The idea behind these policies is to restrain growth where it is excessive in relation to the supply of labour as well as other planning factors, and to encourage new developments elsewhere both by granting planning permissions more readily and by steering entrepreneurs who are denied development in one area, into another. Whether this works or not remains to be seen: a period of recession such as that experienced since 1969 is not the best time to test such policies. Certainly the central government is not disposed to grant industrial development certificates for London under any but the most exceptional circumstances.

The first results of the 1971 census are not encouraging. For London as a whole, of all males who described themselves as economically active, 5 per cent were not in fact working in the week before the census, but the proportion was 10 per cent in Tower Hamlets, 6–8 per cent in most Inner London Boroughs, and 3–4 per cent in the Outer Boroughs.[2]

Should Labour Demand be Stimulated?

In other words, we have moved from an era where the main need was to develop some rational principles for selective restriction, into an era when the management function imposed on the planner seems to demand that he should develop other methods of adjustment, and even stimulate employment in some areas and some branches of activity. Here his duty is clear: if he accepts the economist's forecast of declining labour

---

[1] cf. Greater London Council, SP 371, 'Office and Industrial Floorspace: Consultations with London Borough Councils on Locations for Offices and industry', 18 April 1972. Also, *G.L.D.P. Statement Revisions, op. cit.*

[2] *Census 1971*, England and Wales, Advance Analysis, Greater London, Table I (London: H.M.S.O., 1972). See also *G.L.D.P. Inquiry Background Paper*, B647 (GLC, 1971).

demand, he will need to advocate liberalization of quantitative controls of floorspace, though these will probably be replaced partly by more stringent controls over location and, above all, policies to ensure that what is built will make a worthwhile contribution to the infrastructure and the environment, as well as providing employment.

At present too many office blocks are just ugly lumps destroying the traditional skyline without providing any countervailing advantage: but where the development yields a gain to the public at large (e.g. by the rebuilding of a railway station), it may be permitted.

In fact, developments in 1972 had reached a crisis point, with vast amounts of unoccupied office blocks and three times as much space still in the pipeline leading on one hand to feverish speculation and, on the other hand, to promises of drastic action by the central government. These recent events illustrate the great hazards involved in trying to decide long-term employment policies, but do not invalidate either the objective or attempts to reach it.

The Housing Problem

What is the Housing Shortage?

In the space of a generation, the population of Inner London will have been reduced by well over two million people, counting not only net migration, but also the natural increase foregone as the result of migration. This is the universal experience of old metropolitan cores, though perhaps the full extent of the movement is exceptional in London.

The Census of 1971 has shown that the population fall in London has once again been accelerated. In fact, the Group A (or roughly speaking Inner London) Boroughs have fallen even faster than the most optimistic (or pessimistic) forecasts assumed (Table 1.1). Perhaps the most astonishing falls have been in those boroughs where some of the worst housing conditions obtain (Table 1.2).

Thus, in a mere twenty years since the first post-war census, Inner London alone has lost 701 854 people, and the five boroughs, 304 674 people. At the same time, since 1919, i.e. in fifty years, the LCC, the GLC and the London Boroughs between them have provided some 600 000 dwellings. Since

Table 1.1

Population Decline in Inner and Outer London

	1951	1961	fall (%)	1971	fall (%)
GLC Area	8 196 807	7 992 443	2.5	7 379 014	7.1
Group A	3 681 552	3 492 879	5.1	2 979 698	14.7
Group B	4 515 255	4 499 564	0.3	4 399 316	2.2

Source: Census 1971: Preliminary Report (OPCAS).

1945, public and private agencies have built more than 750 000 dwellings.[1] Fewer than half of these have been built in the Inner London Boroughs, but a great many of those built by the LCC and the GLC in Outer London, or beyond, were for Inner London residents, and so were many of the houses for which nominations were provided in new and expanded towns. We are talking about new local authority housing only, and we exclude conversions, rehabilitations, housing associations and temporary dwellings. On any count, the numerical problem as it was seen before the war, just after the war or even in 1960, should have been 'solved' twice over. Yet taking the evidence of the Milner Holland Committee, John Greve, Barry Culling-

Table 1.2

Population Decline in Five Inner London Boroughs

	1951	1961	fall (%)	1971	fall (%)
Camden	258 318	245 707	4.9	200 784	18.3
Islington	271 002	261 232	3.6	199 129	23.8
Kensington and Chelsea	219 117	218 528	0.3	184 392	15.6
Tower Hamlets	230 790	205 682	10.9	164 948	19.8
Westminster	300 332	271 703	9.5	225 632	17.0

Source: Census 1971: Preliminary Report (OPCAS).

---

[1] Department of the Environment, *Housing Statistics: Great Britain* no. 24, February 1972, p. 13, Table III, which shows 721 000 completions to the end of 1971. The figure of 750 000 was reached by the end of 1972.

worth or our own work,[1] and just looking round us, we know that the day when every Inner London family has its own satisfactory dwelling is once again, on present plans, ten years away. One has a strong suspicion that it has always been ten years away, or perhaps fifteen. There are many and obvious explanations for this: obsolescence is a galloping disease, and because so much of London was built (and built badly) in the last quarter of the nineteenth century,[2] much of it is now falling into almost irretrievable disuse, partly because of long neglect by private owners.

Some Sources of Extra Demand

There are, however, other causes which we cannot yet quantify: the growth of tourism has taken over many former homes, and this particular form of conversion has been spreading fast. It applies not only to old terrace housing, but also to modern blocks of flats which are being converted to short lettings for visitors; 'second homes' are a phenomenon of quite unknown magnitude—they belong to business men who have moved their families into the country and to the increasing number of wealthy foreigners who maintain flats in London, to the swelling mass of diplomats, to firms which maintain short-term representatives in London, and even to people who can afford to keep a flat just in case they want to stay up after a late party or theatre. An unknown amount of residential accommodation has also been turned over to the increasing numbers of students temporarily living in London.

Faced with these problems, there may be an immediate

---

[1] cf. Ministry of Housing and Local Government, *Report of the Committee on Housing in Greater London* (London: H.M.S.O., 1965). GREVE, JOHN, *et al. Homelessness in London*, (Edinburgh: Scottish Academic Press, 1971). CULLINGWORTH, J. B., *Housing Needs and Planning Policy* (London: Routledge and Kegan Paul, 1960). *Report of the Committee on the Rent Acts* (Francis Report) (London: H.M.S.O., 1971). G.L.C. Research Report 4, August 1970 and Research Report 5, August 1970.
[2] PARRY LEWIS, J., *Building Cycles and Britain's Growth* (London: Macmillan, 1965) especially ch. V, fig. 5.1, p. 107, and pp. 135–9. See also DYOS, H. J., *Victorian Suburb: A Study of the Growth of Camberwell*, (Leicester University Press, 1961), p. 81, fig. 4.

temptation to reply with drastic measures: prohibit second homes or at least tax them (as coats of arms on carriages used to be taxed), give foreigners only limited residence permits and forbid them to occupy self-contained accommodation, close our frontiers to foreign students who want to study here and so on. But these options are just not open to us, even if they were legally enforceable: these phenomena are closely connected with London's role, and to stop such practices would only reduce London's significance still further. If businessmen cannot have a *pied-à-terre* in London they will probably move their firm out of London altogether, and if a family with a main home in London is not allowed to have a cottage in the country, it will probably opt to move out. And our learned institutions, our cultural facilities and our historical monuments, which maintain the stream of long-term and short-term visitors, are assets which we must not only keep for the benefit of our own residents but also because their removal elsewhere would make them less useful to all groups of potential users. (Like the proposal to have the National Library at Milton Keynes instead of in Bloomsbury: a typical example of conflict between competing good solutions.)

Household Fission

Then, we have the process of shrinking household size. 'Fission' is the term, and it again has many causes and is becoming an increasingly significant factor. Complex households resolve themselves into nuclear units of parents and children, of old people alone, of single people maintaining a flat, of groups of young who share flats instead of living with their parents, or who become lodgers in someone else's house. This has brought the average household size in London down to well under three persons and is probably heading for 2.5 persons in the near future.[1] Immigrants, in fact, by living in the crowded conditions of their inadequate homes, allow the rest to live at tolerably

---

[1] *G.L.D.P. Inquiry*, 'Notes of Proceedings', Day 231, Wednesday 26 April 1972, pp. 53–6. See also, *G.L.D.P. Inquiry Background Paper B489, op. cit.*, p. 23, Table 6, and Ministry of Housing and Local Government, *Statistics for Town and Country Planning*, Series III: Population and Households, no. 1, 'Projecting growth patterns in regions', 1970, p. 51, Table 9.

low occupancy ratios, and keep up the average per dwelling so as to hide the wide disparity between under-occupation and overcrowding. Moreover, as fertility falls, so does household size, and so the number of dwellings required to house any given total population becomes larger.

The Numbers Needed

All these factors together mean that, although there are far fewer people to house, and there are far more fit and modern dwellings as a proportion of the total stock which itself is much larger than it was, an unknown but very large number of families are still living in dwellings which have reached the end of their useful life, or are lacking in basic amenities, or those who are, against their will, still living with strangers or relatives; the numbers involved are enormous. On the best estimates, London would need another 350 000 dwellings in the next ten years. It may get most of these, but the fear is widespread that even when these 350 000 dwellings have been built, there may still be a considerable number of under-housed families.

Housing the Residue

The process is apparently never-ending, and this makes housing a social, not a building problem. Clearly there is an ill-defined group of people who never get to the top of the housing queue. Net immigration has virtually stopped, and the only overseas families now arriving are mostly of the kind that can solve their housing problem by competing in the open market, so one can assume that the great mass of the underhoused consists of people who have been resident in Britain for many years. The local authorities' rules which enforce a residence qualification may, therefore, not be a good way of allocating housing stock. It is possible that mobile families are among those which always slip through the net—in the census, housing surveys, compulsory housing registration—and they may not, in many cases, even be known to the social service agencies. They certainly do not, as was shown in the 1967 Notting Hill Housing Survey,[1]

---

[1] Notting Hill Housing Service, *Notting Hill Housing Survey*, 1967. Interim Report 1969.

figure on local authority waiting lists. What is it that causes this misery? They move—the word 'nomadism' has been applied to them—and the middle-class 'take-over' of Inner London has been blamed, yet they probably existed long before that.[1] We must regard it as one of the primary tasks of the seventies to deal with this hard core of our housing problem. With the rest we may cope, if the present effort can be maintained.

Then there is the problem of the housing associations and societies, the much heralded 'third arm', neither public nor in the private profit making sector. Modelled on Scandinavian and German examples, much is claimed for these bodies, and a great deal of capital goes into them. In truth they are a mixed group, and the incidence of help, where it is given, is unequal: much depends on the accident of local initiative, and on the attitude of a particular borough. Then again, there are home loans. In theory, local authority lending opens the path to ownership for young people who might be excluded by the commercial lending sector. But if the method is used to lure out from all local authority estates the youngest, fittest, financially most secure applicants, and to give them housing outside London, to free their house for a priority case, will this not eventually lead to even stronger 'polarization' so that in time estates become even more homogeneously the abodes of the not-so-adequate, the not-so-young, the not-so-well-to-do?[2]

Moreover, doubts have recently been expressed whether the provision of 100 per cent mortgages makes much of a positive contribution to the problem. There is evidence[3] that, like all relaxations of credit, the practice raises prices. Moreover, the minimum cost of houses for which 'no deposit' mortgages can

---

[1] cf. *The Sunday Times Magazine*, 16 April 1972, pp. 26–33, for a well-informed survey of the most recent manifestations of 'gentrification' in London. Also, BLAIR, T., 'Rehabilitation', *Official Architecture and Planning*, **33**, no. 2, February 1970, p. 126.

[2] For some of the limitations of housing associations, cf. GREVE, JOHN, *et al.*, *Homelessness in London* (Edinburgh: Scottish Academic Press, 1971), ch. 12; and *Housing Associations: a Working Paper of the Central Housing Advisory Committee* (Cohen) (Department of the Environment, 1971).

[3] cf. WALTERS, S. Z., *The Impact of Rising House and Land Prices in London* (GLC, 1972) esp. p. 5. Also, *The Sunday Times Magazine, op. cit.* pp. 21–4.

be obtained, is so high that even allowing for tax relief (or the option mortgage scheme) no substantial additional income groups are being placed in the category of potential home owners. Annual payments of £600 are beyond the means of households with disposable incomes under £2000.

The Social Geography of Housing

Housing policies involve many other social problems. It is clear that the GLC can only fulfil all its own obligations if it can get housing sites in the Outer Boroughs, and it has been widely urged that the GLC should, with the help of the Department of the Environment, exercise compulsory purchase powers to obtain this land. There is strong feeling, however, against this. One therefore has to decide, given the potential hostility of the new environment, the high cost of travelling to work and the probable lack of local employment opportunities for women (except charring, perhaps), whether one should really exert this pressure? Is this form of compulsory mixing desirable? Would not some of the Outer Boroughs be justified in claiming that this move would destroy their chosen way of life? Could it be that to introduce a strange element into the leafy villages as was done at Roehampton is to create a new and rather frightening sort of ghetto? Once again, the simple solutions are plentiful, but do we actually know what we are doing? The story of the Cutteslowe Walls is still fresh in our memory.[1] The Council in fact decided, in 1972, to solve this dilemma by building houses for sale only, experimentally, in some of those areas where rented GLC housing for rent was most resented, and to concentrate heavily on rebuilding in Inner London and on out of London schemes, to provide the necessary additional houses to rent each year.

Communities

Social Structure

This brief look at incomes, employment and housing brings us to the question of social structure. I do not intend here to

---

[1] COLLISON, PETER, *The Cutteslowe Walls: a study in social class*, (London: Faber, 1966).

discuss at any length the question of what could be meant by such expressions as 'the old communities' or a 'normal social structure'. The historian doubts if there was ever a time when old community patterns were not being disrupted by redevelopment, clearance, migration due to shifting economic opportunities, or when large numbers of people were *not* living in hurriedly built estates on the fringes of built-up areas. It is not a new issue, but it is a live one. The difficulty lies in arriving at a prescription for the forms of residential areas required.

Before we destroy these insanitary, doubtfully cosy slums and twilight areas, we should be quite sure what it is that we aim to put in their places. Each group of experts and politicians has its own priorities: Some think nearness to work is the major factor, others argue for low costs, others for high standards commensurate with future needs, others think that the vital factor should be to facilitate the integration of income and ethnic groups, and age groups; others argue for low densities, for proximity to amenities and services. Others yet feel that the most important task is to keep down costs so as to reduce burdens to tolerable proportions for tenants and taxpayers. Some advocate maximum socio-economic homogeneity,[1] and even the toleration of high concentrations of ethnic groups. For some, the conservation of existing good buildings and townscapes is paramount. Some advocate high densities because this leads to some undefined feeling of 'urbanity'. Land use prescriptions range from total segregation of residential and all other uses to the exact opposite: the Jane Jacobs mixture of private and public uses, commerce, industry and housing, preferably leading to round-the-clock activities so as to prevent boredom, loneliness and the dangers of the deserted city by night.[2] On the surface, it seems that each of these groups advocating special policies is equally well qualified and experienced. Who is, then, to say who is right, who can judge between them, how are we to decide?

---

[1] An interesting recent British survey concluded that community relationships were best fostered where there was a good deal of socio-demographic homogeneity and a chance of visual contact—back to the 'close'. cf. CAREY, L. and MAPES, R., *The Sociology of Planning*, (London: Batsford, 1972) pp. 64 ff. (39).

[2] cf. JACOBS, JANE, *The Death and Life of Great American Cities* (London: Cape, 1962).

The Example of Barnsbury

In Barnsbury an attempt was made to initiate in an organized way the earlier spontaneous developments of Canonbury and Pimlico. The outworn housing of the last century was rehabilitated and traffic and environmental schemes introduced,[1] to try to reintroduce a middle-class, professional, higher income element into an area which with wholesale redevelopment would have produced yet another one-class high-density council estate; and by the conversion of suitable houses through housing associations, to introduce a mixture of ownerships and enable the 'third arm' to give a measure of priority to some special groups of people in housing need.

But, in the event, most of the houses went to the highest income groups, the housing association conversions did not qualify for subsidy and failed to become available for people in acute need, the houses which were rebuilt were cleared, by one means or another, of the poor, the old, those without secure tenure. Loud protests culminated in the direct charge made by an eminent urban sociologist that the GLC hated the poor so much that they were determined to drive them out of London. The word 'gentrification' is heard with increasing frequency in different parts of London. The counterpart scheme, that of enabling lower income groups, disadvantaged minorities, unsupported families and unskilled workers in general, to move to new towns, instead of the predominantly young, skilled and upwardly mobile families of past years, was greeted with the same accusation. Housing associations are roundly condemned as devices to support under-employed architects, or as a means of subsidizing the knowledgeable middle classes.

Polarization or Social Mix?

Behind much of this criticism lies a genuine difference of opinion. The GLC is studying the process of 'social polarization' by which people tend to become segregated into income

---

[1] The residents of Barnsbury expressed satisfaction with the traffic scheme, see 'A Survey on Barnsbury', 28 October–9 November 1971, Opinion Research Centre report no. 1065.

or ethnic groups.[1] Is there any way of measuring this, of assessing whether London is becoming more 'polarized' in any way, or whether it is becoming a 'city of the rich and the poor'? Many planners and sociologists attack the validity and acceptability of these questions. Yet, if we are to plan effectively for people, we need to know what they want and the mechanics of the society in which we live: do people eventually sort themselves into the sort of communities they prefer, in which case is the planner's role to create a freer housing market to enable this sorting-out process to go on; or is it just that some people want to live next door to their 'own kind' and some do not? Is there any consistent pattern in this? We do not know whether we should try to ensure that the pupil composition of each school should be a careful mixture of children with different backgrounds, of innate and environmentally encouraged or stunted ability.[2] We do not even know what kinds of services and amenities in a neighbourhood or small township depend on the existence of some minimum clientèle of better educated people of a certain minimum income.

Housing and Environment

We also have to be aware of the kind of environment we are creating: to 'solve' the housing problem by, for example, creating residential units with minimal amenities, in an otherwise still unpromising environment, is to solve only part of it. Where, as in parts of east London, huge tower blocks have been built right in among the docks, the semi-derelict wharves and warehouses and former industrial plants, it is very hard to see what has been gained.

It is said that such schemes are now out of favour, but they are still being built (new forty storey block schemes were announced in 1972), and one cannot help wondering what kind of people will want to inhabit them. Perhaps 'want' is the wrong word: perhaps it would be better to ask what kind of people will have to move into them if they want to avoid losing their place in the housing queue. The answer must be: those who by reason of their low incomes have no choice, to whom a

---

[1] cf. ch. 5.
[2] cf. ch. 9.

roof over their heads and a clean modern flat, reasonably close to their place of work, must represent the limit of their ambitions.

London is threatened not only by the poverty of the design of so much new housing, but also by other intrusions into the townscape which can vitiate whole areas. One of the most obvious ones was the proposed VTOL/STOL site in Surrey Docks which, if it ever came about, would sterilize 200 acres for any other purpose and blight another 200 so that no private developer would risk a penny on the sites, and would leave them 'free' only for local authorities to take for dwellings for people without choice.

Many public housing schemes could, given a more imaginative urban landscape, be attractive to others besides the poorest. The Barbican is an exciting townscape, and enormous care has been taken over finishes, planting, sculpture—not to speak of interesting and historic buildings close by. But the Barbican is for 'middle' income groups—though the rents there are in fact the same as the cost rents which would be charged in the most unattractive local authority estates, but for the subsidies. 'Environment' is still not well understood, and something that can be attractive and desirable in one setting can be an abomination in another.[1]

Other Problems

This does not by any means exhaust the list of problems of social planning which British cities, and London in particular, face today. We have not dealt with the conflicts which arise over recreation policy in an age when people are becoming more mobile, but an important residue is as immobile as ever. We have not described conflicts over the Green Belt or other encroachments on open space at a time when housing seems to be the most pressing problem, not playspace, and when 'lungs' are less important than they were. We have not referred to

---

[1] For a full bibliography of recent writings on the question of how individuals view their environment, see JOHNSON, SUSAN, 'Perception of the environment with special reference to the urban environment, a select bibliography', GLC Research bibliography no. 36, July 1972. Department of Planning and Transportation.

problems arising from the third London Airport, the new
Dockland Scheme, the Channel Tunnel. All these create new
social and economic difficulties: each can potentially benefit
millions, but ruin the lives of thousands. It becomes ever more
difficult to decide between majority and minority interest. Is
it more important that millions who never had the chance to
have their holiday beyond Blackpool should be able to fly to
Spain or Tunisia? Or are rare birds and plants in the Essex
marshes worth preserving at the cost of the convenience of
travellers?

Towards a Conclusion

In this chapter, only a few of the more important Inner London
social dilemmas have been raised. We have totally left out
public transport, roads, the motor car—not because they do
not offer similar problems and conflicts in the solutions which
have been advocated, but because this chapter is designed to
illustrate approaches rather than to serve as a comprehensive
catalogue of urban planning problems. It is now necessary,
finally, to draw together some of the most salient features of the
urban situation in Britain today to provide at least some
meagre foundations for a new look at our prospects.[1]

We begin with what we might call the general pre-conditions.
First, as always, is the need for yet more research. Only in this
case research needs to be less theoretical, less reliant on abstract
models, more concerned with the kind of problems raised in
this introductory chapter and well represented in the chapters
which follow. There are funds in Britain today to support such
research. But we need more of the better academics to turn their
attention to these kinds of problems. Secondly, education; the
recognition of our urban situation today is still confined to a
minority even of professional planners and other urban
managers; it does not figure to any extent in the syllabus of
most of our planning schools; it does not appear at all in the
curriculum of sixth forms, sociology degrees or courses for
social workers, except in the disguise of general theories about

---

[1] For a fuller exposition see EVERSLEY, D. E. C., 'Urban problems in
Britain today', *GLC Quarterly Bulletin of the Intelligence Unit*, no. 19,
June 1972.

urban social structure, or detailed descriptions of particular problems seen in isolation. Thirdly, new political attitudes towards the city—a determination to keep it alive, to prevent the renewed emergence of a large urban under-class, permanently dependent on means-tested public subventions, and the concentration of such a class in vast urban tracts, in stark contrast to the environment of new towns, green belts, growth areas and prosperous suburbs.

Once we have made some progress with research, education and the formation of new political attitudes, certain courses of action would seem to follow.

Economic Growth

There seems little prospect in Britain today of solving urban social problems unless much larger resources are devoted to housing and the renewal of the infrastructure. The rise in personal real incomes needed to sustain a life with the minimum decencies can only come from full, and adequately paid employment, and this can only be the result of at any rate a moderate rate of economic growth. Therefore the social planner must reject those theories which regard growth simply as a threat to environment. The environment can be protected in other ways than those which injure the poorest sections of society and leave real income distribution as it is, or even allow it to change back in favour of the better-off groups.[1] Growth does not necessarily mean merely additional hardware, diminishing resources of scarce materials and additional pollution. Better real incomes include more education, creative use of leisure, good neighbourly relations and many other intangibles.[2]

---

[1] The main advocate of non-growth in this country is E. J. MISHAN in his books, *Growth—the price we pay* (London: Staples Press, 1969), and *The Costs of Economic Growth* (London: Staples Press, 1967).

No really cogent answer has as yet been given to him, but some indications of a possible reply may be found in JEREMY BRAY, *The Politics of the Environment* (London: Fabian Society, 1972).

[2] For a detailed list of such intangibles, see *G.L.D.P. Statement Revisions*, p. 3, para. 2.3.

Social Structure and Choice

In the kind of society which is envisaged in this introduction, there must be opportunities for every individual and group to make choices. Assuming that they have sufficient basic real incomes, they must be able to choose in what way they will spend them to achieve a life-style which satisfies their aspirations. We have already said that a means-tested population is deprived of such choices. But, on the physical side, choice means how and where one will live, where one will work, how much education one wants for one's children. It means a choice of recreational amenities and leisure activities. It means a choice of goods to buy in shops, and of professional services, a choice of holiday destinations. Above all, it means a choice of association—one's neighbours, one's friends, one's fellow-followers of hobbies and pastimes. It means, negatively, the absence of anything representing a ghetto, or segregated district, through active planning or discrimination. This does *not* preclude the voluntary congregation of Jews in Golders Green or Indians in south-west Crawley. But it does mean avoiding segregation by income, socio-economic group or ethnic origin, by planning or failure to plan. It means preventing the emergence of one-company towns or housing projects where the only employment is that reached by a distant commuter journey to Central London.

Therefore 'social structure' is not another word for the creation of a mythical 'balanced' community, but refers to urban forms in which everyone can exercise choices, without detriment to others.

Community Involvement

We have progressed beyond Skeffington, or the nebulous concepts of participation. We recognize the role of the planner—not to legislate for others, but to build cities *with* the community. The full implications of this have not been discussed in this chapter, but they form part of any system of social planning. We are, in this respect, only in an experimental stage,[1] but it is

---

[1] For the basis of a first experiment see *GLC Council Minutes* 20 June 1972, p. 10 'Swinbrook Road Site'.

For a systematic account of what is involved in a proper community-

widely recognized by the central government and at least some local authorities that unless in schemes like large-scale redevelopment, the building of new roads, and the creation of shopping centres, the community affected is involved right from the start, and takes part in the formulation of the briefs on which architects and planners base their options, from which the community will eventually choose its preference, planning will be dictatorial, arouse resentment and perhaps civil strife, and perhaps fail altogether.[1] It is axiomatic, again, that such options relate not only to the crude physical framework of housing, roads and shopping centres, but include access to education, amenities, social facilities and services, and recreational opportunities, as well as jobs for men and women.

Involvement of Central Government

As we have shown, the magnitude of the tasks involved is such that they are quite beyond the financial strength of local authorities, private incomes and private investors. This means either a very drastic reform of local government finance, or, more likely, a vast increase in central government allocations for the urban infrastructure even in the so-called prosperous cities. Great tracts of London and Birmingham exhibit characteristics of poverty, under-employment and deprivation quite as bad as admittedly larger parts of Glasgow, the Durham coalfield or abandoned rural slums. Hence the need to plan for the further growth of extant policies in the field of main road building, new underground railways for London, new national airports and special features like the Thames Barrier. The greatest test of this new policy will come in the London Docklands, where, for social planning reasons, large national resources must be pledged for the execution of a task which, on

---

based system of planning, see *Community Action*, a journal published in London available from 9, Pattison Road, London, NW2, esp. issue 1, February 1972.

[1] For the place of the planner in the community, see EVERSLEY, D.E.C., 'New horizons for planners', Town and Country Planning Summer School, Southampton, 1971; also *Tomorrow's London* (GLC, 1969), ch. 8; 'Participation: Democracy and Planning' and p. 44: 'The planner in society'.

purely economic grounds would not be performed by any public or private authority.[1]

Control of Land Use

Given the unprecedented rises in the price of land and new housing in the last few years, largely due to muddle and speculation, we can only arrive at a sensible system of land use planning if there is central government control over land use. This does not mean land nationalization, but it does mean that the allocation of land as between housing, agriculture, conservation areas, landscape and recreation must be controlled in such a way that huge fortunes are not made out of delays in the planning process, land hoarding, unfulfilled planning permissions and a trade in options begins to develop. No government has as yet squarely faced this problem, though valiant attempts have been made, ranging from the 1947 Act to the end of the Land Commission. There have been recent signs that the nuisance has gone too far, that it threatens the financial stability of the country, is in itself a main cause of inflation, and may in time lead to insurrection. Central government, therefore, is preparing to amend existing legislation, and to introduce new acts, at the time of writing, to increase the measure of control over land use. Until this is done, the prospects of the inner city will continue to diminish.

Incomes Policies

As we indicated in the section on constraints, local authorities can do little to raise real incomes. Therefore we need new national policies for an incomes and social benefits structure— called for by social planners from Barbara Wootton to the Child Poverty Action Group. Rising costs and static incomes have led to an intolerable squeeze, a vice in which all old urban communities are caught.[2]

---

[1] For the background to the Docklands Project, and the pre-conditions in the form of public investment, see *East London Papers*, **14**, no. 1 April 1972: The New London: replanning the Docklands, esp. EVERSLEY, D. E. C., 'The Docklands, an exercise in Geopolitics', pp. 51 ff., pp. 59 ff.
[2] A more detailed description of these phenomena appears in EVERSLEY, D. E. C., 'Rising costs and static incomes: some economic consequences of regional planning in London', *Urban Studies*, **9**, no. 3, October 1972.

Regional Policies

In the light of all the problems we have tried to identify, a fresh look must be taken at our regional strategies. From the *South-East Study* of 1964 to the *Strategic Plan for the South East* of 1970, regional planners have aimed at a progressive run-down of the big cities, and this, as we have said, seemed at the time the best way of coping with the problems of the inner city. But we have since seen that such a simple prescription of de-centralization, or regional restructuring as it came to be called, might lead to serious imbalances of homes, workplaces and movement. Therefore the process must become more orderly, more controlled, combining the movement of people to new settlement areas with job retraining,[1] and providing for the reception of poor, disadvantaged and minority groups in the new growth areas, even if their prospects of an adequate living standard depend on public subventions. Such policies have been talked about in relation to some of the new cities, like Milton Keynes, but they are a long way from being fulfilled.[2]

Corporate Management

Lastly, both at central government and local government level, the old departmental distinctions and professional demarcation disputes must disappear. This will take a long time, but a start has to be made. In London, a Planning, Programming and Budgeting system has been introduced, with a strong non-financial side of corporate management by social objectives which should, in time, produce a concentration of all efforts—executive, research, advisory, advocatory—on a single and clear

---

[1] A description of the interaction between housing problems, employment and labour training appears in GEE, FRANCES, *The movement of Londoners to new and expanding towns*, Government Social Survey (London: H.M.S.O., January 1972); see also *Manpower in the U.K.*, Organisation for Economic Co-operation and Development, Paris 1970; and MURKHJEE SANTOSH, 'Making labour markets work—a comparison of the U.K. and the Swedish systems', *P.E.P. Broadsheet 532*, January 1972.

[2] See LLEWELYN-DAVIES, WEEKS, FORESTIER-WALKER and BOR, *Milton-Keynes—Interim Report*, London 1968, esp. pp. 18, 135–8.

set of objectives.[1] A whole new generation of administrators will have to be trained to work in this fashion, and they may not come from the ranks of some of the existing professions.[2]

A New Beginning

This introductory chapter ends with a conclusion—but it is not an end. It is only a beginning. It should initiate debates, produce new research, act as a spur to others besides my co-authors to work in the field of social planning. We may expect to see, in the next few years, a spate of new proposals to reform the system of planning, and of government as a whole. But to translate these brave beginnings into action—that is another matter. Only the close collaboration of administrators, professional experts and academic researchers can produce such a new system. At present, they still tend to operate in separate compartments. If this book has illustrated more clearly that we cannot continue to work separately, it will have served its purpose.

---

[1] A detailed description of the planning and programming budgeting system is given by A. W. Peterson (Director-General, GLC) in 'Planning and programming in the GLC—what and why?' in *Public Administration* (Journal of the Royal Institute of Public Administration), Summer 1972, **50**, p. 119.
[2] See EVERSLEY, D. E. C., 'Planning and the environment', *Chartered Surveyor* **105**, no. 4.

Chapter Two

Labour and Life in London

GRAHAM LOMAS

Summary

This chapter examines aspects of the inter-relationship between job opportunities, the housing situation and personal incomes in London, against a background of debate as to whether the continuing decentralization of people and jobs from London is producing disbenefits, particularly for Inner London.

The chapter focuses on the spatial distribution of less-skilled people in the metropolis. Analysis of available data on this, and the distribution of people in low paid occupations, shows that neither group is concentrated exclusively or predominantly in the inner city—though there are parts of the metropolis (such as the East End) where large numbers of less-skilled workers are to be found. Available information, though very inadequate, does not suggest that less-skilled people are increasingly confined to the inner city, since the growth of service jobs in the Central Business District (C.B.D.) is unlikely to outweigh the decline in factory work throughout the inner city.

Problems will continue to arise as the inner city adjusts its function within an expanding metropolitan region—social class competition over the available housing, labour redundancies and under-employment among various elements in the work force are perhaps the principal characteristics, along with the displacement and upheaval associated with urban renewal.

Unemployment, especially of the less skilled, is found to be as high in parts of the inner city as in some Development Areas, with black people significantly represented among the out-of-work. The analysis, however, underlines the severe data gaps which preclude any satisfactory analysis of the social class aspects of metropolitan life.

The chapter concludes that answers to what are essentially socio-economic problems tend to be sought in physical planning, and makes two suggestions in this situation. One concerns the legal framework within which the local authority housing service operates; the other concerns the manner in which the government seeks to help those whose job skills are no longer adequate, or who live in those parts of the metropolitan area where employment contraction is taking place. These are examples of social planning policies required to complement the physical basis in which city planning in the past has been rooted.

For thirty years, ever since the Barlow Report [1] and the Abercrombie plans [2], policies for the metropolis and the wider South-East region have been designed to reduce the level of population in London. Planned overspill together with the spontaneous movement of people to the growing towns beyond the Green Belt have had the desired effect: a slow and steady fall has been discernible since 1940. Governmental policy has also aimed to decentralize economic activity with special emphasis on the movement of factory work away from the conurbation. In this too there has been considerable success [3]. The regional planning reports [4] of the mid-1960s reaffirmed the need for these twin policies.

The preparation of a Development Plan by the newly constituted Greater London Council in the late 1960s, however, provided the first opportunity in many years to appraise these policies, specifically in terms of their impact on London. The Greater London Development Plan (G.L.D.P.) marked a significant watershed for it began to argue [5] that outmigration of population was proceeding so fast as to impair the economic vitality of London, with even more serious imbalances likely to emerge in the demand and supply of labour. The plan urged that the rate of fall of the population should be retarded, and the GLC have pressed this issue strongly at the Public Enquiry into the Development Plan, backing the arguments with data available from 1966 onwards which show that the rate of population decline is in fact accelerating.

A very substantial fall in the level of jobs in London [6] in the late 1960s served if anything to strengthen the Council's determination to challenge long standing regional policies, arguing as they did that far from providing for a more balanced out-migration, with more scope for the creation of a more satisfactory environment in London, the sudden rapid decline of industrial jobs coupled with the decline of population were in fact the beginnings of a cycle of progressive run-down in London with potentially disastrous consequences for the capital. An early revision of the Plan develops this thesis [7].

The revised plan points to a number of features of this run-down. It argues that the continued fall in London's population is depriving London of young, skilled, well educated people, families with young children, and workers with good prospects and rising incomes, leaving London with a burden of the old, the less skilled, the poor and the disadvantaged [8]. The plan stresses the adverse socio-economic effects that will follow if the relatively larger losses of the professional and management groups continues indefinitely [9]. And while the Council continues to be committed to a programme of new and expanded towns in the South-East region, it is nevertheless concerned at the amount of industrial blood London is having to donate to the wider region and the development areas.

Following hard on the heels of the G.L.D.P. came the Strategic Plan for the South East Region of England (S.P.S.E.), aiming to provide a framework for the long-term development of the region. It too pays close attention to the impact of decentralization policies on London and is more explicit about the effects of the economic and demographic trends on the older built-up core of the metropolis. Under the heading [10] of 'Social Problems in Inner London', it concludes:

1 that the continual exodus of 'the middle mass' of people will leave a socially polarized population;

2 that while nationally the trend is for the semi-skilled and unskilled in the workforce to fall, in the particular circumstances of Inner London there is some evidence to the contrary;

3 that a gap is developing in the occupational structure which will cumulatively restrict the job opportunities of the less skilled;

4 that immigrant workers are making little progress in securing more diverse and better paid employment;

5 that low pay is of particular significance in Inner London.

Thus while incorporating the main planning parameters of the G.L.D.P., the S.P.S.E. goes somewhat further than the London plan in postulating social and socio-economic consequences for the inner areas of London if recent trends are allowed to continue.

It would be surprising if all expert opinion were in agreement over the implications of present metropolitan trends. Indeed there is room for considerable debate even about the nature of the trends because successive censuses—the main sources of information in planning at this large scale—have proved awfully weak guides to marginal changes in large urban systems. For example, there is no information on the household and family composition of migrants to and from London, no data on household or personal incomes in different parts of London, no means of discerning the social class of people in poor housing or council housing in different areas of London. It is not possible to say which social groups benefit directly from new building. It is not even possible to show with any measure of accuracy where the coloured population in London lives. And on subjects where the census does provide information—as in the case of households sharing accommodation—its accuracy and usefulness is often open to serious doubt. Comparison of the changes between 1961 and 1966 in the amount of sharing reveals, according to one set of experts [11], an increase of 103,000, and a decline of 10 per cent by another set [12]. There is even argument as to whether the overall number of dwellings in the metropolis has risen or fallen in recent years, with the G.L.D.P. claiming an increase of 100 000 and other opinion claiming a loss of 63 700 dwellings.

It is symptomatic of 'the data gap' that the S.P.S.E., while confident in its conclusions on the trends in the inner city, fails to set out any solid statistical evidence on the five social problems of Inner London mentioned earlier. The GLC too fails to give direct evidence of the progressive run-down mentioned in the Revised Development Plan, though in this particular instance the problem is said to have emerged somewhat dramatically after the date of the last available census. Differences of opinion over the nature of the trends and their significance inevitably lead to differences of view on policy. For example, the S.P.S.E. follows the spirit of previous regional plans in furthering the decentralization of activities, while adding to this traditional approach the need now to decentralize as many semi-skilled and unskilled workers as are not required to maintain Inner London's essential functions [13]. The G.L.D.P., on the other hand, whilst reaffirming the value of the Industrial Selection Scheme, places the emphasis on increasing employment opportunities *in situ* with a rider that only if this fails should the Council seek to solve these workers' problems by outmigration or job training [14]. Again, the Regional Plan asserts that coloured people in Inner London are making little headway in upward social mobility, whereas the G.L.D.P. never refers specifically to problems facing coloured people in London.

The Inner City Problem

This brief review is perhaps sufficient to show that there is no unanimity as to the socio-economic problems of Inner London. In consequence, neither is there any measure of agreement as to appropriate socio-economic policies for the inner city.

In view of the great differences of emphasis, the almost total lack of clarity as to the ways in which the economic base changes in London are thought to be affecting the socio-economic structure of Inner London, indeed the very direction of the changes in the socio-economic composition of the inner city, it may be appropriate in the context of this chapter to try to formulate and test a number of hypotheses.

Six hypotheses might be advanced:

1 that less-skilled workers are becoming increasingly spatially segregated from the rest of society, and concentrated within the inner city;

2 that coloured people are forming an increasing proportion of the less-skilled workforce and therefore that a process of apartheid is occurring as immigrants concentrate in the inner city;

3 that less-skilled labour is less in demand, and that the inner city will increasingly contain an unemployable population;

4 that less-skilled labour is on the lowest rungs of the earnings ladder and getting relatively poorer;

5 that commerce is expanding in the city centre, rendering the less-skilled homeless;

6 that the recolonization of Inner London by other social groups is also affecting the housing chances of the less-skilled.

These are simply *hypotheses*. The theme clearly running through them, however, is of a kind of pincer movement: the less-skilled worker is moving into an economic backwater, a condition which is exacerbated by social and physical forces in modern urban society—the social forces encourage residential segregation; the physical forces ensure it, through the sheer scale of the modern metropolis. The political implication is equally clear: that inequalities in real incomes are being sustained—even extended—by economic forces, and that gross inequalities of opportunity are being sustained by social and physical forces.

The Less-skilled Worker in London

In order to test the notion that less-skilled workers are concentrated in the inner city, the London Boroughs have been grouped into four concentric rings: a central ring, an inner ring, a middle ring and an outer ring, roughly reflecting the phases of London's growth. Census data have been analysed on this basis.[1]

The results, in Table 2.1, show that the number of less-skilled men living in the middle and outer rings of London exceeds those in the central and inner rings by substantial margins. This is the case in each of the three socio-economic groupings (s.e.g.) that comprise 'the less-skilled' [15]. Of course, overall numbers are not the whole story, but even if we take the less skilled as a percentage of all workers in the four zones, the inner ring does not rise above 30 per cent and the outer ring does not fall below 17 per cent, though at a much more local level there will, no doubt, be wider variation. The inner city does not consist wholly, nor even predominantly, of less-skilled workers. But what of the *trends*?

Unfortunately we cannot go back very far since there is no equivalent information in early Censuses, but the trend between 1961 and 1966 might be gauged by comparing Table 2.1 with Table 2.2. The number of semi-skilled and unskilled workers fell consistently over the five-year period in each of the four

---

[1] It was necessary in 1961 to break up arbitrarily the old metropolitan boroughs of Wandsworth and Barking to conform to the divisions adopted. It was possible to align all other boroughs precisely.

Table 2.1

The Less-skilled Male Workers in London (1966)

Males	Central Area	Inner London	Middle Ring	Outer London	Greater London
	Numbers in specified socio-economic groups				
Personal Service	11 290	10 240	9 410	11 130	42 070
Semi-skilled	19 820	74 820	100 620	117 730	312 990
Unskilled	16 410	62 250	62 350	55 630	196 640
	Distribution of each S.E.G. between zones				
Personal Service	26.8	24.3	22.4	26.4	100.0
Semi-skilled	6.3	23.9	32.1	37.6	100.0
Unskilled	8.3	31.6	31.7	28.3	100.0
	Each S.E.G. as proportion of all workers				
Personal Service	5.2	2.1	1.4	1.0	1.7
Semi-skilled	9.2	15.5	14.4	10.9	12.7
Unskilled	7.6	12.9	8.9	5.2	8.0
(Sub-total)	(22.0)	(30.5)	(24.7)	(17.1)	(22.4)
All Economically Active	216 170	481 980	695 960	1 074 190	2 468 300

Source: 1966 10 per cent Sample Census.

The boroughs comprising each of the four rings are as follows:

Central Area
City of London
Camden
Kensington and Chelsea
Westminster

Inner Ring
Hackney
Hammersmith
Islington
Lambeth
Southwark
Tower Hamlets

Middle Ring
Brent
Greenwich
Haringey
Lewisham
Newham
Waltham Forest
Wandsworth

Outer Ring
Barking
Barnet
Bexley
Bromley
Croydon
Ealing
Enfield
Harrow
Havering
Hillingdon
Hounslow
Kingston
Merton
Redbridge
Richmond
Sutton

rings, while the number of personal service workers grew in the central, middle and outer rings. To keep matters in perspective, the addition of 310 service workers in the central area has to be compared with a fall of 5750 in the remaining less-skilled workers in the same area. These are of course workers *living* in the four rings. Overall there is no significant change in the level of less-skilled occupations compared with other occupations, though among the less-skilled there is a slight shift from unskilled manual work to personal service work. The London experience, it should be emphasized, is rather different from that in the provincial conurbations which show a slight rise in the levels of less-skilled workers in the main city compared with other workers over the same five-year period.

The fact that the first hypothesis is disproved does not mean of course that less-skilled workers living in the inner city are not

Table 2.2

The Less-skilled Male Workers in London (1961)

Males	Central Area	Inner London	Middle Ring	Outer London	Greater London
Numbers in specific socio-economic groups					
Personal Service	10 880	10 870	8 870	9 380	40 000
Semi-skilled	21 220	86 050	109 000	129 030	345 300
Unskilled	20 760	71 900	68 630	61 210	222 500
Distribution of each S.E.G. between zones					
Personal Service	27.2	27.2	22.2	23.4	100.0
Semi-skilled	6.1	24.9	31.6	37.4	100.0
Unskilled	9.3	32.3	30.8	27.5	100.0
Each S.E.G. as proportion of total workers					
Personal Service	4.5	2.0	1.2	0.8	1.5
Semi-skilled	8.7	15.9	14.4	11.7	13.1
Unskilled	8.5	13.3	9.1	5.5	8.4
(Sub-total)	(21.7)	(31.2)	(24.7)	(18.0)	(23.0)
All Economically Active	242 830	540 427	754 473	1 104 260	2 641 990

Source: Census 10 per cent Sample 1961.

subject to particular pressures through living there. They may suffer higher costs of living for example. A greater proportion of their income might have to go on housing even though the quality of their housing might be significantly lower than similar workers elsewhere. Many may lack security of tenure. It is certainly the case that a greater proportion of inner city residents live in unfit dwellings [16].

The four rings in themselves do not form meaningful economic zones or social areas within London. *They are merely statistical areas arranged to test a particular hypothesis.* The social geography of the city will be infinitely more complex and subtle than these four rings imply.

The Social Areas of London

Less-skilled workers may not be concentrated in Inner London but this is not to imply that they are spread evenly throughout the metropolis. Male less-skilled workers are in fact closely associated with the traditional manufacturing and warehousing zones of London and the newer manufacturing and commercial

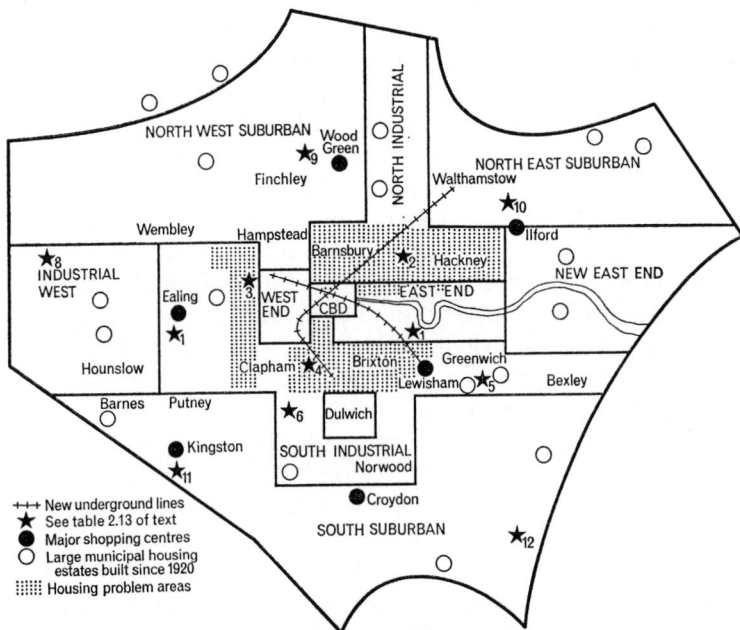

FIGURE 2.1 Social areas

zones of the metropolis. Figure 2.1 presents a diagrammatic view of the 'social area' structure of London. It is based both on the evidence presented in other chapters of this book[1] and on other material [17]. London here is divided into eight broad structural divisions which reflect the layout of the city, the characteristic housing types and conditions, and the socio-economic character of different parts of London:

The Central Business District
The West End

---

[1] Chs. 5 and 6.

The East End
The New East End
The Housing Problem Areas
The Industrial West
The Northern and Southern Industrial Corridors
The Suburban Areas–North-West, North-East and South.

The social class structure of London shows for certain geographical areas a marked degree of social class segregation, most in evidence [18] for example between the East and the West End, and between the interwar working-class suburbs of the New East End and the professional and managerial dormitory suburbs to the north-west and south of London.

The diagram goes some way towards explaining why less-skilled workers are as significant numerically in the outer parts of London as in the inner areas—reflecting radical changes in industrial location preferences, the territorial liberation arising from transport developments, and deliberate public policy over many years. One has to look back to the Housing of the Working Classes movement, the Cheap Trains Act and the development of the LCC out-county estates.

One further point might be mentioned. Even in the most solidly working-class areas of London it is rare to find the number of low-skilled workers exceeding the skilled: at a borough level it happens only in Newham and Tower Hamlets; and even there the scales are tipped the other way again if foremen are ranked with skilled workers. At a ward level [19] there are only twenty-six wards in the whole of London where unskilled, semi-skilled and service workers combine to form more than 40 per cent of the total male economically active population of the ward. These are predominantly in two boroughs—Southwark and Tower Hamlets. Only in one ward in the whole of London do less-skilled workers form 50 per cent of all male workers resident in the ward.

The Coloured Worker in London

The second hypothesis suggests that coloured workers are in low-skill work predominantly in the inner city. There are in reality quite marked socio-economic differences between the different ethnic groups of immigrants in London, but with black Commonwealth immigrants in particular, the socio-economic profile is heavily oriented to less-skilled manual work. British Caribbean workers in semi-skilled and unskilled work, for example, actually outnumber those in skilled work. This is not the case with any other national group and, as we have seen, it is a most uncommon feature in any social area of London. The socio-economic status of black workers as a whole in London therefore is most nearly equivalent to the job profile of the most heavily 'working-class' district of the East End of London—though this statement is not meant to imply that income levels are similar, or that the jobs are the same, or that local employment prospects are no better than those in the East End.

Coloured workers live mostly in the central, inner and middle rings of London. The 1966 census records 380 000 'New Commonwealth' population, of which approximately 290 000 are coloured people from Asia, Africa and the Caribbean. The census, of course, gives no indication of coloured people born in this country—though the Strategic Plan for the South East has commented that adding these to the immigrant totals would give a coloured population of 500 000.

Taking the four concentric rings, the distribution of coloured *immigrants* within London is set out in Table 2.3. The central area, which had a sharp increase in the number of coloured immigrants in the 1950s, shows an appreciable fall in absolute and relative terms in the 1960s. The inner ring shows a steadily increasing coloured immigrant population relative to the whole population of the area, though immigrants still formed less than 6 per cent of the whole population in 1966.

The middle ring shows a substantial increase in numbers in the early 1960s though not sufficient to reach the level of concentration seen in the inner ring. Coloured immigration to Outer London at 1966 was still relatively insignificant.

The inner and middle rings contain extensive areas of 'housing stress'. These areas spread across thirteen London Boroughs. While it is fair to point out that only half of all the coloured immigrants in these boroughs live in the parts designated as 'Stress Areas' in the G.L.D.P. [20], and that the white population still greatly outnumbers the coloured population in these areas, it is nevertheless the case that where housing conditions are at their most acute, the coloured population is the most severely affected [21].

Table 2.3

New Commonwealth Immigrants as Proportion of Total Population in Greater London, 1951, 1961, 1966

	Central Area		Inner London		Middle Ring		Outer London		Greater London	
	New Comm. Immig.	Total Pop.	New Comm. Immig.	Total Pop.	New Comm. Immig.	Total Pop.	New Comm. Immig.	Total Pop.	New Comm. Immig.	Total Pop.
1951 No.	18 224	752 957	?	?	?	?	?	?	62 104	7 770 967
%	2.4	100.0							0.8	100.0
1961 No.	47 366	740 705	81 039	1 601 597	67 556	2 226 523	50 640	3 243 618	246 601	7 992 443
%	6.4	100.0	5.1	100.0	3.0	100.0	1.5	100.0	3.1	100.0
1966 No.	37 700	722 300	89 580	1 566 330	105 060	2 203 420	57 610	3 421 550	289 950	7 913 600
%	5.2	100.0	5.7	100.0	4.8	100.0	1.7	100.0	3.7	100.0

Source: 1951, 1961 and 1966 Census of Population; GLC Special Tabulations, 10 per cent sample for 1966.

It is not possible to make a full area comparison between Metropolitan Boroughs in 1951 and 1961 and the London Boroughs in 1966 because of the lack of comparability of data. For 1951, data by country of birth were available for Admin. Counties and urban areas over 5000, whereas, in 1961, similar data were available for local authorities with population over 2000 born outside British Isles. For areas with less than 2000 born outside British Isles, estimates were used based on total Commonwealth countries, colonies and protectorates resident in England and Wales. Where possible, New Commonwealth countries included only those countries which have predominantly coloured population. Children born in this country to immigrants are not accounted for in the Census.

Census data of course underestimate the level of coloured concentration in these stress areas, as in every other type of area. Whereas the census records 94 000 coloured *immigrants* living in the wards containing housing stress conditions, as against 690 000 people who were born in the British Isles, it may well be at a guess that as many as 90 000 of the latter are coloured. This would mean that, in all, one in four residents in the stress areas of London is coloured. Particular parts of these areas may now consist largely of coloured people. At the time of the 1966 census, for example, twelve wards in Greater London had at least 20 per cent of their population made up of coloured *immigrants* alone.

In very broad terms these characteristics are not unexpected in view of the relatively recent arrival of the bulk of immigrants and the overall housing conditions they encountered in London. But for reasons discussed earlier, it is difficult to demonstrate in what ways the pattern of immigrant and coloured settlement is changing, and how such movements relate to the rest of the population.

Returning to the coloured worker—the location of the less-skilled black Commonwealth workers in London (Table 2.4) underlines the general comments made above: they are predominantly housed in the inner and middle rings, with a high proportion (compared with the indigenous population) doing less-skilled work. Many coloured workers thus face a critical housing situation, one with which their low economic status does not help them cope.

The second hypothesis therefore has validity: there is a marked concentration particularly of black immigrants in less-skilled work, and such workers are significantly concentrated in and around those parts of the metropolis where fierce housing problems exist. Coupled with these two factors there are a limited number of areas in which coloured households form the major element in the community.

Unemployment, Race and the Inner City

The third hypothesis concerns the future employment chances for certain elements in the workforce. This aspect will now be examined.

In America it has long been recognized that unemployment

Table 2.4

The Less-skilled Male Immigrant Worker from the Caribbean 1966

SEG	Central Area	Inner London	Middle Ring	Outer London	Greater London
Service, Semi-skilled and Agricultural Workers	2 750	12 050	12 680	2 860	30 340
Unskilled Manual	1 960	9 360	7 200	680	19 200
Distribution of each S.E.G. between zones					
Service, Semi-skilled and Agricultural Workers	9.1	39.7	41.8	9.4	100.0
Unskilled Manual	10.2	48.7	37.5	3.5	100.0
Each S.E.G. as proportion of total Caribbean workers					
Service, Semi-skilled and Agricultural Workers	29.7	28.6	30.3	29.8	29.5
Unskilled Manual	21.1	22.2	17.2	7.1	18.7
All Economically Active	9 270	42 100	41 820	9 600	102 790
Percentage of Total Economically Active in Each Zone	9.0	40.9	40.7	9.3	100.0

Source: 1966 Census (GLC Special Tabulations), 10 per cent sample census.

is a big-city problem, and a racial one. In this country there is some obscurity about both. *Colour and Citizenship* [22] only went so far as to say that 'when the national trend of unemployment rises, the proportion of immigrants among the total unemployed also rises; thus in times of rising unemployment commonwealth immigrants tend to be harder hit than the general population'. Wright [23] went somewhat further, stating that 'coloured unemployment rates are higher than white, and in all probability at least twice as high; if not higher'. More recently Jones and Smith [24], though not convinced by Wright, have made the point that 'there seems to be a tendency for New Commonwealth unemployment rates to be highest where the coloured population is concentrated, and these regions are those where the unemployment rates for the total labour force are lowest; as a result New Commonwealth unemployment rates exceed total rates'. This latter point is borne out in an analysis of unemployment in London. The rate of unemployment at the time of the census was 3.3 per cent compared with 2.5 per cent for the whole labour force. Male *immigrants* numbered one in sixteen of the total male labour force but one in eleven of the unemployed.

Looking at unemployment more generally, it is interesting to observe that until now government has responded on the basis that it is a product of the industrial structure of certain regions, particularly the peripheral regions of the country—the ones most remote from London; and policies have been geared to this. Yet London has its fair share of unemployment. With 16.9 per cent of the country's male labour force, it has 16.7 per cent of the male unemployment despite the fact that it is in the economically favoured region of the country. Moreover unemployment is prominent in the inner city. Census data in 1966 for wards (Table 2.5) show that unemployment rates exceeding 4 per cent for males under the age of forty-four could be found in 18 per cent of the wards in the central area of London, and 7 per cent in the inner ring, but less than 4 per cent of wards in the middle ring and none in the outer ring. Thus while 1966 was a period of high labour demand—especially in the South East—small parts of the inner city had unemployment rates as high as the Development Areas.

This analysis is based on 1966 census data. Since then, of course, there has been the national economic recession; and the first results of the 1971 census show overall unemployment rates of 6.8 per cent in the central area of London, 7.5 per cent in the inner ring, and 5 per cent in the middle ring.

It is evidence of this kind, reflecting the sudden rapid deterioration in the job vacancy/unemployment ratios, coupled with falling job opportunities—especially in manufacturing and distribution in Inner London—which gives rise to many of the

Table 2.5

Unemployment: Analysis at Ward Level

	Percentage Distribution of Wards where the Male (15–44 yrs) Unemployment Rate was:						Total Ward
	0.99%	1–1.99%	2–2.99%	3–3.99%	4–5.99%	6+%	%
Central Area	24.7	26.0	13.7	17.8	11.0	6.9	100
Inner London	19.1	25.2	35.1	13.7	3.1	3.8	100
Middle Ring	28.4	38.6	23.3	6.3	3.4	—	100
Outer London	56.2	29.8	10.5	2.5	0.6	—	100

Source: Based on data drawn from *Occasional Paper No. 3* (GLC, 1970).

fears expressed at the beginning of this chapter. So much so that there is now talk of long-term, widespread unemployment in the inner city, with coloured people suffering most.

It is the conjugation of events since 1966 which gives rise to the third hypothesis, that the kinds of jobs which immigrants were encouraged to fill in coming to Britain are now disappearing in the automation revolution of these last few years.

The unemployment situation is undoubtedly serious, and as yet there are few estimates as to what the future occupational structure will look like, beyond the assertion that many *unskilled* jobs will not reappear.

It is all the more important therefore to try to see the impact of the events of the last few years on the labour situation in London as clearly as possible. The most comprehensive source of information for this is the Department of Employment records.[1] Though full details cannot be published, an analysis has been made for the post-1966 period in London, including the material which began to be collected in 1971 on the unemployment situation of coloured people. The data on the sixty-one Employment Exchanges enable us to see the picture of coloured unemployment for the first time. Unfortunately we cannot as yet relate the numbers registered out of work in these districts to a population at risk. So it is not possible in the present analysis to refer to unemployment *rates* at individual Exchange levels. Nevertheless a number of characteristics are evident in the London situation.

The unemployment data appear to support census evidence of higher unemployment rates among coloured people generally. For example, in Greater London as a whole, male coloured immigrants comprised 6.9 per cent of the total males unemployed in 1971 whereas they formed only 5.3 per cent of the resident workforce. But even such broad figures as these have to be interpreted with care. The fact is that even in 1966 coloured immigrant workers formed 9.2 per cent of the low-skilled labour force in London. Thus it is somewhat encouraging —in view of the many problems facing coloured workers—that

---

[1] I am grateful to the Department of Employment for access to these records, and wish to make clear that the analyses and interpretations of the data are my own and in no way commit the Department.

by 1971 they formed only 6.9 per cent of the unemployed. Even if we single out black immigrants, half of whom are in less-skilled work, this picture is sustained. They formed 3.7 per cent of the unemployed in London in 1971 (despite being at the 1966 census only 2.5 per cent of the resident male workforce), yet at the time of the census less-skilled Caribbeans were 5.4 per cent of all less-skilled resident workers in London. In the present recession black workers seem to be managing to hold down jobs rather more successfully than one might have feared. This conclusion of course is little comfort to the 2000 or so West Indians in London who are jobless.

These overall figures too will mask significant local variations. Coloured unemployment will be at least as concentrated as the coloured community—and thus certain districts are likely to have large numbers of coloured unemployed.

At May 1971, the Exchange Area figures show that well over half the male West Indian unemployed were concentrated in six Employment Exchange Areas—in Brixton, Hackney, Willesden, Holloway, Tottenham and Lewisham; and in these areas they formed in all 10.5 per cent of the total unemployed (1200 out of nearly 12 000).

Teenage Unemployment

Unemployment among teenagers is now thought to be an emerging feature in Britain's coloured communities, though even as late as 1970, and despite the recession, there was no reference in the literature [25] to particular problems of teenage unemployment. The available evidence from the Youth Employment Offices in London again shows that as yet this is, numerically at least, a small-scale problem. But significantly it is black youths who form the majority of the coloured teenage unemployed: 202 in London in May 1971 out of a total coloured teenage unemployed of 247; that is, about 80 per cent. Once again the picture is one of geographical concentration with 115 of the 202 falling within only six Y.E.O. areas—Brixton, Hackney, Lewisham, Peckham, Tottenham and Willesden. Black youths form 30 per cent of the total teenage unemployed in these areas. These figures cover both immigrants and coloured youths born in the U.K., though the latter seem to form a very small proportion of the total unemployed.

This use of Exchange Area data for 1971 is an attempt to answer the criticism that the 1966 census used earlier is rapidly becoming out of date. It gives a rather more encouraging picture than might have been feared. Nevertheless, however 'up to date' the information may be, the analysis can only be as accurate as the data themselves.

In line with our initial hypotheses, these data emphasise the problem of unemployment in the inner city, though this statement should not eclipse the fact that in parts of Outer London where overall unemployment levels are low, coloured unemployment can be high, as for example in areas associated with the airport industrial complex and Park Royal.

While recognizing the serious situation in parts of the inner city, it is again important to see the effects of the recession on levels of unemployment in different parts of London. Foster and Richardson (in Table 3.12) show that since 1966 the tendency has been for unemployment levels in Outer London to rise towards those in Inner London. In other words the national recession does not appear to have widened the gap between employment opportunities in the inner city as compared with Outer London.

Low Pay as a Factor in the Inner City

Structural changes in London's economy and their effects on the demand for labour raise much larger issues. Our fourth hypothesis concerns the emerging pattern of economic rewards to different groups in the labour force. This is a vast subject which is beyond the scope of this chapter. Its relevance in the context of the present chapter however is that it is sometimes argued that the lowest paid workers (or as it is sometimes put 'the urban poor') are concentrated in the inner city, either because industry there pays badly, because it uses more low-skilled labour than industry elsewhere, or because the only housing available to low income households (wherever they work) is in the inner city among the oldest housing stock. It will be recalled that both the S.P.S.E. and the G.L.D.P. express concern that present levels of selective population migration might mean the virtual abandonment of the inner city to the less-skilled worker.

Looking at the available data, there is cause to doubt whether the lowest-paid workers are concentrated in the inner city. First the evidence of direct household survey [26]. The distribution of households by the size of income of the head of household shows that 25 per cent of households in fourteen Inner London Boroughs earned less than £10 per week. But in the nineteen Outer Boroughs (for this survey [27] London was divided into two groups only) the figure is still 23 per cent. In the income band £10 to £20 per week the figures are 44 and 34 per cent respectively—which means 532 000 households in Inner London and 503 000 households in Outer London. This hardly supports the notion of a significant concentration in the inner city.

The first earnings category may well be elderly retired people but the remaining group of low earning workers confirms the evidence discussed earlier on the distribution of low-skilled workers throughout the metropolis. Supporting evidence is contained in Table 2.6. Occupations containing a high proportion of low-paid workers have been examined in relation to the distribution of these occupations throughout London. The results show that the distribution is not markedly biased towards the inner ring or the central area. More detailed analysis within the group of fifteen occupations shows however that messengers and chefs among male occupations are more significantly concentrated in Central London. But these two occupations in total give rise to only 5000 male workers in the four Central London Boroughs.

Thus *in the London context*, the evidence available at the present time does not support the notion that the lowest paid are concentrated in the inner city. Low income is a condition, and causes problems, over wide areas of the metropolis. This is not to deny however that low economic status in parts of the inner city will present special problems. It may prevent people migrating, getting better jobs or better housing.

The dominant influence on the spatial distribution of less-skilled and low-income workers will continue to be the types of industry employing them. But certain other influences, which are sometimes overlooked, should also be mentioned in this connexion.

Table 2.6

The Lowest Paid Male Occupations

Area of Residence of Workers	Labourers	Clerks	15 Others	Total
Numbers				
Central Area	11 680	20 710	28 120	60 510
Inner London	43 510	42 490	88 630	174 630
Middle Ring	47 100	72 460	94 420	213 980
Outer London	45 030	120 010	113 360	278 400
Greater London	147 320	255 670	324 530	727 520
Percentages				
Central Area	7.9	8.1	8.7	8.3
Inner London	29.5	16.6	27.3	24.0
Middle Ring	32.0	28.3	29.1	29.4
Outer London	30.6	47.0	34.9	38.3
Greater London	100.0	100.0	100.0	100.0

Source: New Earnings Survey 1968.
        Census of Population 1966.

NOTE:

The seventeen occupations in which over 35 per cent of all male workers earn less than £20 week (gross) are included. The residential distribution of male workers in these occupations is calculated from the 1966 census of population. The occupations are as follows: Caretaker, office keeper (83.6 per cent); shop salesman, assistant (72.3 per cent); clerk routine (71.2 per cent); cleaner (69.6 per cent); storekeeper, warehouseman (65.1 per cent) goods porter (64.6 per cent); guard, watchman (59.7 per cent); labourers (56.3 per cent); roundsman, retail sales (54.3 per cent); male nurse (53.0 per cent); chef, cook (51.7 per cent); postman, mail sorter (50.7 per cent); messenger (50.7 per cent); packer, bottler, canner (49.8 per cent); bus conductor (37.7 per cent); painter and decorator (35.3 per cent).

The Economic Base and the Occupational Structure

It is commonplace to point to the long-term shift in occupations from manufacturing to services; shifts which are most pronounced in the conurbations. But there is misunderstanding about what these shifts have involved. They have not come about by men changing their jobs; nor even by significant shifts in the types of occupations taken up by school-leavers. They stem largely from the entry of married women into the labour force. They account to an astonishing degree for the change in the overall occupational structure of London over the last half century.

We can study these trends over half a century with facility. Fortunately the 1921 census compiled data for an area which it called The Greater London Industrial Area and which uncannily resembles the Greater London Council area of today. The boundaries are so close that direct statistical comparison is permissible for 1921 and 1966 using census data. The results are shown in Table 2.7.

The total number of economically active men living in London has remained largely unchanged. The number of female workers has grown substantially, due to the entry of married women into the labour force for the first time. Charles Booth in

Table 2.7

Occupational Structure of the Resident Economically Active Population* of Greater London

Occupation	Males	%	All Females	%	Married Females	%
Greater London (Greater London Industrial Area) 1921						
Basic:	43 526	1.9	4 085	0.3	1 198	0.8
Secondary:						
(a) Metal Manufacture	222 915	9.7	15 585	1.3	1 867	1.3
(b) Clothing Manufacture	90 715	3.9	169 534	14.1	20 177	13.6
(c) Electrical Goods Manuf.	42 705	1.9	10 127	0.8	368	0.3
(d) Others	280 414	12.2	110 166	9.2	14 232	9.6
Sub-total (Secondary)	636 749	27.7	309 397	25.7	36 644	24.8
Tertiary:						
(a) Construction, etc.	559 992	25.0	21 269	1.8	1 089	0.7
(b) Others	1 058 636	46.0	868 531	72.4	109 798	74.0
Sub-total (Tertiary)	1 618 628	71.0	889 800	74.2	110 887	74.7
Total Occupied Population	2 298 903	00.0	1 199 197	100.0	148 729	100.0
Greater London (GLC) 1966						
Basic:	18 610	0.8	2100	0.1	740	0.1
Secondary:						
(a) Metal Manufacture	341 850	13.8	48 910	3.0	30 740	3.4
(b) Clothing Manufacture	37 940	1.5	83 960	5.2	51 890	6.0
(c) Electrical goods Manuf.	90 620	3.7	17 420	1.1	12 040	1.4
(d) Others	296 080	11.2	75 090	4.7	48 100	5.5
Sub-total (Secondary)	766 490	30.0	225 380	14.0	142 770	16.3
Tertiary:						
(a) Construction, etc.	455 640	18.7	41 840	2.6	21 070	2.4
(b) Others	1 208 900	49.6	1 324 730	82.2	701 600	80.0
Sub-total (Tertiary)	1 664 540	68.3	1 366 570	84.8	722 670	82.4
Total Occupied Population	2 468 300	100.0	1 611 140	100.0	877 590	100.0

* Population over twelve years of age at 1921; over fifteen years at 1966.

the 1890s had spotted the social significance of married women working in the East End, but still in 1921 the Report of the census could state, with economy, '. . . the great mass of married women are debarred by their household duties from gainful occupation' [28]. At that time a quarter of all the women workers in the County of London were domestic servants. Half a century later Viola Klein writes, 'Productive work far from being a necessary evil has become a means of self expression and a condition of personal fulfilment; hence it corresponds to a psychological need' [29]. In 1921, one in eight female workers was married; now it is one in two. The married woman has had the largest impact on the industrial landscape since Richard Arkwright and James Hargreaves. As London's employment has grown and become increasingly service oriented, married women have moved into these jobs. The new jobs have not resulted in more workers *overall* living in London. There is thus some prospect that with further shift towards service industries, much of the demand for labour can be met without adverse effect on the housing market, without stimulating migration, and, where low-paid work is involved, without having an adverse effect on average household incomes in London. The evidence for the first two at least is contained in Table 2.8.

A second aspect of importance is the effect that further changes in industrial structure will have on the socio-economic structure. There are three implications here that seem relevant for London, as the metropolis becomes more service industry oriented. Briefly these are as follows. Firstly, the continued change towards a service economy may well extend the social class pyramid since there seem to be more top jobs in service industry than in manufacturing. Secondly, as much low-skilled labour seems to be required in services as in factories; but thirdly, the expansion of the less-skilled service work will afford further opportunities for married women to work, and married women will form a larger percentage of the total less-skilled workforce.

It is not possible to produce a data matrix that would illustrate these points specifically for London—the census does not provide the information—but at a national level data exist to substantiate these points. Tables 2.9 and 2.10 illustrate these themes.

The implications are perhaps that selective outmigration

Table 2.8

Occupation Structure of the Economically Active Resident Population of Inner London

Occupation	Males	%	All Females	%	Married Females	%
Inner London (LCC) 1921						
Basic:	8 255	0.6	442	0.1 ⎫		
Secondary:				⎪		
(a) Metal Manufacture	126 504	9.2	10 027	1.3 ⎬	30 353	27.5
(b) Clothing Manufacture	68 527	4.9	125 162	16.0 ⎪		
(c) Electrical goods Manuf.	24 171	1.7	4 622	0.6 ⎭		
(d) Others	172 479	12.4	77 446	9.9		
Sub-total (Secondary)	391 681	28.2	217 257	27.8		
Tertiary:						
(a) Construction, etc.	351 982	25.4	13 712	1.8 ⎱	79 840	72.5
(b) Others	633 783	45.8	549 200	70.4 ⎰		
Sub-total (Tertiary)	985 765	71.2	562 912	72.2	79 840	72.5
Total Occupied Population	1 385 701	100.0	780 511	100.0	110 193	
Inner London (ILEA) 1966						
Basic:	4 970	0.5	350	0.5	60	0.002
Secondary:						
(a) Metal Manufacture	108 950	11.6	12 680	1.8	8 360	2.4
(b) Clothing Manufacture	19 000	2.0	45 970	6.7	26 520	7.7
(c) Electrical goods Manuf.	32 300	3.4	3 300	0.5	2 080	0.6
(d) Others	116 700	12.4	26 180	3.8	8 320	2.4
Sub-total (Secondary)	276 950	29.6	88 130	12.8	45 280	13.1
Tertiary:						
(a) Construction, etc.	207 100	22.1	17 860	2.6	11 310	3.3
(b) Others	438 070	46.7	568 760	81.3	285 400	82.4
Sub-total Tertiary	645 170	68.8	586 620	83.9	296 710	85.7
Total Occupied Population	939 150	100.0	687 000	100.0	346 230	100.0

from London's population could well continue without adverse effect on the social structure; further that income inequalities will increase under a service economy, and that, ironically, the second household income provided by the wife is unlikely to narrow social class real income differences since female activity rates seem to vary little between social classes [30].

Combined Effects on the Spatial Organization of London

London has always had a tremendous concentration of jobs in and near the centre—today 30 per cent of all jobs in Greater London are still inside the 'Conurbation Centre' of census terminology. But this proportion is falling; the total number of jobs

Table 2.9

A Social Structure and Industrial Structure Matrix for the United Kingdom

Social Structure	Total Employment			Industrial Structure 1961 Males			Females		
	Manu-facturing III–XVI	Con-struction XVII–XVIII	Transport and Services XIX–XXIV	Manu-facturing III–XVI	Con-struction XVII–XVIII	Transport and Services XIX–XXIV	Manu-facturing III–XVI	Con-struction XVII–XVIII	Transport and Services XIX–XXIV
Upper 1	435.2	106.7	1653.2	397.4	102.4	1237.8	37.8	4.3	415.4
3	159.7	70.1	900.4	156.8	69.4	549.3	2.9	0.7	351.1
Total	594.9	176.8	2553.6	554.2	171.8	1787.1	40.7	5.0	766.5
Middle 2	1190.6	154.6	2103.5	519.0	73.7	779.8	671.6	80.9	1323.7
4	307.1	25.4	701.5	265.4	22.5	297.3	41.7	2.9	404.2
5	3219.7	1090.3	1416.8	2652.8	1087.9	1139.3	566.9	2.4	277.5
Total	4714.7	1270.3	4221.8	3437.2	1184.1	2216.4	1280.2	86.2	2005.4
Lower 6	2451.6	253.6	3086.0	1363.6	247.2	1644.7	1088.0	6.4	1441.3
7	1340.0	346.2	1712.2	924.3	331.6	949.1	415.7	14.6	763.1
Total	3791.6	599.8	4798.2	2287.9	578.8	2593.8	1503.7	21.0	2204.4
Total employment	9103.9	2046.9	11 573.6	6279.3	1934.7	6597.3	2824.6	112.2	4976.3
As Percentage of Total Employment									
Upper	6.5	8.6	22.1	8.8	8.9	27.1	1.4	4.5	15.4
Middle	51.9	62.1	36.4	54.8	61.2	33.6	45.4	76.8	40.3
Lower	41.6	29.3	41.5	36.4	29.9	39.3	53.2	18.7	44.3
	100.0	100.0	100.0	100.0	100.0	100.0	100.0	100.0	100.0

Source: Derived from *Manpower Studies No. 6.* Min. of Labour. H.M.S.O. 1967.
Key: 1 Managers and executives   2 Clerical   6 Semi-skilled manual
       3 Higher professional   4 Lower professional   7 Labourers and unskilled
                                   5 Skilled manual

Table 2.10

Changes in Composition of Less-Skilled Categories 1951-61

		Manufacturing		Construction		Services	
		1951	1961	1951	1961	1951	1961
Total employment		3634.3	3791.6	615.4	599.8	4724.3	4T98.2
% change 1951–61		+4.3%		−2.5%		+1.6%	
Males	Nos.	2216.1	2287.9	603.8	578.8	2576.7	2593.8
as % of total		61.0%	60.3%	98.1%	96.5%	54.5%	54.1%
Females	Nos.	1418.2	1503.7	11.6	21.0	2147.6	2204.4
as % of total		39.0%	39.7%	1.9%	3.5%	45.5%	45.9%

in offices, shops and factories in the C.B.D. (Central Business District) and in the inner city is falling (though factories is hardly the right word for some of the manufacturing enterprises near the centre of London) and this has led to fear that London is 'running down'.

It is extraordinarily difficult to distinguish the effects that deliberate governmental policy will have had on the employment levels in the inner city from the effects of the continuing evolution of locational preferences by industry itself. It is equally difficult to say whether the decentralization of economic activity is led by the migration of people, or is the cause of this outmigration. But there are two aspects to the inner city question that should be kept quite distinct. Firstly, the future for manufacturing industry in the inner city, and secondly the role of the C.B.D.

The number of jobs in factories in the inner city has been falling for some considerable time. As measured by the occupational breakdown of inner city *residents* (see Table 2.8) manufacturing employment in 1921 stood at over 600 000 in the old LCC area. By 1966 it had fallen to 365 000. It must continue to fall, both as firms rationalize their manpower needs, as they leave the inner city to find space to grow and expand, as comprehensive redevelopment takes place, and as the price of land in the inner city rises.

The recent economic recession with its high level of unemployment may have cast some doubt on the wisdom of so much redevelopment and compulsory purchase in Inner London in post-war years, but the broad pattern of 'decline' should be seen as inevitable.

The movement away from the inner city however is by no means a straightforward transferal to green fields, new towns and development areas [31]. Much of the movement of firms is over relatively short distances from Inner London to Outer London. Thus, much of the industry that has gone to new and expanding towns has in fact moved from Outer London [32]. It is not the case therefore that regional policies are 'responsible' for the decline of the inner city factory areas.

The diminution of factory work will make future inner city residents more dependent on jobs in the conurbation centre, and thus the long-term trend is for the inner city to become a dormitory area for the C.B.D. The C.B.D. is itself undergoing fairly rapid change but in this case the levelling off of jobs does not appear to herald 'decline'. There are still tremendous economic pressures in the centre. There would be very real grounds for anxiety about the inner city if this were not the case.

The changes in the inner city job structure will certainly have effects in the pattern of household incomes, but it would seem more important and relevant to prepare for these consequences through housing and transportation policies than attempt to manipulate employment opportunities so as to maintain 'the average level of incomes' in the inner city. The general conclusion one is bound to draw is that the transitional problems facing the inner city are unlikely to be helped by steering manufacturing employment to the areas affected, in the context of a metropolitan economy. Such a 'solution' would create far worse problems, as for example, in housing demand and supply.

London is now becoming more polycentric: a megalith instead of a monolith. And this has major implications. First is the development of 'reverse commuting', particularly of the unskilled and semi-skilled. Seventeen thousand men in service and semi-skilled manual work now journey from Inner London (defined here as the former LCC area) to the outer parts of London each day, and 13 000 unskilled manual workers. The movements the other way are 43 000 and 20 000 as Table 2.11 shows. The literature on the pattern of settlement in London by New Commonwealth immigrants illustrates this. Sheila Patterson [33] for example describes how the West Indian 'economic immigrant' lived in Inner London and worked in Croydon. Eventually, slowly, perhaps too slowly, he moves to a house in Croydon. As Miss Gaitskell [34] puts it in another I.R.R. study,

'Croydon becomes the West Indians' Hampstead'. Croydon of course is the archetypal case of a town experiencing the impact of metropolitan 'decentralization'; it continues to send sizeable numbers of its own residents to Central London each day though it is now (since 1951) a considerable job surplus area, drawing in labour from many other surrounding urban and suburban parts of London. Croydon is striking partly because of its unique command south of the Thames. North London has many more centres that are now 'in surplus'.

Table 2.11

Matrix of Workplace and Place of Residence of Selected Employees

Place of Residence	Workplace			
	Workers in Personal Service and Semi-skilled Operations		Unskilled Manual Jobs	
	ILEA Area	Rest of London	ILEA Area	Rest of London
Central Business District	10 550	490	6 280	310
ILEA Area (excluding CBD)	111 570	17 210	70 470	9 490
GLC Area (excluding ILEA)	43 540	136 670	20 130	60 500
Outer Metropolitan Area	6 090	11 670	2 180	4 020
S.E. (Excluding Metropolitan Area)	690	440	130	160
Total Workforce	172 330	166 480	99 190	74 480

Source: 1966 Census of Population (GLC special tabulations).

This raises the second implication: the disposition of jobs more evenly around the metropolis might suggest that labour catchment areas will be more neatly circumscribed. In actual fact, it means they can scarcely be defined at all, if only because jobs in the outer areas are not highly focused—there are no great industrial estates for instance in post-war London. Studying labour catchment in Greater London is like deciphering three or more contour maps of different scales placed on top of one another.

The third implication is that the emergence of stronger labour markets in Outer London should help reduce the degree of social class separation that has developed and emerged over the last century. The spontaneous gentrification process in the inner city is evidence of this, as is the need to provide more public housing in the Outer Boroughs of London. In other words it is very likely that the great need is not to generate this movement but to marshal it. Illustration of the strengthening of these labour markets, both through the movement of industry to Outer London and the development of the strategic and other service centres, can be gained from the current level of female activity rates throughout the metropolis.

Analysis of the married female activity rate obtaining in each ward in London shows an overall high level of participation in the workforce. In nearly every ward, at least one in three wives is working. And Table 2.12 shows that even in Outer London

Table 2.12

Married Women at Work: Activity Rates at Ward Level

	Percentage Distribution of Wards with Activity Rates of:							No. of Wards in Zone
	34.9	35–39.9	40–44.9	45–49.9	50–54.9	55	%	
Central Area	5	8	12	22	26	27	100	74
Inner London	1	1	1	11	43	43	100	131
Middle Ring			1	10	27	42	20	100	176
Outer London	4	8	21	35	24	8	100	314

Source: based on analysis of data contained in *Demographic, Social and Economic Indices for Wards in Greater London*: GLC Research Occasional Paper no. 3, Table 10, Column 2.

on average one in two wives goes out to work. The activity rate is slightly higher in the middle ring, and slightly higher again in Inner London and highest in Central London. But such differences are not dramatic. It seems there is considerable opportunity to work.

Table 2.13 confirms that with a high level of female activity throughout the metropolis reflected in the twelve districts sampled, and a relatively highly dispersed service economy, a considerable proportion of the female workforce can find work locally, and with, in consequence, commuting to the central business district maintained at a fairly constant and moderate level over wide areas of the metropolis.

Encroachment on the Inner City

The two remaining hypotheses suggest that the housing chances of the less-skilled worker in the inner city are constrained by the

Table 2.13

Workplace and Activity Rate Characteristics of Selected Districts in London

Map Ref. No.	Area	Married Women					Men	
		% Econ. Active	Workplace % Distribution				% Service Semi-skilled Unskilled	% Working in C.B.D.
			Same District	Adjacent District	CBD	Elsewhere		
1	East End	60.1	29.9	23.0	23.2	23.6	38.8	26.6
2	Inner Ring: North	58.4	50.0	20.5	13.6	15.9	35.4	22.2
3	Inner Ring: West	59.3	24.2	26.5	33.9	15.4	42.2	28.6
4	Inner Ring: South	63.3	23.9	19.7	30.1	26.3	30.1	37.4
5	East Industrial	52.4	35.2	20.0	19.5	25.3	19.6	30.7
6	South Industrial	57.2	41.9	31.8	10.8	15.5	25.6	21.0
7	West Industrial	53.7	48.1	28.6	9.0	14.3	21.2	16.5
8	West Industrial	46.1	37.8	36.8	5.3	20.1	16.2	18.7
9	N.W. Suburban	50.5	39.3	26.2	15.7	18.8	18.9	24.2
10	N.E. Suburban	44.9	33.3	24.1	19.3	23.3	11.8	28.4
11	S.W. Suburban	56.3	42.7	32.0	6.5	18.8	15.3	17.4
12	S.E. Suburban	44.7	55.9	14.8	15.7	13.6	15.9	31.8

Source: GLC Special Tabulations for Traffic Districts using 1966 Census data.
Notes: The specific Traffic Districts as located on the diagram accompanying this chapter are as follows (with their population and area):

1 New Cross (49 900; 1.8 sq.m.)
2 Hackney (63 200; 2.2 sq.m.)
3 N. Kensington (59 500; 1.4 sq.m.)
4 Clapham (36 500; 1.3 sq.m.)
5 Eltham (48 700; 4.3 sq.m.)
6 Mitcham (53 700; 4.3 sq.m.)

7 Ealing (96 400; 5.9 sq.m.)
8 Ruislip (35 000; 3.9 sq.m.)
9 Finchley (59 500; 4.8 sq.m.)
10 Gants Hill (58 400; 4.60 sq.m.)
11 Surbiton (45 800; 4.2 sq.m.)
12 Orpington (67 500; 12.3 sq.m.)

physical expansion and development of the C.B.D. and by the process of 'gentrification'.

It is extraordinarily difficult to be precise about the social consequences of either at the present time. No data exist on the localized social impact of changes in the C.B.D. There have been no surveys, no monitoring and no public concern until recently. In the case of gentrification, it is paradoxical that the GLC research project which arose out of the public debate over social polarization fails to discern any such thing. It shows a movement towards higher negative unipolarity in certain out-lying suburban areas, and a consolidation of the West End, but no social class change anywhere else in London from a process that has been documented [35] by Westergaard, Glass and others since 1960!

On the same subject, it is astonishing that the recent report on homelessness in London, which arose directly out of concern over the impact of the metamorphosis of Inner London on the less-skilled households, should have failed to pinpoint the effects of 'gentrification' as a cause of homelessness. The issue seems to be eclipsed in Greve's classification [11] of the causes of home-lessness by the description that 'the landlord wanted the accom-modation for himself'.

There has of course been considerable urban renewal in the C.B.D. but the striking feature of the post-war years is that renewal has intensified and consolidated the C.B.D. rather than leading to areal expansion of it. There will have been displace-ment of low-skilled residents in the process—the recent row over Covent Garden is witness to this process—and the 1943 County of London Plan at least showed some willingness [36] to provide local alternative accommodation for displaced service workers, but the overall consequences of commercial expansion at the heart of London in terms of the loss of residential accommo-dation would bear no relation for example to the scale of impact of urban renewal by the local authority itself in the surrounding inner ring.

The falling population, especially in Inner London, might suggest that competition for housing was easing. This is not the case. An astonishing feature of Inner London over the last half century (see Table 2.14) is that despite a fall of $1\frac{1}{2}$ million in population, the number of households has fallen by barely 50 000. One would have expected to see a fall of nearer 500 000,

Table 2.14

Trends in Population, Households, Dwellings and Occupancy Rates in the LCC Area 1921–66

	1921 Nos in Thousands	%	1931 Nos in Thousands	%	1951 Nos in Thousands	%	1961 Nos in Thousands	%	1966 Nos in Thousands	%
Total Population	4.485		4.397		3.356		3.184		3.000	
Population, Private Households	4.244		4.123		3.162		3.025		2.843	
Household Sizes (1,000s in each group)										
1–2 persons	362	32.2	435	36.6	549	48.9	587	51.7	587	55.1
3–4 persons	412	36.8	460	38.7	430	38.4	384	33.9	347	32.6
5‡ persons	347	31.0	294	24.7	142	12.7	163	14.4	130	12.3
Total No. Households	1.121	100.0	1.190‡	100.0	1.121	100.0	1.135‡	100.0	1.064	100.0
Dwelling Sizes										
1–3 rooms	132	18.4	133	17.8	263	32.0	364	38.9	343(153)*	39.6(17.7)
4–5 rooms	196	27.3	215	28.7	274	33.3	334	35.6	311(368)	35.9(42.4)
6‡ rooms	391	54.3	401	53.5	285	34.7	240	25.5	212(345)	24.5(39.9)
Total No. Dwellings	720‡	100.0	749	100.0	821‡	100.0	938	100.0	866†	100.0
Total No. Rooms	4.205		4.348		3.801		3.930		4.188	
Occupancy Rates										
Persons per dwelling	5.9		5.5		3.9		3.3		3.3	
Persons per room	1.0		0.95		0.83		0.77		0.68	

* In 1966 the definition of a room was changed to include all kitchens as rooms. The effect was to increase the size of many dwellings for Census purposes, giving the impression of a fall in the number of small dwellings. In order to facilitate some kind of comparison, all 4-room dwellings in the 1966 Census have been transposed into the 1–3 room category and all 6-room dwellings into the 4–5 room. The figures in brackets show the numbers and percentages of dwellings by size as defined in the 1966 Census, unadjusted for the change in definition.

† This figure has not been adjusted to take account of post-census estimates of 'undercounting' by the GRO.

‡ Because all figures are rounded to nearest thousand, the total is not the sum of the parts.

taking average household sizes. Household fission, lower occupancy rates, second homes and more recently the takeover of dwellings for tourist accommodation, means that for many people housing is as scarce as ever.

A further element is the growth of non-family households, relating directly to the changes in the economic base as just described. The numbers of non-family households increased by 68 000 between 1961 and 1966 in Greater London.

By the mid-1960s, one in two of all households in the central area (Kensington and Chelsea, Westminster, Camden and the City) was without children. The central city has thus become less and less a place for family homes. Many would say that the inner city is no place to raise children anyway (though the present processes of rehabilitation and gentrification may reverse these processes) but for the less-skilled and low-paid worker who has a family, or wants to start a family, there is increasing difficulty in finding accommodation: for him rented accommodation is non-existent, and the price of property places house purchase well beyond his means. Conservation, rehabilitation, gentrification and the consolidation of the C.B.D. will, in many cases, exacerbate his problems.

The planner's basic problem in forming a judgement of these changes is that he still has no model enabling him to equate demand and supply of housing for different socio-economic groups: defining labour catchment areas within the metropolis is difficult; assessing the *availability* of dwellings as against the stock even more difficult. The existing indicators—the number of people in temporary accommodation, the waiting lists, overspill and net migration, the number of new housing starts and conversion—are inadequate guides to housing need and availability.

Conclusions and Policy Implications

Faced with a serious rate of unemployment in parts of the inner city, and continuous redundancy prospects, there is inevitably a tendency to think of solutions along traditional lines: to steer to the areas affected those kinds of industries most appropriate for the available labour surplus. But it is well to remember that these solutions are not readily applicable to conditions in the inner city. Present levels of unemployment are far higher in parts of provincial metropolitan regions, and regional policies are likely to continue giving such areas proper priority; local physical planning constraints are against such remedies for the inner city, and there is the very powerful argument that a policy which does anything to sustain levels of factory work throughout the inner city would have the effect of perpetuating the acute housing situation there.

The long-term *strategic* course is to create opportunities for retraining, for the orderly transfer to other kinds of employment, and outmigration. Unfortunately present machinery at both central and local government levels is inadequate. The I.S.S. is relatively small in scale, restricted to overspill conditions, and geared in practice to more skilled levels of labour. And though there are five Government Training Centres in London, job training of the kind needed for the inner city is linked more with the Development Area type of situation. There is no machinery whereby an individual's housing, employment and income problems, which are inseparably related, can be treated as one problem.

It is increasingly necessary to link central government's employment service with the local authorities' housing service. The only direct link at the moment is on the relatively small scale of planned overspill. The aim, which would involve manpower planning at a regional and metropolitan scale, would be to facilitate the movement of population within the metropolitan areas as the regional economy develops. The Swedish system would seem to point the way.

The emphasis throughout this chapter on the relatively wide distribution of less-skilled workers throughout London and the limited number of districts in which *unskilled* labour is a very significant element in the community gives confidence that such manpower planning and redistribution policies can be managed.

The significance of Outer London might be re-emphasized. Not only are greater proportions of the residents there finding work locally (the numbers travelling to the C.B.D. from Outer London fell by 31 000 in the five years 1961 to 1966) but increasing numbers of Inner London residents are taking up jobs in Outer London—nearly an 11 000 increase in five years. It might help less-skilled workers chasing factory work if the Housing Acts could be amended to require local authorities to meet the housing needs of people who *work* in their areas as well as those who live in them. A statutory requirement of this kind in metropolitan areas might help reduce the long-standing political controversy of ensuring that Outer London helps meet Inner London's housing problems, as the balance of employment tips towards the Outer Boroughs.

Despite the broadly optimistic view taken in this chapter of the economic and physical forces at work in the metropolis, it is quite clearly recognized that the fears expressed in the G.L.D.P. and the S.P.S.E. have foundation in particular local situations within Inner London. But the circumstances of the less-skilled worker in the East End differ from those in Covent Garden and differ again from those in the stress areas. There does not appear to be a single solution or uniform combination of policies for the whole of the inner city.

References

1. BARLOW, SIR MONTAGUE, *Royal Commission on the Distribution of Industrial Population*, Report Cmnd. 6153 (London: H.M.S.O., 1940).

2. ABERCROMBIE, PATRICK, *The Greater London Plan 1944*, prepared for the Ministry of Town and Country Planning (London: H.M.S.O., 1945) and *The County of London Plan 1943* (London: H.M.S.O., 1945).

3. See for example HOWARD, R. S., *The Movement of Manufacturing Industry in the United Kingdom 1945–1965* (London: H.M.S.O., 1968).

4. M.H.L.G. *The South East Study 1961–1981* (London: H.M.S.O., 1964).

5. *G.L.D.P. Statement* (GLC, 1969).

6. *General Strategy and Implementation*, G.L.D.P. Inquiry Proof, E 111/1 (GLC, May 1971) para. 1.14.

7. *G.L.D.P. Statement Revisions* (GLC, February 1972) section 4, para. 4.4.

8. *G.L.D.P. Statement Revisions*, *op. cit.*, para. 3.14.

9. G.L.D.P., E 11/2 (GLC, October 1970) para. 3.32.

10. South East Joint Planning Team, *Strategic Plan for the South East—A Framework* (London: H.M.S.O. 1971), para. 3.29, *et seq.*

11. GREVE, PROF. J., *Homelessness in London*, (Edinburgh: Scottish Academic Press, 1971).

12. G.L.D.P., Inquiry Proof, 11/1 and E 11/2 (GLC).

13. South East Joint Planning Team, *op. cit.*, para. 3.37.

14. *G.L.D.P. Statement Revisions*, *op. cit.*, para. 4.39.

15. The 'less-skilled' categories taken conform with those so called in *S.P.S.E. Studies Volume 2*. Notes to Table 1.1.

16. *The Condition of London's Housing—A Survey*. GLC Research Report no. 4, 1970. Table App. 4.3.

17. (*a*) DALY, M., *Social Characteristics of Greater London Wards*, GLC Research Report, no. 13, September 1971.

(*b*) BUCKINGHAM, M., 'Where to Live in London', *Estates Gazette*, 1971.

(*c*) *Some Aspects of Social Polarization*, G.L.D.P., S 11/113 (accompanying map).

18. GLC Department of Planning and Transportation Research Memorandum 324, September 1971.

19. See for example *Demographic, Social and Economic Indices for Wards in Greater London*, GLC Research Occasional Paper, no. 3, March 1970, Table 9.

20. *G.L.D.P. Written Statement*, Ch. 3.

21. LOMAS, G. M. and LUM, C., *The Housing of Immigrants in London*, GLC Department of Planning and Transportation Research Memorandum 336, Table 7.

22. ROSE, E. J. B., *et al.*, *Colour and Citizenship: a Report on British Race Relations* (Oxford University Press, 1969) 180, Ch. 13.

23. WRIGHT, P., *The Coloured Worker in British Industry* (Oxford University Press, 1968), p. 55.

24. JONES, K. and SMITH, A. D., *The Economic Impact of Commonwealth Immigration* (NIESR, 1970), p. 41.

25. JOHN, AUGUSTUS, *Race in the Inner City*, A Study of Handsworth, Birmingham.

26. *The Characteristics of London Households*, GLC Research Report, no. 5, August 1970, Table 7.2.

27. BOOTH, CHARLES, *Life and Labour of the People of London* (London: Macmillan, 1903), Final volume.

28. *Census of Population 1921*, GRO., Analytical Notes to the County of London Volume.

29. KLEIN, VIOLA, *Britain's Married Women Workers* (London: Routledge and Kegan Paul, 1965).

30. See for example: Registrar General, *Census of Population 1966*, Economic Activity Tables, Part III, Table 29, p. 413.

31. *Mobility of Employment in Greater London*, G.L.D.P. Enquiry B.629. Submitted by the Joint Planning Team of the Strategic Plan for the South East.

32. *S.P.S.E. Studies Volume 2*, Employment.

33. PATERSON, SHEILA, *Immigrants in Industry* (Oxford University Press, 1968).

34. McPHERSON, K. and GAITSKELL, J., *Immigrants and Employment*, IRR Special series 1969.

35. WESTERGAARD, JOHN, *London, Aspects of Change* (C.U.S. Oxford, 1960) Ch. 6.

36. ABERCROMBIE, P., *The County of London Plan* (London: H.M.S.O., 1943), para. 100.

Chapter Three

Employment Trends in London in the 1960s and their Relevance for the Future

C. D. FOSTER AND RAY RICHARDSON

Summary

This chapter considers the problems raised for Londoners by the decline in London's resident and working populations. The first substantive section deals with the problems of specifying the ultimate goals of the GLC authorities. It is concluded that the authorities have been moving towards the position of seeing their fundamental purpose as one of maximizing the *per capita* real income of Londoners subject to the qualification that the relatively disadvantaged are not made worse off by the process of growth. It is suggested that there are particular difficulties in defining precisely the population in whose interests the authorities should seek to act. Also, it is thought that the concept of real income requires a comprehensive specification, for otherwise spurious problems will be posed.

Acknowledgements are made to P. W. Abelson, M. Melliar-Smith and T. Sweetman, and various members of the GLC and DOE who have helped with this chapter but are not responsible for its conclusions.

The second section seeks to present a framework which identifies the major categories of possible social gain or loss that result from population change. It is concluded that emigration by others would tend to benefit those staying behind who were tenants, employees or consumers of certain public services; those who were house owners, employers or users of other public services would tend to lose. Those who emigrate are expected to benefit from their action but it is thought that migration may often be a poor second best to a preferred alternative of improved public decision making.

In the final section there is a discussion of some of the available evidence relating to employment changes, unemployment, vacancy rates, activity rates and earnings. It is concluded that there is no clear evidence that London's population has suffered notable hardship as a result of the decline in the size of the city.

Introduction

The resident population of London has been falling for many years. More recently, it would seem that the number of people working in London has also started to decline. We have heard it suggested that a faster emigration of workpeople than workplaces would cause labour shortages and hence problems for Londoners. We have also heard it suggested that a slower emigration of workpeople than workplaces would cause labour surpluses and hence problems for Londoners. We have even heard both suggestions from the same sources, almost simultaneously.

It is not clear to us that the average Londoner can suffer from both of these alternative events. In this paper we want to consider the problems raised by declining population and workforce and discuss how the GLC authorities should react. We want to consider whether the GLC should seek to reverse or encourage the trends and whether they should seek to change the structure of migration.

The discussion will proceed in three sections. First, we will discuss some ambiguities involved in seeking to express the goals of the GLC authorities. Second, we will consider how a decline in population and/or employment might affect the ability of the GLC authorities to achieve properly expressed goals. Finally, we will marshal some of the available evidence to see how migration actually has affected the welfare of Londoners.

The Goals of the GLC

If one seeks to advise an authority one must have a clear view of what the goals of that authority are or should be. Only then does one have a reference point by which events and alternative policies can be judged. In this section we do not try to suggest what we think the GLC goals should be; rather, we concentrate on what the planning authorities themselves see as their goals. In expressing their goals in the past the GLC has not always been consistent or without ambiguity; here we are trying to state explicitly the goals that we think the GLC is increasingly coming to have.

In discussions of economic planning it is usually suggested that the authorities should seek to maximize the real *per capita* income of the relevant population.[1] In practice the authorities must take into account other considerations, but even with the above planning target at least two ambiguities need to be clarified before coherent policy decisions can be made.

The first of these revolves around the definition and measurement of real income. It is widely recognized that both the structure and level of prices confronting a Londoner differ from those facing a non-Londoner doing a comparable job. It is therefore misleading to make an unqualified comparison of money income between Londoners and non-Londoners or, by extension, between Londoners in one year and Londoners in another year. It is less widely recognized that even sophisticated official price indices do not fully capture the differential costs of being a Londoner. For example, the official indices might reflect some part of the different transport costs faced by Londoners and residents in the rest of the country. However, they will not fully reflect the value of the greater time spent by Londoners in commuting. Similarly, changes in average commuting time between

---

[1] In a more precise formulation there would be a time dimension to the planning target; a preferred target would be the maximization of the discounted flow of real per capital incomes, with some condition imposed on the size of the terminal capital stock if the planning horizon is not infinitely long.

different years are not captured in a time series of average money incomes, even when deflated by the most advanced official price indices. Apart from changing prices and commuting time, we might also wish to include in the full computation of real income such things as differential hours of work, the level of public services, the extent of pollution and the quality of the environment. Putting it another way, for their real income to be high and increasing it should not cost Londoners too much to 'produce' their measured earnings.

There are severe, perhaps insuperable, problems of measurement here, but the concept of real income as opposed to measured income is clear enough. A great advantage at looking at the index of welfare in this comprehensive way is that it helps one to avoid the source of confusion which puts into opposition economic growth and various other goods, for example, the environment. The utility that people derive from their environment *is* part of their real income. If there is growth in measured earnings together with a deteriorating environment there has not been true economic growth unless the value of the former is greater than that of the latter. By now there has been some degree of success in estimating the value people actually set on many of these environmental factors, so that more reliable measures of true economic growth are attainable. However, there is an important difference here between two very distinct valuations placed on environmental change. The first comes from those personally affected, which by definition expresses the effect of the change on their own real incomes; the second is decided by others, official valuers, and is often only tenuously related to how those directly affected will benefit or lose.

The second ambiguity of the above planning target is more difficult to settle; it concerns the definition of the relevant population. Specifically, who is to be considered a Londoner? Consider the following possible definitions:

1 those now resident in London (i.e. at the start of the planning period);

2 those now resident minus those who emigrate;

3 those now resident plus those who immigrate;

4 those now resident minus emigrants plus immigrants;

5 those now resident plus those not resident but working in London;

6 those now resident plus visitors.

The list is not exhaustive but the distinctions between the six definitions are not trivial. As an example, consider the position of emigrants. Definitions 2 and 4 suggest that the welfare of emigrants should be totally ignored, a view held by many people both in the London context and elsewhere. For example, in response to the phenomenon of the international 'brain drain' many people suggest that emigrants should repay to the mother country the cost of much of the human capital they are taking with them. Here the view is that emigrants should at least not impose costs on those who stay behind. An alternative view is that the emigrant has no obligation to repay the cost of his training, just as the child who is leaving home is not expected to repay his parents for all the expenditure incurred by them on his behalf. Here, the interests of the emigrants remain a part of the public interest and there is no case for government action unless the expected gain accruing to the emigrants is smaller than the expected loss suffered by those remaining. A corollary of this alternative view is that the government might properly use the resources of those remaining behind to promote emigration, even if emigrants were the only gainers. Certainly the government should not try to reduce emigration *merely* because those remaining suffer. If the government were to use definition 2 or 4, on the other hand, any losses suffered by those who do not move are a sufficient justification for policies designed to reduce emigration.

There are clear echoes of this brain drain debate in the London context. In one view, the permanent residents of the London Boroughs are suffering because they are helping to finance the education of children, a disproportionate number of whom later live and pay rates outside London. It is also true that the most mobile persons tend to be those on whom the greatest educational expenditure has been lavished. Under definitions 2 and 4 there would be a case in both equity and efficiency for the central government to compensate London for this expenditure. The equity case would derive partly from London being a net loser of human capital and partly from the implication that relatively poor Londoners are subsidizing future relatively rich outsiders. The efficiency case comes from the fact that given definitions 2 or 4, London would want to put too few resources[1]

---

[1] As judged by national interests.

into education and would concentrate unduly on educating and training people for the kind of work expected to be concentrated in London in the future. Under definitions 1 and 3 there would be no such case for external subsidy, although other grounds for subsidy might still obtain.

As a second example of the important differences between the six definitions, consider definition 5, which distinguishes between residents and commuters. The merits of a commuter tax are very different when commuters are considered part of the London population than when they are not. Assume that commuters from outside London could be taxed at a level which more than covered any use by them of London facilities, without inducing a significant number of them to refrain from commuting. Clearly London residents would enjoy an income transfer, but the *per capita* income of 'Londoners' would benefit only if commuters were not included in the definition. Parenthetically this raises an important point of principle. When a tax is levied by a local authority on its residents (or on principles which do not discriminate against non-resident property-owners) it is usually accepted that the authority can raise whatever level of revenue it decides, because there is a democratic check on excess. However, if a local authority levies a tax on non-residents, such as a commuter tax, it may be reasonable for the central government to impose the condition that the tax yield should be no greater than that which can be justified by the costs incurred by the local authority on behalf of commuters. Other principles may be held to apply for a tourist tax, especially when most of the tourists are foreign.

The examples here could be multiplied but the point has perhaps been made. The critical question is, in whose interests should the authorities seek to act? The GLC has not been explicit on this point, but it seems to be increasingly the view that commuters, tourists, and possibly emigrants are seen in the same light as a shopkeeper sees his customers, as sources of income for the true 'Londoner'.

To clarify policymaking these ambiguities in the definition of the GLC's Londoner need to be resolved. Even then there are at least two possible reasons why the goal of maximum real *per capita* income may not be acceptable. First, a maximum might be achieved at the expense of deserving people in neighbouring or distant regions. Partly this revolves around the question of defining the relevant population. To the extent that it does not, that is, to the extent that there is a conflict of interests between Londoners and non-Londoners, it cannot be required of a local authority that it unilaterally moderates its claims. A preferred procedure seems to be that the national government acts as an umpire and rule-maker, but that within the rules each authority takes the maximum advantage it can.

The second, and more important point here is that reliance on maximizing average income is inappropriate because it overlooks the distribution of income. The GLC has recognized this in its concern for actual or impending hardship that might result from large-scale net emigration. In practice there are great limitations on the GLC pursuing the redistributive policies it might favour. Virtually all GLC expenditures must have statutory sanction and many of the services provided must operate within a framework of regulations set by Whitehall, partly in order to achieve greater uniformity between local authorities. For example, the GLC is not at present legally permitted to pay certain kinds of compensation to those made poorer by motorway development. Of course, even if wide redistributive powers were granted to local authorities they would have to be used with some caution because substantial incentives to destabilizing migration are given by large differences in redistributive programmes by area.

For the purposes of the following discussion we assume that the goal of the GLC is to maximize the average real income of those now living in London plus those who migrate into London, with the qualification that the London poor should not be made worse off in absolute terms.

The Effects of a Decline in London's Resident or Working Population[1]

In this section we try to give a relevant framework within which the welfare consequences of emigration can be evaluated. It is not expressed in full detail or rigour but is designed to suggest

---

[1] By 'London's working population' we mean all those who work in London, regardless of their residence, plus officially defined unemployed London residents; by a decline in working population we mean net working population emigration—we thus exclude autonomous reductions in the activity rates of London residents.

the important influences which must be taken into account if population change is to be considered seriously. We will analyse a decline in two steps. First, from a given population we assume that a wholly representative fraction is taken; this may be called a balanced loss of population. Second, we consider the emigration of a group containing a disproportionately large fraction of upper-income, highly skilled members of the labour force; this may be called an unbalanced loss. There is no implication here that London has experienced a balanced loss of population, indeed it is recognized that virtually all emigrant flows are of the second type. In pursuing this two-stage analysis we are hoping to clarify our exposition of some of the difficult analytical points involved.

(a) A Balanced Reduction

It is useful to begin by distinguishing two groups, the emigrants and those who stay. If one has any faith in the ability of people to make decisions in their own interest, it must be concluded that the average emigrant at least expects to improve his situation by moving. An individual may make a mistake and certainly some emigrants lose in the event. On balance, however, it seems reasonable to conclude that the majority of emigrants benefit from moving. It does not follow, however, that the authorities should be passive in the face of emigration, even if those staying behind do not suffer. To see this one must examine the cause of the emigration. For example, if the authorities had mistakenly and inappropriately inhibited the construction of new factories or offices then emigration would take place as an equilibrating reaction. That is, the building ban would limit the number of workplaces and result in a deterioration of job opportunities relative to population. People would then be more inclined to move out, the net advantages of being in London having fallen. The process would tend to continue until the advantages of being in London balanced those of being outside. Even if the movement did not cause those who stayed to suffer, it would still be in the interests of Londoners if the authorities reversed their original decision. In short, emigration may improve an unsatisfactory situation but there may be even better steps that could be taken; it is not the migration that should be criticized but defective policy elsewhere.

Turning to the welfare of those who stay behind, we can pick out a number of areas for analysis, in particular the housing market, the labour market, problems of local government finance and externalities.

1 In the housing market those who rent will benefit from the reduction in population, but those who own housing will lose. Under fairly general assumptions it can be shown that owners lose more than renters gain. This is represented in Figure 3.1.

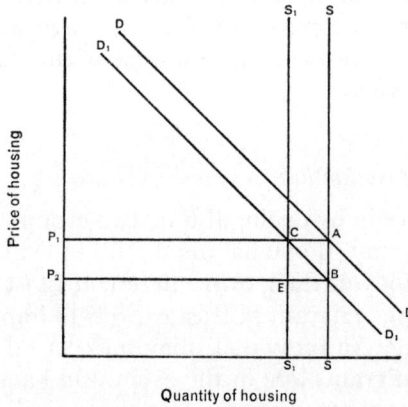

FIGURE 3.1 Affects of population reduction on housing market

On the horizontal axis we measure the quantity of housing in some standardized units; on the vertical axis we measure price. SS indicates the supply of housing, assumed to be fixed; DD represents the demand for housing before emigration and D_1D_1 the demand after emigration. As a result of emigration the price of housing falls to P_2, the owners of the housing stock lose an amount equal to ABP_2P_1, while renters gain an amount equal to CBP_2P_1; the net loss is ABC. In the areas receiving the London emigrants the reverse process takes place.

It is the pattern of house ownership that determines whether those who stay in London lose or benefit in the housing market. We can say that as far as the housing market is concerned, there is no impact on the welfare of the *average* London resident from others emigrating *if* (*a*) the whole housing stock is at all times owned by residents and (*b*) emigrants owned and rented in the same proportions as Londoners as a whole. This is more difficult to demonstrate than the previous proposition, but we can say the following. In Figure 3.1, S_1S_1 represents the supply of housing originally owned by Londoners who do not move; D_1D_1 is the demand for housing from those who do not move. The horizontal difference, at any price, between DD and D_1D_1 indicates the housing that those who emigrated demanded when they were Londoners; the horizontal difference between SS and S_1S_1 indicates the amount of housing formerly owned by emigrants, which is assumed to be sold to London residents when the emigrants leave. The loss suffered on their original holdings by owners who stay, CEP_2P_1, exactly matches the gain enjoyed on their original dwellings by those renters who stay. Renters also gain, by CBE, on the additional housing available to them which results from the decline in the total number of renters. The loss to owners on this additional housing is borne partly by the original owners, the emigrants, and partly by the new owners; in a well-functioning property market the loss will be borne equally, so that the new owners' loss exactly equals the renters' additional gain. Hence, resident Londoners are on average unaffected. The analysis can be extended in a number of ways to introduce greater realism, at the expense of greater complexity. For example, if the long run supply-curve of housing has some positive elasticity, the average Londoner will (on the above assumptions) lose in the housing market but gain in the other markets which use the scarce resources released by the housing market.

Alternatively, if some of the London housing stock were owned by outsiders, the housing market changes induced by emigration would clearly raise the real incomes of London residents. In general, Londoners' real incomes would be more likely to rise from emigration, (a) the more outsiders owned London's housing stock, (b) the more Londoners owned property in the areas receiving London emigrants and (c) the more emigrants owned their own houses in London before moving.

Whatever is true of changes in average incomes, there will tend to be a redistribution away from owners towards tenants. It is not suggested that this redistribution will be instantaneous or uniform, only that the tendency will be in favour of tenants. It might be noted explicitly here that the GLC might wish to attach different weights to the welfare of property owners and tenants, so that even with an unchanged average income the redistribution might be seen as a social gain. One other point is worth stressing. Each of the effects considered here is separately subject to the qualification of 'other things being equal'. In absolute terms rents may be rising over time, and capital gains being realized, for many different reasons; what is being suggested here is that emigration will tend to make, for example, rents lower than they would otherwise have been.

2 In the labour market, balanced emigration would tend to reduce London unemployment levels, and raise both unfilled vacancies and average earnings over what they would otherwise have been. The drift of labour away from London would make London somewhat less attractive than otherwise for employers, so some would react by leaving. The latter change would almost certainly be an equilibrating rather than an explosive reaction however, so that London workers,[1] as a group, would benefit. Nevertheless, some workers might suffer very substantial costs of re-adjusting when their original employer leaves the city. Typically, the costs are relatively severe for the unskilled worker, the older worker, the very specifically trained worker and the secondary worker whose geographical mobility is limited. Even when a given change is beneficial for London as a whole, there is a strong case for government action to alleviate the pockets of distress that the change often implies.

Overall, balanced emigration would therefore be injurious to the average owner of capital. Again, the loss to capital somewhat exceeds the gain to labour, so to know the impact on the average Londoner one would need to know what fraction of fixed capital in London was owned by residents of London and what was the extent of ownership by Londoners of the capital in the areas to which the emigrants moved.

3 The impact of emigration on local government service provision and finance is complicated in full detail but fairly simple in basic form. The main question to be answered is whether the emigration changes the cost of the original level of public services enjoyed by the average Londoner not leaving the city. In considering this problem it is useful (a) to make a clear distinction between economies of scale on the one hand and decreasing costs with respect to output on the other and (b) to pay particular attention to the difficulties involved in defining the output of local government services.

---

[1] This term is used to cover all employees.

Economies of scale may be defined by example. There would be economies of scale in, say, steel production if it took *less* than twice as many units of factors of production to produce, say, 200 000 tons as it took to produce 100 000 tons. There would be constant returns if 200 000 tons required exactly twice as many factor units as 100 000 tons. The whole discussion here, whether of output or factors, is carried out in physical, not value, terms.

Even if there are constant returns to scale, there will still be increasing unit costs as output expands, *if* the prices of factors of production rise as more factor services are employed. Similarly there could be a combination of increasing returns to scale (implying falling unit costs at *fixed* input prices) plus rising factor prices, to give increasing unit costs on balance.

Secondly there is a problem of defining output. Consider a local government financed radio station. One notion of output would be the number of hours the station is transmitting. A second notion, and a better one, would be the number of listeners' hours, i.e. transmitting hours times average audiences. Even though unit costs might rise for the former notion they would fall for the latter. Output would be increased if one more listener tuned in even if other input use (e.g. transmitters, records, etc.) remained unchanged. This is an example of a 'pure public good', where one man's use does not subtract from the availability of the service to others.

With a mixed public and private good, matters are more complex. Consider police services. Assume that we have a given expenditure commitment on police services and a resident population of seven million. Police output may be defined as some index of the number of crimes prevented plus the social satisfaction felt from the punishment meted out to apprehended criminals. What happens when population falls to six million? First potential total crime presumably falls, though whether it falls in proportion to population is less clear. Prevented or deterred crime may rise or fall; (a) with the fall in potential crime there is less crime to be prevented; (b) with no change in expenditure on police services plus a smaller amount of potential crime, the probability of successful crime presumably falls and hence the proportion of potential crime prevented probably rises.

Thus it is not clear what happens to total output, even though output per head of the resident population will probably rise. Financing costs per resident also rise. Whether output per resident rises relative to costs per resident is not clear *a priori*; nor is it clear what would be the new cost per resident necessary to secure the original level of output per head. These relationships depend on the relationship between criminal activity and population size on the one hand, and on the relationship between police expenditure and police output on the other.

We can now sketch an answer to the main question posed in this section. If there are constant returns to scale in the public sector and if factor prices do not change, balanced emigration will not change the cost of the original level of services enjoyed by the average Londoner not leaving the city. This is not to say that the average Londoner will continue to consume that original level of service. Very often with emigration, total public expenditure responds only modestly, with the implication that consumption per head increases, along with the financing burden. In such a case there is often a temptation to conclude that the resident has suffered either because his rate bill has risen or because the cost of service per resident has risen. The temptation should be ignored unless one is confident that average consumption of the service has not similarly risen.

Relaxing the above assumptions, any public services may enjoy economies of scale, so that, other things being equal, the average costs of public services rises with a smaller population.[1] Further, with emigration, relative factor prices will change so that land becomes cheaper and labour more expensive. An implication is that the 'factor intensity' of public service production—i.e. the relative importance of land, labour and capital in production—is an important determinant of changes in average cost from declining city size. Following emigration there will be greater cost reductions in public service provision the more land intensive is the production process.

All of this discussion has implicitly been very long run. In practice there may be severe transitional problems for the public

---

[1] It may be observed that there seems to be very little knowledge relating to the U.K. as to the actual relationships between inputs and outputs for public sector goods. Preliminary work is being done, particularly in education, but generally the picture is empty.

services implied by a reduction in city size. At any time a city has a given inheritance of infrastructure, the necessary maintenance of which may involve substantial burdens on a reduced population until the infrastructure can be slimmed down to an appropriate size.

On the cost side of public service provision, therefore, the effects of emigration are ambiguous. They will be influenced by the nature of the production technology, the course of factor prices and the inherited infrastructure. Residents may have to pay more or less for a given level of service and may be forced in the short run to consume more services than would be optimal if adjustments were rapid.

On the revenue side a balanced emigration will probably help matters because local government revenues are unlikely to fall in proportion to population. A full account here would turn partly on the rating provisions applying to those structures newly vacated and remaining empty and to those structures whose use was altered, and partly on the changes in revenue from local services and from outside. It seems unlikely that revenue would drop by a greater proportion than population.

4 Emigration would have an effect on environmental congestion and externalities. The evidence seems to be that most environmental nuisances are a *progressive* effect of higher population densities. The greater the concentration of noise, traffic, contagious disease, air pollution and many more, the progressively worse are their consequences. These are well-known problems and within the range of population change being considered it is likely that the welfare of those who remain will be raised by others emigrating.

Overall a balanced reduction in population promises anxiety for property owners, employers and, more problematically, consumers of some local services. Tenants, workers, the consumers of other local services and those enjoying reduced congestion all benefit. Of course, some individuals, e.g. property-owning workers, have an ambiguous experience. Many will suffer costs of adjustment. Finally we emphasize again that many of the emigrants, if they are being 'squeezed out', may be suffering unnecessarily. They may be the victims of private decisions that do not fully reflect social valuations; equally, they may be the victims of injudicious planning decisions.

Implicitly we have been discussing a rundown in working population that comes from people leaving the city. It is worth a few words to consider a reduction in working population that comes from a fall in inward-commuting or a rise in outward-commuting, resident population remaining the same. With less inward-commuting, there is a smaller pressure on existing public services and less congestion generally. To the extent that the commuters do not pay the full cost of their public service usage, London real incomes increase. Otherwise the analysis remains the same. Labour market opportunities for the average resident Londoner improve, although some may suffer transitional costs; the housing market is initially unaffected but to the extent that some residents leave in response to the equilibrating drift of workplaces, the rise in house prices is somewhat reduced. The story for increased out-commuting is similar except that there can be no presumption that the demand for public services is directly unchanged.

(b) An Unbalanced Reduction

In many respects an unbalanced reduction has qualitatively the same effects as a balanced reduction. There are, however, additional complexities and qualifications. As far as the welfare of emigrants is concerned the above discussion need not be altered except to observe that the emigrants are, by assumption, wealthier than average and hence an authority largely concerned with the welfare of the poor may put a low weight on the gains accruing to emigrants.

For those remaining behind we may again focus on the housing market, the labour market, local government services and externalities and add explicitly the impact on the price structure of goods and services. In the housing market the main direct impact is on the higher quality sector; over time this impact will filter down to other sectors. As emigrants are now more likely to be property owners there is a greater presumption than with a balanced reduction that those remaining on average benefit in the housing market; as before it may take time for the poorer to benefit.

In the labour market, given a disproportionate emigration of skilled workers, those who are substitutes for the emigrants gain while those that have a complementary relationship lose.

Overall, labour probably gains and employers lose thus setting off some reactive emigration of workplaces. This, as before, will impose adjustment costs on those staying but is not likely to accelerate into an emigration spiral. There is no general indication as to which skill groups are substitutes for others and which are complements; obviously skilled workers themselves will benefit if their fellow skilled workers emigrate.

One point is worth particular stress. Given that the highly paid are heavily represented among the emigrants, the measured earnings of resident Londoners will fall.[1] This arithmetic truism does *not* imply that anyone is worse off, indeed everyone could, in principle, have been made better off. Thus, following a change in the structure of the labour force an unqualified discussion of changes in measured earnings will not be a sound guide to the changes in welfare of the population.

With a change in the structure of the labour force there will clearly be changes in the structure of prices of goods and services. This is most clearly seen with services. The prices of services produced by skilled labour rise in relative terms, while prices of those produced by complements to the skilled labour fall. Also, following the change in the distribution of income coming from the emigration, the pattern of final demand alters, away from luxuries. All these changes are difficult to isolate and impossible to combine in a satisfactory index of change and should perhaps be neglected.

Changes in the public sector are also complicated, but cannot so easily be passed over. Added to all the above problems of returns to scale, factor price changes and definitional problems we must now add the imponderables of changes in demand for publicly provided goods stemming from changes both in the structure of incomes and in the different tastes of different socio-economic groups. To take a simple case, if every group had the same tastes, and if for all government goods an x per cent rise in incomes led to an x per cent rise in demand[2] then nothing need be added to the above discussion. However, we know that this simple case is not realistic, if only because some government

---

[1] This is true in the static, other-things-being-equal context; more generally earnings will be lower than they would otherwise be.
[2] i.e. if all income elasticities are unity.

activity is specifically designed to assist the poor. For such a service the government commitment would be unchanged if only the relatively rich emigrated. In technical language, the more a service faces a low income elasticity of demand the less can government expenditure fall under a condition of unbalanced emigration while continuing to meet the initial commitment.

There is surprisingly little information on the income elasticity of the different local government services in the U.K. We would guess that, for example, refuse disposal and at least some kinds of education have a high elasticity, while public housing and certain social services have a low elasticity. However, guesses are very unsatisfactory so that funding some research into this area promises a high return.

On the revenue side of the account little needs to be added to the above but overall there is a clear possibility that the local government budget is in some danger following unbalanced emigration. That is, on this account alone there is a real possibility that emigration causes those remaining behind to suffer a loss of central government subsidies or transfer payments.

On environmental congestion and pollution the impact of unbalanced emigration is qualitatively the same as before. Quantitatively, it may be that the upper and middle income groups give rise to disproportionate amounts of congestion and pollution. Also, it is likely, as with all these individual effects, that an unbalanced reduction leads to a more spatially uneven distribution of gains and losses than a balanced rundown. Otherwise the picture seems unaltered.

(c) Summary of Effects of Emigration

We have tried to isolate the important strands of principle which determine whether emigration works in the interests of Londoners or not. Net in-migration would have the reverse effects, and an unbalanced change of, say, fewer highly skilled and more low-skilled workers can be analysed by adding components together. Naturally, the discussion is not conclusive in indicating for example what gains or losses will come from a further reduction in London's population. Rather, it sketches the empirical questions needing an answer before a confident evaluation of a particular event can be made.

Table 3.1

Employees (Excluding Self-employed and Unemployed)

	GB Total	GB Male	Female	GLC Total	GLC Male	Female
1960	22 076	14 346	7 690	4 577	2 833	1 744
1961	22 373	14 573	7 800	4 655	2 891	1 764
1962	22 575	14 712	7 860	4 707	2 923	1 784
1963	22 603	14 723	7 880	4 706	2 919	1 787
1964	22 892	14 902	7 990	4 685	2 901	1 784
1965	23 147	14 897	8 250	4 651	2 873	1 778
1966	23 301	14 771	8 530	4 650	2 851	1 809
1967	22 828	14 488	8 340	4 555	2 770	1 785
1968	22 645	14 223	8 420	4 508	2 732	1 776
1969	22 600	14 180	8 420	4 428	2 688	1 740
1970	22 404	13 914	8 490	4 323	2 614	1 709
	S.E.			R.O.S.E.		
1960	7 420	4 672	2 748	2 843	1 839	1 004
1961	7 490	4 717	2 773	2 835	1 826	1 009
1962	7 620	4 791	2 829	2 913	1 868	1 045
1963	7 679	4 825	2 854	2 973	1 906	1 067
1964	7 759	4 861	2 898	3 074	1 960	1 120
1965	7 963	4 974	2 989	3 312	2 101	1 211
1966	8 013	4 948	3 065	3 363	2 097	1 265
1967	7 881	4 846	3 035	3 326	2 076	1 270
1968	7 856	4 821	3 035	3 348	2 689	1 259
1969	7 835	4 803	3 032	3 407	2 115	1 292
1970	7 740	4 717	3 023	3 417	2 103	1 314

Sources: GB and S.E. figures from *DEP Gazette*. GLC figures from DEP, Watford. R.O.S.E. figures estimated.

Recent Changes in Employment in London

Table 3.1 gives the official estimates of the number of employees in employment over the years 1960–70 in the GLC, the South East (S.E.), the South East minus the GLC (R.O.S.E.), and the country as a whole (GB). It will be seen that employment in the GLC has fallen consistently from 1962, that male employment in particular has fallen strongly and that female employment has had a much more uneven experience. Table 3.2 manipulates these data to show employment in the GLC, S.E. and R.O.S.E. as a percentage of GB employment. The London decline is still there, while that for females becomes more distinct; there is a striking contrast between the GLC and R.O.S.E.

Table 3.2

Employees: Regions as Percentage of GB

| | GLC/GB | | | R.O.S.E./GB | | | S.E./GB | | |
	Total	Male	Female	Total	Male	Female	Total	Male	Female
1960	20.3	19.2	22.4	12.6	12.5	12.9	32.9	31.7	35.3
1961	20.5	19.5	22.4	12.5	12.3	12.8	33.0	31.8	35.4
1962	20.6	19.6	22.4	12.9	12.5	13.1	33.3	32.1	35.5
1963	20.5	19.6	22.3	13.0	12.8	13.3	33.5	32.4	35.6
1964	20.2	19.3	21.8	13.2	13.0	13.7	33.4	32.3	35.5
1965	19.9	19.1	21.4	14.1	13.9	14.6	34.0	33.0	36.0
1966	19.7	19.0	21.0	14.2	13.9	14.7	33.9	32.9	35.7
1967	19.6	18.8	21.0	14.3	14.1	14.4	33.9	32.9	35.9
1968	19.6	18.8	20.9	14.5	14.4	14.8	34.1	33.2	35.7
1969	19.3	18.7	20.3	14.8	14.7	15.1	34.1	33.3	35.4
1970	19.0	18.4	19.9	15.0	14.8	15.3	34.0	33.2	35.2

Source: from figures in Table 3.1.

The question to be considered here is whether the GLC should feel any anxiety over these changes, where anxiety has reference to the set of goals suggested in the section on the goals of the GLC, above. If employment is falling because work-places are *leading* the movement from the city, then the GLC has cause for concern. In such a case, unless there were initially great shortages of labour, unemployment would rise and earnings would be depressed. The ensuing induced emigration of employees might improve the situation but on balance

Table 3.3

Unemployment Percentages (For All Unemployed)
(Average of March and September Figures)

| | GB | | | GLC | | | S.E. | | | R.O.S.E. | | |
	Total	Male	Female	Total	Male	Female	Total	Male	Female	Total	Male	Female
1960	1.5	1.7	1.2	0.8	0.9	0.5	1.0	1.1	0.6	1.1	1.3	0.4
1961	1.3	1.5	1.0	0.9	1.0	0.5	1.0	1.1	0 6	1.1	1.3	0.8
1962	1.8	2.1	1.3	1.1	1.3	0.7	1.2	1.5	0.8	1.3	1.7	0.9
1963	2.2	2.6	1.5	1.4	1.7	0.6	1.5	1.9	0.8	1.4	1.8	1.0
1964	1.6	1.8	1.1	0.9	1.2	0.5	1.0	1.2	0.5	1.0	1.3	0.6
1965	1.3	1.6	0.9	0.8	1.0	0.4	0.8	1.1	0.4	0.8	0.9	0.6
1966	1.4	1.7	0.8	0.8	1.1	0.4	0.9	1.2	0.4	1.1	1.5	0.6
1967	2.2	2.8	1.1	1.6	2.2	0.6	1.6	2.2	0.6	1.6	2.3	0.8
1968	2.3	3.1	1.0	1.5	2.2	0.5	1.6	2.2	0.6	1.6	2.3	0.7
1969	2.3	3.2	0.9	1.4	1.9	0.4	1.5	2.2	0.5	1.7	2.4	0.7
1970	2.5	3.4	1.0	1.4	2.0	0.4	1.6	2.4	0.5	1.8	2.6	0.7
1971*	3.0	4.0	1.2	1.6	2.3	0.5	1.9	2.5	0.5	2.2	3.3	0.8

* Average of March and June figures.
Source: *DEP Gazette.*

Londoners are unlikely to benefit.[1] If, to the contrary, employment is falling because workers are leading the movement from the city we have to refer to the taxonomy of the previous section.

In order to see which of these alternative scenarios is more likely to have applied we may refer to Tables 3.3 and 3.4 which give information on unemployment over time for the four regions considered here. From these figures it can be seen that unemployment in the GLC has been consistently below that in

Table 3.4

Unemployment Percentage Relatives

e.g.: $\dfrac{\text{Unemployment GLC (\%)}}{\text{Unemployment GB (\%)}}$

	GLC/GB			R.O.S.E./GB		
	Total	Male	Female	Total	Male	Female
1960	53	55	42	73	76	75
1961	69	66	50	84	87	80
1962	61	61	54	72	81	69
1963	64	65	40	63	69	66
1964	56	66	45	63	72	54
1965	62	63	44	61	56	67
1966	57	66	50	79	88	75
1967	73	79	55	73	82	73
1968	65	71	50	70	74	70
1969	61	59	44	74	75	78
1970	56	59	40	72	76	70
1971	53	57	42	73	83	67

Source: Figures in Table 3.3.

the rest of GB in the sixties. In 1970, the unemployment rate of 1.6 per cent in the GLC was only just over half the rate of 3.0 per cent for GB. The GLC unemployment rate has also been equal to or below the unemployment rate in R.O.S.E. throughout this period. Since 1967, there has been a tendency for the

---

[1] To be certain of what happened to the welfare of the average Londoner in this situation one would also need to know something about the pattern of ownership of capital. For example, if London residents owned all the capital that was moving from London with the migration of workplaces, then the higher return presumably earned by this capital outside London would represent an offset to the losses suffered by the London working population.

GLC's position to improve relative to R.O.S.E. The trends for all unemployment hold also for male and female unemployment separately.

The unemployment rates for the GLC and R.O.S.E. are compared with those for GB by the use of percentage relatives in Table 3.4. These show that unemployment in the GLC relative to that in GB, was at its highest, both for all employees and for males, in 1967; since then it has declined steadily. In 1970 and 1971 unemployment in the GLC relative to that in GB was as favourable as at any time in the sixties. The relative unemployment position in R.O.S.E. has been remarkably constant, especially since 1967, which implies that R.O.S.E. has followed national trends more closely than has the GLC.

To check the interpretation drawn from these data one can also examine the data relating to job vacancies, shown in Tables 3.5 and 3.6. These show that adult vacancy rates for males and

Table 3.5

Adult Vacancies: as Percentage of Total Working Population
(Including Unemployed and Self-employed)

	GB Total	GB Male	GB Female	GLC Total	GLC Male	GLC Female	R.O.S.E. Total
1960	0.85	0.74	1.11	1.13	0.87	1.54	1.32
1961	0.85	0 76	1.08	1.13	0.89	1.53	1.11
1962	0.60	0.47	0.76	0.80	0.61	1.11	0.85
1963	0.57	0.42	0.86	0.82	0.61	0.17	0.93
1964	0.87	0.69	1.23	1.23	0.98	1.73	1.38
1965	1.05	0.87	1.39	1.37	1.02	1.91	1.52
1966	1.02	0.83	1.30	1.21	0.94	1.65	1.70
1967	0.67	0.56	0.92	0.86	0.60	1.27	1.10
1968	0.75	0.57	1.06	0.87	0.61	1.29	1.17
1969	0.79	0.64	1.08	0.91	0.74	1.20	1.38
1970	0.74	0.63	0.94	0.92	0.76	1.19	1.18

Source: *DEP Gazette* and DEP Watford Office. Average of March and September vacancy figures.

females in the GLC were higher than those in GB throughout the 1960s.

The GLC rates between 1967 and 1970 fell from the 1964 to 1966 period but were higher than they had been in the GLC in 1962 and 1963. They were however consistently below the adult vacancy rates in R.O.S.E. Further, GLC vacancy rates were slightly lower in the second half of the 1960s than in the first half compared with GB as a whole. However, there has been *no* tendency towards a relative deterioration in vacancy rates since 1966. Relative vacancy rates in R.O.S.E. were slightly higher in the second half of the sixties than in the first half.

Table 3.6

Adult Vacancy Rates: GLC and R.O.S.E., compared with GB

$$\text{i.e.:} \frac{\text{vacancies GLC (\%)}}{\text{vacancies GB (\%)}}$$

	GLC/GB Total	GLC/GB Male	Female	R.O.S.E./GB Total
1960	133	117	139	155
1961	133	132	142	131
1962	133	130	146	141
1963	144	145	136	163
1964	142	142	141	159
1965	130	117	137	145
1966	119	113	127	166
1967	128	107	138	164
1968	116	107	122	156
1969	115	114	111	175
1970	124	121	127	159

Source: Table 3.5.

All these figures support the view that the loss of workplaces has not been the leading, independent influence on the decline in employment in London. It is possible, however, that these average figures for London as a whole disguise great problem areas. If the data were disaggregated a different interpretation of recent changes might be suggested.

Table 3.7 gives the employment rundown by industrial sector; it should be noted that these figures include employees registered as unemployed. The fall in employment of 350 000 in the manufacturing sector between 1961 and 1970 was by far the most important factor in employment and accounted for three quarters of the total fall in employment. The fall in the manufacturing sector was continuous throughout the period. Other significant falls in employment of about 60 000 occurred in both the construction sector, starting in 1964–5, and in the distributive trades sector from 1966. Part of the fall in employment in construction may have been due to increased productivity, estimated by the Phelps Brown Report [1] at 3.0 per cent p.a.; it is

Table 3.7

GLC Total Employees, Including Unemployed (in Thousands)

	All Manf.	Agric. Forest Fish	Mining Quarry	Construc-tion	Gas Elec. Water	Trans. Comm.	Dist. Trad.	Finance Insure. Bank	Prof. Science	Misc.	Pub. Admin.
1960	1595	13	4	278	81	437	678	249	403	571	301
1961	1611	13	4	291	83	450	687	257	411	573	368
1962	1587	13	4	297	85	466	701	264	424	603	312
1963	1560	12	4	299	84	456	710	280	415	602	326
1964	1516	10	4	306	83	450	705	281	444	603	334
1965	1475	7	6	304	85	445	704	282	449	598	321
1966	1431	6	4	297	85	448	707	274	481	607	339
1967	1402	6	7	282	86	456	675	291	503	587	344
1968	1327	6	7	260	72	466	677	302	509	577	346
1969	1307	5	7	266	78	446	649	306	503	577	338
1970	1253	4	5	239	66	459	627*	456*	504	418*	349

* Revised definition.

Total Employees in GLC by Industry, Including Unemployed (in Thousands)

	Total	All Manf.	Agric. Forest Fish	Min. Quar.	Constr.	Gas Elec. Water	Trans. Comm.	Dist. Trad.	Ins. Bank	Prof. Sci.	Misc.	Pub. Admin.
Males												
1960	2860	1039	9	3	260	72	369	351	143	151	259	204
1961	2918	1050	9	3	270	73	377	356	148	158	265	207
1962	2964	1041	9	3	275	75	392	362	151	163	283	209
1963	2950	1026	8	3	278	73	382	372	157	148	284	219
1964	2935	995	8	3	284	72	376	367	158	171	289	213
1965	2895	966	5	4	281	73	370	364	159	173	287	213
1966	2873	935	4	2	275	73	371	363	153	181	293	223
1967	2829	915	4	5	263	75	375	338	159	186	285	222
1968	2787	876	4	5	249	69	383	338	168	189	281	225
1969	2737	866	4	5	244	65	364	327	172	186	285	219
1970	2664	836	3	4	210	63	371	317	228	191	220	221
Females												
1960	1750	556	4	1	18	9	68	327	106	252	312	97
1961	1771	561	4	1	21	10	73	329	109	254	308	101
1962	1793	546	4	1	22	10	74	339	113	261	320	103
1963	1798	534	4	1	21	11	74	338	123	267	318	107
1964	1793	521	3	1	22	11	74	340	123	273	314	111
1965	1784	509	2	2	23	12	75	343	123	276	311	108
1966	1825	496	2	2	22	12	77	363	121	300	314	116
1967	1794	467	2	2	19	13	81	337	132	317	302	122
1968	1772	451	2	2	21	13	82	329	134	320	296	121
1969	1745	441	1	2	22	13	82	329	134	317	292	119
1970	1716	417	1	1	19	13	88	310	228	313	198	128

Note. Change of classification in 1970 for distribution trades. We have estimated figures consistent with the trend. Definition also changed for insurance, finance, and miscellaneous.

significant however, that commercial and office building declined while the volume of domestic building was more stable.
The controls on office building and the decline in manufacturing were probably the most important causes of the decline in
construction employment in London. The fall in distribution
and trade employment coincided with the imposition of s.e.t.,
but there is some evidence that it was also related to increased
productivity.

The only important increases in employment in the 1960s
were in the professional and scientific services, about 100 000,
and in insurance and banking, about 60 000. The other important groups, transport and communications, public administration and miscellaneous, remained fairly constant over the ten
years without any sign of a trend.

In Table 3.8 the sectoral employment figures are shown for
each sex group. This table shows that female employment fell in
similar fashion to male employment in manufacturing, by about
20 per cent, and in distribution, about 15 per cent, and rose
similarly in professional services, by about 15 per cent. Total
female employment held up better than male employment because it was less heavily concentrated in the manufacturing and
construction industries, which experienced the major declines
in employment in the GLC.

It is also possible to report on unemployment by industry
sector, although these data are usually viewed with more suspicion than the above. Table 3.9 gives unemployment figures for
manufacturing in the GLC and GB from 1960 to 1970. Although the number of employees in manufacturing in the GLC
fell substantially in the sixties, the unemployment rate in GLC
manufacturing was always *lower* than the unemployment rate in
other GLC sectors. The unemployment rate in GLC manufacturing was also consistently *lower* than the GB rate in manufacturing. Indeed the unemployment rate for both males and
females in GLC manufacturing has moved favourably relative
to GB since 1966. Table 3.10 gives some comparison on this
point between the GLC and R.O.S.E. Manufacturing unemployment in R.O.S.E. was very low in 1967, only 0.4 per
cent, but increased to 1.4 per cent by 1970. Some of this
increased unemployment from 5000 to 18 000 was doubtless
due to out-migration from the GLC, where manufacturing,
unemployment fell from 19 000 to 15 000. Nevertheless the

Table 3.9

Unemployment Rates and Relatives in Manufacturing

	Percentage Unemployed GLC		GB		Percentage Relatives GLC (%) / GB (%)		
	Male	Female	Male	Female	Male	Female	Total
1960	0.7	0.4	1.0	1.0	68	41	60
1961	0.7	0.4	0 9	0.8	78	50	75
1962	1.1	0.7	1.3	1.2	81	58	69
1963	1.3	0.7	1.8	1.5	71	49	65
1964	0.8	0.5	1.1	0.9	78	52	64
1965	0.7	0.2	0.9	0.7	81	41	75
1966	0.8	0.4	0.8	0.6	100	72	88
1967	1.7	0.6	1.9	1.1	90	56	85
1968	1.8	0.5	2.0	0.9	91	57	82
1969	1.5	0.4	1.9	0.7	81	50	73
1970	1.6	0.3	2.1	0.9	77	32	67

Sources: *DEP Gazette* and DEP office, Watford. Rates based on mid-year unemployment numbers.

manufacturing unemployment in R.O.S.E. was only slightly higher than in the GLC in 1969 and 1970, and it was still well below the total unemployment rate in R.O.S.E. of 1.8 per cent.

As another dimension of the phenomenon we can consider the duration of unemployment, see Table 3.11. Unemployment has been lower in the GLC than in GB, and unemployed workers have also been out of work for shorter periods in the GLC than elsewhere. Table 3.11 shows the proportion of workers who are unemployed for eight weeks or more. There was consistently a smaller proportion of long-term unemployed,

Table 3.10

Recent Unemployment in Manufacturing GLC and R.O.S.E.

	Total Number Unemployed S.E.	GLC (Thousands)	R.O.S.E.	Unemployed GLC (%)	R.O.S.E.
1967	23.8	18.6	5.2	1.3	0.4
1968	31.4	18.1	13.3	1.4	1.1
1969	30.6	14.8	15.8	1.1	1.3
1970	32.7	14.7	17.9	1.2	1.4

Sources: *DEP Gazette* and DEP Office Watford.

both for male adults and for all workers, in the GLC than else-where, throughout the 1960s. The relative long-term unemploy-ment rates for male adults indicate that the GLC's comparative position *vis-à-vis* GB was equally favourable from 1969 to 1971 as it was from 1960 to 1962.

The percentage of long-term unemployed, eight weeks or more as we have defined the notion here, was both higher and

Table 3.11

Percentage of Long-term Unemployed (8 weeks or more)

| | GB | | GLC | | GLC (%)* / GB(%) | |
	Male Adult†	Total	Male Adult†	Total	Male Adult†	Total
1960	61.4	58.0	50.4	42.0	82	72
1961	58.5	54.4	47.3	38.9	81	72
1962	55.7	51.4	44.8	49.9	80	97
1963	62.9	58.7	54.9	48.6	87	83
1964	61.0	56.1	47.5	41.9	78	75
1965	57.6	52.7	44.4	39.0	77	74
1966	56.5	52.1	40.1	36.7	71	70
1967	59.4	56.1	49.6	45.0	84	80
1968	61.9	58.8	38.9	35.2	63	60
1969	60.6	55.2	48.0	45.2	79	82
1970	59.3	55.5	48.6	45.8	82	83
1971	61.5	57.6	50.4	47.6	82	83

* The percentage relatives are rounded as in earlier tables.
† Twenty one and over.
Sources: *DEP Gazette* and DEP Watford Office.

more stable in GB than in the GLC. Both phenomena could be explained by the relative ease with which Londoners can obtain casual labour jobs in normal times, which are not so easy to find in difficult years like 1963, 1967 and 1970. In these years, the percentage relatives of long-term unemployed have moved against the GLC.

Disaggregating the total data by industry does not change the earlier conclusion that the emigration of workplaces did not seem to precede the emigration of labour. The next disaggrega-tion step is to break down the figures by area within London. This is relatively easy for unemployment but very hazardous for employment.

In Table 3.12 we present some estimates of absolute male

Table 3.12

Unemployed (July) Male

Sectors	1964	1965	1966	1967	1968	1969	1970	1971	1971 as % 1964
NEI	7360	6336	6213	13 824	13 154	10 693	10 931	12 052	163.75
SI	4462	4223	4850	10 836	11 597	9401	10 381	12 286	275.35
NWI	5280	4981	4542	10 289	10 206	7861	7806	8301	157.22
NEO	1445	1943	1611	5066	4746	4387	5139	6163	426.51
SEO	1551	1487	1421	3060	3705	3556	4229	5010	323.02
SO	1986	1964	1987	3530	4146	3479	3563	4899	246.68
WO	1738	1868	1745	4215	4297	3764	3565	5217	300.17
NWO	2281	2094	2141	5129	4506	4362	4356	5280	231.48
GLC	26 347	25 049	24 788	56 618	56 615	47 567	50 118	59 338	225.22

unemployment[1] for the period 1964–71 for eight areas of London.[2] To get an unemployment rate we must refer these figures to a base population and we have a choice either of unemployment as a proportion of resident population or of unemployment as a proportion of employees by place of work. The former is probably more meaningful because we understand that workers typically register as unemployed near to their home. If a man's occupation is spatially concentrated within a small region, however, it may make more sense for him to register near his workplace.

In Table 3.13 we give estimates of unemployment rates by place of residence. In no area was unemployment high over the whole period by national standards, as may be seen by referring back to Table 3.3. In 1967 and 1968 the North-West Inner sector had higher than national rates but thereafter the typical relation was restored. There have been substantial percentage increases over the period but these are related to a small initial unemployment level. Possibly the areas worst hit have been NEO and, especially recently, SI. The former probably was, apart from NWI, the most severely affected region for male employment rundown. The increase in NWI male unemployment is the smallest among the eight regions, followed by NEI; this presumably highlights the importance for these areas of commuting.

It must be concluded from all this information that although workplaces, especially in manufacturing, have left London in substantial numbers, workpeople have left at least as rapidly. More precisely, the rundown in jobs in London seems to have been at least matched by some combination of the following:

1 reverse commuting from London to jobs outside;
2 a drop of commuting from outside to fill London jobs;
3 out-migration from London to take up jobs elsewhere;
4 a drop of in-migration to London.

---

[1] Female unemployment as officially measured is misleading and so it will not be considered here.
[2] viz. North East Inner (NEI), South Inner (SI), North West Inner (NWI), North East Outer (NEO), South East Outer (SEO), South Outer (SO), West Outer (WO), North West Outer (NWO).

Table 3.13

Male Unemployment Rates, by Place of Residence

Sectors	1964	1965	1966	1967	1968	1969	1970	1971
NEI	1.57	1.37	1.36	3.11	3.04	2.53	2.66	3.02
SI	1.05	1.50	1.16	2.64	2.87	2.36	2.64	3.17
NWI	1.67	1.61	1.49	3.46	3.48	2.74	2.76	3.02
NEO	0.65	0.88	0.73	2.30	2.17	2.00	2.36	2.84
SEO	0.75	0.73	0.69	1.48	1.79	1.71	2.02	2.38
SO	0.69	0.68	0.69	1.23	1.44	1.20	1.23	1.68
WO	0.61	0.66	0.62	1.50	1.52	1.25	1.25	1.82
NWO	0.76	0.71	0.73	1.75	1.54	1.50	1.50	1.82
GLC	0.98	0.95	0.94	2.18	2.18	1.89	2.00	2.40

(Unemployed by place of registration; employees by place of residence.)

We would suspect that in-migration has substantially dropped off, if only because migration into London typically falls in recessionary periods. Also the changes that were made after 1965 in the systems of unemployment and redundancy compensation probably had an inhibiting effect on geographical migration generally, particularly on long-distance migration. Regardless of the true combination accounting for the decline in London's working population, it is hard to conclude from the unemployment data that the average Londoner has so far suffered from the migration of jobs. When put into a national context he has at least held his own even in those industrial sectors hardest hit.

Naturally, unemployment figures tell only a part of the story. It is certain, for example, that activity rates of Londoners have fallen in recent years. This means that, expressed as a proportion of the resident population, the number of Londoners either in work or registered unemployed has fallen. However, as Table 3.1 indicates, this has been a national phenomenon since 1966, and even earlier if males are considered separately. The causes of this decline in activity rates are not yet satisfactorily established, but the fact that it is nationwide obviously indicates that London's own decline in activity rates is not predominantly due to the fall in city size. We would also like to know about relative earnings, housing prices, local government services, externalities, changing commuting time and so on, as suggested in the two previous sections of this chapter. By the standards implied in that framework very little can in fact be said about the impact on Londoners' welfare of the decline in population and employment during the last decade. Very little is known on the variables highlighted there. Information is modest indeed on the characteristics of emigrants, the economies of scale in public services, the extent of externalities, the ownership of capital and the housing stock or even of the impact on emigration of the plethora of planning decisions actually made, for sound or unsound reasons. One fragment is available, although the observer should be cautious in interpretation. In Table 3.14 we give estimates of changes in real household income 1965–9. It can be seen that real household incomes have risen more in the GLC between 1965 and 1969 than they have in the rest of Great Britain. That is the finding of the Family Expenditure Survey and it holds true for each quartile range and for the median income level. However real household incomes did not rise so fast in the GLC as in the R.O.S.E. Qualitatively at least this should not be too great a surprise. London has experienced un-balanced emigration, losing relatively large fractions of above average income earners. Conversely, R.O.S.E. has gained many of these migrants. It would follow arithmetically that, other things being equal, average GLC incomes would rise more slowly than those in R.O.S.E. Of course, other things may very well not have been equal, but this is difficult to establish from the available data.

Table 3.14

Changes in Real Household Income 1965–69

		Lower Quartile £	Median £	Upper Quartile £	Inter-Quartile Range £
GLC	1965	17.5	26.5	36.5	19.0
	1969	18.5	29.6	42.0	23.5
	% change	+5.5	+11.7	+15.0	+23.8
R.O.S.E.	1965	13.9	22.7	32.9	19.1
	1969	17.9	27.0	38.4	20.6
	% change	+28.4	+18.9	+16.6	+8.0
RGB	1965	13.9	21.7	29.8	15.9
	1969	14.1	23.8	33.4	19.3
	% change	+1.8	+9.7	+12.1	+21.0

Source: F.E.S. G.L.D.P. Paper S11/113, Table 6.

The New Earnings Survey by the DEP provided evidence that the structural shift in GLC employment away from manu-facturing and construction and towards the service sector, except for distribution, has not reduced the earnings of em-ployees in the GLC. Earnings for some major sectors in the GLC are not available and the sample for some of the sectors not very large, so only the aggregate conclusions for the manufacturing and non-manufacturing sectors as a whole are summarized in Table 3.15.

The average male earnings in the non-manufacturing sector are as high as in the manufacturing sector. This is because there are more manual jobs in manufacturing which reduces the

Table 3.15

Average Gross Weekly Earnings, GLC—April 1970 (£ per week)

(£) Sector	Manual Men*	Manual Women†	Non-Manual Men*	Non-Manual Women†	% Non-Manual Men*	% Non-Manual Women†	Weighted Avge. Men*	Weighted Avge. Women†
All Industry, Services	28.7	15.1	41.0	20.8	28.9	75.6	34.7	19.4
All Manufacturing	30.1	15.0	41.2	19.5	40.3	54.8	34.6	17.5
All non-Manufacturing	27.8	15.2	41.0	21.1	52.7	82.3	34.8	20.1

* Twenty-one and over.
† Eighteen and over.
Source: 'New Earnings Survey', *DEP Gazette* January 1971.

average level of manufacturing earnings. Average female earn-ings in non-manufacturing are slightly higher than in manu-facturing. This conclusion is broadly reflected in the detailed sector results for all GB.

Strictly speaking, the GLC earnings survey related to GLC employees, not only to residents. If GLC residents were mainly manual workers, and commuters were non-manual, then the structural change in employment could still have reduced the earnings of London residents. But, as we have seen from the Family Expenditure Survey, this has not been the case.

Conclusion

From the inadequate information available, it is not easy to discern extensive hardship in London arising from declining city size. Such hardship may appear in the future, or it may exist now but be manifest in ways we have not managed to iso-late. Even if there is no increase in measured hardship the run-down might still be damaging by being the result of foolish planning decisions in London or elsewhere. All these qualifica-tions being made, there is not visible to us a strong empirical case which would justify as yet a dramatic change in policy designed to alter the nature of existing emigration forces.

Reference

1. *Report of the Committee of Inquiry into Certain Matters Concerning Labour in Building and Civil Engineering*, Headed by Professor E. H. Phelps Brown, Cmnd. 3714 (London: H.M.S.O., 1968).

Chapter Four

The Contribution of Public Expenditure and Finance to the Problems of Inner London

RICHARD KIRWAN

Summary

The distribution of public expenditure and the way in which it is financed can have significant impact on urban development. In Britain, local public expenditure is increasing rapidly, partly in response to increasing demands and partly as a result of rising costs. In addition the specific problems of Inner London will require an increasing volume of expenditure. One constraint on expenditure in London is the national allocation of public sector resources, but while there are grounds for arguing that a greater need for public expenditure is a necessary corollary of London's above average productivity and income there would probably be little justification for diverting public sector resources away from other more deserving regions.

Local public expenditure falls into three broad categories: expenditure in response to income-elastic demands, 'neutral' expenditure and redistributive or compensatory expenditure. There is little evidence of how expenditure in Inner London benefits different individuals or households, though the regressive impact of rates as a means of raising finance is well-established. Two alternative models are discussed of the relationship between the distribution of expenditure and the distribution of costs.

Within the London area, there is some evidence to suggest that Inner London is less favourably treated than outer areas, but the main dangers seem to lie in the way in which the demands for public expenditure and the local tax-bases are likely to develop in Inner London and outer areas during the next decade. The process of decentralization prompts a search for alternative systems of finance incorporating the whole metropolitan region. But even now within Inner London the disparities between boroughs prevent the full mobilization of resources to tackle the most severe problems.

If alternative or additional sources of revenue are needed to help to finance the growing volume of expenditure, a local income tax would seem the best alternative for Inner London combined with a system of distributing the revenue raised throughout the metropolitan region.

Introduction

The problems of public expenditure and finance in London are not unique. In most countries of the world, urban growth and development have created severe problems for the systems by which, both nationally and at the local level, the allocation of resources and expenditure priorities are determined and have placed great strain on the methods of raising finance for urban development. The particular problems of different countries reflect of course both the main characteristics of their urban development and the institutional organization of responsibility for urban public expenditure and finance. In France, for example, among developed countries, the problems of rapid urban expansion in many areas outside Paris are currently a source of concern, while in Britain, as in the United States, the problems of decentralization and the reduction in population of central cities are regarded as more important. In the United States again, the problems of urban public finance are considered within the general context of 'fiscal federalism' and 'revenue sharing'; in Britain, they reflect a long process of changing balance between the power of central government and the power of local authorities. The problem is thus not of a specific conflict between public economic activity generally and urban growth, or between a particular system of urban public finance and urban growth or stagnation, but of the responsiveness of institutions and processes whose organization reflects a delicate balance of political interests and compromise to a general process of social change. This process of adjustment acts as a severe constraint on the rate and form of urban change and may contribute significantly to the perpetuation of urban problems. Policies whose implementation takes the form of investment in durable structures may influence for many generations the physical, social and economic structure of an urban area.

The planning activities of the public authorities of course do not all entail public expenditure and the consequent need for revenue. There are many forms of planning and planned action which can affect the welfare of an area and its residents directly. Much of what is traditionally embraced within the category of town planning is an obvious case in point. The control of densities, the location of land-uses, the layout of residential areas and all the many processes of formal and informal regulation which town planning involves have a direct effect on the opportunities available to the residents of an area. Indeed, a large part of any analysis of the problems of Inner London should be concerned with the central role played by the economic, social and physical structure of the metropolitan region as a whole, with the interactions between the markets for land, labour and housing and with the influence of planning over them. Nevertheless, public expenditure is important; much of what needs to be done will inevitably call for public expenditure and the problems of finance can act as severe constraints. Public expenditure, moreover, itself requires planning, so that some discussion of the problems of London's public economy fits naturally into an analysis of planning policy for Inner London.

Public expenditure falls into many different categories and most of these, housing, education, transport and so on, deserve detailed analysis in their own right. There are two main justifications, however, for considering public expenditure as a whole in this context. The first is that there is an especial

interest in the distributional effects of public expenditure—
the effects, that is, of the distribution both between areas, and in
particular between Inner and Outer London, and between
individuals of different social groups and classes. The general
distributional pattern only emerges from an analysis of public
expenditure as a whole. The second justification is that the
problems of raising finance and of the shortage of resources
tend to be common to all categories of expenditure, or at least
to raise the same issues. The broad framework, which limits the
possibilities within individual sectors, such as housing and
education, calls for general consideration.

It is not easy to say exactly how important public expenditure
is in the total economic activity of Inner London. In the London
area as a whole, the local public authorities are probably
responsible for about one sixth of the gross domestic product
generated within the area and for somewhat over 20 per cent
of total incomes (since part of the expenditure for which they
are responsible comprises transfer payments). Such direct
estimates clearly under-estimate the real impact of public
economic activity. Apart from the fact that any public expenditure has some multiplier effect on the general level of economic
activity in the area, the types of activity in which the local
authorities are engaged are peculiarly important to the viability
of other types of economic activity. Education, transport facilities, refuse collection and street lighting—to quote only an
arbitrary set of examples—are all things which in one way or
another make possible a host of other types of economic
activity.

Public expenditure policy within local areas in Britain is
influenced directly and indirectly to a very significant extent by
the actions of central government. There is a large volume of
public expenditure which is under the direct control of the
central government and which can have a significant impact on
the economic welfare of the residents of a small area. At the
most general level, there are the examples of defence, foreign
trade and central administration. The residents of Inner
London presumably benefit, if anyone benefits, from expenditure on defence and external relations. The merchant bankers of
the City may benefit more directly than most from the provision
of export credits to developing countries. And the total level
of economic activity in Inner London is certainly greatly

increased by the location of central government offices and army barracks. These are merely examples. More significantly, however, expenditure on the National Health Service and on universities and the provision for pensions and social security payments represent a very important contribution to the well-being of a local area. This is particularly true in the case of low-income residents and areas, since there is a greater redistributive component in central government expenditure of this type than in local authority expenditure. To this extent the solution, or rather mitigation, of some of the fundamental problems of an area such as Inner London lies in the hands of central government rather than the local authorities. There are of course very sound reasons why many of these services should be administered centrally but one effect of this is that, while the level of provision of health and social security services varies to some extent in accordance with needs and can reflect local conditions through such things as the variable rent allowance in social security payments, generally speaking, there is less scope for a variable response to local needs and problems. However, to the extent that the problems of any area like Inner London which reflect a maldistribution of opportunities and incomes do flow from factors which have a genuinely local and spatial content, rather than from the national employment structure and income distribution, the role of social security payments and such types of expenditure is more palliative than curative; to this extent the local authorities may have more real leverage.

Central government policy on income distribution, of which policies on pensions and social security payments are two of the more obvious examples, sets the limits within which a whole range of local public expenditure and other policies must operate. Such policies therefore have a direct impact on the success of local policies designed to improve urban living conditions in areas like Inner London. A large part of all local public expenditure takes the form either of investment in new urban structures or of expenditure on compensatory social services and facilities. Too often the long-term value of such expenditure is dissipated because of the lack of a basic command over resources among the resident population. Housing is a very good example, where the value of local expenditure on the renewal and improvement of the stock is reduced by the continuing low level of effective demand for maintenance. The importance, therefore, of central government policy in determining the over-all economic framework within which the local authorities attempt to find solutions to the problems of areas such as Inner London cannot be over-estimated.

Central government, moreover, maintains a very widespread influence over the public expenditure policies of local authori-ties, which seriously constrains their exercise of power. In the exercise of its general control over the allocation of resources to different sectors of activity, the central government retains many specific powers over the conduct of local authorities and through the mechanisms of expenditure control, loan sanctions and grant payments can effectively determine the allocation of resources at the local level, particularly in the field of capital investment. This is not necessarily a bad thing. The arguments about the appropriate location for the control of local public expenditure are complex; they are essentially arguments about the distribution and balance of political power. Such a dis-cussion would be beyond the scope of this chapter; but there can be no doubt where one is looking for change, that a large part of the initiative for change must rest with central government.

Equally important in this context is the way in which the administrative arrangements adopted by central government can influence local authorities. The structure of central govern-ment grant payments, for example, can introduce specific biases into local expenditure. Supplementary grants for specific services may encourage substitution in favour of other activities, if the local priorities do not match those of central government. The formula distribution of general grants may encourage local policies designed to influence the eligibility for grant in later years—for example, a deliberate failure to tackle some problem which features in a 'needs' formula in order to attract more unattached funds to spend on other activities. High rates of specific grant on capital expenditure, such as the 75 per cent grant on major roads and public transport investment, en-courage local authorities to regard these goods almost as 'free goods', while capital grants generally introduce a serious bias into the choice between investment and the support of current services. London's transport policy provides good evidence of the strength of these influences.

The Scale and Growth of Public Expenditure

The authorities concerned with local expenditure (Table 4.1) in London are the GLC (including ILEA), the London Boroughs (including the City of London), the Metropolitan Police and the Metropolitan Water Board. In 1969/70 (the last year for which consolidated accounts are readily available) these authorities together spent over £910 million on current services and £356 million on capital investment. This was equivalent to £2.30 per resident per week for current services. GLC is responsible for a much larger share of London's capital investment than of current expenditure. GLC and ILEA are the largest spenders individually, although the Boroughs are more important in total.

The really 'big business' is in education and housing. About one third of the current budget of the London authorities is

Table 4.1

Distribution of Expenditure in London by Category and Authority, 1969/70

Revenue Expenditure (Gross)	GLC/ILEA £m	BOROUGHS £m	TOTAL* £m	%
Education and youth employment	139	187	304	33.2
Public libraries, museums, etc.	—	14	14	1.5
Local health services	8	27	33	3.6
Local welfare services	—	25	24	2.6
Child care, etc.	—	17	15	1.6
Sewerage	12	6	17	1.9
Refuse collection	7	16	22	2.4
Parks and open spaces	6	11	16	1.8
Baths and public health	—	21	26	2.2
Town and country planning	5	10	14	1.5
Highways, public lighting	12	30	40	4.3
Housing loans	14	14	27	3.0
Housing revenue account	54	123	175	19.0
Fire service	13	—	13	1.4
Police (Metropolitan Police)	87	—	87	9.3
Water supply (Metropolitan Water Board)	23	—	23	2.5
Total (*including others*)	402	585	917	100.0
Capital Expenditure				
Education	14	17	30	8.5
Sewerage	8	5	13	3.8
Refuse collection	4	1	4	1.2
Highways, public lighting	21	8	29	8.2
Housing loans	20	15	34	9.6
Housing revenue account	53	147	200	56.1
Police (Metropolitan Police)	4	—	4	1.2
Water supply (Metropolitan Water Board)	5	—	5	1.4
Total (*including others*)	134	222	356	100.0

* Adjusted to eliminate double-counting.

absorbed by education and about one fifth by housing. Even so, the average expenditure per head on education of some £0.73 per week is less than the average weekly expenditure on alcohol and tobacco (though obviously the value of education is much greater than this in those families which benefit directly from it). On capital account, the situation is reversed: housing is the most important category of expenditure (absorbing about two thirds of the budget), followed by education and highways.

Over the last two decades, local authority expenditure has been one of the fastest growing sectors of the economy, and this is reflected in the figures for London (Table 4.2). Between 1960

Table 4.2

Increase in Expenditure in London, 1965/66 to 1969/70

£ million

Revenue Expenditure GLC/ILEA, etc. (Gross)		Boroughs	Total*
1965/66	295	409	624
1966/67	348	459	717
1967/68	360	513	796
1968/69	388	555	861
1969/70	402	585	917
Capital Expenditure			
1965/66	142	183	326
1966/67	127	199	326
1967/68	133	216	349
1968/69	114	233	347
1969/70	134	222	356

* Adjusted to exclude double-counting.

and 1970, for example, total local authority current and capital expenditure (including interest) nearly trebled. During the same period the gross domestic product increased by about 87 per cent (equivalent to a real rate of growth of about 2.8 per cent). In the five years since GLC was formed, total local expenditure in London has increased by over 30 per cent. This was a slower rate of increase than for local authority expenditure generally, which increased by 50 per cent in the same period, owing to the very small increase in capital expenditure in London.

There appear to be three main reasons for this general increase in the share of local public expenditure in the national income. Firstly, many of the services provided by the public sector have high social income-elasticities: that is to say, they are things on which we do and shall want to spend an increasing proportion of the national resources. Education, housing, mobility and the environment are all sectors of increasing concern. Secondly, the public sector is responsible for many of the undesired consequences of economic growth and urban social, economic and physical development. Given the present structure of the economic and social system, these effects increase inevitably with the rate of change of the urban structure. I am referring of course to such things as obsolescence in housing, homelessness, technological unemployment, pollution, deteriorating public transport and so on. And thirdly, the costs of urban public services increase rapidly,[1] since they comprise by and large labour-intensive services, among which productivity increases have been slow, and income-related transfer payments. Taken together, these reasons suggest an inevitable and continuing relative increase in local public expenditure and hence an increasing problem of financing.

The difficulty of financing an increasing demand for urban public services has prompted a search for alternative solutions. It has been argued, for example, that, given the difficulty of diverting resources into the public sector, it is inappropriate for that sector to provide goods and services which have a high income-elasticity and hence that a larger share of these activities should be undertaken by the private sector. The argument will be familiar in the fields of housing, education and health. Unfortunately, the case is not so simple. Many of the fields of concern, unemployment, environmental pollution and public transport, for example, are by definition fields in which only public action is possible. And in other cases there is a severe risk of generating new problems at least as serious as those caused by the problems of finance if the alternatives proposed were adopted. In particular, since a major part of the aim of

---

[1] The price index for public authorities' goods and services, which is some reflection of costs, reached 154 in 1970 (1963 = 100) compared with 136 for all final goods and services.

public expenditure in these fields is to compensate for the inequities of the market distribution of basic goods and services, there is a necessary contradiction between the goals of local authority policy and reliance on private sources of finance. On the other hand, one could produce a more convincing argument that many of the unwanted consequences of urban growth are the product in part of the size of urban areas and in part of the systems of allocation which operate within them, and hence that a valuable approach to a reduction in the need for public expenditure would be through an increase in the sphere of public control and more forceful regional and urban settlement policies. Housing provides a good example of a field which directly and indirectly generates a need for public expenditure to relieve the poor conditions in which large numbers of people are condemned to live in an area like Inner London. These conditions are the product of the low level of effective demand represented by middle-to-low income families in the housing market, which are exacerbated in the conditions of a very large metropolitan area with a high degree of centralization in employment. So there are some pointers towards reducing the scale of these problems by exercising more control over the workings of the market. Furthermore, the cost of urban services may also be capable of being reduced by technological innovation in more ways than is generally recognized. Too little attention has generally been paid to the scope for increasing labour productivity, largely because the incentives to economy are not as great as in the private sector. To quote one example: it might be argued that the emphasis on increasing the teacher–pupil ratio in schools is misguided and that it would be better to concentrate on more effective use of teachers' time through the assistance, for example, of pupil-controlled teaching-machines. To discuss an issue such as this would obviously take us beyond the scope and competence of this chapter. But undoubtedly too little attention has been paid within many spheres of public sector activity to the long-term implications for the costs of urban public services of increasing real incomes and leisure preference and more generally to the implications for urban planning of the changing cost structure. Overall, one is bound to conclude that even if within limits developments of the types discussed above could make a useful contribution to reducing the increase in the demand for public expenditure, the long-term prospect for urban areas generally is still likely to be of a continuing rapid increase in the demand for expenditure and hence of a continuing problem of obtaining finance.

In Inner London, the demand for urban public services is also likely to continue to expand rapidly. The structure of the population is changing as a direct result of the process of de-centralization, with an increasing proportion of old people, students and children of school age. This generates a direct demand for local authority services, while at the same time entailing an increasing dependence on central government transfer payments (pensions, grants, etc.). In addition to the problems of an obsolescent housing stock, the authorities face large areas of environmental deprivation, congested roads, a decaying public transport network, pollution, and flood risk, and a wide range of social needs which are symptoms of the depri-vation and self-selection of the resident population. And on top of all this, of course, Inner London must continue to cater for a million and more commuters, for tourists and business visitors and for the whole range of administrative, business and cultural activities which go with being the capital and seat of govern-ment. While the labour costs of providing services rises at least as fast in London as elsewhere, London faces a particularly rapid increase in the price of land for development.[1] It is clearly not necessary to attempt a detailed forecast of the likely demands for public expenditure in Inner London to see that these are going to continue to be heavy. Thus the original Greater London Development Plan estimates (for what they are worth) forecast that public investment (in construction) would increase by about 6 per cent per annum during the 1970s in real terms (that is at constant prices). Expenditure on

---

[1] It is generally hard to reconcile the very high price of land in London with the basic trends of declining population and manufacturing employ-ment. While inflation generally and planning controls in specific instances may be partially responsible, there is sufficient evidence to suggest that in the valuation of land for public acquisition too much attention is paid to the few transactions between private developers and sellers (where high prices can often be explained by an in-built tendency to concentrate high-value development) and too little to the general structural influences, including such things as the trough in land-values usually found in inner areas around the C.B.D.

Table 4.3

Sources of Finance for Public Revenue Expenditure in London, 1969-70

£ million

	Gross Expenditure	Government Grants	Other Receipts	Net Expenditure	Needs Element	Rate Support Grant Domestic Element	Rate Support Grant Greater London Equalization	Own Requirement	Total Rate Call
City of London	14.8	1.4	5.4	8.0	0.1	0.0	−2.4	10.1	28.6
Camden	16.9	1.4	5.7	9.8	3.4	0.8	−0.2	6.3	21.3
Greenwich	11.9	0.8	4.7	6.4	3.0	0.4	+1.1	1.8	7.3
Hackney	15.6	1.3	5.8	8.5	3.5	0.5	+1.1	3.8	10.0
Hammersmith	10.5	0.6	3.4	6.4	3.0	0.4	+0.6	2.8	8.8
Islington	13.1	1.3	3.9	7.9	3.8	0.5	+0.1	3.6	12.2
Kensington and Chelsea	8.0	0.5	3.1	4.4	3.3	1.0	−1.5	3.1	13.3
Lambeth	17.1	1.1	7.6	8.5	4.8	0.7	+0.7	2.4	11.1
Lewisham	14.1	0.8	5.3	8.0	5.0	0.6	+1.1	1.3	6.5
Southwark	18.5	1.3	5.9	11.2	4.2	0.5	+1.8	4.9	12.8
Tower Hamlets	12.1	1.1	3.1	7.9	2.8	0.3	+1.4	3.2	9.1
Wandsworth	15.0	1.1	5.5	8.4	4.5	0.7	+0.8	2.0	9.0
City of Westminster	24.0	1.0	11.8	11.2	3.7	1.4	−6.6	11.0	58.1
Inner London	191.6	13.7	71.2	106.6	45.1	7.8	−2.0	55.3	208.1
Outer London	393.2	13.4	121.9	257.1	113.9	11.6	+2.0	134.5	188.2
GLC/ILEA	295.0	13.7	86.8	194.5	29.3	—	—	168.8	—
Met. Police	84.0	39.4	7.4	37.3	—	—	—	38.3	—
Met. Water Board	22.6	0.6	21.9	0.1	—	—	—	—	—
Total	916.7	80.8	239.4	595.7	188.3	19.4	—	396.9	396.3

current services, where productivity increases are more difficult to achieve, will probably have to increase at an even faster rate.

On the other side of the account, the main sources of revenue for public expenditure in London are central government grants, the rates and other charges and payments for specific services. The absolute and percentages contributions of each source are indicated in Tables 4.3 and 4.4. The amount of

Table 4.4

Sources of Finance for Public Expenditure in London 1969/70

Percent of Gross Revenue Expenditure	Inner London Boroughs	Outer London Boroughs	GLC/ILEA	All Public Authorities in GLC Area*
Government specific payments	7.2	3.4	4.6	8.8
Other receipts	37.2	31.0	29.4	26.1
Rate Support Grant				
needs element	23.5	29 0	9.9	20.5
domestic element	4.1	3.0	—	2.1
Greater London equalisation	−1.0	+0.5	—	—
Local contribution to expenditure	28.9	34.2	57.2	43.3

* Including Metropolitan Police and Metropolitan Water Board.

public expenditure financed from local sources is above the national average, although it would appear less if cash grants for capital works such as highways were included. In common with other parts of the country, the contribution from central government funds has tended to increase.

With this background, one should be asking what the effects of this level of public expenditure are going to be and how it may best be organized and financed. The process is bound to have a significant effect on Inner London, but it is important to con-consider the distribution of the impact. And at the same time, we might ask whether the present systems of financing will be capable of generating a sufficient flow of funds.

London in the National Context

One major constraint on the level of public expenditure in London is the national allocation of resources between regions. With the publication of Woodward's (1970) estimates [1] of the United Kingdom regional accounts, we are in a better position to discuss the implications of this distribution (Table 4.5). Not surprisingly, it appears that London and the South East make the highest contribution per head to the Domestic Product of all the regions—Woodward estimates about 13 per cent above the national average (which means nearly 75 per cent above Northern Ireland)—and are roughly in balance with

Table 4.5

Regional Deviations in Net Public Beneficial Expenditure Per Head, 1964

£ per capita

	Excluding Debt Interest	Including Debt Interest	Including Debt Interest and Trading Surplus
North	+31	+26	+27
Yorks and Humber	+13	+11	+8
North West	+5	+2	+4
East Midlands	+14	+11	+5
West Midlands	−22	−25	−23
South East	−39	−34	−34
South West	+25	+30	+34
Wales	+45	+40	+38
Scotland	+32	+31	+33
Northern Ireland	+82	+77	+84

Source: WOODWARD, V. H., NIESR and DAE, Cambridge.
Note: + indicates better off than national average.
      − indicates worse off than national average.

the rest of the country in inter-regional trade. But if one excludes expenditure on national administration, public authority current and capital expenditure per head in the South East is only slightly above the national average and considerably less so than private expenditure. Current expenditure on the social services (excluding national and local administration and defence) in 1964 was only 2 per cent above the national average. Woodward's estimates of public sector 'beneficial' expenditure—i.e. current expenditure on goods and services excluding defence and central administration and capital expenditure excluding trading services and dwellings—and receipts per head suggest that the diversion of expenditure in favour of Wales, Scotland and Northern Ireland has left the North and the Midlands the least favoured areas, the South East benefiting from an average level of expenditure; but that when expenditure is set against the tax income of the public authorities it is the South East (together with the West Midlands) which is the prime source of the national redistribution of resources to the tune of nearly £40 per head per annum, or about one third of the beneficial expenditure actually enjoyed by the region.

It is difficult to say what one should conclude from this. If one aim of the redistribution of public sector expenditure is to compensate for the inequalities in regional incomes, then London and the South East must clearly expect to enjoy a relatively lower level of expenditure than the more depressed regions. If the aim is not merely to achieve a static redistribution, but to contribute to overall economic growth by means of a dynamic shift in the productive potential of the depressed regions, then the evidence of the success of the national redistributive policy is less clear. Throughout Scotland and the North there are monuments to the redistributive policies of the early 1960s, in the form, for example, of little-used rural and urban motorways, which testify to the inadequacy of infrastructure investment in isolation as means of solving the regional problem. None the less, a successful regional policy must undoubtedly depend among other things on a redistribution of public sector resources. The South East region does not suffer from a below-average level of public expenditure; the question is whether it would be justified in retaining a somewhat larger share of the above-average public sector revenues generated in the region. The distribution of earned incomes in the London area tends to have much the same shape as in other regions (though the distribution of total incomes is likely to be more 'top-heavy' than elsewhere), but the whole distribution is typically some 10–12 per cent above the average for the U.K. as a whole. To plead for a greater share of the national resources, the Londoner must argue that at least and perhaps predominantly at the bottom end of the scale the costs of London living are proportionately greater.

What we are really discussing in this context are the economies and diseconomies of urban scale. In recent years there have been a number of studies of urban size on both sides of the Atlantic [2], partly in reaction to what were thought to be exaggerated statements of the problems and disadvantages of large urban areas. Most of these studies have tended to conclude that large urban and metropolitan areas still generate significant net economies: the benefits of the agglomeration of economic activities and of 'connectivity' outweigh the disadvantages. But in this context it is necessary to add some important riders to this conclusion. Firstly, the conclusion is based on an assessment of aggregate benefits and costs; we need to ask to whom do the benefits flow and who bears the costs. There are good grounds for saying that a disproportionate share of the benefits of agglomeration flow to the landowner, the profit-taker and the upper-income employees, while low and middle income groups bear a disproportionate share of the costs. (To some extent the balance will reflect the internal spatial distribution of activities within the area, but even in the most equitable conditions the proposition would have some truth.) And secondly, it is right to point out that the diseconomies or increasing disadvantages of urban size are an intrinsic part of the package, even if in total they are outweighed by the advantages. These costs or disadvantages are not simply financial costs (though these may be included) but such things as long average journeys to work, traffic congestion, crowded public transport, noise, dirt and pollution, poor quality and high rent housing for many low income groups, inadequate facilities for children and so on. These are very serious problems. If this model of agglomerative economies is right, the resident of Inner London might justifiably argue that London ought to be allowed to retain a larger share of the public sector resources generated in the area. While part of the public expenditure which is diverted away from London, mainly capital expenditure, would most likely have been devoted to such things as highways, a large part would normally be expected to go into sectors, such as housing and education, from which the low-income residents of Inner London would stand to gain most. So there is a sense in which the national redistribution of public sector resources is at the expense of the low-income groups in London and the South East. By the same token, it would be essential to ensure that any rediversion of resources in favour of London was used to benefit these deprived communities within what is admittedly the most prosperous region of the country.

To some extent this is generally accepted in the allocation of resources by means of Rate Support Grant: special weight is given to some London costs. Unfortunately the system of allocation cannot ensure a more equitable distribution within London between groups of potential beneficiaries. In this connexion it has been suggested that central government is bound to develop an increasing concern with inter-personal equity (and with equity between communities at a local and neighbourhood level), the logic of which suggests a return to more general use of specific grants and goal-oriented programme funding. The Urban Aid programme would be taken as indicative of this trend. Unfortunately, apart from the obvious conflict between the goals of local autonomy and central allocation, specific grants do not always achieve their effect, as local authorities tend to substitute these funds for expenditure out of general finance. There have already been accusations of substitution in the case of the Urban Aid programme.

However, although the elements of a case exist for a larger allocation of resources to Inner London, it is unlikely that this would be justified. It is very much a case of special pleading. London remains a very rich area with a very high level of public expenditure and even if the absolute numbers of poor and unemployed and deprived are very large in London, the potential exists within the London area for a radical redistribution of wealth. In comparison with parts of Scotland, Wales and the North, one is bound to conclude that London does not come off badly.

The Distribution of Public Economic Activity in London

So we are left to consider the future of the public economy within the London Metropolitan Region itself. Within that area public expenditure has a considerable impact but do we even know who benefits from it and who bears the costs and to what extent? The simple answer is that we do not. To start with, the measurement of benefits in the field of public services is fraught with difficulties. The traditional economic approach states that we can measure benefit in terms of the amount that someone is willing to pay. In this context, though, in addition to the well-known problem of the wide difference in individuals' abilities to pay, we are faced with a situation in which there is by definition no market in the major public services. Attempts have been made to derive measures based on physical measures of output, such as the number of collections of refuse per week, or on real measures of the inputs into the service provided, such as the number of hours of teacher–pupil contact in education, but inevitably such measures are less than complete and beg the major questions about the quality of, and value set on, the services enjoyed. Still more difficult is the establishment of any measure that can take account of both differing needs and differing preferences. We must admit, therefore, that this is an area about which we are generally very ignorant; we can only fall back on qualitative assessments.

There are basically three types of service provided by local authorities: those provided in response to an income-elastic demand, such as highways; those provided in some sense 'neutrally' on the basis of need, such as refuse collection; and those with an explicitly redistributive or compensatory aim such as housing. Into which category education falls is more doubtful. It clearly has elements of all three types, and much of the argument about educational provision is about whether one or other of these three approaches should be allowed to dominate the organization of the service. The provision of services of the first type will by definition have a regressive effect on the distribution of real income, just as provision of the last group will have a progressive effect. A true picture of the benefits of these services would have to be more complex, since they have many indirect effects. In many cases, these effects are what are technically called 'pecuniary', that is they do not themselves reflect a real change in the conditions which determine the productivity of urban economic activity or the range of goods and services available for consumption, but they do affect the relative prices at which goods are available. In any analysis of the overall impact of local public expenditure it would be right to ignore these effects, but if we are interested in the distribution of benefits, they can be critically important, since they determine how the benefits of public action are shared. Thus highway improvement tends to be of greatest direct benefit to upper-income groups, but its secondary effects are much more complex. If it tends to encourage decentralization of employment this may work additionally to the detriment of low-income groups, but if it encourages decentralization of housing it may work to some extent to the advantage of low-income groups by taking pressure off the housing market in inner areas. On the other hand the increase in traffic which may be attracted to the central area will adversely effect all inner area residents through the noise, danger and disturbance of passing traffic and the growth of non-resident parking. In any event the total impact is likely to be made up of a number of contradictory elements.

If we turn to the revenue side of the public economy, there is the same problem of the distinction between the direct impact of the costs of provision and their final incidence; but at least the problem of establishing a unit of measurement is easier. Local authorities obtain their revenue from three main sources:[1] the rates, central government grants and subsidies, and local charges, rents, etc. (Local authorities can also borrow funds but in the last resort the finance to meet their debt service must come from one of the sources mentioned.) The origin of the central government contribution to local finance could only be traced through a study of the origins of central government taxation, but the direct incidence of the rates charged locally is much easier to trace. It is well-known that rates are a very regressive form of taxation whose impact on low-income households is proportionately much greater than on the rich. The Allen Committee of 1964, for example [3], showed that while households with incomes of less than £312 in 1963–64 paid as much as 9.1 per cent of their disposable income in rates, households with incomes of £1560 and over were paying only 2.5 per cent. (See Table 4.6). More recent studies confirm this. In their final incidence, however, rates may not be so regressive, since a part at least of their impact is probably shifted back on to land and property-owners.

Alternative Models of the Public Economy

It is hard to assess the impact of public economic activity on a community, still harder to propose an appropriate system for its organization, without some 'ideal' model in mind. There are

---

[1] It is partly a matter of convention, partly of theoretical approach, whether one regards the revenue from the charges and rents charged for specific services as equivalent to revenue from the other two sources. One approach is to regard the net cost of the services for which charges are levied as the real item of public expenditure, all of which must be financed from rates and grants.

two fundamentally opposed models of the operation of the public economy between which one has to choose. One is a market-surrogate model. This accepts that local authorities are charged with the provision of certain services for various institutional or historical reasons, but proposes that as far as possible they should aim to satisfy individual preferences on the basis of what people would be willing to pay for the services enjoyed, whether or not specific user-charges are imposed. Costs should similarly be distributed in such a way as to reflect the value of

Table 4.6

Rates Paid by Different Income Groups, 1963–64

	Household Income Group						
England and Wales	*Under £312*	*£312 £520*	*£520 £780*	*£780 £1040*	*£1040 £1560*	*£1560 & over*	*All*
Households (%)	10.1	9.9	12.9	18.5	26.8	21.8	100.0
Household income (5)	236	411	662	909	1280	2333	1169
Rates % household income	8.1	6.0	3.8	2.9	2.4	1.8	2.6
Rates % disposable income	8.1	6.2	4.1	3.2	2.7	2.2	2.9
Rates % housing costs	30.5	20.3	28.3	27.9	28.4	28.8	28.8
London							
Households (%)	11.4	11.4	8.2	15.8	29.8	23.4	100.0
Household income (5)	240	406	664	906	1276	2115	1147
Rates % household income	8.8	6.4	4.8	3.2	2.4	2.1	2.8
Rates % disposable income	9.1	6.6	5.4	3.6	2.8	2.5	3.2
Rates % housing costs	30.8	30.2	21.6	25.8	26.6	25.4	26.1

Source: Allen Committee, 1964.

the services demanded and enjoyed. The trouble with this model is that even in theory it would be wrong to follow its prescriptions too closely for a number of reasons. For one thing, public services typically do not have a single class of beneficiaries. Many different people benefit from the provision of a service like highways and in many different ways. And even where there is a predominant class of users or beneficiaries— say, library-users or school-children or council tenants—there are still other groups who derive indirect benefits from the provision of these services, whose needs should also be recognized. Indeed at the extreme there are services from which everyone can derive some benefit without using up the available supply, that is true public goods, like an unpolluted atmosphere, for which the individual's willingness to pay in a market situation is not a practicable criterion. More important, there is a fundamental objection to this type of model, where, as in local urban services, the redistribution of real income through the provision of services to those most in need is an avowed aim of policy.

The alternative model proposes a complete divorce between the principles appropriate to the provision and distribution of public services and those appropriate to revenue-raising. The distribution of services should be predominantly based on need, while the distribution of costs should be based on ability to pay. The problem with this model lies, as always, with the concept of need. To make it operational, we are faced with difficulties at least as great as in defining the concept of benefit.

The most significant differences between these two models lie in the presence or absence of a specific link between the enjoy-ment of urban public service and payment for them, and in the distinction between the market-based concept of benefit and the non-market concept of need. In practice, there is no doubt that the second of the two models tends to dominate the plan-ning of urban public expenditure and in general it is right that it should. But the real answer to the search for a model for urban public expenditure policy should lie in a synthesis of both these models. And this is implicit in the three-fold classification of urban public expenditure that I have introduced above. For, while one may accept the predominance of need as a criterion for providing many services, it is hard to avoid the feeling that in many cases services should only be provided when those who stand to gain from them are prepared to meet the full social cost. Highways are a good example. Investment in additions to the network cannot be justified unless at the least the potential beneficiaries are prepared to meet the cost, including the social costs of pollution, congestion, environmental deterioration and so on. This suggests that one can draw a clear distinction in terms of the threefold classification just mentioned, between, at the extremes, the income-elastic category of urban public services which should be provided only where the beneficiaries are prepared to meet the costs and whose costs should be distributed accordingly, and the income-redistributive or compensatory category of services where the need and ability to pay criteria should predominate.

The Conflict between Inner and Outer London

Even if we cannot say much about the distribution of the costs and benefits of public expenditure in Inner London between individuals, we may look at the broad distribution within the London region as a whole between Inner London, the outer GLC area and the Outer Metropolitan Area. Once again we are faced with severe analytical problems. It is difficult enough to say how the costs and benefits of different services are distributed spatially in static conditions but when individuals cross the boundaries between areas daily in millions imposing costs, creating benefits, enjoying benefits and bearing costs on both sides of the boundary the problems are multiplied many times. Even without any physical flow of people or goods or funds, it is possible for some of the benefits and costs of public services to cross boundaries. A small peripheral area, for example, may benefit greatly from the police services[1] or the anti-pollution programme or the further education facilities of its larger neighbour, just as it may suffer from atmospheric pollution or a heavy volume of through traffic. Looked at in this light, Inner London provides a range of metropolitan services in education and the arts, in recreation facilities, in the police services and in transport which are of great benefit both to those from outside the area who travel into it and more generally. But at the same time Inner London residents must suffer the direct disbenefits caused by commuters and other visitors to the capital—traffic congestion, noise, dirt, pollution, car parking in residential areas, over-crowded and irregular public transport services and so on—as well as the costs of the investment that these entail. The community must also bear the costs which are the direct product of the way in which the housing market tends to allocate households of different income-groups and classes within a large metropolitan area—the costs of renewing outworn and overcrowded housing, of providing adequate social services in areas of severe stress and of establishing an education system that is fully capable of compensating

---

[1] The importance of cross-boundary effects in the provision of police services is implicitly recognized in the fact that they are the only major current service for which a specific central government grant is now paid.

for the severe concentration of deprivation. These are simply examples. Such a list cannot be complete; for each sphere of activity is bound to generate some reciprocal interaction between inner and outer areas.

On the other side of the account, of course, there is the very high rateable value enjoyed by the Inner London Boroughs, a form of wealth that is itself a direct product of the size of the metropolitan economy and the concentration of activities in Central London. To the extent that rates can be regarded as a contribution to local tax revenue from the capitalized wealth of land-owners, Inner London benefits in this case from the centralization of activities. But even with rateable values there can be problems for Inner London. Changing spatial distributions of activity lead to shifts in land values and hence to some extent in rateable values within the metropolitan area as a whole. And Inner London only benefits from the concentration of commercial and industrial premises; much of the valuable domestic property, whose residents work in and use the facilities of Inner London, is in the outer areas. While land values tend to be highly concentrated within the metropolitan area, income earners are highly dispersed, with those enjoying the upper levels of income tending towards the periphery. So long, however, as the contributions to the local tax revenue of those who earn income from employment and profits are routed via the central government through general taxation and grants to local authorities, this is less of a problem; and it constitutes of course a significant argument in favour of the continued use of this form of funding for local expenditure.

What happens when we put the two sides of the equation together? The two models of the public economy mentioned above are relevant here. If one thinks in terms of linking benefits and costs strictly together, one is likely to conclude that it is very difficult to determine exactly which way the sum of costs and benefits flow. There seem to be some grounds for saying the commuters obtain some benefits for which they do not pay, while Inner London residents bear costs without equivalent benefits. But the case is not clear. The alternative model, however, offers a rather simpler approach. Instead of attempting to ascribe the generation of costs and benefits to particular groups or areas, which would raise a set of problems that defy simple analysis—joint costs, social costs, diseconomies of urban scale and so on—we may attribute the whole bundle of costs and benefits, distributed as they are, to the scale of the metropolitan area as a whole. In so far as commuters and the residents of the outer areas are part of the total metropolitan system and therefore in some degree beneficiaries of it, they should contribute to its costs according to their ability to pay. The same argument can be expressed in terms of land-values. Urban land-values, in excess of agricultural use-value, are created by the agglomeration of economic activities and, so long as proximity to the metropolitan core creates additional value, a common tax fund should be established for all residents and all areas.

In practice, the rate poundages in the outer metropolitan area are generally above those of Inner and Outer London,[1] (Table 4.7) but the average amount of rates paid on domestic

Table 4.7

Rates and Rateable Values in London and the South-East 1971–72

	Total Rateable Value £million	Rateable Value per Resident £	Average Rate Poundage p	Rate Call Per Resident £	Domestic Rate Call Per Resident £
Inner London	370.0	126	78.0	94	26
Outer London	309 5	66	78.9	51	24
Brighton CB	12.6	78	67.5	51	26
Reading CB	8.1	64	75.0	47	18
Southend-on-Sea CB	9.0	55	79.5	42	23
Bedfordshire	15.6	54	85.4	45	19
Berkshire	24.4	48	78.3	37	20
Buckinghamshire	35.7	61	77.0	47	21
Essex	57.3	49	82.0	39	18
Hampshire	45.6	46	77.5	36	18
Hertfordshire	59.1	65	76.5	49	22
Kent	58.7	43	86.1	36	19
Surrey	58.8	58	80.5	47	25
East Sussex	24.5	56	79.1	43	28
West Sussex	29.3	61	81.6	48	28

property per resident tends to be lower in the Outer Area (except in Surrey and Sussex, where the relatively low proportion of non-domestic activity puts more of the burden on domestic rate-payers). To this extent, the residents of the Outer

---

[1] This is consistent with the phenomenon generally observed in the United States that areas with wealthier tax bases (*per capita*) tend to have lower tax rates, but to spend more (*per capita*) than poorer areas.

Metropolitan Area 'get off cheap', since the value of land and hence of housing falls with distance from Central London. The incorporation of peripheral areas within a common rate fund would not therefore at present result in a shift of the burden of costs away from Inner London, and would only benefit Inner London if less relatively was spent on services benefiting the residents of the Outer Metropolitan Area. This is simply another way of saying that the rating system does not provide an equitable method of sharing costs over areas within which there is a very sharp variation in land and property values. But the thesis that those who commute from the outer area are off-loading some of their costs on to Londoners must be regarded as not proven. Certainly there is no evidence of an inverse correlation at the small area level between the rate poundages in the outer area and the proportion of resident workers commuting to London. It may well be that some of the variations that do exist could be explained by differences in the quality of the available services.

The real problems of Inner London, however, do not lie so much with the distribution of the burden of the costs of public services as with the way in which this is likely to change over time [4]. Inner London is by any standards a prosperous area, but the level of wealth may be less important than its rate of increase. Certainly history suggests that the urban areas which have been able most easily to undertake massive programmes of capital investment and a high level of expenditure on current services, have been those which have been growing at the fastest rate. In London, the increasing demand for capital investment is generating a growing burden of debt, so that between 1956–66 and 1969–70 the total net debt increased by nearly 50 per cent and loan charges increased by over 80 per cent, while capital investment (valued at prices current in the year of expenditure) increased by only 10 per cent. Loan charges as a percentage of gross current expenditure increased from 19 to 23.5 per cent.

Decentralization tends to exacerbate these difficulties. The loss of activities does not always lead to a *pro rata* reduction in costs. A recent GLC paper [5], for example, suggests that there may be particularly strong economies of scale in education which the loss of population operates against. Indeed, in some cases—for example, the costs associated with transport and commuting—it is conceivable that decentralization actually increases costs. More important is the effect on the tax base. Decentralization has meant a relative reduction in the rate of increase of rateable value compared both with outer areas and with other urban areas. In the recent past the loss of population has kept pace so that the rateable value per resident in Inner London has still increased faster than in many other parts of the metropolitan area. But even so this has not been sufficient to prevent a rate of increase in rate poundages much faster than in most other urban areas and other parts of the London region.

It would be wrong to exaggerate the seriousness of the situation. By some standards, Inner London and the GLC area generally have come through the last decade of decentralization remarkably successfully. The relative decline in rateable values in Inner London has not been as great as might have been expected and by way of contrast it has been the Outer Metropolitan Area which has felt the greatest impact from the rapid process of urbanization and the consequent need to increase public expenditure. But figures based on the resident population do not tell the whole story; while the resident population has fallen rapidly, the number of commuters to Central London has fallen only marginally. More important, however, is the question whether this success in retaining rateable value will continue. For if, as seems generally true, Inner London is unable to reduce its costs as fast as it loses population, it will not be sufficient merely to remain even in terms of *per capita* rateable value. The danger is, as Eversley has pointed out, that what was true of Inner London in comparison with Outer London in the 1950s, could become true of Greater London in comparison with the Outer Metropolitan Area.

This is not specifically a problem of the rating system, though it has particular features which are peculiar to that system. It would be a problem in any system of local taxation. Ideally it suggests the incorporation of the whole metropolitan area within a common local taxation unit. One obvious objection to this proposal would be the administrative size of the resulting unit. But this is only if one has in mind the type of reform which the creation of the GLC represented for London in the early 1960s. It might be argued that the economies of scale associated with such a large unit would in any case point in the direction of a larger administrative area, though these economies have not been well demonstrated [6]. But most people would accept that the loss of local political identity and participation is too large a price to pay, once one is talking of a population of up to 15 million in a very large geographical area.

This is a question of the distribution of political power and initiative as much as of cross-boundary externalities and economies of scale. What we should be talking in terms of is a more

Table 4.8

Increases in Rates and Rateable values in the London Metropolitan Region and Other Urban Areas, 1965–66 to 1971–72

	Total Rateable Value	Rateable Value per Resident	Rate Poundage	Domestic Rate Call per Resident
Inner London	+6.6	+15.9	+68.5	+75.2
Outer London	+9.9	+12.6	+52.6	+48.1
Berkshire	+29.8	+11.5	+38.1	+84.3
Buckingham	+24.8	+11.3	+46.7	+111.2
Essex	+31.4	+14.4	+45.6	+142.7
Hertfordshire	+22.9	+14.3	+49.1	+131.9
Kent	+21.8	+10.5	+56.5	+136.7
Surrey	+19.5	+13.4	+59.7	+163.5
Birmingham CB	+8.6	+10.8	+57.9	+65.6
Leeds CB	+13.1	+14.6	+56.1	+53.7
Manchester CB	+6 5	+16.6	+56.9	+54.0
Newcastle-on-Tyne CB	+6.6	+17.6	+70.2	+72.6
Bristol CB	+16.3	+17.9	+78.6	+69.3
Coventry CB	+13.7	+11.5	+58.3	+59.6
Leicester CB	+16.3	+12.1	+37.1	+29.5
Nottingham CB	+9.5	+13.6	+35.4	+39.3
Sheffield CB	+17.1	+9.6	+58.7	+61.8
Southampton CB	+14.0	+13.5	+55.1	+45.7
Wolverhampton CB	+86.7	+6.0	+50.4	+57.3
All CB's in England and Wales (average)	+22.2	+14.7	+55.1	+57.0

radical alteration of the present system of urban government, involving an upper-tier covering a larger area than at present and a lower-tier with real expenditure powers at a much lower level where there exists a real identity of community. Within such a structure, the benefits of scale could be obtained without vesting extensive administrative powers in the upper-tier by hiving services off into independent organizations [7], as is done in the case of the Metropolitan Water Board, the Metropolitan Police, London Transport and the Passenger Transport Executives of other metropolitan areas, with which local areas could contract for services. Of course such a system would create new problems—problems of monopoly and vested interest in the independent public services, problems of the loss of direct political control over their operation and of determining appropriate budgets and charges, problems of the relationship between the upper and lower tiers. But these are not insoluble; and at least in this context it begins to suggest how the future physical and economic development of the metropolitan area could be accommodated within a framework that would avoid some of the problems of public expenditure and finance which are endemic to the present system.

The Allocation of Resources within London

It would be wrong, however, to give the impression that the problems of Inner London all flow from its relations with the Outer Metropolitan Area. Even within the GLC area and in Inner London itself, it is reasonable to ask to what extent the current allocation of resources and the current distribution of rateable values contribute to the solution or aggravation of the problems.

Within the GLC and the ILEA, the declaration of a standard rate of precept helps to equalize the disparities in the area and the poorer parts of Inner London undoubtedly gain as a result. In addition, there is a rates equalization scheme [8] which contributes towards borough expenditure. By allowing poor areas to obtain access to part of the revenue collected in richer areas, the scheme attempts a partial equalization within London by a means of a formula similar to the Central Government Rate Support Grant, based on a definition of resources (non-domestic property plus expensive housing minus poor housing) and of needs (a modified version of the Rate Support Grant needs element calculation). The merit of the scheme in comparison with the Rate Support Grant is that the rich authorities have to pay so that the poor areas can receive. To this extent it is more genuinely a scheme of equalization. But the disparities after the equalization are still great; such a scheme cannot be more than a political compromise and real needs are not adequately equated.

These disparities are reflected in the large variations in expenditure between different sectors of activity which exist

Table 4.9

Per Capita Expenditure on Selected Services by London Boroughs, 1969–70

£ per resident per annum (gross expenditure)

	Local Health Service	Local Welfare	Child Care, etc.	Parks, Open Space	Town & Country Planning	Housing Loans	Highways, Etc.	Housing (Revenue A/C)
Camden	5.5	5.3	3.6	1.3	1.2	3.8	3.2	30.3
Greenwich	5.0	3.8	2.6	1.1	0.8	3.4	3.3	16.4
Hackney	5.2	3.4	3.7	0.7	0.3	0.6	2.5	26.2
Hammersmith	5.3	5.4	4.9	1.4	0.8	2.1	3.8	16.6
Islington	3.9	5.4	3.6	1.0	0.6	0.7	3.9	22.1
Kensington & Chelsea	3.3	3.7	3.5	0.3	0.5	1.2	3.4	8.2
Lambeth	4.1	3.6	4.2	0.3	0.9	0.7	3.0	16.2
Lewisham	4.0	5.1	2.9	1.0	0.5	2.6	3.0	15.0
Southwark	5.1	5.4	3.7	1.3	0.5	0.2	4.2	25.1
Tower Hamlets	3.8	4.7	5.9	0.8	—	0.1	4.7	24.3
Wandsworth	3.1	3.9	3.7	0.6	0.3	2.4	2.6	18.2
City of Westminster	4.8	5.0	3.9	1.0	1.2	3.4	7.4	21.3
Inner London Boroughs	4.4	4.5	3.8	0.9	1.7	1.8	4.2	20.8
Outer London Boroughs	3.0	2.6	1.2	1.9	1.0	2.0	3.7	13.3
All London Boroughs	3.5	3.3	2.2	1.5	1.3	1.9	3.9	16.2

between different London Boroughs (Table 4.9). For example, even if we ignore the very rich Cities of London and Westminster, gross current expenditure per resident in 1969–70 on all services except education varied between £76 and £34, while the total sum required from local revenue sources (after taking account of central government grants, the equalization scheme and other sources of income, but before GLC/ILEA and other precepts) varied between £28 and £6. We cannot tell to what extent this reflects differences in needs or in costs, in the level of service provided or in the tax base, but it is clear that within Inner London the variations do to a significant extent reflect the constraints of different volumes of available resources in the face of widely differing problems and needs. For despite the equalization scheme, the rate poundage in the areas with the most serious problems is consistently higher than in the richer areas, even though the yield from their domestic property per resident remains consistently lower. Undoubtedly they also reflect very marked differences in political priorities as well as in needs. How else can one explain the fact that Kensington and Chelsea spent £8.2 per resident in 1968/69 on items chargeable to the housing revenue account, while Camden spent £30.3 and Tower Hamlets £24.3? Or that Islington spent £0.7 per resident on housing loans while Lewisham spent £2.6 and the City of Westminster £3.4? Or again that Hackney spent nearly as much per resident on local health services as Camden, while Kensington and Chelsea, like Tower Hamlets, spent only about two thirds as much? None the less, whatever the scope for political disagreement about priorities and needs, there can be little doubt that if the areas with the most serious problems had access to the resources of the richer areas those problems would be tackled more forcefully. For while it is possible for a rich borough to turn its back on the worst problems within its boundary, less fortunate boroughs which do have some of the most serious and widespread problems in housing and the social services consistently demonstrate their readiness to attack these problems by spending more per resident and by having as a result to charge a higher rate poundage.

Looking more generally at the allocation of London's resources to the different categories of local service, one is bound to conclude that the only major shift which would be generally beneficial to Inner London would be a reduction in the allocation to highways.[1] While public transport is of critical importance to the welfare of Inner London, both because of its relationship to the physical structure and the employment distribution of the area and because of the large number of non car-owning and low-income households in the area, major investment in highways is very unlikely to bring any benefit to the area unless it is very carefully kept in step with a whole range of other policies relating to housing and the distribution of employment. Not merely is highway investment likely to generate worse problems for the residents of Inner London in the form of increased traffic volumes, congestion, noise, dirt, pollution, deterioration of the bus services, increased parking and destruction of the physical and social environment, but it is also likely seriously to add to the physical, social and financial problems of Inner London by encouraging further unplanned decentralization of residents and employment. And to add insult to injury, where improvements to public transport are proposed, the current grant system encourages wasteful investment in additions to the system which generate little additional benefit at high cost rather than a balanced programme of current and capital expenditure designed to get the most out of the fast-deteriorating existing network of public transport services.

Additional and Alternative Sources of Finance

Granted the problems of Inner London and the low probability of attracting additional resources from elsewhere, it is natural for those who are concerned with problems of Inner London to turn to consider additional sources of revenue. The most traditional method of attempting to increase the supply of local public sector resources is by attracting high value land-uses to the area. In the case of London, which is already experiencing a rapid decentralization, retention must be

---

[1] The central government must of course take a major share of the blame for the exaggerated propensity to spend money on highways. For despite the compelling logic of a block grant for transport (or addition to Rate Support Grant) it insists on providing 75 per cent capital grants—a rate which cannot conceivably be justified by the size of the benefits enjoyed by those who live beyond the boundaries of the local authority.

substituted for attraction. In the commercial sector, this means continuing to encourage office development and attempting to retain a major share of the shopping trade. This is undoubtedly one of the factors that has encouraged the GLC to reconsider the limitation of office building in Central London and lies behind proposals for the redevelopment of Covent Garden and other areas. In the domestic sector, where, as those who are concerned about the prospects of the social polarization of Inner London recognize, the very rich show little sign of wanting to move out of London and the stock of expensive housing is undiminished, it means retaining the middle-income households. Unfortunately, both these policies reveal classic examples of the conflict between the short-term constraints of financial policy and the long-term development of the urban area. Thus in the case of commercial development, we should be aware that there is a very direct relationship between the volume of employment in Central London and the housing conditions of low-income households in Inner London generally (and the condition of the housing stock), a relationship which is mediated through land values in the office development and housing markets. Could it be that the development which may generate more funds to tackle Inner London's housing problem will also exacerbate that problem? In the domestic sector, London seems to have been more successful than, for example, many North American cities in retaining the middle-income groups. But to the extent that this success has depended on the availability of public housing, the net contribution to public sector resources may not have been very large (though in future this will depend on the implementation of the Housing Finance Act). In general though, it must be true that the retention of a balanced population would be preferable from the standpoint of the local tax base to a process of social polarization, assuming that there are no changes in the system of local finance. But whether or not such social balance is desirable on other grounds or whether the goal of social balance can justify housing policies which aim to upgrade and improve outworn housing but result in worse housing conditions for the very lowest income groups are other questions.

If rateable values cannot be increased, one must turn to other sources of finance. This is not because rates have not been a buoyant form of taxation, but because the perverse effects of

attempting to raise the Inner London rate even faster relative
to other parts of the metropolitan area to compensate for the
slower growth of the tax base would be likely to contribute more
to the exacerbation of Inner London's financial problems than
to their solution. In fact it would be more reasonable to be
talking in terms of substitutes for rates rather than of supple-
ments. For it is well established that domestic rateable value is a
proxy neither for the income of residents nor for wealth nor for
the market value of the property nor for the value of the benefit
received from local services nor for the costs imposed. They are
simply a specific tax on the occupation of housing[1] whose direct
incidence, as the 1964 Allen Committee demonstrated, is
strongly regressive [9], even if in the final analysis some of their
impact is shifted back to land and property owners. To some
extent their effect is offset by the contribution of other forms of
taxation to local revenue through the central government
grants and subsidies, but the impact on low-income groups is
still severe, especially when rate poundages rise rapidly. Rate
rebates and the partial de-rating of domestic property (through
the domestic element of the Rate Support Grant) can only
relieve the situation partially, while the fact that they are needed
alongside the Rate Support Grant and the London equalization
scheme, is sufficient evidence that the system is unsound, leading
as it does, to unequal treatment of equals, disincentives to
improve obsolescent housing and improper incentives to locate
firms and residences in areas with low rates [10]. Even the much
vaunted administrative simplicity of the system—collection
costs are low and evasion is minimal—proves to be illusory when
the periodic attempts are made to cope with the formidable
task of revaluation, during which in the name of objectivity
valuers attempt to make essentially political decisions about the
future distribution of the costs of urban services. Nevertheless,
no taxman is likely to do away lightly with a source of revenue
that yields more than £1700 million per annum and whose

---

[1] In this instance also the local finance system reveals a remarkable
perversity, for, as Netzer has pointed out, the effect of a high rate of
taxation on the consumption of housing must be to reduce the real quantity
and quality of housing enjoyed (especially at low-income levels)—a
phenomenon which in other circumstances is of great concern to policy-
makers.

yield has grown at a rate of some 5 per cent per annum. In this instance, those who would argue in favour of a change in the system are faced by an unhealthy coalition of politicians and bureaucrats.

The alternative (or more probably additional) sources of revenue that could be introduced in London have often been discussed [11]: local income tax, sales tax, employment tax, vehicle and petrol duties, tourist poll tax and so on. Of these, local income tax is undoubtedly practicable and is the most attractive on grounds of fiscal equity. It is unpopular with many local authorities, partly because income tax is itself unpopular and therefore they would feel more constrained in fixing rates and partly because, since the most practicable schemes would make the local tax an adjunct to the national, they feel too much power to limit the rates permitted would naturally be retained by central government. Sales tax tends to be regressive (in income terms) though if such things as housing, food and public transport are excluded such a tax could be made to cover something like 30 per cent of the purchases of the lowest income groups and 50 per cent of the highest; this would still be more regressive than income tax. On the other hand, very small rates of tax could yield a sizeable revenue; for example, a theoretical 1 per cent tax could yield as much as 5 per cent increase in rates. Unfortunately, without a full 'cents/centimes' element in the decimal currency, it is impossible to apply uniform low percentage rates of sales tax, though a tax on purchases over 50 p might be workable. The administrative costs of such a tax tend to be high. A payroll tax is more problematical, at least without an extension of the boundary of local taxation, since any differential tax on employers is likely to increase the propensity to decentralize and thereby add to Inner London's financial and other difficulties. The most attractive form of tax on employers would be one which could discriminate in terms of the propensity to decentralize, which suggests a tax related to high income per employee office employment; but this sort of discrimination would almost certainly not prove practicable. The assignment of a part of the vehicle excise duty or of petrol duties to local authorities would not assist Inner London if the new revenues were ascribed to the Boroughs (except in so far as partial adjustments were made to the rates equalization scheme and rates support grants) since car ownership levels are higher in the relatively rich Outer Boroughs. There would also seem to be a serious risk that local authorities would be more ready to accept the argument of the motorists' lobby that these funds should be devoted to highways and that the benefits of the Treasury's stalwart refusal to admit the principle of hypothecated funds would be lost. Local petrol taxes have some merit as an additional tax on the use of cars—despite the risk of petrol-fetching journeys—provided once again that the boundary is drawn fairly wide; otherwise the redistribution of benefits between those inside the area who would mostly have to pay the tax and those outside who could avoid it, while still enjoying the benefits of access to, and imposing costs within, the urban core, would be unacceptable.

The proposals for tourist taxes—e.g. taxes on hotel beds—is usually justified on the grounds that tourists make considerable use of the 'free' public facilities of Inner London, but that their expenditure is not sufficiently large to generate an equivalent return to the public authorities through existing forms of taxation. So long as rates are the only direct form of local taxation this is likely to be true, though the indirect contribution of earnings from tourists through national taxation and the yield of purchase tax are also important. But another consideration in this case must be the elasticity of tourism with respect to such things as hotel prices, in the light of the shadow price attached to tourist expenditure both from the national standpoint as a source of foreign earnings and from London's standpoint as a fundamental component of the local economy. Certainly it is possible over a number of years for tourist areas to price themselves out of the market.

A more fundamental method of achieving an effective increase in local revenue within an area like Inner London would be by increasing the level and range of charges imposed on specific services. This type of proposal is canvassed as a solution to the general problems of the rising cost of, and increasing demand for, urban public services. The merits of such a proposal relate directly to the two models of public expenditure and finance discussed earlier in this paper. Specific user-charges are the corollary of the so-called market model. In terms, therefore, of the threefold classification of urban public services introduced earlier, charges are most appropriate in the case of the income-elastic group of services and inappropriate for compensatory or redistributive services. Housing of course is a special case with its own special rules. In practice, however, short of the introduction of some form of road pricing or congestion tax, there seems to be little scope for increasing revenue in this way.

Conclusion

The conclusion I would draw from this brief survey is that in the medium-term, if not the short-term, the prospects for Inner London are somewhat bleak. In so far as the solution of some of its outstanding problems will depend on the availability of resources within the public sector, it would be optimistic to predict a radical improvement in the general level and distribution of welfare. Inner London is and will remain a very prosperous area within the country as a whole but its prosperity is declining relatively and with it the capacity to achieve, without more radical programmes than are at present admitted, the considerable tasks of renewal and redistribution which are still needed. A number of changes could help Inner London: for example, the recognition that the net contribution which London makes to the national pool of public sector resources does not adequately reflect the costs which are an intrinsic component of the process of achieving a high level of productivity; some method of incorporating the whole metropolitan area within a common local taxation unit; a more equitable distribution of resources within Inner London; a shift away from highway investment towards expenditure directly related to the more pressing problems; and the replacement of the rating system by a system of local income and capital gains taxation. These are obviously only a selection of possibilities. But even with such changes the problems of an area such as Inner London, at the centre of a rapidly decentralizing metropolitan economy, at a time when there is a sharp increase in the demand for local public services and the prospect of a continuing rise in the real costs of providing them, are likely to remain a persistent source of concern.

References

1. WOODWARD, V. H., 'Regional Social Accounts for the United Kingdom', *Regional Papers 1*, National Institute of Economic and Social Research, London, 1970.

2. Papers by WINGO, L., RICHARDSON, H., EVANS, A., FOSTER, C., THOMPSON, W. and MILLS, E., in a special issue of *Urban Studies*, **9**, no. 1, February 1972, and references attached thereto.

3. *Committee of Inquiry into the impact of rates on households*, Report Cmnd. 2582 (London: H.M.S.O., 1964).

4. EVERSLEY, D. E. C., 'Rising costs and static incomes—some economic consequences of regional planning in London', *Urban Studies* **9** no. 3, October 1972. Also EVERSLEY, D. E. C., *Cutting our Cities Down to Size* (Institute of Municipal Treasurers and Accountants, London, 1971).

5. *Factors affecting the annual revenue expenditure of London local authorities*, G.L.D.P. Background Paper 526, 1972.

6. HIRSCH, W., *The Economics of State and Local Government* (New York: McGraw-Hill, 1970).

7. FOSTER, C. D., 'Public finance aspects of national settlement patterns', *Urban Studies*, **9**, no. 1, February 1972.

8. ILERSIC, A. R., *Rate Equalisation in London* (Institute of Municipal Treasurers and Accountants, London, 1967).

9. OLIVER, F. and STANZER, J., 'Local government finance', in WISEMAN, H. (ed.), *Local Government in England 1958–1969* (London: Routledge and Kegan Paul, 1970).

10. NETZER, D., 'Federal, state and local finance in a metropolitan context', in PERLOFF, H. and WINGO, L. (eds.), *Issues in Urban Economics* (Washington D.C.: Resources for the Future Inc., 1968).

11. Department of the Environment, *The future shape of local government finance* (H.M.S.O., 1971). See also MARSHALL, A. H., *New Revenues for Local Government* (London: Fabian Society, 1971).

Chapter Five

Some Aspects of Social Polarization

MARGARET HARRIS

Summary

In this chapter an attempt is made to distinguish the various ideas subsumed under the heading of 'polarization' and the use of an appropriate terminology is suggested. 'Social polarization' is defined here as a change in the distribution of social classes in a defined geographical area such that, either the proportion of the population at the two extremes of the social class continuum increases; or the proportion of the population at one point only on the continuum increases; or the distribution becomes more unlike an actual or hypothetical 'norm' distribution. Some of the theories and concepts which appear to be relevant to discussions of 'social polarization' are examined in this chapter in an attempt to set the discussion within a wider sociological context. Finally, the possibility is examined of measuring 'social polarization', and the results of work completed so far are presented. It is concluded that, although social class distribution (and therefore 'social polarization') on the one hand, and social problems on the other hand, are not necessarily related to each other, they are, in themselves, of great concern to local authorities. A more fruitful line for future research, therefore, might be

The author wishes to acknowledge the help and advice she received in the preparation of this chapter from John Lyons, Maurice Marchant and Chris Mellor of the Greater London Council's Intelligence Unit. Maurice Marchant prepared the computer program upon which much of the empirical material is based and Chris Mellor analysed the results obtained.

to attempt to distinguish the generators of different social class distribution patterns and, separately, the generators of various social problems which beset city regions.

Introduction

In the last few years, there has been much speculation and discussion about 'polarization' in urban areas, particularly London [1–5]. The most frequent argument has been that there is a danger of London becoming a city of the very rich and very poor with middle income groups moving away from its expense. There has also been concern about an apparent tendency for low-income and unskilled workers to become geographically isolated within inner city areas. The concern about trends in British urban areas almost certainly derives from knowledge of North American urban problems; the 'flight' from the cities on the one hand and the increase in the number of ethnic and income-based ghettos on the other hand. It may also reflect the traditional dichotomous theories of the organization of society.

The elements common to practically every reference to 'polarization' have been:

1 a reference to one or more urban geographical areas;

2 an interest in the spatial distribution of one or more variables;

3 an implication that polarization is undesirable or has undesirable consequences.

However, there are a number of points on which users of the term 'polarization' have differed or have failed to make clear their attitude. These are:

1 The size and nature of the urban geographical area or areas referred to.

2 The variable or variables under discussion: I have found references to the distribution of at least eight different variables, including social class, occupation, income, age, family cycle, career cycle, housing tenure and life chances. Naturally, there are relationships between these variables and it is sometimes possible to draw conclusions about one by examining another; but confusion can be minimized by considering each, separately, as has been shown elsewhere [6].

3 The adverse and undesirable *consequences* foreseen: the consequences foreseen have been social, economic and political but have varied according to the variable under discussion and the size and nature of the area referred to.

4 The pattern of the distribution of a variable within geographical areas: the type of distribution pattern which is of interest does not necessarily vary according to the variable under discussion. Some writers have been generally concerned about 'abnormality' or 'imbalance' in the distribution of a variable, and others have been concerned about concentrations at specific points of the distribution scale.

5 The time scale: we should distinguish between the situation at one point in time (that is, a state), and the change that may occur over a period of time (that is, a process).

6 The population referred to: when the characteristics of an area are mentioned it is not always the total residential population that is described, but sometimes the working population or some specific section of the population defined, for example, by sex, age or economic activity.

For ease of reference, and in order to distinguish the various elements discussed above, the term *degree of polarity* will be applied in this chapter to the distribution of a variable in the residential population of a specified geographical area at one point in time, and the term *polarization* will be applied to a change over time in the distribution of a variable in a geographical area.

The terms 'polarity' and 'polarization' may be qualified according to which variable is under discussion; for example, 'social polarity' and 'social polarization' may be used to refer to the distribution of social classes, 'income polarity' and 'income polarization' may refer to the distribution of income, and so on.

Three types of polarity may be distinguished according to the nature of the distribution pattern which is of most interest:

1 Bi-polarity: A state in which the distribution of a variable within the defined population of a defined geographical area is such that a relatively high proportion of the population are at the two extremes of the distribution.

2 Uni-polarity: A state in which the distribution of a variable within the defined population of a defined geographical area is

such, that there is a relatively high proportion of the population at one point only on the distribution.

3 Abnormality: A state in which the distribution of a variable within the defined population of a defined geographical area differs from a hypothetical or actual, norm or ideal distribution. This type of distribution could include 1 or 2.

The adoption of this framework does not imply that the terms 'polarization' and 'polarity' have any intrinsic meaning or value. If the terms are to be useful they must be applied to clearly defined situations and not to a large number of differing ones. This suggested terminology may be seen, therefore, as a means of clarifying the various issues involved in discussions of 'polarization'.

In the rest of this chapter, discussion will concentrate on the distribution of the social class variable; that is, on 'social polarity' and 'social polarization'. In the following section some of the theories and concepts which may be regarded as relevant to discussions of 'social polarization' are listed in an attempt to set discussions within a sociological context.

Social Stratification

Sociological theories of social stratification can provide the basis for a discussion of social class distribution. The term 'social stratification' refers to the hierarchical ranking of individuals and groups in society. Theoretical and practical studies of stratification in Great Britain and the United States have led to the conclusion that no one factor can account for or be used to measure the 'social class' of an individual, that is, his place in the hierarchy of society.

Social class may be seen as a multi-dimensional concept of which the three main dimensions are position in the economic system, status in society and power. Thus, an individual's social class must be related to a wide range of variables including his occupation, his income, his accumulated wealth and property, his educational experience and achievement, his ethnic origin, his dwelling area, his social contacts and his leisure-time pursuits. Any one of these variables, alone or in combination with others, could affect an individual's position in the economic system and the prestige and power which he enjoys in society.

The variables listed above are generally interdependent, and this fact, combined with the paucity of published data on many of the variables, has resulted in one or two of the variables only being selected as indicators of social class in many empirical studies of social composition. The results of such studies have to be interpreted bearing in mind the variable or combination of variables used as an indicator of social class.

Social Balance

One of the reasons why users of the term 'social polarization' have implied that it is undesirable may have been that they regarded social polarization as a movement away from a desirable and ideal state of 'social heterogeneity', 'social balance', 'social mix' or 'balanced community'. Let us examine some of the reasons which have been advanced for regarding social balance as desirable.

1 It is suggested that where communities are unbalanced there will be a shortage of people willing to lead, question, agitate and pressure local authorities. Politicians at both the national and local level could then become extremely powerful since the British democratic process depends to a large extent on questioning and criticism from the public and the press. A more immediate effect of a lack of leadership and agitation could be that pressure to improve and provide community facilities would be low. Judy Hillman, for example, has viewed with concern the apparent development of one-class communities in London [2]. 'There have always been concentrations of better-off people in Westminster, Kensington and Chelsea and of the less privileged or poor in Tower Hamlets and Southwark. But there used to be a healthy balancing factor in these areas as well. Small cottages in Chelsea provided homes for people with smaller incomes; in the East End there were groups of former merchants' homes housing middle-class people who were prepared to put pressure on the authorities for better schools, transport, shops and the general standard of environment.'

Similarly, Jo Grimond has discussed the implications of a 'ghetto society' [7]: 'If more of the top industrialists and bureaucrats lived in the poorer districts a great deal would be done to improve the services offered'. The argument that middle-class people provide balance in an area and that a lack of middle-class people is a disadvantage for the poorer sections of the community is applicable even if the highest social class remains in an area. The facilities demanded by and provided for the rich are not generally those that also benefit poorer people. It is argued that middle-class people, on the other hand, will agitate on behalf of the less affluent and/or will demand facilities for themselves which will also benefit other social groups.

2 The argument that a mixture of social classes can lead to an improvement in the facilities provided by public authorities in an area, can be extended to the provision of facilities by private developers, such as supermarkets, new housing for owner-occupiers and employment opportunities.

3 It is suggested that many facilities which the middle and upper classes demand or supply for themselves may be of the kind which manual workers or less educated people may not regard as particularly important, attractive or interesting. However, it is thought that the very existence of facilities such as libraries and art galleries in an area may have a long-term 'improving' or 'uplifting' effect on the less interested sections of the population.

4 It is thought that children of the lowest social classes within a balanced community should benefit from mixing at school and socially with less 'culturally deprived' children. This need to compensate children who are educationally deprived at home and school was one of the concerns of the Plowden Committee [8].

5 It is argued that, when a community is socially balanced, it will benefit from the fact that essential professional workers, such as teachers, doctors, social workers and solicitors will live within it or will be encouraged to do so. The Cullingworth Report [9], for example, drew attention to the need for local authorities to ensure that those who man community services have opportunities to find homes within the areas they serve.

6 It has been said that in a society with an unbalanced social structure, social mobility will be hindered as there will be less opportunity for people at the bottom of the social scale to move upwards and less incentive for them to try [3].

7 It has been argued that the useful life of existing buildings in an area is likely to be prolonged in a socially mixed area.

Those with higher incomes are likely to improve their own property and thus encourage other owner-occupiers, landlords and local authorities to do the same.

Policies of local and national government have, intentionally or unintentionally, fostered 'social mix' through (*a*) encouragement of private capital investment in low-income housing areas; (*b*) provision of housing improvement grants for landlords and owner-occupiers; (*c*) improvement and provision of facilities and amenities favoured by middle-income groups; examples may be roads, schools and record libraries; (*d*) the exercise of control over the selection of movers to new towns and the industries provided in them.

Arguments for social balance seem, then, to be based on an assumption that certain social composition patterns within a geographical area are associated with certain social advantages. It is apparently assumed that: (*a*) one social class may raise the social, political and cultural conscience of another when the classes live in close proximity; (*b*) in acting on behalf of its own interests, a class may benefit not only itself but also other sections of the local community; and (*c*) the knowledge and culture of people of one class may be modified or improved by living in close proximity to another class.

I think that the arguments in favour of social mix must be treated with caution for a number of reasons.

1 Nobody has attempted to suggest what social composition pattern might constitute an ideal social mix. In fact, it is unlikely that there are one or two particular social class distributions which could be demonstrated to be related to all the social advantages suggested above. If the hypothesis of the relationship between social composition pattern and social advantages is valid at all, it is most probable that for every advantage there is an associated social composition pattern within which it is likely to arise.

2 The size of the area for which social balance may be the aim is not clear. Gans [10] has distinguished four levels of community—the house, the block, the neighbourhood and the political community. He has argued that it is most realistic to plan the street block as a homogeneous unit, but that as a political entity the community should encompass a mixture of classes

and ethnic groups so as to secure the benefits of diversity at that level. Although Gans's terminology is directly applicable to the United States, we can see from his arguments the necessity to distinguish clearly the size and nature of the geographical area within which social mix might be associated with social advantages.

3 It cannot be assumed that the population of areas which do not contain a middle-class 'balancing' factor is inarticulate and incapable of putting pressure on the appropriate authorities when necessary. It is true that amenity groups and other pressure groups are usually led or dominated by middle-class people. But there are other methods of presenting a case (for example, protest marches, lobbying and demonstrations), which do not appear to be dependent on middle-class leadership or encouragement. The majority of the GLC rent strikers and the Isle of Dogs rebels, for example, were not from socially mixed geographical areas.

4 The argument that good or improved facilities will not be provided in an area unless the middle-class element is strongly represented seems to rest on the erroneous assumption that only 'effective' demand (that is demand that is clearly backed by money or votes) is worthy or capable of satisfaction. It is implied that only the operation of the political and economic 'market' can or should lead to the provision of facilities.

It is true that where facilities are provided by private enterprise, the ability of the population to buy will be the foremost consideration in the mind of potential investors. Public authorities, on the other hand, should not and do not give priority to purely economic and political considerations when deciding whether or not to provide good or improved facilities in an area. If a public authority assesses an area to be lacking in certain essential facilities, irrespective of whether these facilities are generally provided by private or public enterprise, that authority has the power, and some might argue an obligation, to attempt to provide these facilities whatever the social composition of the area. Indeed, social policies of positive discrimination which have been adopted (for example, educational priority areas) are an acknowledgement of the viewpoint that a middle-class element in a population is not a prerequisite for improving the facilities of that area.

5 A clear distinction must be drawn between arguments for

social class balance and those for a balanced distribution of other variables. Some of the arguments presented for residential social mix may really reflect a concern for occupational mix (a wide range of employment opportunities to facilitate social mobility); for an even income distribution (to encourage a variety of private investment); or for a range of housing tenures (to relieve the burden on local authority housing departments).

6 There are practical and moral difficulties involved in creating or maintaining areas of residential social mix. Janet Cochrane [11] has discussed the consequences of houses in working-class or multiple occupation being bought up and converted into single occupation housing or bedsitters for the more prosperous. She has argued that although the working-class person may benefit at first from improved shopping and cultural facilities, 'this is a transitory phase and rising prices will sooner or later force him to leave'. Thus the process of creating social balance through the movement into a predominantly one-class area of people of another class may not halt at the point where balance is achieved; it raises a moral difficulty in that the effect of the process appears to be mainly to the material advantage of the newcomers and to the disadvantage of the original residents of the area. It may be noted at this point that it is generally assumed that social mix will be achieved in areas by moving middle-class people into areas of lower-class residence rather than by the opposite means. This in itself is an assumption that may be criticized, but the problem outlined here is applicable however social mix is achieved.

Another practical difficulty has been pointed out by Alonso [12]. He has shown that, although social balance is a traditional objective of new town theorists who want new towns to contain substantial proportions of diverse social, economic and ethnic groups, there have been few suggestions as to how social integration might be achieved in practice. Moreover, recent studies of new towns [13] have indicated that the higher classes have tended to leave the new towns and that residential areas within the towns are becoming differentiated by social class. Broady [14] has pointed out in a similar way that efforts to mix social classes in new towns through housing and community facilities have been unsuccessful, largely because deep economic and educational divisions in society cannot be changed by physical layout.

7 As the discussion in the previous paragraph suggests, even where areas are socially mixed, it cannot be assumed that there is understanding and meaningful contact between people of different social classes. A review of 'propinquity' and 'homogeneity' theories of neighbouring by Gans [15], for example, has led to the conclusion that although propinquity initiates many social relationships and maintains less intensive ones, it is not sufficient by itself to create intensive relationships. Friendship requires homogeneity of social composition.

8 The educational advantages of social mix for school children are the subject of some debate. This is reflected, for example, in Chapter Ten.

Mass Society Theory

Discussion of the situation which I have termed 'bi-polarity' has included suggestions that there are dangers inherent in a decrease in the 'middle' sections of society. For example, the authors of *Tomorrow's London* have said [1]: 'We want to retain all groups of the community . . . because the good functioning of government and society demands that we should prevent extreme polarization.' This concern with the intermediate section of society bears some resemblance to theories about the adverse political consequences of 'mass society'. Mass Society theorists, e.g. Kornhauser [16], suggest that adherence to democratic norms and the maintenance of democratic institutions are dependent upon the existence of a pluralistic social and political system. When conditions of 'mass society' develop, that is, when some groups or institutions of pluralist society are eroded and there are no integrating intermediate groups between the mass of individuals and the ruling group, individuals become susceptible to mobilization for political participation in 'anti-democratic' and 'extremist' movements.

These 'mass theories' generally assume that the 'intermediate groups' are the formal and informal institutions which can relate individuals to the wider society, rather than intermediate social classes. Moreover, their pessimistic viewpoint is subject to many criticisms [17]. Nevertheless, the common concern of social polarization theories and mass society theories with the consequences of the erosion of intermediates is interesting. This is all the more so because some of those who have discussed social polarization have used language that has overtones of mass society theory. The South-East Joint Planning Team [3], for example, saw social polarization as a process that could occur in Inner London 'as a consequence of the "middle mass" leaving due to high costs and unacceptable living conditions'.

Social Composition Change

The term 'social polarization' has been taken to refer to certain types of change in the social class distribution of a geographical area. By measuring the social composition of an area at two points in time, we could discover whether any change had occurred; but we would not then know the reason for any found change. Three main factors which could contribute to a change in the social class distribution of an area may be distinguished.

Migration or Geographical Mobility

The social composition of migration flows into and out of a geographical area and the size of the flows will affect the overall social class distribution pattern within an area at any one time. Since migration may contribute to change in social composition, we can see that an understanding of motives for migration would be a useful adjunct to studies of 'polarity' and 'polarization'. Work at the University of Kent [18] has thrown some light on why people move to private residential developments in the Outer Metropolitan Area, but more work is needed on the motivation of migrants, especially migrants into and out of large urban areas.

Social Mobility

Irrespective of the pattern of geographical mobility, the measured social composition of an area may change if some of the individuals or groups who remain in the area move from one social class to another. We may refer to such a movement between social classes as 'social mobility'. The question remains as to what generates social mobility.

Some of the variables which are related to and contribute to an individual's social class have been discussed already. It follows that any factor which encourages, enables or forces an individual or group to change his or its 'score' with respect to one or more of these variables, may be regarded as a generator of social mobility. Such factors include: change in employment structure and employment opportunities; change in overall income distribution such that an individual's or group's relative position in the income scale changes; change in national economic climate affecting the value of different types of property; change in the nature and extent of education provision; and change in society's mores with respect to the prestige attached to types of occupation, types of dwelling area, social contacts and pastimes.

Demographic Change

Independently of the effect of geographical and social mobility, demographic changes can lead to alterations in the size and characteristics of a measured population. For example, if the social classes in an area have different fertility or mortality rates, the overall social class distribution of an area is almost certain to undergo some change in the long term. Similarly, both the absolute and relative size of the employed sections of a population will be influenced by differential rates of entry to and retirement from the labour market.

Each of these three factors may contribute to change in the social class composition of an area over time and is itself subject to the influence of a variety of factors (see Figure 5.1). It is

Some of the factors that control the 'Generators'

'Generators' of Change in Social Class Distribution

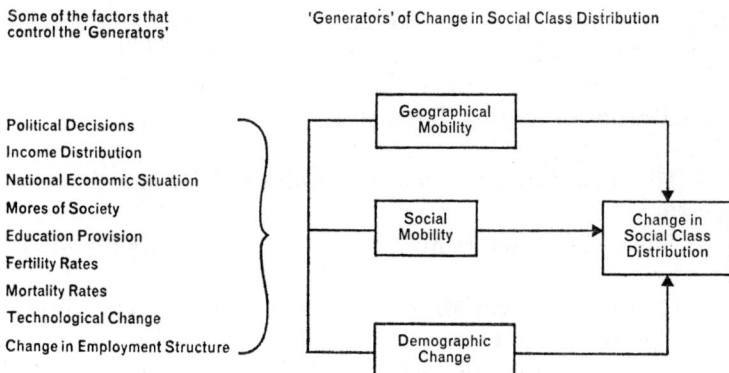

Political Decisions
Income Distribution
National Economic Situation
Mores of Society
Education Provision
Fertility Rates
Mortality Rates
Technological Change
Change in Employment Structure

Geographical Mobility

Social Mobility

Demographic Change

Change in Social Class Distribution

FIGURE 5.1 Change in social class distribution

therefore clear that, for any particular case of social composition change, it would be difficult to distinguish all the contributory factors unless sufficient data were available to allow for the examination of each possible factor in turn.

An interesting example of the way causes may be inter-dependent and inter-related has been discussed by Waugh [19], who has studied the changing distribution of professional and managerial manpower in England and Wales between 1961 and 1966. He suggests that conurbations provide opportunities for social mobility:

> The continuing concentration of wealth and expertise in the Midlands and South-East can no longer be attributed mainly to selective immigration; cities provide opportunities for upward socio-economic mobility among their residents and conurbations are major generators of high status groups. Rising socio-economic status round Greater London is unparalleled elsewhere in the Country.

Spatial Structure and Social Structure

We are now using the terms 'polarity' and 'polarization' to refer to spatial arrangements of the population with respect to social class characteristics. We have also seen that there have been suggestions that spatial arrangements of the population may be related to certain social advantages and social problems. Let us consider briefly the possible nature of the relationship between the spatial or geographical distribution of a population, facilities, employment and so on, on the one hand, and other aspects of the social structure on the other hand.

There seem to be three possible types of relationship between spatial structure and social structure:

1 The spatial structure may determine or influence the social structure.

2 The social structure may determine or influence the spatial structure.

3 One or more variables may be related independently to both the spatial structure and the social structure, so that there is only an indirect, non-causal relationship between spatial structure and social structure.

Presumably the type of relationship or the combination of types of relationship will vary from one society to another according to the factor whose spatial distribution is under examination and according to the aspect of the social structure considered. Pahl [20], however, emphasizes the importance of the first two types of causal relationship and suggests that they are likely to occur together; he is among the writers who assume that in urban society the spatial structure partly reflects and partly determines the social structure.

Since 'polarity' is a particular type of spatial arrangement of a population with respect to social class, it is relevant to consider the suggestion that it is related to some other aspects of social structure. The questions that remain to be answered are: of what type or combination of types is the relationship between 'polarity' and other aspects of the social structure and to which aspects of social structure is polarity most closely related when it occurs?

Janet Cochrane [11] has suggested that large, urban, economically specialized societies are conducive to the development of a high degree of social class polarity. She has written:

Modern cities develop and advance by progressive specialisation. Attempts to encourage intimate social mixing of people of widely differing background are often based on a nostalgia for rural life, where the isolation of the village community, its relative smallness, compactness and self-sufficiency encourage face to face contacts and intimate knowledge of everyone's past and ancestry. It is impossible to recreate this in a city such as London, where the pace of life is swift and where people are so mobile and specialized.

On the other hand, the arguments for 'social balance' which were discussed earlier assumed that the spatial structure could influence and even determine some other aspects of social structure; in particular, that social class heterogeneity could produce social advantages. Social polarity, conversely, would be likely to encourage or facilitate the occurrence of social and economic problems.

It would be reasonable, then, to hypothesize that the occurrence of social polarity is related in some way to other aspects of the social structure. However, the exact nature of the relationship and which are the aspects of social structure most concerned, are not at present clear.

Poverty and Deprivation

It has been mentioned already that we should examine separately the distribution of different variables, such as social class and income. However, income, as well as being a variable in its own right, can be used alone or in combination with other variables as an indicator of social class. Therefore, discussion about distribution of real income and poverty in Great Britain and concern about some sections of the population being 'left behind' in spite of a general trend of increasing affluence, are relevant to discussions about social polarization. So also are references to 'deprivation'.

'Deprivation' may be used as a synonym for poverty; not only low income but also the inadequate social and physical environments which generally accompany it. In this context, we may make the following observations about the relationship between deprivation or poverty and social composition patterns:

1 If polarization occurs in the sense that degree of bi-polarity increases, it is probable that the section of the population which may be termed 'deprived' will be more clearly delineated. This is not an argument that 'deprivation' in fact increases as degree of bi-polarity increases, but merely an assertion that situations of deprivation may be more apparent when social bi-polarity increases within an area.

2 Uni-polarity or polarity in the sense of 'abnormality of social composition' could cause or aggravate situations of deprivation in an area if people remaining there were not able or willing to pressure the authorities for the provision and improvement of services and facilities. However, this argument must be balanced against the point made earlier, that it cannot be assumed that particular social classes are less capable than others of putting pressure on appropriate authorities when necessary.

3 The existence of a large number of deprived people in an area could lead to an increase in the degree of uni-polarity or bi-polarity by encouraging those who could afford to do so to move away to areas where the provision of facilities and the physical environment were better. Violence could be the intervening variable in such a chain of events, as has been suggested by the 1969 report of the U.S. National Commission on the

Causes and Prevention of Violence. *The Times* on 24 November 1969 explained that the Commission found that poverty was the basic cause of violence. A spread of violence could aggravate a social polarization trend. *The Times* report said that the Chairman of the Commission told reporters that if poverty and crime were not eradicated in cities, the city of the future would be 'a guarded mixture of business enterprises and high-rise apartments'. There would be a 'flight of people to the suburbs where they will be guarded, some by private and some by public police . . . where houses will have every kind of burglar device known . . . where sanitized highways will connect these areas with the cities'.

'Deprivation' is essentially a relative term. 'Poverty' and 'low income' are similar terms. People are termed 'deprived' when there are people who are demonstrably better off than themselves with whom they may be compared. Another term which conveys a meaning similar to that of 'the deprived' is the term 'the less privileged', which was used by the South-East Joint Planning Team [3] to refer to the population at the lowest end of the social class and income distribution: those whose situation compared unfavourably with the rest of the population.

This inherent property of the word 'deprivation' may account for the use of the term 'relative deprivation' by politicians and journalists, often in conjunction with a reference to social polarization. In labelling people or groups 'relatively deprived' they have been emphasizing the fact that they regard 'deprivation' as a relative term. In fact, this use of the term 'relative deprivation' can be confusing since the same term has been widely employed for many years by social psychologists and sociologists to refer to a different but related concept.

For the social scientist, 'relative deprivation' is a special concept arising from reference group theory. Merton [21] has explained that an individual may be oriented towards any one or more of various groups of people and he derives from them his values and attitudes. If an individual assesses himself to be less privileged than members of his reference group or groups he is 'relatively deprived'. The term is thus applied to a feeling rather than to an objective situation. As Runciman's book [22] has made clear, a distinction should be drawn between the facts of a situation and a person's perception of it. Runciman says:

Relative deprivation should always be understood to mean a *sense* of deprivation; a person who is 'relatively deprived' need not be 'objectively' deprived in the more usual sense that he is demonstrably lacking something. In addition, relative deprivation means that the sense of deprivation is such as to involve a comparison with the imagined situation of some other person or group.

'Relative deprivation', then, is not a term that is usually applied by social scientists to objective situations. Nor is it applicable only to income and physical environment. For these two reasons the term should be used with care.

The question remains as to what may be the relationship between polarity and polarization on the one hand and 'sense' of deprivation on the other. Following the arguments of Merton [21] and Runciman [22] we may surmise that the existence of such an association would depend upon whether, or to what extent, individuals selected their reference group or groups from within their geographical area of residence. For example, if an individual chose his reference group from among his neighbours he might feel less relatively deprived in an area of high degree of polarity than in a socially mixed area. In the latter case, he might select as his reference group people of slightly higher social class and status than himself and make unfavourable comparisons with his own situation. In the former case, where the individual was geographically and socially isolated from those at the next stages up on the social scale, he might take as his reference group people of similar social class and status to himself and thus he might be less relatively deprived. However, at the moment we do not have enough empirical evidence about how reference groups are selected to reach any firm conclusions on this question.

Having set the discussion of social polarity and social polarization within a sociological context, the next question must be 'Can we measure social polarity and social polarization?'

Given adequate data, the ability to measure social polarity in a meaningful way would allow the calculation of polarity scores for sub-areas of a given urban region, thus describing the polarity pattern for the region at a point in time. If these scores were also obtained at intervals of time, their movements could be studied so that hypotheses related to social polarization in areas, that is, change in pattern over time, could be tested.

Most of the writers who have discussed social polarization have been concerned about it because they suspected or assumed that it was associated with the occurrence of undesirable social, economic and political phenomena. Therefore, the next stage of an empirical study would be to examine the association between measures of polarity and a number of phenomena relevant to planning policy. Two further areas of research work that follow from the measurement of social polarity are noted in Figure 5.2 which sets out the stages of research in this area that can be tentatively identified at the present time.

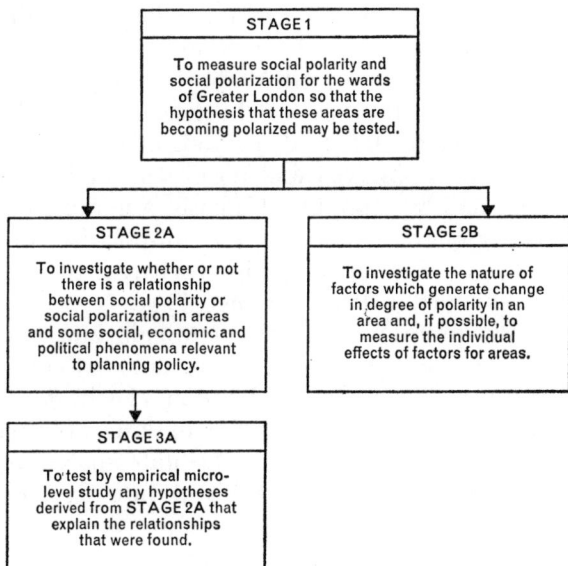

FIGURE 5.2 Stages of research

It is apparent, then, that the social polarization of Greater London is not self-evident but is, in fact, a hypothesis which awaits careful testing. In the meantime, what conclusions can be drawn from work already completed?

Stage 1

In developing measures of polarity, two main points were considered. First, social polarity refers to particular patterns of the distribution of social classes. It was apparent then, that

measures that merely related to the proportions of particular
classes and not to the overall picture of class distribution in sub-
areas would not be of use for this exercise. Measures were
needed that were based on total distribution and were capable
of identifying particular types of pattern. This was not, incidentally, a prerequisite of the study by Peter Willmott and Michael
Young described in Chapter 6. They had a broader aim of
seeking to identify which social classes live in which areas; this
led them to adopt different measures, more suited to their particular aims.

Second, polarity is a relative concept. It was therefore necessary to base measures on the difference between an observed
social class distribution in sub-areas and a 'norm' social class
distribution. Peter Willmott and Michael Young also recognized
the importance of this, as will be explained in Chapter 6.
There are two basic statistical methods of measuring the relationship between observed and norm distributions; namely,
by difference and by ratio. On this basis, a number of possible
polarity statistics were proposed for uni-polarity, bi-polarity
and abnormality of social composition pattern; these measures
have been explained in detail elsewhere [23].

A computer program was written to calculate some of the
measures using 1961 and 1966 Census data on economically
active males in wards of Greater London, classified into seventeen socio-economic groups. In order to ensure comparability
of 1961 and 1966 s.e.g. data and to facilitate analysis of results,
these seventeen s.e.g.s were combined into five groupings,
broadly representing:

  1 professional and managerial workers (s.e.g.s 3, 4, 1, 2 and
13)
  2 skilled manual workers (s.e.g.s 8, 9, 12 and 14)
  3 non-manual workers other than those in section 1 (s.e.g.s
5 and 6)
  4 semi-skilled and service workers (s.e.g.s 7, 10 and 15)
  5 unskilled manual, armed forces and unclassified workers
(s.e.g.s 11, 16 and 17)

Two of the calculated measures of social polarity were examined
in detail. The first social polarity measure may be regarded as
a measure of uni-polarity in that it indicates the extent to which
the social class distribution of an area at one point in time tends

towards one or other of the extreme ends of the distribution when compared with the 'norm' distribution. Taking the 'norm' socio-economic distribution to be 'balanced', the measure calculates the extent to which the 'point of balance' or 'centre of gravity' of the sub-area socio-economic distribution, differs from that of the norm distribution. A positive score represents a concentration towards unskilled and semi-skilled workers; a negative score represents a concentration towards the professional and managerial classes. The second measure is one of bipolarity and indicates the extent to which the social class distribution of an area is above the 'norm' at the two extremes of the distribution. The measure is based on the difference between the standard deviation of the norm socio-economic distribution and the standard deviation of the sub-area socio-economic distribution. It should be noted that the measure takes into account the total social composition pattern of sub-areas and does not merely reflect the existence of percentages of particular groups. The norm for these measures was taken to be the GLC average distribution in the year under examination. The results of the calculations of these two measures of social polarity were examined using as a basis for summary a cluster analysis of Greater London wards [24].

The purpose of a cluster analysis is to derive a classification of a set of objects (in this case the wards of Greater London) into groups or clusters in such a way that each object is allocated to a cluster and that objects in the same cluster are as similar as possible with respect to the input variables. The input variables to the cluster analysis used were the 1961 Census s.e.g. data for 1961 wards which in 1966 fell within the Greater London area. The output chosen to provide a basis for the summary consisted of eleven ward clusters.

Table 5.1 shows the number of 1961 wards contained within each cluster and the location of wards in post-1965 London Boroughs. It also indicates the approximate geographical position of the Boroughs in the Greater London area. It was found that within each cluster, the polarity scores fell within a reasonably small range. It was possible, therefore, to use the mean polarity score of a cluster as an indicator of the polarity score of every ward in that cluster and to use the clusters as a means of identifying the geographical location of different degrees of polarity.

Table 5.1

Greater London Wards Classified by Cluster and Borough

Borough (and location in Greater London)	Clusters 1	2	3	4	5	6	7	8	9	10	11	Total*
Hackney	Inner N						5	24		8			37
Islington	Inner N							13	2	3	1		19
Tower Hamlets	Inner NE							11	21		1		33
Greenwich	Inner SE		6	2		1	4	5	5	5	5		33
Lewisham	Inner SE		4				7	5	5	7	2		30
Lambeth	Inner S		4			3	3	7	5	2	6		30
Southwark	Inner S		3			1	1	16	17	3	3		44
Wandsworth	Inner SW		6			1	7	6	1	7			28
Hammersmith	Inner W		2				3	5	5	2	4		21
Kensington and Chelsea	Inner W		1	5	2	1		1	1		2	2	15
Westminster, City of	Inner W		4	11	4	1	1	1	3		9	8	42
Camden	Inner NW		5	4	3			1	6		5		24
Sub-total	Inner Boroughs		35	22	9	8	31	95	71	37	38	10	356
Enfield	Outer N		2		3	2	2	3		5			17
Haringey	Outer N		1	2		1	5	8		5			22
Newham	Outer NE							5	12	9	1		27
Redbridge	Outer NE		6		2	7	5			1			21

Borough (and location in Greater London)		Clusters 1	2	3	4	5	6	7	8	9	10	11	Total*
Waltham Forest	Outer NE		3		1	1	6	4		8			23
Barking	Outer E		1			1		11	1				14
Havering	Outer E		2		2	3	4	3		4	1		19
Bexley	Outer SE		6	1	2	7	6			3			25
Bromley	Outer SE	3	7	2	9	7	3			6	3		40
Croydon	Outer S		2	2	7	4	6			2	1		24
Hounslow	Outer SW		5		1	1	10	1		4			22
Kingston upon Thames	Outer SW		7	1		7	3		1	3			22
Merton	Outer SW		5	1	1	3	6	1		7			26
Richmond upon Thames	Outer SW				5	3	6	1	7	7			29
Sutton	Outer SW		2	6	4	10	3	3		3	1		24
Ealing	Outer W		7	2	5	5	2	2	1	5	1		30
Hillingdon	Outer W		4	2	1	3	6	4	1	7	1		29
Barnet	Outer NW	3	2	4	2	11	2	1		5	1	1	35
Brent	Outer NW		5	2	2	3	6	5		1	1	1	26
Harrow	Outer NW		3	3	1	3	5		1	2			15
Sub-total	Outer Boroughs	6	77	28	54	78	93	55	17	73	9	—	490
Total	Greater London	6	112	50	63	86	124	150	88	110	47	10	846

* A small number of 1961 wards do not lie wholly in one post—1965 Borough. In these cases, the ward has been allocated to the Borough that contains the largest part of the ward area.

Polarity in 1961

The group of wards which had the highest average positive uni-polarity score, that is, the highest uni-polarity towards the bottom end of the scale, (cluster 8, see the key on Figure 5.3) was examined and it was found, as expected, that this group was characterized by a relative lack of all non-manual and skilled manual workers. Service, semi-skilled and unskilled workers were greatly over-represented relative to the GLC norm. This group comprised approximately 10 per cent of all wards. The majority of the wards were in Inner London and there were also several wards from the area just outside Inner London, to the east and north-east.

There were also two other groups of wards with fairly high positive uni-polarity scores. First, there was a very large cluster of wards, 18 per cent of the total, (cluster 7) characterized by a higher than average proportion of all manual workers, not just the unskilled, semi-skilled and service ones. Again, the majority of wards in this group were concentrated in Inner London but there were also several wards in boroughs extending to the east and north-east of Inner London and a few in areas formerly in the County of Surrey. Second, there was a smaller cluster of wards, about 5 per cent of the total, (cluster 10) that were not geographically concentrated although there were more wards in Inner than in Outer London. This cluster of wards was charac-terized by the fact that the social class distributions of wards differed very little from the norm except for the fact that they had a far higher than average proportion in the lowest s.e.g. grouping. (This last s.e.g. grouping includes members of the Armed Forces who are on average a very small fraction of the grouping; normally the grouping would contain an over-whelming majority of unskilled workers. However, the presence of barracks there may have distorted the figures for Westminster and in that case the high uni-polarity score was caused by the presence of armed forces rather than unskilled workers.)

It was found, again as expected, that the cluster of wards with highest negative uni-polarity, 7 per cent of the total (cluster 4) was characterized by great over-representation of all non-manual workers, particularly professionals and managers, as compared with the GLC norm situation. The wards of this cluster were geographically scattered, mainly throughout the outer suburban boroughs of Outer London.

In sum, the uni-polarity measures for 1961 suggested that high uni-polarity, positive or negative, was generally a phenomenon scattered throughout the GLC region. Wards of high positive uni-polarity were not confined to Inner and East London. Similarly, high negative uni-polarity scores were scattered throughout wards of Inner and Outer London. Thus, there were few extensive areas of Greater London which justified a general description of 'having a high degree of uni-polarity'.

The examination of 1961 bi-polarity scores did not identify any clusters of wards with exceptionally high bi-polarity scores. It seemed that, at least in 1961, there were few, if any, wards of Greater London which contained, simultaneously, high concentrations of social classes at the two extremes of the social class distribution.

Polarization between 1961 and 1966

The polarity statistics for 1961 and 1966 were calculated with respect to the norm, that is, the GLC socio-economic distribution, in the two years. It is of interest to consider the change in the norm distribution between these two years, and this information and the polarity statistics for the 1966 GLC distribution based upon the 1961 GLC norm are given in Table 5.2.

Table 5.2

| Year | S.E.G. grouping (%) | | | | | Total (%) | Measure of Uni-polarity Based on 1961 Norm | Measure of Bi-polarity Based on 1961 Norm |
	1	2	3	3	5			
1961	16.3	35.0	22.9	14.7	11.1	100.0	0.00	0.00
1966	17.4	35.1	23.8	14.4	9.3	100.0	−0.06	−0.03

A decrease of 1.8 per cent in the unskilled category (from 11.1 to 9.3 per cent) resulted in a small negative uni-polarity score for the 1966 GLC norm with respect to the 1961 GLC norm. There was also a small decrease in bi-polarity. Observed movements in the polarity scores of clusters had to be considered in conjunction with the above analysis of the movement in the GLC distribution.

FIGURE 5.

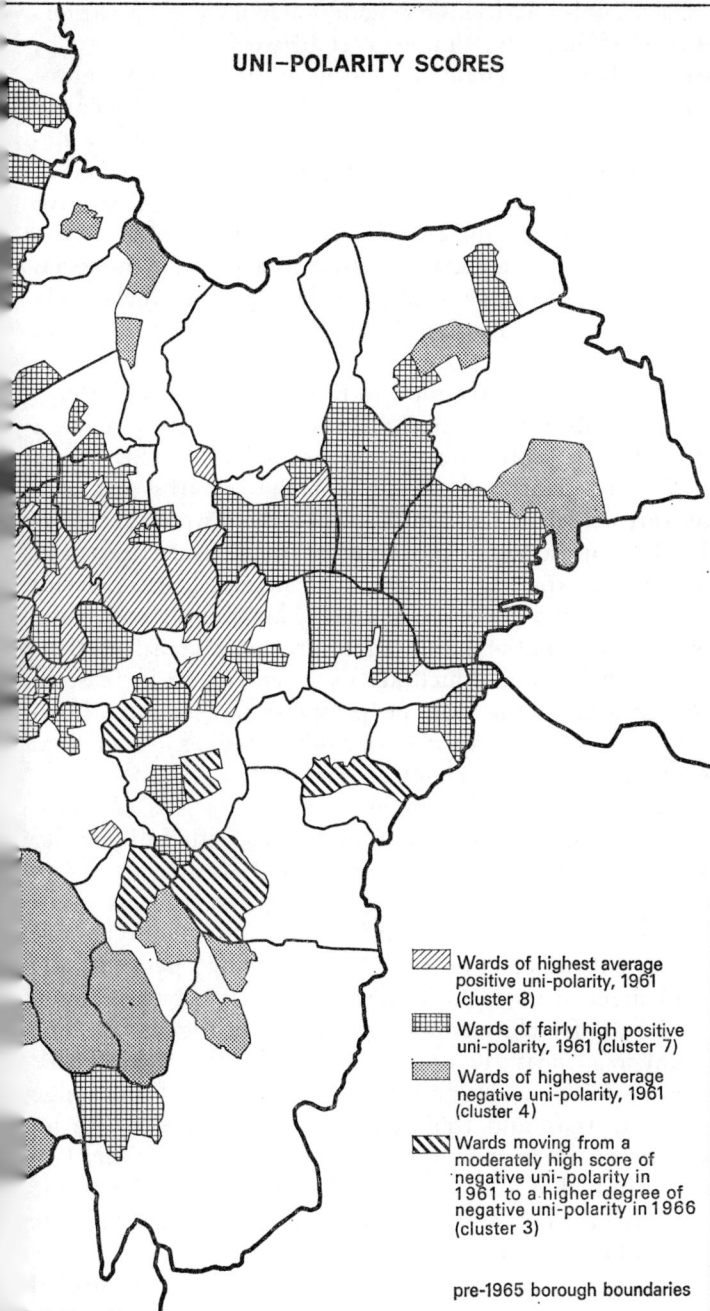

UNI-POLARITY SCORES

Wards of highest average positive uni-polarity, 1961 (cluster 8)

Wards of fairly high positive uni-polarity, 1961 (cluster 7)

Wards of highest average negative uni-polarity, 1961 (cluster 4)

Wards moving from a moderately high score of negative uni-polarity in 1961 to a higher degree of negative uni-polarity in 1966 (cluster 3)

pre-1965 borough boundaries

scores

As regards uni-polarity, the general tendency was for clusters of wards to retain a very similar score between 1961 and 1966; if anything, there was a tendency for uni-polarity scores to move towards the norm; the standard deviation of the uni-polarity scores decreased by 3 per cent. The movement towards a decrease in uni-polarity scores was apparent in clusters 4 and 8, the two groups of wards which had in 1961 the highest positive and negative average uni-polarity scores. This confirms the impression of a tendency between 1961 and 1966 for the social class distributions to move towards normality of social class mix and away from concentration at one or other end of the social class distribution scale.

The one noticeable exception to this tendency was cluster 3 a group of wards, 6 per cent of all wards, which in 1961 has a moderately high score of negative uni-polarity. This group included wards scattered throughout the suburbs and also several wards of Inner London Boroughs which were characterized by flat and bedsitter accommodation. Between 1961 and 1966 this group experienced a moderate increase in uni-polarity towards the top end of the social scale. This finding lends some support to the hypothesis that there are some areas, particularly in Inner London, which are experiencing an increase in the concentration of the 'rich' or 'prosperous'. This must, however, be put into the context of our other findings, mentioned above, of a general tendency towards normality.

On examining the changes in bi-polarity scores of wards between 1961 and 1966, it was found, as with uni-polarity scores, that the tendency over the period was for scores to approach the norm. The average bi-polarity score of every cluster moved towards the norm between 1961 and 1966 and the standard deviation of the scores decreased by 4 per cent.

The changes in uni-polarity and bi-polarity scores between 1961 and 1966 for clusters are represented in Figure 5.4. The horizontal axis measures uni-polarity while the vertical axis measures bi-polarity. Two points are given for each cluster: these represent the 1961 and 1966 average polarity scores with an arrow between them indicating the change between the two points of time. For each cluster, the extreme points of the diamond are based upon ± one standard deviation and indicate the spread of the scores within that cluster.

The absence of any marked degree of bi-polarity is illustrated by Figure 5.4 as is the universal movement towards a lower degree of bi-polarity between 1961 and 1966. One or two relatively small increases in uni-polarity may be observed but these appear to be confined to those clusters with only moderate uni-polarity in 1961, the base year.

Thus to sum up, it was found that there was a general tendency for the social class distribution of small areas within London to approach the average GLC distribution over time. However, some areas of London were found to have exhibited a tendency for the upper social classes to concentrate within them.

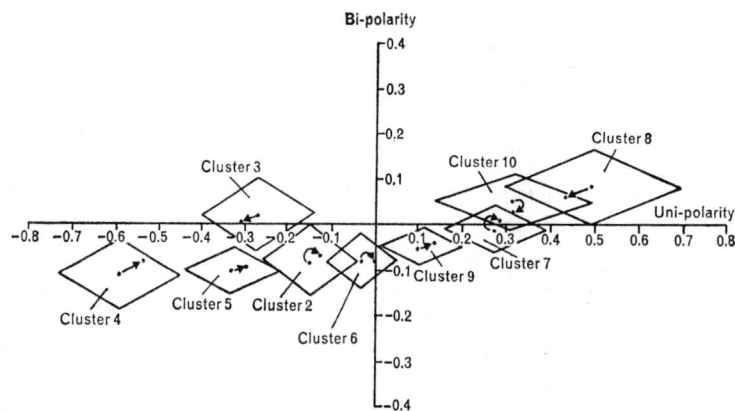

FIGURE 5.4 Changes in cluster polarity scores (1961–1966)

Stage 2A

Having obtained polarity scores for area units, the next stage of an empirical study would be to examine the relationship between those scores and the occurrence of a number of phenomena. This would be a way of testing the hypothesis, implied in social polarization discussions, that there is a relationship between the social composition of geographical areas and the occurrence in them of social problems.

Some writers on social polarization have referred only vaguely to symptoms of 'social malaise' but others have been quite specific about the problems they envisage as being associated with social polarization. Some of these problems were mentioned earlier when I listed reasons which have been advanced for regarding social balance as desirable and by implication, for regarding social polarity as undesirable. Phenomena selected for empirical tests would probably fall into one or more of the following broad categories of public authority concern:

1 the state of the physical fabric and environment: including for example, buildings and open spaces;
2 the provision of facilities and services by both public authorities and private enterprise;
3 the physical and mental health of the population;
4 the education and care of young people;
5 the ability of groups and individuals to deal with their own problems without recourse to public agencies;
6 the formation of the population into communities and the mutual support functions performed by such communities;
7 the demographic characteristics of geographical areas;
8 the maintenance of public and social order;
9 'the public good'.

Of course, these are not discrete categories; they overlap to some extent, and category 9, in particular, may be regarded as covering all the areas of authority concern listed. It must be emphasized, also, that the list represents broad, general categories and is derived from a number of separate hypotheses contained within various statements on 'social polarization'.

Having selected some appropriate phenomena, a study of the relationship between the occurrence of the phenomena and the social composition pattern of area units would be done separately for each phenomenon. It could not be assumed that any found relationship was either linear or causal. One, or more than one, of the following three sub-hypotheses could be applied to such a relationship. (In the following, the dotted line represents a found relationship and the unbroken line the actual relationship or sequence of events.)

(a) Social Selection

That the occurrence or non-occurrence of the phenomenon has been, directly or indirectly, conducive to the development of a particular social composition pattern. The relationship could be of the type:

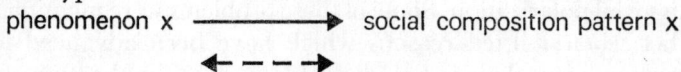

phenomenon x ⟶ social composition pattern x
◀ − − ➤

This situation might arise, for example, if an increasingly high incidence of violent crime in an area induced people to move from that area and if these out-migrants contained high proportions of particular social classes only.

Alternatively, the relationship could be of the type:

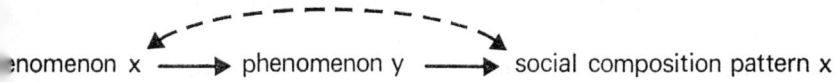

nomenon x ⟶ phenomenon y ⟶ social composition pattern x

An example of this type of situation might occur if a shortage of teachers in an area (phenomenon x) resulted in a low general level of education achievement (phenomenon y). This in turn might induce selective out-migration by social class, although measurements using available data might merely show the existence of a relationship between teacher shortage and a particular social composition pattern.

(b) Social Causation

That the existence or development of a particular social composition pattern has been, directly or indirectly, conducive to the occurrence or non-occurrence of a phenomenon. The relationship may be of the type:

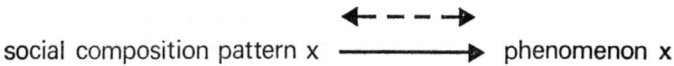

social composition pattern x ⟶ phenomenon x

This relationship might exist where, for example, the existence of a particular mixture of residents by social class in an area resulted in a general movement to improve the external fabric of buildings. A relationship would then be found between social class pattern and the condition of buildings in an area.

Second, the relationship could follow the model:

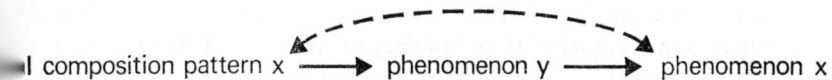

l composition pattern x ⟶ phenomenon y ⟶ phenomenon x

This type of relationship could occur where the existence of a particular social composition pattern in an area directly encouraged the local authority to improve its standard of education provision in an area (phenomenon y). If the level of education achievement (phenomenon x) improved in the area as a result, a relationship would then be found between a particular social composition pattern and level of education achievement.

(c) Other Factors

That a particular social composition pattern and the occurrence or non-occurrence of a phenomenon are independently related to another common factor or to other common factors. At its simplest, such a relationship could approximate the model:

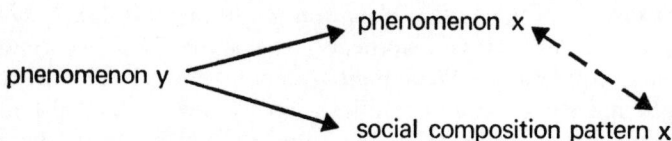

In this case the found relationship would be spurious. An example might exist where there was a particular pattern of employment opportunities in an area (phenomenon y). This pattern could then be directly conducive to both the social composition pattern in the area and to the school leaving age pattern (phenomenon x). Measurements would merely reveal the existence of a relationship between school-leaving age and social composition pattern although no account had been taken of the prime causative factor.

It is apparent then, that there are a number of different possible types of relationship that could exist. It would be important for a local authority to be satisfied that a phenomenon was a prime causative factor in any found relationship before attempting to influence that phenomenon.

What can be said at the present time about the relationship between social composition pattern and social phenomena relevant to planning policy? The main work in this field up to now[1] has been based on data on education achievement and uses for social composition description data on proportions of particular social classes, rather than polarity measures [25]. However, it is noteworthy that this work has not shown significant positive relationships between social class 'mix' and education achievement.

---

[1] Some work to relate polarity measures for wards of Greater London in 1966 to some variables has now been done in the Department of Planning and Transportation of the GLC; but at the time of writing there has been insufficient analysis to permit any reporting of results.

Stage 2B

The many factors which can generate change in the social composition pattern, and therefore the degree of polarity, in geographical areas have been discussed earlier in this chapter. Two further points can be made at this stage. First, the generators of change are so many and so interdependent that it seems doubtful whether it would ever be possible to distinguish by empirical investigation the factors contributing to specific cases of change. It would probably only be possible to make 'informed guesses'. Apart from this difficulty, it must be realized that many possible generators of social composition change, for example, technological change and fashion, are not subject to the manipulation of local authorities. Indeed, some of the generators, for example, fertility rates, are barely subject in any way at all to the control of public authorities.

Conclusions

In this chapter I have looked in detail at the implications of what has been said in the last few years about polarization. I have attempted to provide a theoretical framework, in order to distinguish the various elements in references to polarization, and I have concentrated subsequent discussion on the distribution of the social class variable; that is on social polarity and social polarization. I have also drawn attention to the several theories and concepts which are relevant to a consideration of social polarization.

The main conclusion must be that social polarity and social polarization are of concern for Greater London and other large urban areas if there is truth in the hypothesis that they are related to the occurrence of social problems. Work to date does not suggest that there is a tendency for social polarity to increase in Greater London and, in any case, the relationship between social polarity and social problems is by no means self-evident. Nor is the empirical testing of the relationship a straightforward task. Thus, the 'social polarization' concept seems to be of very limited value in so far as it is a means of relating two aspects of social structure; namely, social class distribution and social problems. On the other hand, these two aspects are, singly and in themselves, of great concern to local authorities and to

Greater London authorities in particular. Indeed, social class distribution and some of the social problems of Greater London are in fact, the subject of separate chapters in this volume.

I believe that a fruitful line for future research would be to attempt to distinguish the generators of different social class distribution patterns, and separately, the generators of various social problems which beset Greater London. In this way, we might eventually discover not only the extent of the relationship between social class pattern and social problems, but also the extent of the relationship between each of these factors and other factors as yet untested for Greater London.

References

1. *Tomorrow's London: A Background to the Greater London Development Plan* (GLC, 1969).

2. HILLMAN, JUDY, 'London', *The Observer*, 14 December 1969.

3. South East Joint Planning Team, *Strategic Plan for the South-East* (London: H.M.S.O., 1970).

4. WILLMOTT, P., 'Some social trends', *Urban Studies*, **6**, no. 3, November 1969, pp. 286–308.

5. WILSON, A. G., *Metropolitan Growth Models* (London: Centre for Environmental Studies WP 55, 1969).

6. *Some Aspects of the Polarization Issue*, G.L.D.P. Inquiry Document, S11/113, 1971.

7. GRIMOND, J., 'Rich Man, Poor Man', *The Guardian*, 18 May 1970.

8. Central Council for Education (England), *Children and Their Primary Schools—Vol. 1, The Report* (London: H.M.S.O., 1967).

9. Central Housing Advisory Committee of Ministry of Housing and Local Government, *Council Housing Purposes, Procedures and Priorities* (London: H.M.S.O., 1969).

10. GANS, H. J., 'People and Plans', *Essays on Urban Problems and Solutions*, Ch. 2 (New York: Basic Books, 1968).

11. COCHRANE, JANET, *Social Balance (2)*, GLC Planning Department, unpublished Research Paper, 1967.

12. ALONSO, W., 'What are New Towns for?', *Urban Studies*, **7**, no. 1, February 1970, pp. 37–55.

13. See, for example, HERAUD, B. J., 'Social class and new towns', *Urban Studies*, **5**, no. 1, 1968, pp. 33–58.

14. BROADY, M., 'Social aspects of a town development scheme', in: *Planning for People* (London: National Council of Social Service, 1968).

15. GANS, H. J., *op. cit.*, Ch. 12.

16. KORNHAUSER, W., *The Politics of Mass Society* (Glencoe, Illinois: Free Press, 1959).

17. See for example GUSFIELD, J. R., 'Mass society and extremist politics', *American Sociological Review*, **27**, February 1962, pp. 19–30 and

SHILS, E., 'The end of ideology?', *Encounter*, **5**, November 1955, pp. 52–8 and ALLARDT, E., 'Social sources of Finnish communism', *International Journal of Comparative Sociology*, **5**, no. 1, March 1964, pp. 47–72.

18. Summarized in South East Joint Planning Team, *Strategic Plan for the South East, Studies Volume 2, Appendix 2c*, (London: H.M.S.O., 1971).

19. WAUGH, M., 'The changing distribution of professional and managerial manpower in England and Wales between 1961 and 1966', *Regional Studies*, **3**, no. 2, September 1969, pp. 157–69.

20. PAHL, R. E., *Spatial Structure and Social Structure* (London: Centre for Environmental Studies, WP 10, 1968).

21. MERTON, R. K. and ROSSI, ALICE S., 'A contribution to the theory of reference group behaviour', in, *Social Theory and Social Structure*, enlarged edition (New York: The Free Press, 1968).

22. RUNCIMAN, W. G., *Relative deprivation and social justice* (London: Routledge and Kegan Paul, 1966).

23. HARRIS, MARGARET and LYONS, J., *Social Polarization*, GLC Department of Planning and Transportation RM 324, London, 1971.

24. Described in KELLY, FRANCES, 'Classifications of the London Boroughs', *GLC Intelligence Unit, Research Report no. 9*, London, 1971.

25. See, for example, MEYER, J. W., 'High school effects on college intentions', *American Journal of Sociology*, **76**, July 1970, p. 60.

Chapter Six

Social Class and Geography

PETER WILLMOTT AND
MICHAEL YOUNG

Summary

In connexion with a larger study of family life, work and leisure in the London Metropolitan Region, this chapter is concerned with the attempt to measure changes in the social class structure of different parts of the region. Some special analyses of Census material for 1951 and 1966 have been used; because of changes in the official classification scheme, a special procedure has been devised to allow a comparison of the social class distribution at the two dates. This was done, inside Greater London, on the basis of pre-1965 local authority areas.

The first step was to examine the social class composition of areas in 1966. The analysis suggests that inside Greater London, instead of the conventional concentric zones, the class pattern formed the shape of a cross. The three elements distinguished are the Central Residential District, the Cross itself and the suburban Quarters bound by it. The Cross, into which workingpeople were concentrated, is from east to west along the Thames Valley, to the north along the Lea Valley and to the south, coinciding to some extent with the valley of the River Wandle. This pattern of distribution is explained mainly by the location of docks, industry and communication routes, which have mostly been located on the low land. The more favoured residential areas, conversely, are commonly on higher ground. Thus the physical geography of London has helped to shape its class geography.

An examination of changes between 1951 and 1966 shows that a process of differential migration was taking place. Higher-class people became relatively more concentrated in the Central Residential District, the suburban Quarters and the Outer Metropolitan Area. Working-class people, especially the less skilled, became more concentrated in the Cross. Thus economic and social trends in the London Region were, if anything, reinforcing its class geography.

In London, as in any other city, an important clue to the processes of urban change is the residential distribution of the social classes. Which of them live in which kinds of area, and how are the patterns changing?

In the course of a wider enquiry into some of the long-term changes in family life, work and leisure among Londoners[1] we tried to explore these questions, mainly by means of special analyses of Census material for 1951 and 1966. The discussion in this chapter concentrates on Greater London, but some reference is also made to the Outer Metropolitan Area.

Methods of Analysis

For the analysis we had first to decide on an index of social class or socio-economic status. The one we selected was that used in the Census, which groups occupied and retired men into five social classes on the basis of their occupation. The classes are as follows:

Social Class	Title
I	Professional
II	Intermediate
III	Skilled
IV	Partly-skilled
V	Unskilled

For our analysis we combined these into three classes: I and II,

---

[1] Reported more fully in *The Symmetrical Family: a Study of Work and Leisure in the London Region* (London: Routledge, and Kegan Paul, 1973), supported mainly by the Centre for Environmental Studies.

III, and IV and V. As explained in Appendix 1, this had to be done to make it possible to compare 1951 with 1966.

As well as showing the proportions in these three classes in each district, we needed a single measure—one figure for each district—which would give an indication of its relative 'classiness'.[1] Three of the possible indices are explained and used in Moser and Scott's statistical comparison, based on the 1951 Census, of 157 British towns [1]. The first method was to take the proportion of occupied and retired men in the Registrar-General's highest social classes (Professional and Intermediate, or I and II). The places with the largest proportions in these classes would be considered the 'classiest'. The second method was to look at the other end of the class range and compare the proportions in the bottom two classes (Partly-skilled and Un-skilled Manual, or IV and V); the more 'classy' areas would this time be those with the lowest proportions. The third method was to calculate for each area some measure which expressed the relationship between the proportions at the 'top' and the 'bottom' (thus, automatically, taking into account the 'middle' as well). Such a composite scale was devised by Moser and Scott [2], who called it the Social Class Index.

We tried all three methods and compared the different sets of figures. We found, as Moser and Scott themselves had done [3], that the results were similar, and that when each area in Greater London was listed by the three methods according to the data in 1966 the order was almost identical: in general, places that rated high by one method also rated high by the others. An important exception was a cluster of central districts which were unusual in having relatively high proportions at both the top and bottom of the class scale; this peculiarity is noted later. But, as a single measure of the class of a district, the proportion of men in Classes I and II seemed the best one to choose. It correlated slightly better with the so-called Social Class Index than did the proportion in Classes IV and V. It was less elaborate than the Social Class Index and easier to understand. It was also the measure used by Westergaard who had, in a paper based on 1951 Census data for London, pioneered this kind of geographical analysis of social class [4].

---

1 Alternative approaches to this question are shown in chs. 2 and 5.

Areas to Choose

The next decision was about the areas we should use as spatial reference points. We recognized, of course, as every Londoner must, that the heterogeneity is great, with the rich and the poor sometimes living in neighbouring streets or even in the same street—like Ladbroke Grove which has large houses in single occupation at one end and similar large houses divided up for immigrants and other poor people at the other. This mixture is particularly noticeable in districts with older buildings once occupied by better-off people. The point may be worth a word of explanation. One rule (with exceptions to it, as with all rules) is that new houses are built for people of one particular class. It follows that the newer the houses, the more likely is the area to be homogeneous in social class. A second rule is that houses, whether privately or council owned, do not usually go up in class as they age. Their 'social mobility' is usually downwards. Their price goes down with their cost of upkeep and with their class—goes down relatively, that is, to the price of new houses of the same size in as favoured an area. A third rule is that a district does not go down uniformly. Some of the houses in it stay with the original occupiers or their like, while others are taken over by newcomers of a different social background. So if one wants to look for heterogeneity, one should look first for an area with older houses in it. It follows that on the whole the nearer the centre, either of London itself or of some old settlement on its outskirts, the more heterogeneous the area. There are, however, exceptions even to this rule; there are some areas near the centre, in parts of Kensington and Westminster for instance, which have become fashionable in recent decades—and therefore *more* homogeneous—partly because some old houses are actually valued *for* their age.

In many places, however, the classes are, as we have said, very much mixed up. It would be best, therefore, from one point of view if the areas we considered were small. The finer the grain the less damage to the truth would be done by generalizations. But we had to do what was possible rather than what was desirable. We were limited by the fact that we wanted to make the comparisons between 1951 and 1966, and the smallest unit for which comparable statistics at both dates could be derived were the local authority areas as they were before the creation of the Greater London Boroughs. These, then, were the districts of our analysis. They should not be confused with the larger London Boroughs, some of which bear the same names; in the analysis of Social Class in 1951 and 1966, when we talk about 'Westminster' or 'Lambeth', for instance, we refer not to the present larger unit but to the smaller—and earlier—one.

The 1966 Results

Given a definition of class and of area, the next thing was to bring the two together. This is done in Figure 6.1, which shows the proportions of occupied and retired men in Social Classes I and II as shown by the 10 per cent Sample Census of 1966. We decided to treat as 'more middle class' the districts with 25 per cent and over in the top classes and as 'more working class' those with 76 per cent or more in the other classes. The choice of 25 per cent was somewhat arbitrary; we wanted a round figure a little higher than the mean for the London Region, which was 24 per cent.

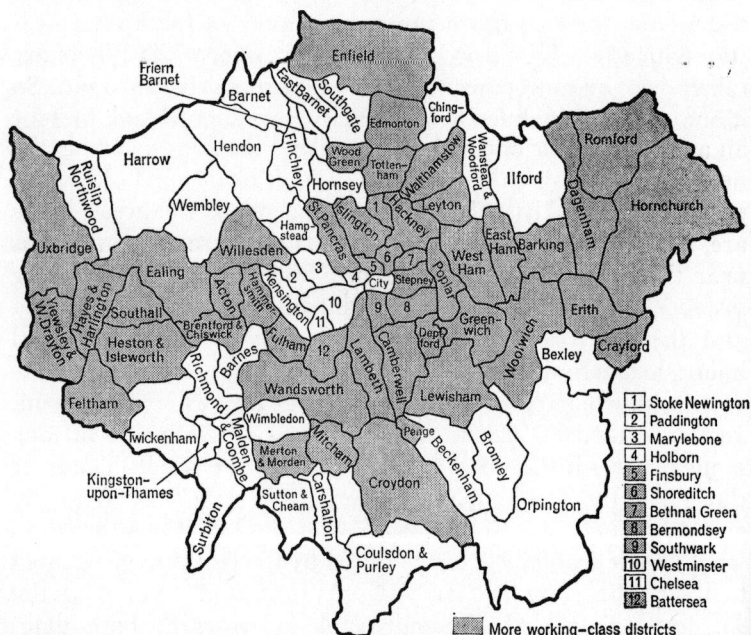

FIGURE 6.1 Social class in Greater London, 1966

Other people may see different shapes in the mist. What we see is the sign of a cross, made up of the more working class districts of Greater London.[1] The more middle-class districts are at the centre and the four quarters (a term not used here to mean 'quartiers'). We discuss below the main elements of Greater London as shown by Figure 6.1.

Central Residential and Business Districts

In London, as in nearly all cities, there is what can be called the Central Business District. Alongside it and to some extent intermingled with it, there is also a Central Residential District. (The Residential District is to the west of the Business District.) The districts in it are the adjoining ones which satisfy our condition of having 25 per cent or more of their population in the Professional and Intermediate Classes, i.e. Chelsea, City, Holborn, Kensington, Paddington, St. Marylebone and Westminster. The historic twin cities—the City of London and the City of Westminster—survive in the junction of the Business District and the Residential District, which has grown outwards from the Court and its circle, from Parliament and from Whitehall.

We suggested earlier that the proportion of people in the top classes is in general a good measure of the 'classiness' of a district, but that the class distributions were different at the centre from elsewhere. All the central districts had a deficiency in the middle of the class spectrum—a low proportion of skilled manual workers and clerks.[2] Some of them had, as well as above average proportions at the top, above average proportions at the bottom. The distributions for Greater London as a whole were: Social Classes I and II, 22 per cent; III, 52 per cent; IV and V, 26 per cent; but Holborn had 31, 39 and 30 per cent respectively and Westminster 36, 34 and 30 per cent. In such places there was therefore a degree of what has been called class bi-polarity—an emphasis at the extremes and a

---

[1] The cross is clearly visible in the alternative map, based partly on ours, presented by Graham Lomas (Figure 2.1). It is also evident in an earlier such generalized map by Westergaard on page 101 of reference 4.
[2] Class III includes, as well as skilled manual workers, clerks and other routine non-manual workers such as shop assistants.

relative deficiency in the middle.[1] This is due in part to the juxtaposition of richer people able to afford the high prices of housing in the centre and of poorer people employed particularly (and needing to live near to their work) in the service industries which are booming on the strength of the increase in the numbers of foreign and British tourists for whom the historic centre is the major attraction.

The centre is, quite apart from tourists, the most 'cosmopolitan' part of London. In 1966 there were three Greater London Boroughs with over 10 per cent of their population born in 'foreign' countries (that is, people who were not born in the British Isles or in present or former Commonwealth countries). These were Camden, Kensington and Chelsea and Westminster—the Boroughs which, with the City, are the closest approximation to the Central Residential District as we have identified it in terms of pre-1965 districts.

Cross and Quarters

Outside the centre, the Cross forms the dominant pattern. The four Quarters outside it contain all the more middle-class areas, apart from those in the central district. The most unusual Quarter in shape is the north-western. Hampstead is the corridor that joins it to the Central Residential District. The most unusual districts in class were Beckenham and Coulsdon, which were not only above average in the top classes but also even lower than the others in the proportion at the bottom.

The more working-class districts inside the four arms of the Cross are not all equally marked. The eastern arm, in particular, south of the Thames as well as north, had a low proportion of men in the top two classes and also a high proportion in the bottom two—Partly-skilled and Unskilled. This was particularly true of Bermondsey, Poplar, Stepney and West Ham.

The Cross is of course different in other ways from the rest of Greater London. The *Report of Studies* prepared for the Greater London Development Plan showed, for instance, the distribution of industrial floor-space per acre. There is markedly more industry in the Cross than in the Quarters [5]. The same

---

[1] See ch. 5.

report also showed the areas of bad housing—what it calls the 'Areas of Housing Stress' and the 'Housing Problem Areas'— in Greater London in 1966/7 [6]. Apart from a few areas at the edge of the Central Residential District, these are all in the Cross, with the difference that the eastern houses are physically dilapidated but not overcrowded, whereas in the other arms there is more overcrowding as well as, or without, dilapidation.

Despite these correlates with social class, it is possible that the pattern of the Cross showed up because of the size of district that we were using. We were able to make some check on this by comparing our results with those given with smaller and with larger units. The *Atlas of London* contains a map showing the proportions of economically active men in 1966 in the top five socio-economic groups (which roughly correspond to Classes I and II) in the wards of Greater London. There is, as we noted earlier, much heterogeneity—high-class wards mixed up with low-class ones—but the general shape of the Cross is discernible [7].

Another analysis based on differences between wards in 1966 was carried out by the Greater London Council. This was an elaborate statistical exercise using a combination of eleven variables, including indices of age, housing, birthplace and residential mobility as well as of social class. The map summing up the results shows the Central Residential District with the corridor linking through to the north-western Quarter. It also shows at least some elements of the Cross, with the northern and eastern arms particularly in evidence [8].

One can also go to the other extreme of scale and look at social class in terms of the larger Greater London Boroughs. When this is done, the southern arm is truncated. Although the London Boroughs of Lambeth, Lewisham, Southwark, Merton and Wandsworth are 'more working-class', the former Croydon, which showed up as 'more working-class' on the basis of the smaller units, becomes 'more middle-class' when united with Coulsdon and Purley into the London Borough of Croydon. Apart from this change the pattern of the Cross stands out. Another statistical analysis by the GLC set out to classify the London Boroughs according to eight variables (again including other things as well as an index of social class). The diagram plotting the results shows that the Boroughs group into three clusters—three different kinds of London Borough—that correspond fairly closely to what, on the basis of the smaller districts, we have described as centre, Cross and Quarters [9]. In general, therefore, these various other ways of looking at it support our own.

The customary way of describing London has been in terms not of a Cross but of concentric zones—for instance, centre, inner districts and suburban ring.[1] This is the sort of pattern suggested by the most famous theory of urban growth, that of the founders of the Chicago school of urban sociology in the 1920s [10]. Is there any sign of this alternative configuration in the distribution of social classes? It does show up to some extent on Figure 6.1, in that there is the Central Residential and Business District and that the angles of the Cross are filled in— forming, as one way of describing it, an inner concentric zone which has arms. But to what extent are there variations inside each arm of the Cross? The answer is given in Table 6.1.

Table 6.1

Proportions of Unoccupied and Retired Men in Social Classes I and II, 1966, in Zones within the Arms of the Cross

		per cent
Northern	Inner	12
	Outer	17
Eastern	Inner	13
	Outer	14
Southern	Inner	16
	Outer	22
Western	Inner	15
	Outer	18

There is virtually no difference in the eastern arm. In the others the districts further out are rather 'higher' in class.

The Quarters are different. They are (with the exception of Hampstead) all in Outer Greater London. It is more difficult to make subdivisions there according to the distance of the districts from the centre. In the north-east it is indeed impossible, as the areas are more or less equidistant. We did subdivide the other three Quarters. In the south-eastern and south-western Quarters the proportions in Classes I and II were if anything slightly lower in the further-out districts than in the further-in;

---

[1] Such zones appear in the discussion by Graham Lomas in ch. 2.

only in the north-west was the proportion higher in the outer districts.

In considering social class in London it is helpful to take account of the Outer Metropolitan Area, which together with Greater London makes up the London Metropolitan Region. Figure 6.2 shows the distribution of class in the O.M.A. in

FIGURE 6.2 Social class in the Outer Metropolitan Area, 1966

1966. The units are local authority areas (which did not in general change in 1965, as did those inside Greater London). The index of class is the same: the more working-class areas, shown in black, are those in which 76 per cent or more of the occupied and retired men were in 1966 in the bottom three Social Classes. It is obvious that the Cross itself is a feature only of Greater London. It does however have a 'shaft', which extends along the Thames Estuary both north, to Basildon and Canvey Island and beyond Southend, and south, to the Medway ports and down to Maidstone. There is also something of a clustering to the north-west of London—places alongside the M1 and the main rail routes like Watford, Luton, Luton Rural

District and Dunstable—but otherwise the working-class areas are some of the towns, such as Aldershot, Aylesbury, Reading, Slough and Crawley.

Change between 1951 and 1966

We now turn to the question of how the class distribution altered between 1951 and 1966. What we have done is to compare the results of the two Censuses, on the basis of data either published or supplied specially by the Census Branch of the Office of Population Censuses and Surveys. The procedure that we followed, and in particular the adjustments that we made to allow for the changes in the scheme for classifying occupations into social classes, are described in Appendix 1. This also shows for each area the distribution of occupied and retired men between the three classes (I and II, III, IV and V) at both dates. We have to warn that, given the data with which we had to work, the method used for converting 1951 distributions to the same basis as that used in 1966 could give only an indication of the 1951 distributions on the new basis; we cannot claim precise accuracy for them. Too much should not therefore be made of small percentage changes.

The first question we have to answer is whether Greater London showed in 1951 the same broad pattern of centre, Cross and Quarters. We have of course to take into account the general changes taking place over Greater London—and the region as a whole—during the period. These are shown in Table 6.2.

There was a general up-grading. Both Greater London and the O.M.A. showed an increase in the proportion at the top and a decrease at the bottom, with the intermediate class staying much as it was. In this sense the whole London Region became 'more middle-class' over the fifteen years. If the class map of Greater London were redrawn for 1951 using 25 per cent or

Table 6.2

Changes in Social Class of Occupied and Retired Males, 1951–1966—Greater London, OMA and London Metropolitan Region

	1951			1966		
	I & II	*III*	*IV & V*	*I & II*	*III*	*IV & V*
Greater London	17	53	30	22	52	26
Outer Metropolitan Area	20	50	30	27	49	24
London Metropolitan Region	18	52	30	24	51	25

The figures quoted are percentages.

more as the measure of a high-class district, it would obviously
show fewer of them. Beddington and Wallington, Chislehurst
and Sidcup and Sutton and Cheam are among the places that
would be shown as 'more working-class'. But we clearly wanted
to make a comparison which allowed for the general rise. To
determine which category each district belonged to in 1951,
we took as our dividing line, not 25 per cent in the top two
classes (as for 1966) but 20 per cent. Districts which in 1951
had this proportion or more in Social Classes I and II
were judged 'more middle-class'; those with 81 per cent or
more in the remaining classes were judged 'more working-
class'.

Measured in this way, there was little change over the fifteen
years. Of the eighty-six districts (as defined earlier) in Greater
London, seven had moved from one category to the other. The
districts that changed are shown in Table 6.3.

Table 6.3

*Proportions of Occupied and Retired Men in Social Classes I and II in Districts that
Changed as Between 'More Middle-Class' and 'More Working-Class' Categories,
1951 to 1966*

	1951	1966
Bexley	19	25
Brentford and Chiswick	22	23
Carshalton	15	26
Croydon	20	23
Ealing	21	24
Kingston-upon-Thames	16	28
Merton and Morden	20	24
Definition of 'More middle-class'	20 or over	25 or over

The figures quoted are percentages.

The changes, as the table shows, were mainly small ones,
especially when set against the background of a rise of 6 per
cent in Social Classes I and II in the London Region as a whole.
Bexley, Croydon and Merton and Morden switched categories
by virtue of a mere 1 per cent; had Bexley been 20 per cent in
1951 and Croydon and Merton 19 per cent, they would have
stayed in the same category at both dates. Nor did Ealing and
Brentford change very much. Carshalton and Kingston, however, were more markedly up-graded. In so far as there were

changes over the fifteen years, their effect seems to have been to sharpen the distinction between Cross and Quarters, rather than weaken it.

But, since the general pattern shown in Figure 6.1 existed in 1951 as well as 1966, it seemed to us sensible to take the 1966 pattern as a base and try to summarize the changes in Greater London in social class between 1951 and 1966 in terms of the main types of area we have already distinguished. The comparisons are given in Tables 6.4 and 6.5. Table 6.4 lists

Table 6.4

Social Class of Occupied and Retired Men in Sectors of Greater London, 1951 and 1966

	1951			1966		
	I & II	III	IV & V	I & II	III	IV & V
Central Residential District (Chelsea, City, Holborn, Kensington, Paddington, St. Marylebone, Westminster)	29	40	31	36	39	25
Cross, Northern Inner (Finsbury, Hackney, Islington, St. Pancras, Shoreditch, Stoke Newington)	10	54	36	12	53	35
Outer (Edmonton, Enfield, Leyton, Tottenham, Walthamstow, Wood Green)	12	56	32	17	56	27
Cross, Eastern Inner (Bermondsey, Bethnal Green, Deptford, Greenwich, Poplar, Stepney, Woolwich)	9	48	43	13	50	37
Outer (Barking, Crayford, Dagenham, East Ham, Erith, Hornchurch, Romford, West Ham)	10	53	37	14	54	32
Cross, Southern Inner (Battersea, Camberwell, Lambeth, Lewisham, Southwark, Wandsworth)	13	54	33	16	54	30
Outer (Croydon, Merton, Mitcham, Penge)	19	57	24	22	56	22
Cross, Western Inner (Fulham, Hammersmith)	12	52	36	15	53	32
Outer (Acton, Brentford, Ealing, Feltham, Hayes, Heston, Southall, Uxbridge, Willesden, Yiewsley)	16	58	26	18	58	24
North Eastern Quarter (Chingford, Ilford, Woodford)	23	57	20	27	54	19
South Eastern Quarter (Beckenham, Bexley, Bromley, Chislehurst, Orpington)	26	51	23	33	50	17
South Western Quarter (Barnes, Beddington, Carshalton, Coulsdon, Kingston, Malden, Richmond, Surbiton, Sutton, Twickenham, Wimbledon)	26	53	21	34	49	17
North Western Quarter (Barnet, East Barnet, Finchley, Friern Barnet, Hampstead, Harrow, Hendon, Hornsey, Southgate, Ruislip, Wembley)	28	52	20	33	49	18

The figures quoted are percentages.

comparative figures at the two dates for the Central District, the various arms of the Cross (each divided into Inner and Outer) and each of the Quarters. Table 6.5 presents the same material in terms of the changes in percentages.

Table 6.5

Summary of Changes in Social Class of Occupied and Retired Men in Sectors of Greater London, 1951 and 1966

		Change in percentage of:		
		I & II	III	IV & V
Central Residential District		+7	−1	−6
Cross, Northern	Inner	+2	−1	−1
	Outer	+5	No change	−5
Cross, Eastern	Inner	+4	+2	−6
	Outer	+4	+1	−5
Cross, Southern	Inner	+3	No change	−3
	Outer	+3	−1	−2
Cross, Western	Inner	+3	+1	−4
	Outer	+2	No change	−2
North Eastern Quarter		+4	−3	−1
South Eastern Quarter		+7	−1	−6
South Western Quarter		+8	−4	−4
North Western Quarter		+5	−3	−2
All Greater London		+5	−1	−4
London Metropolitan Region		+6	−1	−5

The figures quoted are percentages

In terms of changes in Classes I and II, the increase was in general largest in the Central Residential District and the sub-urban Quarters. Inside the Cross, the largest gain was in the outer part of the northern arm, the increases being mainly in Enfield and Edmonton. Class III changed relatively little in most sectors. A number of areas in the Cross had little or no decrease in Classes IV and V—in this sense, they 'declined' in social class—particularly inner northern (mainly Hackney, Islington and Stoke Newington), outer western (Willesden and to a lesser extent Acton, Brentford, Ealing, Heston and Southall) and outer southern. The north-eastern and north-western Quarters also lost less than average proportions of Classes IV and V.

The general conclusion that we would draw from this set of comparisons is that most parts of the Cross became more working-class over the fifteen years from 1951 to 1966. Because of increasing class concentration, the Cross of London became more marked. At the time of writing, the results of the 1971 Census are not available. In view of the continuing pressures on housing demand over recent years, discussed later in this paper, we would expect the up-to-date figures to show that the process had continued.

A similar process was going on in the Outer Metropolitan Area between 1951 and 1966. There was again an up-grading almost everywhere, but the places that showed a higher-than-average increase in Classes I and II were those that already had high proportions of them. These were the rural areas, and particularly those in Surrey, Sussex, Hampshire and Berkshire. At the other end of the occupational scale, the largest relative increases among people in Classes IV and V were in Thameside Essex and Kent—the shaft of the Cross—the Luton/Watford area, and the other towns that were 'more working-class' to start with.

These various sets of changes, inside Greater London and in the O.M.A., are shown and summed up in Table 6.6. The table

Table 6.6

Summary of Changes in Social Class of Occupied and Retired Men in Main Types of District in London Metropolitan Region, 1951 and 1966

(a) Distributions	1951			1966		
	I & II	*III*	*IV & V*	*I & II*	*III*	*IV & V*
Central Residential District	29	45	31	36	39	25
Cross	13	54	33	16	54	30
Quarters	26	53	21	32	50	18
Outer Metropolitan Area	20	50	30	27	49	24
(b) Changes 1951–1966	*I & II*	*III*	*IV & V*			
Central Residential District	+7	−1	−6			
Cross	+3	No change	−3			
Quarters	+6	−3	−3			
Outer Metropolitan Area	+7	−1	−6			
London Metropolitan Region	+6	−1	−5			

The figures quoted are percentages.

confirms that the centre, Quarters and O.M.A. had high gains in Classes I and II, while the Cross gained less than average. Conversely, the Cross lost a less-than-average proportion of men in Classes IV and V, while the centre and the O.M.A. had relatively large decreases among them. The Quarters do seem rather different in this respect. They, like the Cross, showed a relatively small decline at the bottom. This is thus a qualification to the general theme of increasing concentration: the Quarters may have acquired a higher-than-average proportion at the top, but they also gained more than average (in the sense of losing less than average) of the partly skilled and unskilled.

An Alternative Approach

We have so far measured the changes only in one way, by taking the absolute change in the percentage and comparing this with the change over the London Region as a whole. The trouble with this is that it does not take into account the starting point; on an initial percentage of say 16 per cent in 1951, a rise from 4 per cent to 20 per cent is more of a relative increase than a similar 4 per cent rise from a base of 36 per cent to 40 per cent. Nor does the method used take any account of the relative deviance that a particular area shows from the norm—that is, the difference between the distribution of the three classes in the one area and that in the region as a whole. A relatively high increase in a particular class might help to make a place either less different from the norm, or more so.

We therefore tried various ways of measuring the degree of deviance in each place at both dates. The index that we finally settled on was simple and, it seemed to us, about as meaningful as the alternatives. We added up, for each particular area, the number of percentage points by which it differed from the average for the region, ignoring plus or minus signs. Thus, the 'deviance score' for Battersea in 1951 was calculated as follows:

	Battersea	London Region	Difference
Classes I and II	9 per cent	18 per cent	9
Class III	58 per cent	52 per cent	6
Classes IV and V	33 per cent	30 per cent	3
		Total	18

Battersea's score for 1966 was calculated, by the same method, as twenty. So the change between the two dates was an increase of two; Battersea became slightly less 'normal' in its class distribution between 1951 and 1966.

This procedure is applied to all the areas in Appendix 1.

The deviance at both dates and the changes over the fifteen years are shown by type of area in Table 6.7.

Table 6.7

Main Types of District in London Metropolitan Region, Extent of Deviance from Class Distribution of London Region in 1951 and 1966, and Change in Deviance between 1951 and 1966.

| | Degree of Deviance | | Change |
	1951	1966	1951–1966
Central Residential District	24	24	No change
Cross	10	16	+6
Quarters	18	16	−2
Outer Metropolitan Area	4	6	+2

We can sum up the various changes shown in Table 6.7 in this way:

The Central Residential District was at both dates the most deviant of all, but it became in general neither more nor less deviant between 1951 and 1966.

The Cross became more deviant over the fifteen years. This was as a result of the changes already noted—a relative decline at the top and a relative increase at the bottom.

The Quarters became rather less deviant. Though they had a relative increase at the top, they also had some relative increase at the bottom, which made them rather less 'abnormal'. They remained, in 1966, as deviant as the Cross, though in the opposite direction—that is, more high-class rather than more low-class.

The O.M.A. was at both dates relatively normal, but over the fifteen years it became slightly less so.

The main conclusion of this alternative approach is the by now familiar one: over the period there was an increasing concentration of working-class people into the Cross.

Patterns of Movement

The discussion of the changes from 1951 to 1966 has been in terms of broad changes in the proportions in one class or another.

The information is not available to allow us to describe with any certainty the complex patterns of movement in and out that add up to the net changes shown. But we must now try to put some interpretation on the figures.

The first point is that the changes in class took place over a period of general movement outwards from London. From 1951 to 1966 the population of Greater London fell by more than half a million to just over seven and a half, while that of the O.M.A. increased by one and a half million to nearly five. The concentration in the Cross that we have discussed earlier was a relative concentration, not an absolute one.

The decline inside London would have been even greater had it not been for the immigrants from the Commonwealth. Most of them arrived before the Commonwealth Immigration Act of 1962, but the consequences over the fifteen years from 1951 are apparent. Figures are not available for both dates for all London Boroughs, but those for Inner London are. There the numbers of people born in the 'new Commonwealth' increased from 59 000 in 1951 to 231 000 in 1966. Among Outer London Boroughs for which there are figures, Ealing had an increase from 4000 to 18 000 and Haringey from 2000 to 26 000. As one would expect, most of the immigrants have moved into the Cross. West Indians are concentrated in the northern arm, particularly in Hackney, Haringey and Islington; in the southern arm, notably in Lambeth, Lewisham, Southwark and Wandsworth; and in the western arm, especially in Brent [11]. There are fewer Asians but those there are live mostly in the Cross, with an especially high concentration in the Southall part of Ealing. Irish immigrants are mainly in the northern and western arms. The eastern arm, although the most 'working-class' of all, has not become the home of immigrants in the same way as the other three. This is partly because of the kind of housing it has. The East End was built for working-class people in the first place. Dwellings are small, whereas in the other arms of the Cross there are more of the large Victorian houses that lend themselves to subdivision and to overcrowding by people whose bargaining power on the housing market is lower than anyone else's.

Another reason for the pattern of immigrant settlement is the location of the point of arrival. The Jews who fled from the pogroms of Eastern Europe in the last century settled near the

Port of London where they disembarked, as the Huguenots had before them. Beatrice Webb has described how the Jews founded the tailoring industry of Whitechapel and Bethnal Green in the 1890s [12]. Many of the Irish who came when railways were the mode of transport took up residence near the two stations where they arrived, Euston (for Camden Town and Islington) and Paddington (for the district of the same name and also Willesden). The West Indians, when they came, arrived at Waterloo from Southampton and formed a series of settlements in South London, with an early cluster at Brixton; or Euston from Liverpool and moved into Islington and Finsbury Park. The Indians and Pakistanis who came by air and landed at Heathrow have stayed not far away.

This movement of immigrants into London has been, as we have said, an exception to the trends. Although others also have moved in—inside Greater London itself, from the O.M.A. into Greater London, or from elsewhere in the country into the region—the net balance of movement has been outwards.

We can—with the help of some speculation—try to distinguish the various patterns of class movement between 1951 and 1961. Among people in Classes I and II, some moved into the Central Residential District and into adjacent districts (examples are Barnsbury, Canonbury and Kennington) which have acquired something of a similar character. But most people in Classes I and II who were already living in the London Region moved out of the Cross into the Quarters or the O.M.A., and most Class I and II people who came into the region from outside similarly went to those areas.

Among skilled manual and clerical people (Class III), many who left their previous district moved outwards along the arms of the Cross. Others moved out to the Quarters or the O.M.A. Most of these moves were probably from privately rented property, some into owner-occupation, others into public housing (council estates in the Cross or Quarters and new or expanded towns in the O.M.A.).

As for people in Classes IV and V, some of them moved from the Cross into the Quarters. This is what helped to make the Quarters somewhat less unbalanced in their deficiency of such people than they had been in 1951. But such people also moved from the centre and the inner parts of the Cross out-

wards along its arms. The reason for these latter kinds of move
has been described thus by Donnison [13]:

> As slum clearance and redevelopment, privately or publicly
> sponsored, modernise many of the central parts of London, those
> who cannot escape to the suburbs, or find a home in the council
> flats or the more expensive private housing left in the centre, are
> squeezed into the larger rented houses a little further out. These
> houses are sub-divided, overcrowded, sold at prices that reflect
> the high rents paid for such intensive use and sub-divided yet
> again.

The process has been charted in detail in the London Borough
of Enfield in particular. There overcrowding and multiple
occupation were found to have increased between 1961 and
1966 in certain wards containing older housing. The newcomers, who were overwhelmingly working-class people, had
mainly moved outwards along the northern arm of the Cross,
from Islington, Hackney, Wood Green and Tottenham [14].
It is clear from Appendix 1 that something similar happened
in Willesden, Wood Green, Brentford, Heston and Hornsey
between 1951 and 1966. These are among the places in the
Cross which had higher than average increases in Classes IV
and V. It is also clear that coloured immigrants, whom we
have formerly mentioned as coming into London over the
fifteen-year period, were among those who, after their arrival,
later moved along the arms of the Cross to such districts as
these.

Why the Cross?

The puzzle is why the class geography of London should have
taken this distinctive form. We have seen that it has been
becoming not less marked but more. We must try to offer an
explanation.

The clue has been given earlier in the concentration of
industry in the arms of the Cross. Figure 6.3, a contour map of
Greater London, shows that there is a connexion between
physical geography and working-class residence. The explanation is obvious enough. The geography of London has given
rise to a particular distribution of docks, industry, road and
rail routes, and in general working-class people have tended to

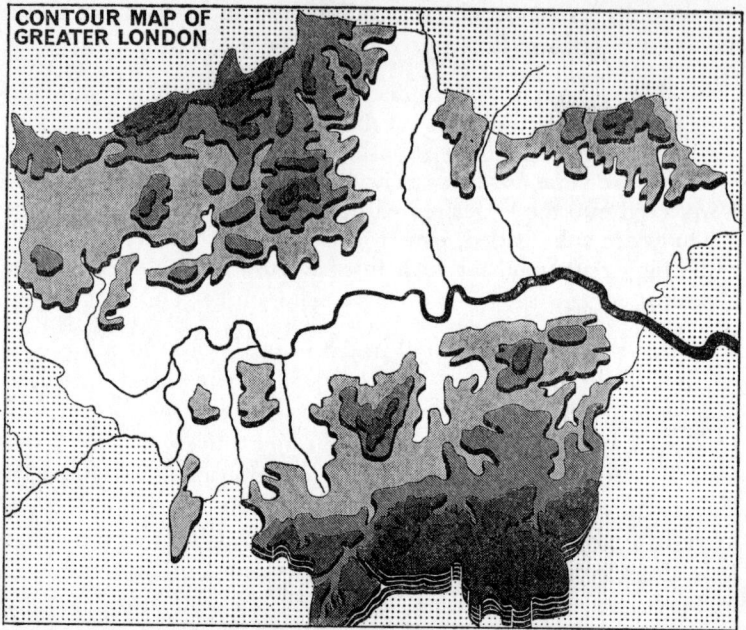

FIGURE 6.3 Contour map of Greater London

live nearby. The surface railways, which have usually avoided the high land, tended to blight the land around them, so that the nearby housing more often went to working-class people. In the nineteenth century a good deal of industry clustered on the low land of the East End to be near the docks; in the twentieth century on the low land to the west to be near to the new roads like the Great West Road and Western Avenue and, later on, to Heathrow. Industry also clustered along the Lea Valley. The land was flat in these three arms of the Cross, as well as in the southern one (in the valley of the River Wandle and elsewhere), and much of it was also near water which was useful for transport and processing.

The reasons why the low ground was good for industry are the reasons why it was not for residential housing. Much of it, except in the central districts, has been bad building land, more liable to flooding. It has been damper and it used to be less healthy. As a result richer people have, again except at the centre, kept to the high ground which had the opposite virtues. It had better drainage, less air pollution, better views. All the old villages established on relatively high ground, in such places as Highgate, Hampstead, Harrow on the Hill, Campden Hill, Richmond Hill, Kingston Hill, Sydenham Hill, Blackheath and Buckhurst Hill, became nuclei for surrounding middle-class settlement when the population of London expanded. Most of these old villages are outside the Cross; the few that are in are exceptions that prove the rule.

The Cross, and our suggested explanation for it, does not tally with the principal theory to explain urban growth—the Chicago 'concentric zones' to which we have referred earlier. We think that the mistake made by Park and Burgess was to ignore two special features of Chicago. The first was that it was, unlike London, a city without a history, without pre-existing villages, to constrain and help shape its growth. The second was that Chicago is on a plain. It could only be in flat country that a city could be thought of as expanding in terms of concentric circles. As it was, they neglected the contours almost completely. They regarded even Lake Michigan as a sort of irrelevance to their ideal scheme, although it made such a bite into the concentric regularity of their maps. Other cities, they seemed to be saying, do not have Lake Michigan, and will expand according to the model. What they should have said was that this will tend to happen, then stating the two chief limiting conditions: *if* the city is (*a*) on perfectly flat ground and (*b*) without water, that is river, lake or sea, as a primary feature of its environment. They happened to live and work in a city that was an extreme case, and yet did not realize it. They treated the extreme as though it were the general.

Another American student of the city produced an almost equally famous monograph on the subject in 1939. Hoyt investigated the tendency in American cities of high-rent areas to move from the centre outwards—a tendency, incidentally, which is not apparent at all in London. But in other respects what he said was very relevant, especially his observation that expansion outwards was often in rather distinct sectors. Hoyt summarized [15] the considerations that govern the pattern of growth in nine propositions. One of these was that:

> The zone of high-rent areas tends to progress toward high ground which is free from the risk of floods and to spread along lake, bay, river and ocean fronts, where such water fronts are not used for industry.

We ourselves would go a good deal further even than that in stressing the formative power of physical geography upon the shape the city takes, and, above all, the two linked features of that geography that we have already mentioned—water and contours.

Conclusions

To sum up, we are suggesting two propositions. One is that in the past the physical geography has determined the location of industry and communications, and thus given rise to the Cross of Greater London. The other, which follows from our comparison of the social class distribution of 1951 and 1966, is that the pattern of Central Residential District, Cross, Quarters and O.M.A. is being reinforced by a process of differential migration. Higher-status people have moved out of the Cross and into the already high-status sectors of London and the O.M.A. Above all, there has been a great concentration, relatively, of working-class people in the Cross—a process that has been intensified by the arrival of the Commonwealth immigrants.

Should these trends be welcomed, accepted or, if the choice is open, reversed? The question is not easily answered; despite the contributions made by some of the other papers in this collection, social researchers and policy-makers alike are still a long way from being able to judge with any confidence how, for example, people's living standards, opportunities and social networks are affected by the particular mixture of social classes in the district in which they live. The research that would allow such evaluations has yet to be done. Meanwhile, our own opinion is that the increasing class concentration of London is on balance probably more harmful than beneficial and therefore that policy should seek to check it.

One possible reversal is suggested by what we have said about the influence of the River Thames. The key is in the double role that water can have in the city. The river is for the rich a magnet and a repellent, a repellent if the water is also a port and a gateway to the industry that is usually sucked on to a port; a magnet if they can get near to an edge unencumbered by commerce. The Thames below the Pool has (except for the one jewel of Greenwich) been a repellent. It has been lined with docks and industry for fifteen miles. East London has had its back to the river, with a hinterland for the people who work in the industries and cannot afford to live anywhere except in the low-lying areas nearby. The Thames above the Pool, or at any rate above Westminster, is a magnet. Chelsea, Barnes, Chiswick, Kew, Twickenham, Richmond, are on the route that the Royal Barges used to take between the palaces of St. James, Hampton Court and Windsor; they are all desirable places for people who have the money to make their desires effective. The attraction of the river in such districts is, we suggest, the explanation of the Quarter that stands out in Figure 6.3 as exceptional. It is in the south-west Quarter only that relatively low land is relatively high in social class.

The implications are clear for the eastern arm of the Cross in particular. Surrounding the Port of London, it has been the most working-class sector of the city. With the movement of the port down river—the result of containerization and larger cargo ships—the estuarial shaft of the cross is likely to be further reinforced. But inside Greater London the same thing need not apply. The traditional role of the Thames as an industrial and commerical river can give way to a new role as an amenity and residential river. The same process is happening all over the world, in other large cities which were established where they are to be beside water. If the opportunity is seized in East London, this can help at one and the same time to make the eastern arm of the Cross less overwhelmingly one-class and bring recreation and pleasure to Londoners generally—and to visitors to the capital.

References

1. MOSER, C. A. and SCOTT, WOLF, *British Towns* (Edinburgh: Oliver and Boyd, 1961) pp. 104–5.
2. *Ibid.* p. 105.
3. *Ibid.* p. 63.
4. WESTERGAARD, JOHN, 'The structure of Greater London', in Centre for Urban Studies (ed.), *London—Aspects of Change* (London: MacGibbon and Kee, 1964).
5. *G.L.D.P. Report of Studies*, 1969, p. 63.
6. *Ibid.*, p. 27.
7. JONES, EMRYS and SINCLAIR, D. J. (eds.), *The Atlas of London and the London Region* (Oxford: Pergamon, 1968).
8. DALY, MARTIN, *Characteristics of 12 Clusters of Wards in Greater London*, GLC Research Report 13, July 1971.

9. KELLY, FRANCES, 'Classification of Urban Areas', *GLC Quarterly Bulletin, No. 9*, December 1969.

10. BURGESS, E. W., 'The growth of the city in an introduction to a research project', PARK, R. E., BURGESS, E. W. and McKENZIE, R. D., *The City* (University of Chicago Press, 1967) (first published 1925), p. 50.

11. See the maps in DOHERTY, JOE, 'The distribution and concentration of immigrants in London', *Race Today*, December 1969. Also DEAKIN, N. and COHEN, B. G., 'Dispersal and choice for ethnic minorities', *Environment and Planning*, **2**, no. 2, p. 197.

12. POTTER, BEATRICE (later WEBB), 'The Tailoring Trade', reprinted in BOOTH, CHARLES, *Life and Labour of the Poor in London*, First Series, Vol. 4 (London: Macmillan, 1889).

13. DONNISON, D. V., *The Government of Housing* (Harmondsworth: Penguin, 1967) pp. 336–7.

14. *Report on the Changing Nature of Residential Areas*, (duplicated) London Borough of Enfield, April 1969.

15. HOYT, H., *The Structure and Growth of Residential Neighbourhoods in American Cities* (Federal Housing Administration, Washington D.C., 1939).

Chapter Seven

Beyond the Ghetto: The Illusion of Choice

NICHOLAS DEAKIN AND
CLARE UNGERSON

Summary

The paper starts by examining some of the more frequent usages of the word 'ghetto', pointing to its indication of common racial characteristics, or class characteristics, or even common housing tenure type. The crucial importance of 'choice' in discussions of the ghetto is elaborated.

We then turn to a discussion of the determinants of life-chances for black people living in London. Which is more important in determining where people live and their access to other goods and services—the housing market or the employment market? And are the difficulties black people encounter in both these markets due mainly to their colour or as much to other characteristics they share with other white groups? We conclude that everything is important: jobs, housing, colour, poverty; and that all combine to provide the context for the possible—although not yet actual—formation of ghettos.

A more detailed discussion of possible and actual interventions by government in the housing market follows. The Rent Acts, Housing Advice Centres, the Cullingworth reports, the Race Relations Act, the Urban Programme, are looked at critically and proposals are made about their use. Particular emphasis is laid on the need to introduce legislation to cope with the growing problems of furnished rented accommodation where black people are increasingly housed.

The paper ends with a discussion of 'dispersal'. What do we mean by it? Is it a relevant concept when we are concerned to extend *voluntary* dispersal? Should we not rather be asking questions about 'choice' and how we extend that?

This chapter began as an attempt at an examination of a single concept: that of the ghetto, and the extent to which it can legitimately be applied to the situation in London. Historically, the notion of the ghetto is both stigmatizing and restricting; it identifies a group which a society wishes to define as a separate entity, not forming part of the main body of that society, nor entitled to rights that are common property within it. In the past, such groups have carried a literal stigma—an ineradicable sign setting them apart: the black skin of the slave, the Star of David of the Jew. This stigma has permitted the majority to exercise control over their physical location and movement, and, in extreme cases, to destroy them.

Yet the application of the term to groups in our society now can lead not to illumination but to the generation of a great deal of heat—and heat, in turn, to haziness of outline. For it is striking how often the term is used loosely or in contradictory senses. We think that we can distinguish at least three different usages. First, and most obvious, there is the definition based on ethnic difference ('race'). There is no need to labour the point that the concept of the black ghetto has been employed freely in the British situation, often with reference to London. But in order to establish how meaningful the application of this term to the present situation is we will need to examine closely the evidence about the distribution of ethnic groups in London—a task which we will return to later. There is also another common usage, based on economic circumstances. In this usage, the term 'ghetto' is applied to deprived areas and by extension to their inhabitants. The definitions employed vary, depending on whether the focus is on deprivation in the geographical area as such—in schools, the social services available, or simply the general environment; or on the individual, his income, his skills or his class—defined in socio-economic terms. By extension, the term is also applied to certain tenure groups, conceived of as separate housing classes: it is quite common to find reference made to 'council house ghettos' [1]. Reference has even been made recently by the Chairman of one London Borough Housing Committee to 'upper-class ghettos' in part of his local authority area.

Beyond this, the term is applied more widely still, to groups distinguished by certain general characteristics, such as sex or age (references to ghettos of the old—'Sun Cities'—or the young). Clearly at this point the usage is so loose as to become almost meaningless—unlike the other definitions we have cited in the previous paragraph, which are important enough to be worth further consideration.

But before we do consider the other usages we should also note in passing that they all appear to be based on a geographical definition—the separation of the particular group is defined spatially. It is, however, perfectly possible for a minority (however defined) to be separated from the main body of society or stigmatized in some way while at the same time being distributed evenly throughout the whole population. The 'spiritual ghetto' of a minority is a familiar concept. It can be applied to the advocates of the counter-culture as much as to the exiles and refugees who, while often spatially dispersed, still take pride in and adhere to the customs and ideologies of their lives elsewhere. Although not susceptible to precise measurement, this 'spiritual ghetto' is often of considerable importance in considering the future development of the society of which that group forms a part.

The Importance of 'Choice'

In general, the common usages of the term 'ghetto' imply either areas of ethnic concentration, areas of one-class concentration, areas of multiple deprivation or a combination of the three. In all these usages the concept of 'choice' plays a crucial, although differing role. This is fitting, since one of the common implications of the word 'ghetto' is that it is a place from which the inhabitants cannot escape—they have no choice but to stay within the actual or metaphorical walls of the ghetto. But the different usages imply that choices are available to the people living within the defined area. And these choices vary in kind.

For example, a 'racially distinct ghetto' might exist because the people living within it wish to live together, and can do so, in areas where the services are good enough to maximize their satisfactions in other ways. The Jews of Golders Green are a good example of a group who have chosen to live together in such circumstances. On the other hand such a concentration may exist because the majority society wishes to confine such a group within certain areas. In that case, the majority society has severely restricted the choices of the minority group. In contrast, areas of multiple deprivation are areas where choice for all the inhabitants is severely restricted—not necessarily deliberately— by factors at work within the wider society. Poor schools, poor wages, bad housing and overcrowding, combine to keep the inhabitants in such conditions. Without the money to buy them- selves out, or the skills to agitate for better services at home, these people are stuck almost as firmly as if their areas were literally surrounded by walls. Thirdly, in 'one-class neighbour- hoods' which are not 'areas of deprivation' the concept of 'choice' has yet another emphasis. It may be, as in the com- muter villages of Hertfordshire, that in middle-class, one-class neighbourhoods the occupants have deliberately chosen that it should be like that, just like the Golders Green Jews. But in working-class one-class neighbourhoods, which in London will probably be areas with a very high proportion of council hous- ing, it is arguable that some kinds of choice are limited. For example, it is impossible even for a well-paid worker living in East London to buy a decent house in that area and thereby gain access to the considerable financial advantages attaching to owner occupation.

The Significance of Housing

In considering these problems of absence of choice, especially in areas of deprivation, we will need to return to fundamentals and try to answer one of the perennial and basic questions: whether the place of residence of disadvantaged groups is determined by the workings of the housing market, or whether employment is the critical factor. In the broadest terms, the pattern of the housing market has been changing rapidly over the last twenty years. Whereas twenty years ago almost three-quarters of the dwellings of England and Wales were rented, by 1967 half were owner-occupied; and of those that were not, more than half were rented from the local authority. But these changes did not take place evenly throughout the stock of dwellings. Generally, the rapid growth in owner-occupied dwellings has taken place on the periphery of our major cities and in new housing developments; the equally rapidly shrinking privately rented sector is confined increasingly to the centre of these cities. Local authority housing is more evenly distributed between the two; but access to such housing is controlled by a series of rules operated by local authorities, which tend to restrict the access of newcomers. To be specific, there are at least six ways in which discrimination by local authorities against newcomers—and specifically coloured ones—can take place. First, in the framing of points systems for the allocation of housing from the waiting list which lay stress on local residence; second, by omitting areas of high concentration from slum clearance schemes; third, by rigid definition of the categories of persons considered eligible for rehousing; fourth, in the type of property offered to them when they are rehoused; fifth, in the assessment of their suitability for accommodation by housing visitors; and, finally, by making selective attacks on the problems of multi-occupation and thereby squeezing minorities into certain specific areas. The Political and Economic Planning report of 1967 indicated that there were grounds for supposing that discrimination is occurring under all these heads [2].

At the same time, access to other sectors of the housing market has been severely restricted. Access to owner occupation is of particular significance, because it is often the solution which the immigrant himself would most like to adopt [3]. But the attitude initially adopted by building societies towards coloured house purchasers (especially before the Race Relations Act of 1968), and towards the type of property which is within their means to purchase, restricted their opportunities at the crucial earlier stage in the migration. Often, such purchasers have been forced to raise short-term loans at high rates of interest. The attitudes of estate agents towards black clients has been an additional restriction: often they have interpreted their role as entitling them to 'steer' coloured people to certain 'suitable' areas. That so many immigrants have been able to purchase their own property, despite a relatively low *per capita* income, is a striking illustration of the desire to escape the disadvantages inherent in housing in the private rented sector—the remaining sector open to them.

Nevertheless, it will be seen from Table 7.1 that the majority of immigrants in London are still to be found in the private rented sector, and that they are very considerably over-represented in the most vulnerable part of that sector—in furnished accommodation. We shall be returning to the significance of this particular facet of distribution later.

Table 7.1

Housing Tenure Groups of Coloured Immigrants in the London Conurbation

Area of Residence	Owner-Occupiers		Renting From a Local Authority		Renting Unfurnished		Renting Furnished	
	All Coloured immigrants	English	All Coloured immigrants	English	All Coloured immigrants	English	All Coloured immigrants	English
London Conurbation	32.6	38.9	4.2	22.3	18.1	29.0	43.6	7.3

Source: 1966 10 per cent Sample Census.

Not only are immigrants concentrated disproportionately in one tenure group: they are also disproportionately concentrated in the inner areas of major cities. The evidence about the extent of concentration is taken from the 1966 Sample Census. There are a number of well-known objections to its use, particularly with reference to immigrants. First, this Census is, of course, out-of-date—we await the results of the 1971 Census which will allow us to confirm the possible trends we indicate later on. Secondly, we know that the Census seriously under-enumerated the immigrant populations. Thirdly, the smallest unit for which numbers were large enough to be significant was the electoral ward, which for our purposes may well be too large when we talk about 'areas of multiple deprivation'. Nevertheless, the 1966 Census is the latest data we have and with these caveats in mind we shall proceed to use it.

On concentration itself, the evidence is confusing. Since immigrants form such a low proportion of the London population, the proportion of one particular group living in one particular area would have to be very high indeed to fill a defined area.

Table 7.2 shows how small are the proportions of various ethnic groups in the whole of the Greater London area.

Table 7.2

Proportions of Various Ethnic Groups in the GLC Area in 1966

Irish	Asian	W. Indian	African	Cypriot/Maltese
3.70	1.53	1.98	0.56	0.76

The figures quoted are percentages of the total population.

As Table 7.3 indicates, there are some wards in London where, in 1966, nearly a quarter of the population belonged to one ethnic group. At the same time, nearly half (43 per cent) of the West Indian population of London lived in wards where they comprise less than 5 per cent of the population. What sort of areas are they where immigrants of one kind or another constitute nearly a quarter of the population? As Joe Doherty has pointed out: 'The major problem now is not "how concentrated" but "where concentrated".' In all the areas of substantial settlement, the density of occupation is high, the proportion of occupied dwellings with all facilities low, the proportion of households in privately rented furnished accommodation is high the proportion of economically active men in skilled, semi-skilled and service employment high, while the proportion in 'other non-manual' work is low. Thus a clear picture emerges of 'typical' areas of multiple deprivation with poor housing stock, low social class, insecure tenure. This picture is most marked in Harrow Road ward where 21 per cent of households were West Indian in 1966, and very nearly half the households were lacking in one facility, nearly one-third of the households were in furnished accommodation, and nearly a quarter of the men were in service or semi-skilled occupations.

Although concentrations of unskilled workers, or poor housing circumstances are not exclusively a feature of Inner London, areas of multiple deprivation with a substantial proportion of black inhabitants are characteristically found in the inner city. These also tend to be the areas where the social services are at their least adequate. This inadequacy affects all the inhabitants of these areas—the 'twilight zones' of our major cities where the housing stock is sinking to the end of its useful life. But there is one section of the population that suffers particularly from the

Table 7.3

Major Settlement of Immigrants by Wards, London 1966 (Percentage Population)

Wards with large Irish concentrations	% Irish	% Asian	% W. Indian	% African	% Cypriot/Maltese
Kilburn (Brent)	24.41	2.37	6.84	2.09	0.28
Mapesbury (Brent)	22.26	4.14	1.85	3.27	0.00
Cricklewood (Brent)	18.95	3.06	3.26	2.27	1.58
Kilburn (Camden)	18.68	3.33	4.31	3.09	3.01

Wards with large Asian Concentrations	% Asian	% Irish	% W. Indian	% African	% Cypriot/Maltese
Northcote (Ealing	24.41	2.89	4.56	1.44	0.17
St. Mary's (Tower Hamlets)	9.30	3.67	0.86	0.12	2.08
Soho (Westminster)	8.23	1.52	0.30	0.00	1.52
Spitalfields (Tower Hamlets)	8.13	7.33	1.96	1.02	5.37

Wards with large W. Indian concentrations	% W. Indian	% Irish	% Asian	% African	% Cypriot/Maltese
Kensal Rise (Brent)	21.13	6.00	0.46	1.39	0.12
Harrow Road (Westminster)	20.88	10.81	0.97	2.73	0.46
Rectory (Hackney)	14.37	3.74	1.18	1.67	0.47
Tulse Hill (Lambeth)	13.84	5.20	0.58	1.81	1.17

Source: 1966 Census.
This table was taken from: JOE DOHERTY, 'The Distribution and Concentration of Immigrants in London', *Race Today*, **1**, No. 8, December 1969.

handicaps imposed by residents in such areas: the children. Children in these areas are more likely to die at birth, or shortly after it, will get inferior health care at the beginning of their lives, are more likely to be run over by traffic because there are no adequate play facilities available, are more likely to catch illnesses as a result of playing among rubbish or from bad housing conditions. One investigator [4] who has recently worked in an area of this kind with a high proportion of black inhabitants stresses that the absence of adequate provision of day nurseries forces parents to place children in 'establishments' where

> . . . the children had little or no play facilities; even three year olds had no books or writing tablets, nor did they get enough attention from the child-minders. . . . In view of the almost total absence of any formative education, it would hardly be surprising if their children did not become 'problems' during their first years at school. They will certainly require special attention, and if the teacher does not have the resources to provide special attention or fails to recognise the need for it, then their children might well start and finish in the bottom stream—today's 'problem child', tomorrow's drop-out or delinquent.

The obstacles encountered by children in these areas will continue to affect them into adult life: their poverty will, in most cases, be perpetuated and transmitted to the next generation. Unable, because of inadequacies in their education, to obtain better jobs than their parents, with better pay, they cannot escape from the underprivileged area in which they were brought up, and are forced, in their turn, to bring up their families in these conditions of severe deprivation. At some point in the vicious cycle they may qualify, by operation of the points system or of the bulldozer, for local authority housing. But entry into local authority housing is restricted, as we have already indicated: and for inhabitants of Inner London, at least, it is often delayed beyond the span of a child's passage from birth to adulthood. Nor is decent housing a guarantee of freedom from poverty. In the light of the Housing Finance Act, the costs of decent housing may be so high as to make other areas of life very difficult indeed.

All those handicaps affect all inhabitants of the twilight zone, and coloured people are conspicuous among them. Thus we see that access to particular types and location of housing is certainly a major determinant of the quality of life, in that, with its type and location, come a whole bundle of other services and disservices, opportunities and deprivations. But the question remains: do these people have this differential access to good services, which puts them at such a disadvantage compared with the inhabitants of the leafy suburbs, because they are poor, because they are black or because of the jobs they do?

Employment and Housing

There is general agreement, based initially on G. C. K. Peach's examination of migration flows [5], that it has been the availability of jobs that has determined the distribution of coloured people among the major conurbations. Once in these areas, the coloured population are affected by a series of developments within the employment market in major conurbations. A rather over-simplified view of the current situation is this: there is a growing demand for service workers in the centre of our cities: these jobs are frequently filled by black people, particularly— in the case of London—by black women; jobs in the transport, postal, hospital and catering services are comparatively low paid; the operation of discrimination in the employment market, particularly against coloured people and women, will mean that large proportions of these groups are effectively prevented from working in other industries; since they are low paid they cannot afford to purchase good housing and are forced either to pay rent or buy inadequate accommodation in the centre; moreover, they have to live near their work because fares for public transport are high, and anyway they often do shift work and go to and from work at times when public transport is not operating; they are thus made poor and forced to live in areas of multiple deprivation near the city centres.

Against this view, it is argued that—in London, at least—the opportunities for semi-skilled and skilled workers are not disappearing as rapidly as has been suggested. Nor (see Chapter Two) is there any convincing evidence of a concentration of semi-skilled or unskilled workers in any specific areas. In some areas, the city has in fact generated new employment opportunities within the inner core: and other areas outside the traditional industrial belts are providing new opportunities. One specific example is Croydon, where a whole range of new jobs has become available over the last decade, and West Indians from the Lambeth area have taken full advantage of the opportunity provided [6].

But these new opportunities, though they help to correct the impression of an inevitable decline in the inner city, can necessarily affect only a minority. The restrictions placed on coloured householders by the operation of the housing market are compounded by the additional restrictions on the type of employment available and the levels of pay.

Table 7.4 shows that in certain London wards where there were concentrations of immigrants, West Indian men were

Table 7.4

Percentage Socio-economic Distribution* for Different Immigrant Groups for Selected Areas, 1966: Males—Selected Inner London Boroughs 1966†

Birthplace	Caribbean	Ireland	England and Wales
Number economically active‡	20 500	14 400	206 750
1 Professional workers	0.4	1.0	3.1
2 Employers and managers	0.3	3.6	8.3
3 Non-manual	4.6	13.2	22.1
4 Skilled manual and foremen	40.5	36.5	39.6
5 Semi-skilled manual	26.7	19.7	15.7
6 Unskilled manual	25.1	24.8	9.9
7 Armed Forces and inadequately described	2.3	1.2	1.2

Source: 1966 10 per cent Sample Census, Special Tabulations.

* Categories used consist as follows:

Category	Registrar General's S.E.G.
1 Professional workers	3, 4
2 Employers and managers	1, 2, 13
3 Non-manual	5, 6
4 Skilled manual	8, 9, 12, 14
5 Semi-skilled manual	7, 10, 15
6 Unskilled manual	11,
7 Armed forces and inadequately described	16, 17

† For areas covered by seven selected metropolitan boroughs (Stoke Newington, Hackney, Paddington, Battersea, Lambeth, Camberwell, Deptford). Figures for India and Pakistan born not included, because the birth-place criterion employed in the Census is misleading.

‡ Figures for the number economically active have been multiplied by ten as the size of the sample was 10 per cent of the total population.

heavily over-represented in semi-skilled and unskilled manual work, and while a very similar proportion were in skilled work, compared to the English born men the West Indians were very under-represented in non-manual work.

To say that the housing market is rivalled by the employment market as a determinant of where people live is not to deny the impact of housing conditions on the quality of people's lives. Overcrowding, high rents or mortgage interest, poor maintenance, insecurity of tenure, coupled with an inability to escape from the effects of these circumstances, add up to an appalling burden for individuals and families. However, even if people are forced to live in certain areas as a result of economic factors beyond their control, there are some measures that can be taken to alleviate housing hardship, despite the operation of the broader economic and social imperatives.

Are Immigrants in a Special Position?

A view taken by many race relations experts on this question has been neatly summarized by Elizabeth Burney. She takes the view that immigrants as a group have many of the characteristics of other deprived groups and hence suffer from all their disadvantages [7]:

> The chief losers in the battle for a fair share of housing are working-class families with young children in big cities, especially if they are newcomers supplying essential labour. Among them are the overseas immigrants, whose plight is unique only in its particular combination of circumstances. Many of those circumstances are shared with, for example: young families; large families; low-paid workers, mobile workers, shift workers; unmarried mothers; and almost any non-English-looking, non-English-speaking, non-conforming people. Any of these features is equivalent to a minus mark in the competition for housing space. Racial discrimination is perhaps the biggest single minus; but even this can generally be overcome unless combined—as it nearly always is—with at least one, if not several, of the other factors listed.

Sir Milner Holland's Committee on London Housing came to broadly the same conclusions [8] commenting that:

> The basic nature of the differences of coloured immigrants is the same in quality as that of all the newcomers to London without

adequate means, arriving at a time when many local authority housing lists are very overcrowded or even closed, and in conditions where they obtain very low priority for allocation of housing.

Others have taken rather a different view. John Rex and Robert Moore, in their study of the Sparkbrook area of Birmingham [9], argue that immigrants constitute a distinct housing class, whose access to housing is restricted as a result of competition with other classes in the city, defined by their control of access to superior kinds of housing—the suburban middle class with their access to owner occupation and the white urban working class with their access to local authority housing. In these circumstances, the immigrant is forced back on the ethnic colony, where his needs are catered for by the immigrant landlord.

More recent evidence, from an extensive enquiry conducted in Notting Hill, enables us to examine in detail the relative circumstances of black and white in an inner urban area of a similar kind to that described by Rex and Moore. The Notting Hill Housing Survey [10] showed that a very high proportion (33 per cent) of households living in the survey area were living at more than $1\frac{1}{2}$ persons per room—black or white. Poor housing conditions, in terms of absolute numbers, affect many more whites than blacks. Proportionately, however, blacks generally suffer more. In Notting Hill, 59 per cent of the West Indians, 53 per cent of the Africans, 33 per cent of the Asians were living at this rate compared to 22 per cent of the households where the head was born in the United Kingdom. But this cannot be said to be purely a question of colour: 44 per cent of the Irish households were overcrowded—which seems to indicate the relative significance of poverty, size of household, newcomers, as opposed to the single factor of colour.

At the same time, there is no doubt that being black makes the struggle for decent, secure housing even more difficult than it is for the deprived white household. The survey showed that households with 'coloured' heads paid more rent than households with 'white' heads. It is clear that part of this is due to 'black' households being comparative newcomers and so not getting the advantage of controlled tenancies where median rents were considerably lower than in other tenures. The survey also used a device for measuring value for money in all tenures and found that furnished tenants got least value, controlled tenants the most. It is the concentration of black households in furnished accommodation which is clearly a crucial determinant of the high rents paid by coloured householders.

According to the survey, two-thirds of the West Indian households and three-quarters of the Asians and Africans lived in furnished accommodation in Notting Hill in 1967 as compared to one-fifth of the English households. This connexion between furnished accommodation and colour is not restricted to Notting Hill, it is typical of the rest of London. The 1966 Census showed that 43.6 per cent of all coloured immigrants living in London were in furnished accommodation as compared to 7.3 per cent of the English (Table 7.1).

The picture that emerges from these findings is not completely clear cut. It is certainly the case that there are many more whites living in dreadful housing conditions than there are blacks. Moreover, some of the reasons why blacks find themselves in particularly bad circumstances is no doubt because they do— as Elizabeth Burney suggests—find themselves in a situation which combines many of the different features of those households that are most often found in housing need. Nevertheless, the Notting Hill evidence provides general confirmation that, as far as rent and type of tenure are concerned, colour operates as a separate handicap.

This would be less disturbing if it could be shown that the situation is improving. It is often argued that immigrant groups must expect, simply because they are newcomers, to encounter some additional difficulties in obtaining decent housing and well paid jobs. But in fact the position of blacks in the housing market showed very little improvement between 1961 and 1966, a period in which the housing circumstances of white families living in similar kinds of areas showed a substantial improvement. When allowance is made for the change in definition of a room between Censuses, the position of Indian and Pakistani migrants, taken together, actually deteriorated [11].

We urgently need to know whether the situation has changed since 1966: whether, for example, a large black family is likely to be in as good or bad housing as a large white family, or whether colour has become even more important as a source of differential access to better circumstances. Only the 1971 Census can answer that question: but the indications seem to be that in certain areas of multiple deprivation in London, the problems of blacks in the housing market are becoming relatively greater, particularly when account is taken of their concentration in the furnished sector.

The evidence we have available about West Indians living in London [12] shows that just over 40 per cent of West Indian households in Greater London were living in privately rented furnished accommodation in 1966 compared with 8.6 per cent of all households. The Francis Committee has indicated that many people live in furnished accommodation not because they want to, but because they cannot get anything else [13]. It is also the tenure category from which, according to the Cullingworth Committee, some local authorities still refuse to rehouse the tenants. In Kensington and Chelsea, where 67.7 per cent of the West Indian households were in furnished accommodation in 1966, the local authority still refuses to rehouse such tenants from redevelopment areas except 'on their merits'.

This means that this sector of the housing market could be construed as the place where the significant concentration takes place. Not only does it compare badly with other sectors of the market in terms of amenities and security, but also it is very difficult indeed to move out of it, particularly if you are black and poor.

But, as we saw earlier, the Census evidence shows that a substantial proportion of West Indians are owner occupiers. In Greater London as a whole 32.7 per cent own their houses compared to 38.5 per cent of all households, and in the eleven Inner Boroughs where 79 per cent of all West Indian households live, 28.4 per cent of West Indian households had bought their houses compared to 21.8 per cent of all households [12]. A second important point concerns the conditions in which these large groups of furnished tenants and owner occupiers live. Haddon found that in all the boroughs—whether they had high proportions of immigrant residents or not—lower proportions of West Indian owner occupiers were overcrowded than in any other sector. Only 12.5 per cent of West Indian owner occupiers in concentrated boroughs were living at more than $1\frac{1}{2}$ persons per room, compared with 25.0 per cent of West Indian local authority tenants, 30.1 per cent unfurnished tenants and 34.8 per cent furnished tenants. Thus even in areas which are afflicted by multiple deprivation, movement into owner occupation

appears to be an effective way of escaping the severe overcrowding that West Indians suffer in other tenure categories.
But if we turn to overcrowding patterns in the boroughs with
lower proportions of West Indians, we find that movement out
of the inner areas, particularly for unfurnished tenants, does not
completely resolve problems of overcrowding. Even in the non-
concentrated boroughs 10.4 per cent of the West Indian households were overcrowded, which is still a fairly high proportion
although it compares favourable with 20.5 per cent in the
'intermediate' boroughs and 27.0 per cent in the 'concentrated'
boroughs. 'Dispersal' clearly brings some comparative benefits
for many, but it does not remove housing hardship for all. Thus
the links between a particular form of housing hardship—overcrowding—and particular areas of concentration are not firmly
established. Many West Indians continue to suffer from bad
housing wherever they live.

The Scope for Alternatives

Before embarking in a discussion of any new measures that
might be introduced, it is important to assess the range of devices for intervention in the local housing situation that already
exist, and in particular to examine their significance for the
problems of coloured householders.

In present circumstances, the scope for direct intervention by
central government is limited. The legislative framework is
provided at the centre; and the succession of Housing Acts and
White Papers of the post-war years mark the various changes in
priority in housing policy. The emphasis in the period immediately following the war was on new building in the public sector,
which shifted, in the fifties, to slum clearance in the public
sector and the construction of new housing for owner occupiers
in the private sector. Since 1961 there has been increasing
emphasis on the problems of the inner cities and in particular
the multi-occupation of large properties with inadequate facilities. The new powers with which the 1961 Housing Act armed
local authorities have been supplemented on two occasions
since, and the goals of policy redefined so as to permit local
authorities to deal with the problems of underprivileged areas
as a whole, with the emphasis increasingly on rehabilitation as
well as on the clearance of really bad property. At the same time

the notion that the problems of the private rented sector were best resolved in the market, partially implemented by the Rent Act of 1957, has been progressively reversed, most significantly by the 1965 Rent Act which allowed for the rent regulation of most unfurnished decontrolled property.

Within this framework, the role of central government has been to provide the resources: the subsidies for local authorities (and housing trusts) for the construction of new dwellings, the funds for the improvement and conversion grants that are an increasingly important element in the campaign against poor housing facilities, and the sanctions for the loaning of money by local authorities for mortgages. The chief responsibility lies with the local authorities, both for dealing with the inadequacies of existing housing stock, and provision of new housing to replace it, for using various Housing and Public Health Act powers to manage and control conditions in their area, and for managing and controlling the housing that they own. In all these matters, the role of central government has in the past been essentially advisory, although the provisions of the Housing Finance Act mean that in future local authorities will no longer set their own rent levels. The impact of 'fair rents' on inner city areas cannot yet be assessed, but it is likely that, particularly in London, council housing will become rather less attractive than in the past.

Nevertheless, while it is true that the major share of responsibility for the execution of policy lies at the local level, this does not mean that the general orientation which housing policy takes cannot have a critical effect on the day-to-day policies that affect the lives of black people. The most dramatic example is probably the Rent Act of 1965. While the swing from unfurnished to furnished tenancies was not an intention of the Act, it is probably true that this has been its most important effect. There is very considerable evidence now available to show that this Act and the legislation affecting furnished tenancies has been very considerably underused. In evidence to the Francis Committee, the Notting Hill Housing Service commented [14]:

As in other areas (see e.g. Michael Zander, *New Society* 12.9.68) we have discovered extensive ignorance of the law on the part of tenants, and much less use of the machinery than seems justified in our view.

It has been estimated that in the worst part of North Kensington there are about 3000 households living in unfurnished accommodation eligible for registration under the 1965 Rent Act. Up to the end of 1969 only 172 tenancies had been registered in this area. While we do not have comparable figures for applications to the Rent Tribunal, the Notting Hill Housing Service suggested that [15]:

> There is an extreme reluctance on the part of the furnished tenants to apply for rent reductions to the Rent Tribunal because of fear, wholly justified, that it will lead to their eventual eviction.

We are certain that these figures and statements apply over the whole population—black and white. But we think that the existing differential in security of tenure between furnished and unfurnished accommodation has very serious implications for race relations. All over London a far higher proportion of blacks than whites live in furnished accommodation, where rents are higher and security is less. At the same time, there is evidence from all over the country that landlords are taking advantage of this differential and, where they can, they are furnishing previously unfurnished accommodation. If immigrants also find difficulty in buying their own houses, an increasing proportion are going to have to live in furnished accommodation, with all its associated handicaps [16].

Many furnished tenants will be continuously on the move within the furnished sector either because they are seeking better accommodation, or because they are forced to move either through pressure from the landlord or because the local authority refuses to rehouse them when they redevelop the area in which they live. In this way, movement within the furnished sector will be accelerated and the attitudes of some local authorities to furnished tenants reinforced. But, as we have seen, the evidence suggests that an increasing proportion of these people will be black, and there is additional confirmation of this in the evidence gathered by the Francis Committee [17]. Nevertheless, the majority on the Committee opted to preserve the present distinction between unfurnished and furnished tenancies. The Government has accepted this view, which is likely to have far-reaching and very damaging implications for race relations in this country. Furthermore, they have carried the distinction into the provisions of the Housing Finance Act, although subsequently the Government has had second thoughts.

The powers of advice and enquiry available to the Government are also of considerable significance. The enquiry made by the subcommittee of the Central Housing Advisory Committee under the Chairmanship of Professor J. B. Cullingworth has been of particular importance in exploring the crucial issues in the interlocking field of housing and race relations. The same cannot, unfortunately, be said of the Report of the Select Committee on Race Relations and Immigration [18], which considered this subject in the Session 1970/1. Their report is something worse than a damp squib: it takes us no further than the Cullingworth Committee—indeed, in some senses it represents a retreat from the earlier position.

The most important issues that the two Committees considered show up the limitations of the present system of dividing responsibility. Professor Cullingworth's Committee strongly urged that unless there were exceptional circumstances there should be no residential or other qualification for admission to a housing list, and that records should be kept and used by local authorities for operational progress. These recommendations were endorsed, with a degree of caution, by the Select Committee. Both these reforms are of considerable significance for the situation of coloured people: but the Secretary of State does not, under present legislation, have the power to enforce them. Moreover, although most local authorities have accepted the Secretary of State's recommendations, some have not: and among those who have not are some whose policies are of the greatest importance.

There are other ways in which the role of central government can have a direct significance for coloured people. A good many practical difficulties stem from differences in practice between different local authorities—variations in policy for dealing with overcrowding or rehousing of certain tenure groups. More important, there are problems which have a disproportionate impact on authorities in areas under particular stress, to whose solution other local authorities can make a significant contribution. Reference has been made by Professor Cullingworth in the case of London to the problems of Inner London and the contribution that Outer London Boroughs might make to solving them—a problem to which he has drawn attention in a further report [19]. The role of the department in encouraging the pooling of resources in this way and the evolution of common policies through co-ordination could have very great practical value.

Similarly, the role of the department can be of great import-ance in bringing to the attention of local authorities various innovations in housing policy and practice. A relevant example is the introduction of the Housing Advice Centres now being operated by some local authorities, notably Lambeth. Many—although not all—of the difficulties that affect coloured people —and other inhabitants of deprived areas—can be traced to lack of access to vital information at critical stages in their housing circumstances. The extension of such services to other areas could be of substantial practical significance: it is encouraging to learn from the Select Committee's Report [20] that ministers are considering the possibility of urging this upon other local authorities.

Anti-discrimination Legislation

The effects of this kind of intervention are necessarily indirect. However, there are a few areas in which the intervention of central government in matters that affect black people is expli-cit and direct, the most obvious of which is through the Race Relations Act of 1968. The purpose of the race relations legis-lation has been widely misunderstood. The intention of the legislation was not to create a specially privileged class: the dangers of doing so are particularly clear in the field of housing. Here—as we have tried to show—black and white share many difficulties resulting from factors not directly connected with colour. Rather, the intention was to deal with certain specific difficulties arising directly out of discrimination on grounds of colour.

Specifically, the Act makes it unlawful to discriminate on grounds of colour, race, or ethnic and national origin, in selling or letting housing accommodation, business premises or land, or in the treatment of tenants. The Act applied in both the public and private sectors, but it exempted a person who had the power to provide or dispose of residential accommodation if he lived (and intended to continue to live) on 'small premises' and shared some of the accommodation with other people who were not members of his household.

'Small premises' were defined as those which provided sepa-

rate residential accommodation for not more than two households under separate letting agreements in addition to the landlord's accommodation, or provided accommodation for not
more than twelve people in addition to the landlord and his
household. In November 1970 this number was reduced to six
people in addition to the landlord and his household. The Act
was also extended so that 'small premises' were exempted from
the application of the Act if (*a*) the landlord lived on the
premises and (*b*) the landlord shared relevant accommodation
(e.g. kitchen, bathroom and lavatory) with people other than
his own household.

In the most recent full year for which statistics are currently
available (1 April 1970 to 31 March 1971), the Board considered
151 complaints under Section 5 of the Act which deals with
housing. The outcome of the complaints is shown in Table 7.5.

Table 7.5

Subject	Total	Opinion: discrimination	Opinion: no discrimination	Others
Private housing (rent)	65	18	22	25
Private housing (sale)	22	3	18	1
Private housing (other)	30	2	18	10
Local authority housing	34	2	26	6
	151	25	84	42

Source: Select Committee on Race Relations and Immigration, *Housing*,
Vol. 3 (H.M.S.O., July 1971), p. 586.

Both the number of complaints made and the number of
cases of discrimination found proven seem low, and are reason
enough to presume that a great many cases of discrimination
are never reported to the Board. In areas of housing stress, in
particular, a coloured person who encounters a discriminating
landlord knows that the place could be let many times over
within a few hours. To complain is merely to cause trouble for
himself.

Nevertheless, in several instances the Board has been able to
deal with problems of great significance for the pattern of race
relations. For example, they were able to persuade Wolver-
hampton Borough Council to amend the practice which they
had formerly followed, of applying an increased period of qualification before entry to the housing list in the case of those born
outside the United Kingdom. And in a case before a County

Court in February 1971, they were able to secure a ruling about the practices which had been adopted by many accommodation bureaux. Della Nevitt of the London School of Economics emphasizes [21] how the Act has significantly affected the exercise of discretion in an area of the greatest importance for minorities.

My own experience of building society middle management officials is that one can rouse a passionate debate amongst a group of them by the mere mention of twilight area problems. Meetings I have addressed have divided almost equally 50 per cent *for* coloured savers and borrowers and 50 per cent against. The vehemence with which some managers defend the coloured population gives great hope for the future. I have been assured that families from the Caribbean area are 'better' savers, 'better' payers and 'better' householders than the indigenous population. Other managers will deny this but my general impression is that the Race Relations Act curbs those who wish to discriminate improperly; and the more open-minded managers are actually discriminating in favour of coloured applicants when funds are limited, because from experience they have found them to be a very responsible group of savers and borrowers. This seems a proper exercise of a manager's discretion.

Nevertheless, the Board has not been—and would not profess to be—able to deal with the underlying causes of discrimination in the housing market. The substantial discrimination in the private sector so dramatically revealed in the situation tests conducted in the course of the P.E.P. investigation will yield only slowly to the effects of legislation which must be, at least in part, educative in its efforts. A complaints-based procedure, although it may be apt—when it is used—for the remedying of individual grievances, does not provide the means for dealing with the structural handicaps which affect immigrants as a group, rather than as individuals. Many of the problems that affect black people in areas of high housing stress arise from these general difficulties, and although the Board has the power under Section 17 of the Act to make investigations on its own initiative into cases of discrimination which have not been the subject of individual complaints—and has employed them in cases affecting the public sector—it does not have the power to make the fundamental changes necessary to provide a lasting remedy.

Other Central Government Action

There is, however, another area of central government activity that does relate directly to these problems. This is the series of initiatives usually grouped together under the general title of the Urban Programme. The Urban Programme could in our view have very important consequences for the situation of all deprived people living in the inner city. It represents an attempt to improve the quality of life by direct intervention from the centre. We singled out earlier in the paper the situation of children in these areas: 70 per cent of the Programme's funds has been allocated for the provision of play centres, day nurseries and nursery classes. There is also considerable emphasis on the provision of aid and advice services, some of them relating specifically to housing; and, finally, there is separate provision made in a related programme for the parallel issue of community development.

It is arguable that the channelling of funds through local authorities has been one of the less satisfactory features of this programme, and that it has inhibited the growth of genuinely representative grass roots organizations, which are necessarily often in conflict with local authorities and thus unlikely to obtain their approval for funding purposes. There is evidence that local authorities and voluntary organizations are often in direct conflict with each other for money for projects, and such competition is made worse by the small amount of money made available under the whole of the Urban Programme scheme [22]. Nevertheless, the potential of the Urban Programme remains. Ultimately the solutions of many of the problems of deprived areas must come from below, from the inhabitants; they cannot be imposed from above. But the organizations that have appeared in such areas are often seriously handicapped by their lack of resources and expertise. We would strongly stress the importance of making such resources available, even—perhaps particularly—in areas where the organizations concerned have set their faces firmly against 'collaboration with the power structure'. We would argue that the existence of such organizations is a sign, not of breakdown, but of community cohesion which should be welcomed and wherever possible encouraged. But the clear implication is that such organizations cannot and should not be manipulated in order to establish goals different to those which they came into existence to achieve. As Robert Holman of Birmingham University has put it [23]:

> The specific role of the Urban Programme, I suggest, is to facili-
> tate the gaining of power by the deprived by funding their move-
> ments. In addition, it should stimulate their development in the
> most deprived areas of all, those so bereft of organisations that
> grants are never applied for.

One activity in which some of these organizations have become involved relates directly to housing: the setting up of voluntary housing advice services, and, in one or two cases, a move towards forming housing associations, organized on a co-ownership basis. The part that they can play in the provision of accommodation for groups suffering from specific handicaps and not catered for in the inner city housing market can be of some significance. Moreover such co-ownership schemes can provide the basis for genuine tenant participation. The provisions of the new Housing Act based on the White Paper *Fair Deal for Housing* [24] may, however, make it less easy for new associations to get going, since, as Miller and Filkin point out [25], where there are deficits between cost-less-subsidy and 'fair' rents, new associations will not be in a position to pool the rents from older properties.

Dispersal: The Ongoing Debate

In our view, the major debate that has taken place over the past few years—broadly, since Roy Jenkins produced his famous redefinition of integration in pluralist terms [26]—about the relative merits of concentration and dispersal is based on a misconception. No amount of dispersal by physical planning or inducement will ensure that people live fully integrated lives. Everyone, regardless of ethnic origin, exercises some selection over the social contacts that they value: most people choose to live within a fairly restricted—'concentrated', if you like—circle with broadly similar social characteristics. The important thing is that everyone should be free to choose, and to move outside such circles if they wish to do so: there should be as few constraints as possible on the exercise of choice by individuals.

To this extent, the resolution of the practical problems of limited access detailed in earlier sections are the first priority; and to talk about dispersal as a first aim of policy is to put the cart before the horse. The opportunity of freely exercising the option to disperse is not yet available; our first objective should be to provide it. This will mean making widely available information on which to base a choice, providing easier access to the particular institutions that can best provide it, and cutting down on the exercise of arbitrary powers by those who now take the crucial decisions about people's housing chances. When the options are opened up in this way, it will then be possible to talk more realistically about voluntary dispersal.

Nevertheless, although we would argue strongly for concentrating attention on short-term priorities that affect people's life-chances now, it is useful to attempt to get the long-range objectives into focus, and to consider the alternatives that may later open up. In evidence to the Cullingworth Committee, one of the present writers took the view that to argue for a policy of dispersal without any qualification was wrong, on at least three grounds. First, such a policy failed to distinguish between the different needs of different ethnic groups at different stages in the migration process. Second, it failed to allow for the fact that concentration confers certain positive benefits, especially during the earlier stages of a migration—communal support and the growth of special facilities in particular. And, third, he argued that a policy of directed dispersal is ultimately indefensible, because it introduces coercion into what should be essentially a matter of choice. The Committee, after quoting this evidence in some detail, came to broadly the same conclusion, stating that [27]:

> We are convinced that any policy of dispersal in the field of housing must be implemented with great sensitivity, with no element of compulsion or direction, and can proceed only at the pace of the needs and wishes of the people involved.

There are arguments on the other side that should not be brushed aside. First, it is clear that in certain circumstances dispersal can provide access to better material facilities. Data from 1966 Sample Census showed that the situation of those West Indians living in boroughs with low concentrations of West Indians was considerably better than that of those living in areas of high concentration (see Table 7.6) [28]. Furthermore, it is probable that the improvement in housing circumstances would be matched by access to better educational facilities. In

Table 7.6

Proportion of Households where Head was Born in the West Indies Living at Different Densities (Persons Per Room)

Persons Per Room	Concentrated Boroughs	Dispersed Boroughs
Under 0.5	4	15
0.5–0.74	15	23
0.75–0.99	8	14
1.00	27	22
1.0–1.50	20	16
over 1.50	26	10

Boroughs of high concentration are defined as those containing more than 5000 persons born in the West Indies—Brent, Hackney, Hammersmith, Haringey, Islington, Lambeth, Lewisham, Newham, Southwark, Wandsworth, Westminster.

Boroughs of low concentration are defined as those containing less than 2500 persons born in the West Indies—Barking, Barnet, Bexley, Bromley, Enfield, Greenwich, Harrow, Havering, Hillingdon, Hounslow, Kingston-upon-Thames, Merton, Redbridge, Richmond-upon-Thames, Sutton.

Sources: Special tabulations by the Research and Intelligence Unit, GLC, of 1966 Census.

view of the importance of equal educational opportunity in determining the future of the second generation of black Britons, this is an important consideration. Second, it now seems likely that some of the countervailing advantages of concentration have been exaggerated. In political terms, the fact that the numerical concentrations are not as great as is generally believed effectively removes any immediate possibility that the voting strength of minorities can be used to obtain political leverage or elect candidates from minority groups to local office or to Parliament. A partial exception can be glimpsed in one or two areas of Indian settlement, though even here there are sharp intra-communal divisions [29]. Third, there is real risk of an association being made between the presence of black minorities and the existence of poor facilities in a squalid environment. Such a connexion makes it easy to blame the minority concerned for creating the poor conditions with which they have to put up. If there were any serious prospect of eliminating the root causes of underprivilege forthwith, by the direct injection of substantial additional resources, this would matter less. But for the reasons given above in the discussion of the Urban Programme, this seems most unlikely.

The arguments are therefore finely balanced, and no clear cut conclusion is possible. But some misconceptions can be cleared away. In their evidence to the Select Committee, Lambeth Borough Council refer to three obstacles that have, in their experience, inhibited dispersal [30]. They argue, first, that dispersal may pose serious problems for officials and set them undesirable tasks—like setting and maintaining coloured quotas in 'dispersed' local authority estates. Second, they argue that dispersal is still rejected as a goal by the majority of West Indians because of the risks involved in 'pioneering'. Third, they argue that the skills necessary to obtain work in a 'dispersed' area are not present.

The first objection seems to be based on a misunderstanding. A policy of scattering blacks around council estates in exactly equal sized penny packets does not have any relationship to dispersal as we conceive it. Far more important is the breaking down of the remaining institutional barriers to the exercise of free choice. For example, it is of very great importance that categorical distinctions are not drawn between persons of different tenure categories when decisions are made about offering to rehouse residents of clearance areas. The evidence gathered by the Cullingworth Committee, and quoted above, shows that practice varies very widely. To decline to rehouse furnished tenants—among whom, as we have seen, coloured people are grossly over-represented—is to close off what will probably be the only real possibility of escape from the twilight area, thereby restricting freedom of choice in the most drastic possible way, and increasing, in all probability, the extent of involuntary concentration.

There are other constraints that hinder choice, even when people are offered rehousing. The Cullingworth Committee has drawn attention, in Chapter Three of their report, to the crucial role of housing visitors in determining where people are rehoused. At the same time, housing visitors had little or no training or common practice. In our experience, housing visitors themselves are frequently not equipped with information about the range of council housing available and the rents charged, which in turn makes it impossible for them to give the information necessary for people to make a genuine choice between types of housing and different locations. Training specifically for housing visitors and a willingness in local authorities to provide the information about rents, rent rebates and type of housing that people need to make a real choice, would be a significant step towards 'voluntary' dispersal or concentration. Local authorities could ensure that in future tenants really do know what type of housing is available: where necessary transport should be provided so that people can have a whistle-stop tour around the estates. Such transport is already provided for their employees by firms intending to move to new and expanding towns, and a few local authorities are intending to provide such services for their residents. But, even though the distances are much smaller, we suspect there are a great many immigrants living in areas of multiple deprivation who have never seen the local authority housing that lies in the 'leafy suburb' end of their borough. Even if, once they have seen it, they reject it in favour of greater concentration elsewhere, at least they themselves will have made that choice.

Another answer to this difficulty about dispersal that has been widely canvassed lies in increasing the opportunities for movement to new and expanding towns, which have for some time now taken 20 000 Londoners a year. On paper, many immigrants possess the skills that are at a premium in these towns—in 1966, over 40 per cent of the West Indians living in London were skilled workers. Initiatives have been taken both by local authorities and the new towns to ensure that the opportunities are more widely known among immigrants in London.

If, despite the efforts being mounted by public bodies of all kinds, coloured people continue to be, as they are now, grossly under-represented in new towns, then one conclusion would be that the persistent reluctance on the part of black and brown minorities to take the social and economic risk of dispersal from the inner city must be in part the consequence of the climate of race relations in Britain. It may be that there is an information gap (though efforts are being made to close it); there are also quite clearly some economic obstacles—though these are not peculiar to coloured people. If, even allowing for all these efforts, coloured people remain under-represented, it will be because of the anxieties to which Lambeth Borough Council refer in their evidence to the Select Committee on Race Relation and Immigration.

In these circumstances, to talk of dispersal as a policy goal is premature, and it may be that we should not only be re-examining the short-range alternatives detailed above but also fundamentally rethinking the whole broad question of race relations in Britain, and how change can be achieved.

Some Conclusions

We have set out in this paper to explore an apparently straightforward issue; but our discussion of it has involved us in considering a whole series of complex issues and the deploying of a good deal of detailed evidence. But briefly, and at the risk of gross over-simplification, we would summarize what we have said so far as follows:

The distribution of housing and different types of housing tenure are of importance in determining the quality of life of black and brown people in Britain, but has to be seen within the context of constraints within the economic system: restriction of employment and educational opportunity for all groups living and working in run-down areas and industries, low wages in certain sectors and unemployment.

Moreover, immigrants are in a special position in the housing market, to the extent that discrimination on racial grounds exists and is reflected in the restrictions on the standard and location of housing available to them. But they are also the victims of the general handicaps that affect all the inhabitants of the stress areas in which they are largely to be found.

Third, we do not at present have black ghettos, in the American sense. There are, in fact, other situations in the British Isles that correspond far more closely to the American models—the Catholic enclaves in Northern Ireland, for example—and groups as grossly underprivileged as certain non-white groups in the United States, like the gypsies. But in any event the probability is that there will be an increasing concentration of coloured people in a limited number of areas. The argument as to whether this is a desirable process or not is a complex one, on which no clear-cut conclusion can be reached.

The Government has tended to concentrate on policies which might ameliorate some of the problems of grossly deprived areas, on an area basis. The Educational Priority Area programme, the Urban Programme, the Community Development Project, local authority slum clearance programmes, all set out to alleviate territorial injustice and deprivations. Social security payments (in particular the Family Income Supplement) and the Rent Acts are examples of efforts to counteract inequalities in the housing and employment markets. But such policies are undermined by unemployment, particularly where it is highly localized as on Clydeside, and continued insecurity for furnished tenants. Where it has had any direct policy about race relations, central government has leant towards encouraging the break-up of concentrations of immigrants, particularly in the schools, on the grounds that black and white ought to mix; and a variant of this policy has recently been canvassed at a local authority level to encourage social class mixing by allowing private developers and housing associations access for building purposes to council-owned land. This, it is suggested, will leaven otherwise working-class areas with the necessary middle-class qualities of articulate leadership. But such attacks on concentration by public intervention, especially in the housing field, where middle-class occupation is encouraged in what could otherwise be areas of total working-class occupation, in effect maintain inequalities and deprivations by disallowing working-class claims to better housing in favour of the fulfilment of a planner's dream of 'social mix'. Thus attacks on concentration can, in some cases, actually counteract attacks on deprivation.

As far as London is concerned, the particular position of the different immigrant groups needs to be seen in the context of the broader social and economic problems of the metropolis. The apparent malaise revealed by evidence of population declining by migration, both of the skilled and unskilled; the danger that the loss of population will lead to significant damage to the economic infrastructure that sustains the capital; the contest between the prosperous and the poor for accommodation in the inner areas, where land prices are the highest in the country: all these factors may have crucial consequences.

It is true that immigrants are substantially represented among owner occupiers. But what appears at first sight to be a form of protection against the worst consequences of insecurity produced by the workings of the housing market may in practice provide little or no protection. Many immigrant householders who have bought property in inner areas will find themselves caught up in redevelopment schemes. Even when they are not, the security that property ownership would normally confer may turn out to be illusory if adequate job opportunities are not available for the head of household. But even here many Indian families will be cushioned by the support provided by the extended family; and in many households the children of migrants will shortly be reaching wage-earning age and making substantial contributions to household income.

But although the overall prospects for black and brown people in London are not necessarily wholly depressing, it is a mistake to place too much emphasis on the aggregate perform-ance of immigrants as a whole. The evidence so far available suggests that the effect of the economic advance that has taken place implies a tilting of the incipient colour line in this society rather than a crumbling. It is a matter for speculation whether this situation will lead to the settling in of black and brown minorities, as a bloc, at a certain point in the social class struc-ture of our society or whether internal ethnic divisions will re-sult in different ethnic groups following different patterns. A picture which at first sight seems less disturbing than it is often painted may conceal the growth of a sub-group of the severely underprivileged within the general population. The Pakistani—or Bengali—single man isolated in the shrinking rented sector and contending with insecurity and rising rents; and the young West Indian couple with small children, totally unable to com-mand the financial resources that would enable them to afford the house they want to buy, at current London prices: their problems are going to be especially difficult to resolve, in any foreseeable circumstances. They are not unique: and it may well be that solutions, when they come, will be reached in the context of a concerted assault on the problems of poverty in our society. But on present indications it is difficult to see such an assault being mounted on a sufficient scale to mop up the persistent pockets of underprivilege that still disfigure London.

References

1. See for example HILLMAN, JUDY (ed.), *Planning for London* (Harmondsworth: Penguin, 1971), p. 14.
2. DANIEL, W. W., *Racial Discrimination in England* (Harmondsworth: Penguin, 1968).
3. Select Committee on Race Relations and Immigration, *Housing*, Vol. 2, (London: H.M.S.O., July 1971), p. 68.
4. JOHN, AUGUSTINE, *Race in the Inner City* (London: Runnymede Trust, 1970).
5. PEACH, G. C. K., *West Indian Migration: A Social Geography* (Oxford University Press for Institute of Race Relations, 1968).
6. McPHERSON, KLIM and GAITSKELL, JULIA, *Immigrants and Employment: Two Case Studies in East London and in Croydon* (Institute of Race Relations, 1969).
7. BURNEY, ELIZABETH, *Housing on Trial* (Oxford University Press for Institute of Race Relations, 1967).
8. Report of the Committee on Housing in Greater London (Milner Holland Report), Cmnd. 2605, (London: H.M.S.O., 1965).
9. REX, JOHN and MOORE, ROBERT, *Race, Community and Conflict: a study of Sparkbrook* (Oxford University Press for Institute of Race Relations, 1968).
10. *Interim Report: Notting Hill Housing Survey* (Notting Hill Housing Service, 1969).
11. DEAKIN, N., *et al.*, *Colour, Citizenship and British Society* (London: Panther, 1970).
12. HADDON, ROY F., 'A minority in a welfare state society: location of West Indians in the London housing market', *The New Atlantis*, 1970, **2**, No. 1.
13. Report of the Committee on the Rent Acts, Cmnd. 4609 (London: H.M.S.O., March 1971), ch. 20.
14. *The Rent Acts and the Housing Market in North Kensington* Memorandum of Evidence to the Francis Committee (Notting Hill Housing Service and Research Group, May 1970), p. 49.
15. *Ibid.*, p. 23.
16. Cullingworth Committee, *Council Housing: Purposes, Procedures and Priorities* (London: H.M.S.O., 1969).
17. Report of the Committee on the Rent Acts, *op. cit.*, p. 298.
18. Select Committee on Race Relations and Immigration (H.M.S.O., July 1971).
19. CULLINGWORTH, J. B., *Report to the Minister of Housing and Local Government on proposals for the transfer of GLC housing to the London boroughs* (Ministry of Housing & Local Government, 1970).
20. Select Committee on Race Relations and Immigration, *op. cit.*, vol. 1, p. 52.
21. NEVITT, DELLA, 'Housing and the Race Relations Act', *Venture*, *23*, no. 1, Fabian Society, January 1971.
22. See SMITH, TERESA and SMITH, GEORGE, 'Urban First Aid', *New Society*, 30 December 1971.

23. HOLMAN, ROBERT, 'The Urban Programme', *Venture,* **23**, no. 1, Fabian Society, January 1971.

24. *Fair Deal for Housing,* Cmnd. 4728 (London: H.M.S.O., July 1971).

25. MILLER, Kay M. and FILKIN, CAMILLA J., *Housing Associations —Three Surveys,* University of Birmingham, Centre for Urban and Regional Studies, Research Memorandum no. 7, September 1971.

26. 'Equal opportunity, accompanied by cultural diversity, in an atmosphere of mutual tolerance', in an address given to a meeting of the Voluntary Liaison Committees on 23 May 1966.

27. Cullingworth Committee *op. cit.,* p. 135.

28. This table, and the supporting argument, comes from DEAKIN, N. and COHEN, B. G., 'Dispersal and Choice', *Environment and Planning,* **2**, pp. 193–201.

29. JOHN, DEWITT, *Indian Workers' Associations in Britain,* Oxford, 1969.

30. Select Committee on Race Relations and Immigration, *op. cit.,* vol. 2, p. 46.

Chapter Eight

Some Sociological Implications of Slum Clearance Programmes

B. JOHN PARKER

Summary

Over the past twenty years, slum clearance has occupied a very important place in our national housing priorities. But as clearance has proceeded, devastating large tracts of old but familiar housing, many people have queried the wisdom of destroying existing communities on such a large scale. Among the fears expressed are those which suggest that the life style of the slum dweller has a certain romantic quality which is worthy of preservation, or more seriously that it provides valuable support mechanisms for poor and deprived people. It is also suggested that rehousing from slums to suburban housing estates causes significant and detrimental effects on those forced to move. This paper reviews research into these matters.

The evidence reviewed throws up contradictory findings, but on the whole it is suggested that the break up of working-class communities by slum clearance has no more than a minor and short-term effect on most people. It is important to place slum clearance within the context of other social changes which are much more important, for example, the economic progress of recent years has helped to reduce the interdependence of kin and neighbours, and the extended family group is fast disappearing. For many years middle-class and better off working-class families have been voluntarily migrating away from the inner city to suburban locations, and there is some survey evidence to indicate that slum dwellers share the general desire for better housing and suburban living. Evidence of mental ill health arising from rehousing from slum to suburb is conflicting but seems to indicate that serious difficulties are experienced by only a minority and that these difficulties do not last.

Although generally we can conclude that the effects of slum clearance are not serious we must be particularly cautious about the problems posed by transitional areas. Here there may be concentrations of ethnic minorities, newcomers to the city, the poor and deprived and deviants. In these situations the likely consequences of large scale slum clearance are much less easy to judge. The social life of these 'communities' is likely to be much more complex than it is in the traditional working-class slum areas and the inhabitants much more susceptible to disturbance. Generally the whole area of study requires much more research effort.

Introduction

Evidence of the scale and importance of slum clearance and urban renewal to our contemporary society are dramatic and immediate. Go to the run-down residential areas which almost inevitably cluster around the central business districts of our major cities and one soon finds large cleared sites, boarded-up houses and new residences emerging from the rubble. Slum clearance has of course occupied an important role in our housing policy for over a hundred years, but over the last two decades, it has become more dominant as local authorities, encouraged by central government subsidies, have become involved in a sustained drive to clear away their outworn houses. All the evidence suggests that these processes will continue for many years to come, for a recent survey has shown that there are still 1.2 million unfit houses in the country, and the present government has expressed its commitment to securing the rapid clearance of all slums, a commitment it has backed up by providing for generous subsidies in the Housing Finance Act. An indication of the scale of the problem in London has been illustrated by the house condition survey carried out in 1967 which found that the number of houses becoming obsolete seems to double each seven years.

But as people see once familiar landmarks disappearing rapidly before their eyes, misgivings are bound to arise and from time to time doubts about the social consequences of these programmes are expressed. A whole range of questions is raised. Are we destroying an important social environment of value to the people who live there? Are the new estates built to house those displaced, many of which are located on the periphery of town, far away from the slums they are replacing, an adequate substitute for what has been lost? What of the people displaced, do they really want to move? Are their interests protected by the local authorities responsible for the scheme, and are they properly compensated? Issues like this are widely debated and quite regularly featured in the press and on radio and television programmes.

The usefulness of these debates is often not assisted by the existence of a number of popular stereotyped images of the slum. One version sees them as rather quaint friendly places, rather like Granada Television's 'Coronation Street', which are worthy of preservation because of their unique social character. Another sees them as places of vice, crime and anti-social behaviour of all kinds, and this latter view more often than not colours the attitude of suburbanites who think that the slum dwellers have socially unacceptable habits which render them undesirable as neighbours. The resistance of the Outer London suburban boroughs to housing people from areas of housing stress in Inner London bears witness that attitudes of this kind are not completely dead.

It would be wrong, however, to assume that opposition to slum clearance is only based upon popular mythology. People from a wide range of responsible professions have reflected the general concern that some desirable qualities of social life in slums will be lost. Town planners, for example, have for many years been almost obsessively preoccupied with the idea of fostering 'community feeling' following a brand of determinism strongly expressed in the neighbourhood unit concept, which was such a characteristic feature of so many early development plans. Although the original neighbourhood unit idea has become largely discredited as a planning concept upon which new estates should be designed [1], this has not prevented continued doubts being expressed about the consequences of destroying existing 'communities', particularly in slum areas which may have a social life shaped by over a hundred years of history. Social and community workers have often shared these doubts, for example, Birmingham [2], in evidence to the Greater London Development Plan enquiry, pointed out some of the possible dangers arising from the disruption of existing patterns of community life in the East End of London.

Behind these misgivings is an implication that there is a quality to the social life of the slum which has some intrinsic value worthy of preservation, and also that the alternatives available are lacking this desirable characteristic. At the most frivolous level this view reflects a romantic and nostalgic attachment to a way of life which is fast changing but it also reflects a much deeper and more serious concern that slum life has distinctive features which provide desirable or even necessary support for people who are poor and deprived in other ways, i.e. the slum performs a social function. Questions of this sort have been of interest to sociologists for many years and there is a considerable volume of theoretical and empirical literature available. This chapter reviews some of this literature in an attempt to throw light on two main questions; first what is it in social terms that we are destroying when we clear slums; and second what is the evidence for significant changes in the way of life of people rehoused and can any of these changes be in any way regarded as detrimental. These two questions are related because we can reasonably hypothesize that if the slum community performs valuable functions for its inhabitants then we could expect some overt signs of maladjustment on the part of those disturbed and rehoused elsewhere.

The City

Concern among intellectuals about the social consequences of uprooting people from urban 'communities' is relatively recent and is something of an about face, for from the mid-nineteenth century onwards writers were more worried about the social consequences of the trend to an urbanized society from a folk society. In particular, there was a widely held notion that the change from a predominantly rural to a predominantly urban society meant a change from a personal to an impersonal life style which encouraged a state of social disorganization or anomie brought about by removal from well regulated village communities which provided all their inhabitants with a structured frame of reference which governed all their social actions. Tonnies [3] saw society moving from a social system based upon close and satisfying personal relationships (gemeinschaft) to one based upon impersonal, transitory and superficial relationships (gesellschaft). Durkheim [4] took a more optimistic view considering that 'anomie' although a danger, was an abnormal feature of the development of society brought about by exceptional circumstances such as recurring financial and economic crises and too rapid industrialization.

Sociologists writing after Durkheim, however, concluded that anomie was an essential characteristic of city life. Redfield [5] described urban society as disorganized and less harmonious than folk society and considered the term urban community was a contradiction. Park and Burgess [6] attributed the social problems of cities to the transition of great masses of population from a society based upon primary group relationships into the looser and less controlled existence of life in urban areas. The Chicago School of Sociology in the 1920s to '30s stressed the importance of social disorganization in the city especially in slums and other downtown areas, and their views were summed up by Wirth [7] in an essay written in 1938. In this he attempts a sociological definition of the city based upon folk society-urban society contrasts, and he uses terms like superficiality, anonymity and transitory to describe the character of social relationships in the city and says that 'overwhelmingly the city dweller is not a home owner, and since a transitory habitat does not generate binding traditions and sentiments, only rarely is he truly a neighbour'.

Criticisms of the Chicago School are well known and are most succinctly summarized by Gans [8] who re-analyses Wirth's essay and concludes that his view of the urban way of life applies only, and then not too accurately, to residents of the inner city. He points out that many of the empirical studies upon which Wirth's formulations are based were conducted in the inner city in rather specialized types of area, typically slums invaded by waves of recently arrived European immigrants. Furthermore within the city fairly homogenous groups emerge with social and cultural cohesion and located in fairly well-defined areas which shield their members from the disadvantages suggested by Wirth of size, density and heterogeneity. Gans suggests that the way of life of many neighbourhoods within a town may be described as quasi primary. Indeed a considerable number of empirical studies have shown that within the city primary contacts are still important [9], thus while such sociologists as Merton [10] would still use the concept of anomie to explain various forms of social deviancy few would regard it as an essential or harmful general feature of urban life.

The Slum

Definitions

In the Oxford Dictionary [11] we find a slum defined as 'a street, alley, court, etc., situated in a crowded district of a town or city and inhabited by people of a low class or by the very poor; a number of these streets or courts forming a thickly populated neighbourhood or district of a squalid and wretched character'. A definition which rather clearly illustrates the range of value judgements involved. Seeley [12] points out that defining the slum is not a matter of absolutes, but that the slum as a social fact is judged by subjective and relative criteria. Gans [13] has stressed that the term is evaluative rather than analytical and that any definition must be related explicitly or implicitly to the standards of the age, which of course can vary considerably over even relatively short periods of time. Clinard [14] has made an interesting attempt to focus attention on to the life style of the slum dweller rather than on the physical and social indices of decay which are normally applied. He suggests that a slum is characterized by a specific way of life 'a subculture with a set of norms and values which is reflected in poor sanitation and health practices, deviant behaviour, and characteristic attributes of apathy and social isolation. People who live in slum areas are isolated from the general power structures and are regarded as inferior, and slum dwellers, in turn, harbour suspicions of the outside world.'

The slum then is a notion which depends upon a number of

rather loose concepts which makes it difficult to define operationally. The English housing law has for the most part concentrated upon physical criteria, for example, the 1957 Housing Act states that 'a house shall be deemed to be unfit for human habitation if and only if it is so far deficient in one or more of the following matters as to be not reasonably suitable for occupation; repair, stability, freedom from damp, natural lighting, ventilation, water supply, drainage and sanitary conveniences, facilities for storage, preparation for cooking of food, and for the disposal of waste water'. The Act further defines clearance areas in which the houses are unfit for human habitation, or 'are by reason of their bad arrangement or narrowness or bad arrangements of the streets, dangerous, or injurious to the health of the inhabitants of the area, and that of the other buildings, if any, in the area are for a like reason dangerous or injurious to the health of the said inhabitants'. This definition is directly descended from the earliest slum clearance legislation which was very firmly based upon sanitary principles, yet even so it provides the legal basis of much of the housing redevelopment carried out in the inner areas of our cities today, and as a result most of the slums cleared in this country, until relatively recently, have been traditional two-storey working-class cottages.

It is only recently that official definitions of slums and perceptions of their problems have widened, although in these cases a variety of terms serving as euphemisms for slum have been used. Of course, for many years local authorities have had powers to deal with problems like overcrowding and multi-occupied premises, but for the most part, these have been little used. But over the last ten years as a result of a series of Government sponsored reports, there has been increasing evidence of the need for a much wider and more comprehensive set of criteria by which slums are defined. For example, the Milner Holland Committee [15] emphasized that poor housing conditions in London were no longer restricted to the traditional working-class cottage areas, nor were they restricted only to the very poor but that the worst conditions were in dwellings which were structurally sound but which had become slums as a result of over use and overcrowding. Also the Plowden Committee [16] described the poor physical amenities of many primary schools in inner areas and introduced the concept of educational priority areas. As a result of these broadened perceptions of the nature of the slum problem, a much wider range of policies are being implemented; the renewed emphasis on rehabilitation, concern with alleviating the causes of poverty, greater efforts to ameliorate overcrowding, the Government's urban programme and community development projects are all examples of this trend.

The Slum Community

Hillery [17] reviewing over ninety definitions of community found little agreement between any of them. It would seem therefore a somewhat fruitless task to attempt any kind of precise definition of a slum community. It would appear more useful to attempt a description of the social and demographic characteristics of areas which have typically been regarded as slums, to outline some of the features which have been recognized as characteristic of the social life in the slum, and to review the theories which have sought to explain these characteristic features. Gittus [18] has emphasized that in this country it is necessary to distinguish between two distinctive types of decaying area; the first characterized by the inadequacy and obsolescence of the buildings themselves, and which have been slums from the time they were built; and the second, where the houses were originally built for upper- and middle-class occupation but whose social character has changed through the retreat of their original occupiers to the suburbs and their subsequent multi-occupation or conversion into flats. The former type are termed residual areas and the latter transitional. The distinction is important because there are sociological differences between the two types of area. The residual areas in London typified by the East End and Southwark tend to have an average proportion of families with young children, high fertility rates and a low ratio of females. These are traditional working-class areas with a homogeneous social class composition and the majority of men working in the lower occupational grades. The transitional areas, typically Islington and North Kensington, have low fertility, a high female sex ratio and a high proportion of young single adult households. They are also areas which may have a high foreign born element and an above average proportion of newcomers to the city. They frequently have a social-class composition which is more varied than average. This sort of area with its furnished flats and bed-sits, is a place where newcomers to the city get their first foot-hold in the housing market. Although it is plain that these differences have sociological significance, it is perhaps necessary to add that there are also similarities between the two types of area. The majority of people living in them are working class and whether they be newcomers, or long standing residents, they share this common attribute and all the social consequences which flow from it. Furthermore, we may regard the two kinds of area as ideal types which are rarely, if ever, found in pure form. Fried and Gleisher [19], when reviewing the results of American empirical research in this field, felt confident that they could see strong similarities between different kinds of slum area.

A wide range of studies have described the characteristic ways of life of working-class people living in slum communities. These studies have shown a remarkable degree of similarity in some of the essential elements of social life between such widely differing areas as West End, Boston and Bethnal Green [20]. A somewhat simplified 'traditional' pattern of working-class life in such areas may be summarized thus: it is family and com-munity oriented, there is sharp sex segregation in family roles, and husbands and wives tend to lead rather separate lives. Particular value is placed upon kinship and neighbour re-lations, with perhaps the most significant social relationship being between the mother and the married daughter. The term 'matrilocal' has been applied to this life style.

Social Theories

A number of theories have been developed seeking to explain this characteristic form of social life in the slum. Some of these depend on the idea that the pattern of social life performs a function which is useful and necessary for the individuals who live there. One group of theories in this category stress the transitional function of slum communities as places where strangers to the city learn about and adjust to urban ways of living; and another group emphasizes the utility of the distinc-tive life style as a mechanism built up over the years as a defence against continual poverty and hardship. Other theories pay less attention to functions but seek to explain the social life of the slums in terms of constraints either cultural or situational which act as a barrier to upward social mobility for those trapped in decaying areas.

It was the Chicago sociologists who first developed the notion that slums could provide an initial base from which rural immigrants could start to integrate themselves into city life. They pointed out the importance of migrations to the growth of the city, and also the fact that most migrants were from rural areas and many were also from abroad and with low educational attainments. They were forced, therefore, to crowd into deteriorating slum tenements or into the large houses of the better-off, converted for multi-occupation, in areas which became associated with extremes of poverty, disease and social pathology. It was postulated that these symptoms of social disorganizations were consequent upon too rapid a transition from a rural to an urban environment and this proposition was supported by the fact that as each migrant wave prospered so it moved outwards and the symptoms of disorganization declined.

This idea has been taken up again more recently in a series of papers published as a result of a study carried out in Boston's West End, and all of which have warned of possible dangers resulting from the destruction of working-class communities by forced relocation. Fried and Gleisher [19] stress the importance of locality to the working class and the way in which individuals closely identify themselves with their local area and of the importance to their lives of the dense system of social networks based upon kinship and neighbour relations. The use of the street as a physical extension of the home, as a place to meet and talk is quoted as an example of this. Ryan [21] in his paper, develops the idea that the inhabitants of the West End subscribe to a sub-socio cultural system at variance with dominant American values. These sub-cultural values are constantly challenged by outside influences such as radio and television, but the essential rightness of local values are almost ritually reinforced whenever social interaction between groups of people in the West End takes place.

Perhaps the most important of this series of papers, is that by Fried [22] who, echoing the Chicago school, develops the concept of preparedness for displacement and found that such preparedness was closely related to social class and pre-displacement situation. He concludes that for many working-class people displacement through slum clearance and re-housing comes too soon and causes undue stress. This paper is undoubtedly an important contribution, but, in that it stresses a rural-urban contrast, we must doubt its applicability in a setting like the East End of London, which has experienced little rural migration for fifty years or so (the rural transition having taken place at the end of the last century). Thus Fried's work may be a partial explanation of the Chicago situation, but lacks general applicability.

Rex [23] has used a similar proposition as part of a conflict model designed to explain the sociology of the zone of transition. This postulates an ideal type of immigrant, newly arrived in the city and going through the first stages of adjustment to the new urban society in which he finds himself. In these circumstances, the immigrant is passing through a difficult but transitional stage between integration in his home community and integration with the city. He therefore turns naturally to his fellow immigrants from his own area, with whom he shares a linguistic and cultural meaning and becomes a member of a small group which perform important functions for him, such as solving personal problems and discussing adjustment to the host society. Gradually the immigrant becomes less dependent on such groups as he grows more confident in the new community and eventually he is able to dispense entirely with this kind of primary community.

Young and Willmott [9], in their study of Bethnal Green, describe the matrilocal working-class community, and suggest that some of the essential characteristics of this system are due to the insecurity resulting from widespread unemployment, poverty and early death which are so much part of the history of this area. They conclude that most people do not wish to leave the East End because of their deep rooted and long lasting attachment to their families and advocate more emphasis on renewal rather than redevelopment and lettings policies which allow the movement of street and kinship groups as a whole which 'would enable the city to be rebuilt without squandering the fruits of social cohesion'.

Vereker, Mays, Gittus and Broady [24], however, come to different conclusions following their study of Crown Street,

Liverpool. Two types of area are identified from this survey, one a relatively homogeneous working-class area (residual), and the other a previously upper-class area in decline (transitional). They found a striking dichotomy in the desire to move away from the area between the high proportion who wished to move in the stable area and the low proportion who wished to leave the more socially disturbed transitional area. They seek to explain the greater satisfaction found in the transitional area, by suggesting that such areas function in a way which may satisfy some of the basic requirements of the population. In the residual areas, however, they consider that many of the residents no longer regard their surroundings as adequate in the light of alternatives which their improved economic circumstances permitted, and conclude from this that the influence of the close knit matrilocal life style is of lesser importance than the attainment of better housing on suburban estates.

In recent years a number of writers have developed theories which seek to explain the sociology of the slum in terms of constraints which limit the life chances of people born into these situations. Some emphasize the importance of the sub-culture of poverty as a means of preventing upward social mobility, while others have stressed the importance of structural barriers erected within the social system which prevent people from breaking away from slum conditions. One form of the sub-culture of poverty argument is the cycle of poverty theory which suggests that the poor or deprived are unable to break away from their situation in society because low income and occupational skills reduce their ability to participate in the wider society.

This eventually leads to negative attitudes to wider society and to behavioural patterns which reinforce their inability to escape. An alternative viewpoint places more emphasis on the consequences of the class system, which restricts life chances through the distribution of urban resources and the controls of social gatekeepers. This approach has led to empirical studies [25] and indeed Pahl [26] has suggested a redefinition of urban sociology which strongly advocates this approach.

In America a strong discussion of these issues has been stimulated by the poverty programme and the plight of the deprived in cities [27]. Gans [28] has divided the views of those involved in this debate into two principal schools of thought—those who take a situational view of social change and who believe that people respond to situations and opportunities made available to them, and change their behaviour accordingly; and those who take a cultural view of social change, which suggests that people react to change in terms of prior values and behaviour patterns and adopt only those which fit in with their own culture. Oscar Lewis [29] for example, strongly argues that behaviour conditioned by culture can be an important causal factor to poverty. He feels that the poor have a set of behavioural and attitudinal norms which resist change. These norms which he considers grew up as a defence mechanism against their deprived and marginal social status, have become so internalized as to perpetuate their poverty in spite of public policies designed to assist them.

Gans criticizes both schools regarding the 'situational view' as being too simple, because individuals respond to situations in different ways, and that even within a fairly well defined subcultural group such as the working class, there are a great variety of different types of person. But the brunt of Gans's attack is on those who adopt the cultural view of change. He considers that the orientation of this school is towards behavioural norms, but they pay little or no regard to aspirations —or values which express the desire for alternative forms of behaviour. Walter Miller [30] for example thinks that the aspirations of the working class are for their own culture. Gans considers that the views of the behaviourists originates from their intellectual origins in anthropology and the study of preliterate societies, and points out that in America the poor may be fatalists but this is not because they have no idea of alternatives.

In Gans's view, there are enough data to affirm the existence of a gap between aspirational norms and behavioural norms. In a pluralist society, aspirations diffuse freely between groups and he suggests that the poor retain the aspirations of the affluent society while having a much reduced range of options open to them. The culturalists are also criticized for taking too static a view of culture. Gans sees culture as a response to economic and social conditions which are situational in origin. His view is that 'some behavioural norms are more persistent than others, but over the long run, all the norms and aspirations by which people live are non-persistent; they rise and fall with changes in situations'. Norms vary in depth and intensity with which they are held, some are built into personality structure and a generation or more of living in a new situation may not dislodge them, others disappear quickly in a changed situation.

Housing Aspirations of Slum Dwellers

Social surveys provide us with some guides to the aspirations of slum dwellers, at least as far as their desire to move away from the area is concerned. The interpretation of the results of these surveys is, however, very difficult. To the respondents, the question of a move is often hypothetical and unless placed in a very specific context can produce very misleading results. Even more serious difficulties arise because of differences between surveys in the way questions are asked and the importance attached to the particular question about moving and attachment to the area. In view of these difficulties, it is hardly surprising that the results of such surveys are somewhat contradictory.

Jennings [31] in Bristol found that many inhabitants were 'only too conscious of the poor structural conditions of their own homes'. She found some reluctance to move, but the only organized opposition to the redevelopment proposals was primarily designed to secure amelioration of the disturbance caused by the move; she suggests that the lack of opposition compared with that encountered in some northern industrial towns can be attributed to the generally high level of housing in Bristol, so that most people were well aware of better alternatives. However, in surveys carried out in typical working-class areas in two small Lancashire towns [32], a reluctance to move was indicated. In Deeplish, 60 per cent were very well satisfied with their house and about the same proportion were well satisfied with the neighbourhood. In St. Mary's, Oldham, there was evidence of wider discontent with the houses, but a strong desire to stay in the neighbourhood after redevelopment. Norman Dennis [33] in Sunderland found 40 per cent very satisfied with their living conditions, but this figure was as high as 70 per cent among owner occupiers.

In larger towns, however, there seems to be much more evidence of discontent. In Leeds, Wilkinson and Sigsworth [34] found 82 per cent in favour of a move, and only 16 per cent against, while Coates and Silburn [35] in St. Anne's, Nottingham, found 66 per cent of their sample were glad the area was scheduled for redevelopment and nearly 50 per cent wanted to leave the area altogether. They also report the results of a Nottingham Corporation Survey which showed 38 per cent would not mind moving right away from the area. Liverpool Corporation [36] in its survey of the inner ring of the city found about half the households wanted to move away from their present locality, particularly willing to move were young people and car owners. Rex and Moore, in Sparkbrook [37], found a majority of the English, 77 per cent of men and 81 per cent of women, would prefer not to be in Sparkbrook and that while some people were held by ties of property, kinship or loyalty to the area, the majority stayed because of their sheer inability to move. The majority of the Irish also wanted to move out, but West Indians showed signs of a more ambivalent attitude, being split evenly on the desire to stay or move out.

Conflict in the Slum

Our discussion of the slum community cannot be complete without reference to conflict, for it is easy to romanticize about the matrilocal way of life and ignore the fact that slums are areas where social tension can be very high. In fact it may be that the close knit community which expects conformity from its members and exercises strong sanctions against those who break the rules will generate conflicts of greater intensity than those in wider society where things are less strictly controlled. Juvenile delinquency for example is more common in respectable working-class areas like the East End of London than in other areas.

Class, race, competition for houses and jobs are all potential sources of conflict. In some situations these conflicts can reach high levels of intensity, for example the race riots of Notting Hill in 1958 and more recently the so called class war in the Barnsbury area of Islington. Rex following his study with Moore in Sparkbrook, Birmingham [37] would go as far as to explain the sociology of the zone of transition in terms of conflict between housing classes [23]. But some American writers claim to have found a surprising degree of tolerance between disparate groups living in slum areas. Both Gans [20] and Ryan [21] comment upon this, while Suttles [38] in Chicago found that, although Mexicans, Puerto Ricans, Negroes and Italians living in the Addams area formed separate groups and were occasionally in conflict, there seemed to be a general assumption on everyone's part that the area had a unity to it and that in the face of real or imagined threats from outsiders they had little alternative but to act together. Suttles considers that the fact that all groups had to live in close proximity to each other in a small area meant that they simply had to get on together.

Of course, the existence of conflict within slum areas of itself cannot be used as an argument either for or against slum clearance, for many would argue that conflict is an essential part of the social system. What is important is that the nature and causes of conflicts should be understood so that hand in hand with slum clearance other policies are adopted which will tend to resolve conflicts rather than aggravate them.

The Suburb

For those disturbed by slum clearance, rehousing is a major event. Inevitably it involves the disruption of ways of life which may have developed over many years. But is there any evidence to suggest that such forced moves give rise to undesirable social consequences? Obviously the nature of the change experienced varies greatly from one individual to another. A typical local authority will own a range of houses from brand new to the very old purchased in advance of slum clearance, and it will use this stock of houses to rehouse most of the people affected by clearance schemes. However, because most new houses are built in suburban locations and because the majority of council houses have been built since 1920 and because more often than not densities are lowered on redevelopment, there is a general tendency towards suburbanization as a consequence of clearance.

A number of studies have attempted to look at the effects of relocation from slums to suburbia, but there are quite serious difficulties over the methodology of this kind of study. Ideally, we have to find subjects for study who are to be rehoused, follow them over many years of post relocation experience and also at the same time find a control group with matched characteristics, who are not rehoused and remain in slums—a well nigh impossible task. Another possible approach is to make comparative studies of the old and new housing estates and to observe the differences between them. In these cases, however, the bias occasioned by individual choice and by bureaucratic selection procedures, causes difficulty, and of course all those rehoused from slums are not moved to new estates. It is also difficult in these instances to decide to what extent observed differences are due to relocation or to other characteristics which give rise to variation between areas.

It is reasonable to suppose that one of the consequences of relocation from a slum to a suburb would be change in the behavioural patterns of the relocatee to fit into a more suburban way of life. In Scotland, a post relocation survey was carried out by Hole [39]. Initial reactions to the new dwellings were found to be good, but to the estate, poor. This study also noticed reduced kinship visits and withdrawal from neighbouring. Hole suggests that the methods of selecting tenants may have influenced this pattern. Most people adjusted to their new situation by friendly but reserved intercourse with neighbours, and she considers that people lacked an ideology of behaviour in which suitable social relationships could be developed. Young and Willmott [9], in their survey of a new estate housing East End overspill, also commented on the emergence of a more home centred pattern of life with fewer kinship visits and less friendly relations with neighbours.

Norman Dennis [1] has argued, however, that on new estates one observes in exaggerated form social changes which are occurring much more widely throughout society and that 'it is only a matter of time before our Bethnal Greens become socially indistinguishable from housing estates'.

This view is supported by data gathered by Hall and Whittaker [40]. In a survey of a slum area, a new estate built on an old slum site and an overspill estate they found that many people complained about the loss of the old 'community spirit', but that this complaint was just as strong in the slum area as on the new overspill estate and they conclude that the loss of community was really part of the 'things ain't what they used to be' syndrome. They also suggest that rehousing was not the direct cause of any change in social behaviour, but that it could be attributed to more general social changes in our society which affect both old and new areas. They point out four factors which could account for these changes; the great reduction in overcrowding which must change the quality of life in slum areas; the fact that poverty is much less widespread and tends to be relative rather than absolute; that probably the slums never were quite as neighbourly as people remember them; and lastly there are many more alternative ways which people can spend their leisure time than in less affluent times. Hall and Whittaker acknowledge that life is probably much more family centred on new housing estates than it used to be, but point out that this is also true of the slum areas. If this is the pattern which is emerging we may applaud or deplore the trend but the question of whether slum clearance contributes to this process is largely irrelevant because it is happening with or without it.

A much more serious proposition is that rehousing can cause stress which leads to increased rates of mental illness. One hypothesis suggests that individuals forced to move away from familiar surroundings, their kinship ties and the formal and informal associations which help them to organize their lives and possibly asked to bear increased housing and other costs, a longer journey to work, and other substantial changes in their life style, will not be able to cope. Such problems are likely to be particularly felt by slum dwellers whose income may be lower and who may face other difficulties. Another line of argument suggests that it is the quality of life on new estates which leads to increased mental illness rather than the stress of rehousing.

A number of studies have examined these problems although in addition to the methodological difficulties outlined above they have faced the problems of defining mental illness and dealing with sources of data which are more liable than most to produce biased results.

The West End Boston Survey, which has been described, also included post relocation interviews, and some of these results have been described by Fried [22]. This study noticed that the majority of relocated people showed symptoms similar to grieving after a bereavement. These symptoms included 'painful loss, the continued longing, the general depressive tone, frequent symptoms of psychological or social or somatic distress, the active work required in adapting to the altered situation, the sense of helplessness, the occasional expressions of both direct and displaced anger, and tendencies to idealize the lost place'. The study considered this phenomenon to be widespread and serious. Relocation was likely to increase social and psychological pathology in a limited number of instances, and although it was also likely to create new opportunities for some, 'for the greatest number, dislocation is unlikely to have either effect, but does lead to intense personal suffering despite moderately successful adaptation to the total situation'. The report concludes that there is a need to maintain a sense of continuity for those affected by rehousing schemes, and suggests such methods as reducing the amount of drastic redevelopment and encouraging more moves within the former area of residence.

Coleman [41] reporting from East Kilbride New Town in Scotland found a higher incidence of neurosis in new towns than in more settled areas, but that the great majority of those suffering from neurotic illness became wholly or partially relieved of their symptoms within a period of months or at most two years. He termed this 'transitional neurosis' and attributed these symptoms to the rapidity of social change which was a crisis point in most people's lives 'to which the majority adjusted well sooner or later'.

Martin, Brotherston and Chave [42] in a study of the incidence of mental illness among the population of an LCC housing estate in Hertfordshire, thought that 'it seemed plausible that the strains consequent on rehousing in a new estate of suburban character combined with the preponderance of small families unsupported by extended kinship ties, might predispose to an increased incidence of at any rate the minor psycho-neurotic and psycho-somatic disorders'. Their study suggested that mental health problems were in fact more common than might be expected on demographic grounds and that the effects of rehousing and the conditions of life on the estate were to blame. Some of the factors thought to be important were the dislocating effect of the rehousing process itself, the changes in family life and the new patterns of expenditure and employment. Also the attitude of keeping oneself to oneself was thought to contribute to a degree of loneliness and social isolation not conducive to good mental health. Analysis of juvenile delinquency figures and child guidance cases showed higher rates immediately after the move but stability occurred later—

which tends to support Coleman's transitional neurosis syndrome.

A later study by Taylor and Chave [43] developed this study by looking at a New Town and a decaying London Borough as well as the same LCC estate. It was thought that in the case of the New Town, because of careful social planning, the mental health of the inhabitants would be better. The conclusions were somewhat surprising. It appeared that social planning had no effect on sub-clinical neurosis but that the incidence of psychosis was reduced. The level of sub-clinical neurosis was virtually the same (between 30 and 35 per cent) in the London Borough the LCC estate and the New Town, and it was concluded that this syndrome is not a product of the immediate environment but is constitutionally deeply embedded within the central nervous system. Contrary to expectations it was concluded that psychosis is much more influenced by the social environment, the New Town rates being much lower.

Hare and Shaw [44] looked at old and new parts of Croydon in a study designed to compare the mental health of the two types of area and to find out how far the mental health of the people on the new estate reflected the lack of certain social amenities. They found, for the majority of indices of mental health, no difference in the prevalence of mental ill health between the sample population, and no association between mental ill health and length of stay in the district. A third of the sample expressed specific dissatisfaction at the lack of various social amenities; but even higher proportions in the older districts expressed dislike of the inconveniences of industrial urbanization. The authors conclude that there is no important difference between the mental health of the two populations and no measurable effect could be attributed to lack of social amenities.

Hopper [45] in Rotherham found little difference in the incidence of mental disease in old and new parts of the town, although many more children required child guidance on new estates. In American, Schroeder [46] found a higher proportion of mental hospital admissions from areas lying near the centre of a city but Wilner, Walkley, Pinkerton and Tauback [47] found no statistically significant difference in the incidence of mental illness between a group of subjects who had been rehoused and those who had remained in the slums except for women between thirty-five and fifty-nine. In this age group, the findings were erratic, being at first lower then higher, in the new housing area.

A. E. Martin [48] in trying to reconcile the somewhat conflicting results of these surveys, stresses the great variations that exist between individual families and individual personalities within families. Individuals can show opposite reactions to the same environment and the effect of rehousing must also depend on the cultural background and the kind of facilities which exist on new estates. It would be rash to come to firm conclusions on the basis of such a limited set of studies, but it would appear on the evidence which we have so far, that people rehoused have a quite strong adaptive capability and that fears about the adverse psychological consequences have been overstated.

Conclusions

We can now return to our two original questions—what is it in social terms that we are destroying when we clear slums? And what is the evidence for significant changes in the way of life of people rehoused and can any of these changes be regarded as detrimental? The review of the literature which has been presented illustrates a wide range of views and some contradictions, but, on the whole, evidence from British sources seems to suggest that the break-up of existing working-class communities by slum clearance has no more than a minor and short term effect on most people. The evidence most contradictory to this comes from America, particularly from the Boston West End research. But although we must bear in mind the similarities which have been reported between working class styles of life there and in this country, there are important differences. Most of the West Enders were of Italian immigrant origin, which probably strengthened their local orientation and since the American equivalent of council housing is relatively unimportant, it is unlikely that they fared as well as their English counterparts in terms of their new home on redevelopment. We must qualify this generally optimistic conclusion by pointing out that as a recent study has shown [49] there is a high degree of unhappiness and disturbance caused by the manner in which local authorities carry out rehousing. It is this rather than the break up of the 'community' which should cause concern.

It is probably most important to place slum clearance within the context of other social changes which are much more important. There is a great deal to suggest that the emergence of the matrilocal system was a response to the hardships which people faced when they migrated to the towns in the late nineteenth century, and for many years faced economic uncertainty, unemployment, hard physical work and the prospect of early death. For many working-class communities, the functions of the matrilocal community are now obsolete. Rural migration into areas like Bethnal Green probably ceased to be significant fifty years or so ago, and the economic progress of the last twenty years has weakened the interdependence of kin and neighbours, and the extended family structure has virtually disappeared.

For many years now, families have been migrating away from the decaying residential areas of our inner cities and seeking more congenial surroundings in the suburbs or beyond. This outward migratory movement has been clearly illustrated by successive censuses, and without doubt as far as the majority are concerned is a voluntary and desired change, which has been participated in by working-class as well as middle-class people. In a sense therefore we can say that local authorities are reacting to, rather than precipitating, social change. Survey evidence indicates that many slum dwellers share the general aspiration for better housing and suburban living and that most of those forced to join the outward movement because of slum clearance settle very quickly into their new way of life, and that the difficulties encountered by a minority are for the most part temporary.

These arguments, however, are not conclusive. Many societies retain social customs which are highly valued but which originated under social conditions very different from those existing today. Moreover, the obsolescence of social structures for the majority, does not necessarily mean their obsolescence for all groups of the population. We can stress here perhaps that the situation in residual and transitional areas, is likely to be rather different. The combination of economic disadvantage and newness to urban life, which encouraged the matrilocal system to develop in the residual areas in the late nineteenth century, is a characteristic of some transitional areas today, with many having the additional complication of ethnic differences. In this kind of area a minority, perhaps a substantial minority, are much more likely to be dependent on local social networks and much more sensitive to change. In this situation the likely consequences of putting in the municipal bulldozer are less easily predicted, and local authorities in Inner London are tending to look more closely at this kind of area.[1]

In these areas, which have problems arising from overcrowding and racial minorities as well as those arising from bad housing facilities and conditions, we face some difficult policy decisions, matters which are more fully discussed in Chapter Seven. Such areas cannot simply be left to get worse, but because of their social structure neither can the policies of wholesale slum clearance, successful elsewhere, be indiscriminately applied. In such situations there would appear to be a need for the development of much more sensitive public participation techniques than we have at present so the needs and wishes of residents can be much more fully understood.

In carrying out this study, one cannot but be struck by the limited scope of the research available. Authoritative, well thought out surveys are few in number, the sample sizes are small, they apply to a limited number of specific situations and yet from these studies we have to make the generalizations upon which reasonable policy decisions can be made. Society in recent times has placed a good deal of faith in slum clearance as a means of doing away with the depressing legacy of our early industrialization and of reducing social and economic inequalities. It would seem sensible to back-up the large scale investment which this faith has stimulated by a programme of research designed to tell us exactly what long term social effects result from the forced movement of people away from their homes and from their familiar surroundings.[2]

[1] Some of the reasons for this in Lambeth are illustrated in ch. 10.
[2] There have been more encouraging signs recently. The Centre for Environmental Studies, for example, has sponsored research into the social implications of urban renewal at the Institute for Social and Economic Research at the University of Glasgow.

References

1. The best critique of the neighbourhood unit idea is to be found in Norman Dennis' paper, 'The popularity of the neighbourhood community idea' in *Sociological Review*, 1958, **6**, (2).

2. G.L.D.P. Inquiry, *Notes of Proceedings of the Hearing held on Wednesday, 28 October 1970*, 19th day, Produced and Distributed by the Greater London Council, pp. 15–24.

3. TÖNNIES, F., *Community and Association* (London: Routledge and Kegan Paul, 1955) (First published 1877).

4. DURKHEIM, E., *The Division of Labour in Society* (New York: Free Press, 1964) (First published 1893).

5. REDFIELD, R., *The Little Community: Viewpoints for the Study of a Human Whole* (Phoenix: University of Chicago Press, 1955).

6. PARK, R. and BURGESS, E. W., *Introduction to the Science of Sociology*, (Phoenix: University of Chicago Press, 1969) (First published 1921).

7. WIRTH, L., 'Urbanism as a way of life', In HUTT, P. K. and REISS, P. J. (eds.), *Cities in Society* (New York: Free Press, 1957) pp. 46–63 (Original essay 1938).

8. GANS, H. J., 'Urbanism and suburbanism as ways of life', in PAHL, R. E., *Readings in Urban Sociology* (Oxford: Pergamon Press, 1963) (Original essay 1962).

9. The best known English example is YOUNG, M. and WILLMOTT, P., *Family and Kinship in East London* (London: Routledge and Kegan Paul, 1957).

10. MERTON, R. K., *Social Theory and Social Structure* (New York: Free Press, 1957).

11. *The Shorter Oxford English Dictionary*. Third Edition (Oxford University Press, 1944).

12. SEELEY, J. R., 'The slum: it's nature use and users', *Journal of the American Institute of Planners*, 1959, **25**, no. 1.

13. GANS, H. J., 'The human implications of slum clearance and re-location', *Journal of the American Institute of Planners*, 1959, **25**, no. 1.

14. CLINARD, M. B., *Slums and Community Development. Experiments in Self-Help* (New York: The Free Press, 1966).

15. *Report of the Committee on Housing in Greater London*, Cmnd. 2605 (London: H.M.S.O. 1965).

16. Central Advisory Council for Education (England), *Children and Their Primary Schools*, (London: H.M.S.O., 1967).

17. HILLERY, G. A., 'Definitions of community: areas of agreement', *Rural Sociology*, 1955, **20**.

18. GITTUS, E., 'Sociological aspects of urban decay', in MEDHURST, F. and PARRY, LEWIS, J., *Urban Decay, an Analysis and a Policy*, (London: Macmillan, 1969).

19. FRIED, M. and GLEISHER, P., 'Some sources of residential satisfaction in an urban slum', *Journal of American Institute of Planners*, 1961, **27**.

20. See GANS, H., *The Urban Villagers: Group and Class in the Life of Italian-Americans*, (New York: Free Press, 1962) and Reference 9.

21. RYAN, E. J., 'Personal identity in an urban slum', in DUHL, L. J. (ed.), *The Urban Condition* (New York: Basic Books, 1963).

22. FRIED, M., 'Transitional functions of working class communities: implications for forced relocation', in KANTOR, M. B. (ed.), *Mobility and Mental Health* (Springfield: Charles Thomas, 1968).

23. REX, J., 'The sociology of a zone of transition', in PAHL, R. E. (ed.), *Readings in Urban Sociology* (Oxford: Pergamon Press, 1968).

24. VEREKER, C., MAYS, J. B., GITTUS, E. and BROADY, M., *Urban Redevelopment and Social Change* (Liverpool University Press, 1961).

25. See the approach of M. Harloe *et al.* ch. 10.

26. PAHL, R. E., *Whose City? And Other Essays on Planning and Sociology* (Harlow: Longmans, 1970).

27. A wide range of differing views is presented in MONIHAN, P. (ed.), *On Understanding Poverty* (New York: Basic Books, 1970).

28. GANS, H. J., 'Culture and class in the study of poverty: an approach to anti poverty research', in *People and Plans—Essays on Urban Problems and Solutions* (New York: Basic Books, 1968) Ch. 22, pp. 321–46.

29. LEWIS, O., *La Vida* (New York: Random House, 1966).

30. MILLER, W., 'Lower class culture as a generating milieu of gang delinquency', *Journal of Social Issues* 1958, **14**.

31. JENNINGS, H., *Societies in the Making: A Study of Development and Redevelopment within a County Borough, Bristol* (London: Routledge and Kegan Paul, 1962).

32. Ministry of Housing and Local Government, *The Deeplish Study*, (London: H.M.S.O., 1966) and Ministry of Housing and Local Government, *Living in a Slum, a study of St Mary's Oldham* (London: H.M.S.O., 1970).

33. DENNIS, N., *People and Planning* (London: Faber and Faber, 1970).

34. WILKINSON, R. K. and SIGSWORTH, E. M., 'Slum dwellers of Leeds', *New Society*, 4 April 1963.

35. COATES, K. and SILBURN, R., *Poverty: The Forgotten Englishmen* (Harmondsworth: Penguin, 1970).

36. Liverpool City Planning Department, *Social Survey: A study of the Inner Areas of Liverpool*, Unpublished.

37. REX, J. and MOORE, R., *Race Community and conflict. A Study of Sparkbrook* (O.U.P. for Institute of Race Relations, London, 1967).

38. SUTTLES, G. D., *The Social Order of the Slum* (Phoenix University of Chicago Press, 1968).

39. HOLE, V., 'Social effects of planned rehousing', *Town Planning Review*, 1959, **30**.

40. HALL, J. F. and WHITTAKER, J., *The Social Effects of Urban Renewal*, paper given to British Sociological Association Conference 2 April 1968. Unpublished.

41. COLEMAN, S. D., *Mental Health and Social Adjustment in a New Town. An Exploratory Study in East Kilbridge*, Glasgow University, Department of Economic and Social Research, 1966.

42. MARTIN, F. M., BROTHERSTON, J. H. F. and CHAVE, S., 'Incidence of neurosis in a new housing estate', *British Journal of Preventative and Social Medicine*, 1957, **2**.

43. TAYLOR, LORD and CHAVE, S., *Mental Health and Environment*, (London: Longmans, 1964).

44. HARE, E. H. and SHAW, G. K., *Mental Health on a New Housing Estate*, Maudlley Monograph, no. 12 (Oxford University Press, 1965).

45. HOPPER, J. M. H., Disease, Health and Housing, *Medical Officer*, 1962, **107**.

46. SCHROEDER, C., Mental Disorders in Cities, *American Journal of Sociology*, 1942, **48**.

47. WILNER, D. M., WALKLEY, R. P., PINKERTON, T. C. and TAUBACK, M., *The Housing Environment and Family Life* (Baltimore: Johns Hopkins Press, 1962).

48. MARTIN, A. E., Environment, Housing and Health, *Urban Studies*, 1967, **4**, no. 1.

49. UNGERSON, C., *Moving Home*, Occasional Papers on Social Administration, no. 44 (London: Bell, 1971).

Chapter Nine

Reading Attainment and Social and Ethnic Mix of London Primary Schools

ALAN LITTLE AND
CHRISTINE MABEY

Summary

In this chapter we explore the relationship between the social and ethnic mix in primary schools and children's reading attainment. We have attempted to answer four main questions:

1 How mixed, in social and ethnic terms, are our primary schools?

2 How far is the 'mix' in a neighbourhood reflected in the schools which serve that neighbourhood?

3 How does the class/ethnic mix of the school affect attainment?

4 What are the policy implications?

The research evidence which forms the basis of this chapter is derived from the Inner London Education Authority's Literacy Survey. This survey included all eight-year-olds (over 30 000 children) in ILEA schools in 1969. The children were given a group reading test by their class teachers who also completed questionnaires about their education and home background.

The principal conclusions we reach are that:

1 The 'mix' of a neighbourhood is not necessarily, or even generally, reflected in the 'mix' of the schools which serve that neighbourhood.

2 Neither the immigrant nor lower working-class concentration of the school has as strong a relationship with the reading standards of pupils as do the pupil's own social and ethnic origin, the extent to which the school is in an education priority area and probably the support, encouragement and interest of the home.

3 Pupils attending schools which are heavily middle class or contain few immigrants appear to read better than their age peers in other schools but this means schools with less than 10 per cent immigrants and more than 50 per cent middle class: clearly impracticable in an authority with nearly 20 per cent immigrants and only 25 per cent of the pupils middle class.

4 The educational gains from social and/or ethnic mix in schools, in so far as they are measured by reading standards at the age of eight years, at best appear to be small. Further the degree to which a school is in an education priority area appears to be a much more significant factor in reading progress.

5 That what is needed is a national and local policy of dramatic positive discrimination of educational, and other resources in favour of educational priority areas, and the proper utilisation of such resources.

Introduction

In this chapter we are concerned with examining the relationship between the social and ethnic composition of schools and the academic performance of children from different social and ethnic backgrounds. Our interest stems from the current interest, of planners and politicians, in 'socially mixed' neighbourhoods, allied to the suspicion that we are witnessing growing social polarization in central urban areas. Although precise definitions are numerous, we interpret a 'socially mixed' community as meaning one in which all social classes or occupational groups are represented and 'social polarization' as the absence in an area of middle-class or middle-income groups so that either there is a predominance of only the better-off or the poor, or in some cases of only both poles. Margaret Harris in Chapter Five has dealt in much greater detail with this: both the various definitions used and the undesirable consequences attributed to social polarization. Allied to this is the extent to which immigrant neighbourhoods or ghettos have developed during the past decade in some metropolitan areas. Various reasons, social and economic, have been put forward for socially and ethnically mixed neighbourhoods. A common and important one is educational: it is claimed by some that disadvantaged children, in particular, will benefit, socially and academically, from being educated in schools with children from more economically and culturally advantaged homes. In this context probably the most relevant research is that of Coleman [1] who found, when examining the attainment of disadvantaged whites and Negroes in schools of varying class and ethnic concentration that the most important factor associated with pupil performance and narrowing differentials was the social composition of the school and the classroom.

There are four questions which we attempt to answer in this chapter.

1 How mixed, in social and ethnic terms, are our schools?
2 To what extent is the social/ethnic mix of a neighbourhood reflected in the schools which serve the neighbourhood?
3 How does this class/ethnic mixture affect attainment overall and of specific groups?
4 What are the policy implications of this?

Limitations of Analysis

Before proceeding to examine these questions, the limitations and constraints of our analysis must be outlined. In the first place we had access to educational data for the Inner London Boroughs only, and we do not know how typical our schools are of schools in other areas of London. Our framework of reference, then, is Inner London and the variations within it. Secondly, most of the data for this chapter are drawn from a literary survey carried out in 1968–69 of reading standards in ILEA primary schools. For this survey all eight-year-old children were given a group reading test administered by the teachers who also completed questionnaires on the children's educational and home background. Several points must be made about the test: it is a group test and not an individual one and inevitably a relatively blunt measure of reading attainment. Further, it measures reading comprehension and not other aspects of literacy (reading fluency, oracy, etc.); other basic primary skills (writing and numeracy) have been ignored, as have other aspects of the curriculum (social adjustment and personal relationships). More varied and comprehensive testing might have produced results different from those we report. In particular, testing of a different, older, age group might have produced different results. For the purpose of this chapter it is necessary either to assume a high correlation between the reading skill measured by the test used and/or that the skill is of such intrinsic importance that the results are of intrinsic interest. Thus, the analysis is limited in two important ways: first, a single measure of attainment is used—reading—and as measured for one age group at one particular point in time: secondly, by the quality of the sociographic data provided by the teachers. Further we have no measure of the quality of teaching provided in different schools, so that the question as to what area of deficit we are measuring—the child and his attainment or the teacher and his ability to teach—cannot be adequately assured. However, such information as we have on the teaching force (on qualifications and length of service) suggests that there are not great differences overall between schools of different type.

As far as the information used for this chapter is concerned there are two key characteristics: immigrant status and social background. The teachers were asked to classify each child as 'non immigrant' or 'immigrant' and for the latter to assign each to a nationality group. The use of the term 'immigrant' and its definition is not one with which we or other workers in this field are entirely satisfied. The definition used was: 'Children born outside the British Isles who have come to this country with, or to join parents or guardians whose countries of origin were abroad; and children born in the United Kingdom to parents whose countries of origin were abroad and who came to the U.K. less than ten years ago.' However, the definition used is the statutory one employed by the Department of Education and Science in its annual return. It is, therefore, one with which teachers are familiar, is probably applied fairly constantly throughout the Authority and, to an extent, is accepted by teachers.

The second characteristic with which we are concerned is the pupil's social background. Teachers were asked to give the occupation of the child's father or guardian grouped into the following categories: professional/managerial, other non-manual, skilled manual, semi-skilled manual, unskilled manual. This categorization was expanded in the instructions and numerous examples were given of each occupational group. For comparative purposes the occupational groups can be equated with the Registrar General's socio-economic groups: professional/managerial s.e.g. 1, 2, 3, 4, 13; other non-manual s.e.g. 5, 6; skilled s.e.g. 8, 9, 12, 14; semi-skilled s.e.g. 7, 10, 15; unskilled s.e.g. 11. This grouping, it should be noted, is the same as that used by Margaret Harris in Chapter Five. The quality of response on this question is limited in two ways: the knowledge of teachers of parental occupations and their accuracy in assigning them to broad occupational groups. On the first point, a category of 'do not know' was included and this accounted for a significant proportion of all children in the survey (nearly one-sixth overall). On the second point, an independent and rough check of the accuracy of categorization is provided by the Census. The survey distribution was compared with that of the socio-economic groups of heads of households in Inner London Boroughs in 1966. The two samples are not strictly comparable; they were enumerated at different dates, the Census describes *heads* of *households* and the school survey the *guardians* of *eight-year-old* children in ILEA schools. Two adjustments were made, therefore, to the Census distributions taking account of both differential fertility of different occupational groups and the loss to the private sector of education. Overall, the survey distribution and the adjusted Census distribution were markedly similar with almost identical proportions of non-manual but slightly higher proportions of semi- and unskilled and smaller proportions of skilled in the survey population.

There is one further characteristic of the schools which is used in this chapter; that is, the education priority ranking of the school. How this was arrived at is described in more detail elsewhere. Briefly, the education priority ranking (E.P.A. index) was devised in response to the Plowden report which advocated positive discrimination in favour of deprived, E.P.A. schools.

The index is composed of ten factors which attempt to measure different facets of educational and social deprivation. It is a multi-dimensional index of deprivation. On each of the ten factors each primary school (roughly 900 schools in all) was scored, the scores summed and the resulting total score used to derive each school's rank position. Resulting from this exercise there was no attempt to identify 'E.P.A. schools' as such, but simply to use the index as a measure of relative deprivation among ILEA schools.

Social and Ethnic Mix of London Schools

In trying to answer the question—how mixed are London schools?—we became involved in the critical problem of defining 'social mix'. This in turn hinges on two factors; whether it is defined in terms of the *whole* social distribution or focuses on elements within it and, secondly, the norms which one employs. The very concept 'social mix' has, to our mind, the flavour of an ideal or correct balance (in culinary terms, a 'mix' consists of different elements in fairly rigorously defined quantities). One could, therefore, construct an ideal based on value judgements. Alternatively, and operationally an easier task, it can be defined with regard to the *observed pattern* of the population as a whole. Again, however, this raises problems as to which population should be considered to be the norm: a national, regional (i.e. South East), sub-regional, (i.e. GLC) authority, borough, or possible smaller unit? As indicated earlier we are restricted for much of our data to Inner London, and thus the frame of reference must be the Authority or smaller units within it. In principle, we would prefer when considering the social composition to examine the whole distribution. However, there are methodological problems in comparing distributions in a meaningful way, and so for the purposes of this paper we have concentrated on two measures: a crude measure of proportion of middle class, that is, those from non-manual backgrounds, and the proportion of lower working class, that is, those with parents in semi-skilled or unskilled manual jobs. Furthermore, we have to some extent bypassed the problem of the norm by examining, in terms of the two measures, the distribution of the population and how attainment varies between schools of different composition. Examination of immigrant concentration is much simpler since we have only data which produce dichotomies. We have examined the two factors—of social and ethnic composition—separately.

Distribution of Middle-class Children

Overall, children from non-manual background account for exactly one-quarter of the survey population. Thus, it can be argued that if all schools were 'socially mixed' all children would be found in schools with the same population of non-manual. Of course, this is a naïve assumption since Inner London itself is so varied in social composition.

However, it is perhaps useful in this and the following five tables to focus on the extent to which schools with a similar population of non-manual to the Authority as a whole, say within 10 per cent limits, account for the survey population. From Table 9.1 it can be seen that just over two-fifths of all children are in schools with a middle-class composition comparable with that of the Authority as a whole, i.e. 15–35 per cent. One third are in schools with less than this (and 6 per cent in schools of under 5 per cent) and one-fifth are in schools with a higher proportion. Of course, these limits of ±10 per cent are arbitrary. If we focus on the proportion of children in schools with a middle-class proportion, ±5 per cent of the ILEA average, we find only 20 per cent of all children. Nearly one in ten children are in schools which are predominantly middle-class

Table 9.1

Percentage Distribution of Children in Schools of Varying Middle-class Composition

Non-manual in Schools (%)	Children (%)
≤5	6
5.1–15	26
15.1–25	31
25.1–35	15
35.1–50	13
50.1–65	5
65.1–75	3
>75	1
Number of children	25 304

(i.e. 50 per cent or more). Incidentally, it should be noted that the percentage distribution of *schools* is almost identical with the distribution of *children* shown in Table 9.1.

Perhaps more interesting and more relevant is the extent to which middle-class children are found in predominantly middle-class schools.

Table 9.2

Percentage Distribution of Middle-class in Schools of Varying Middle-class Composition

Non-manual in School (%)	Non-manual Children (%)
≤5	2
5.1–15	13
15.1–25	21
25.1–35	19
35.1–50	21
50.1–65	12
65.1–75	8
>75	4
Number of Children	**6231**

Once again approximately two-fifths of children from middle-class backgrounds are in schools with a middle-class composition similar to that of the Authority as a whole. However, a much larger proportion of non-manual children are in predominantly middle-class schools (one-quarter), and only 15 per cent are in schools with an unusually low middle-class composition.

Distribution of Lower Working-class Children

In the survey population, children from a lower working-class background accounted for approximately two-fifths of the population (42 per cent). If the same indicator is used as in Tables 9.1 and 9.2, it can be seen that two-fifths of all children are in schools with a lower working-class composition similar to that of the Authority as a whole. Nearly one-third are in schools which are predominantly lower working-class (half or more), while just over a quarter are in schools in which less than one-fifth of the pupils are lower working-class. Again we looked at the distribution of *schools* and found that it was almost identical with that shown above of *children*.

Once again approximately two in five are in schools with a proportion of lower working-class comparable to that of the

Table 9.3

Percentage Distribution of Children in Schools of Varying Lower Working-class Composition

Unskilled and Semi-skilled in School (%)	Children (%)
≤10	3
10.1–20	8
20.1–30	15
30.1–40	20
40.1–50	22
50.1–60	15
60.1–70	8
>70	8
Number of Children	25 304

Authority as a whole. Nearly half of the lower working-class children are in predominantly lower working-class schools as compared with just under one-third of all children. Further, one in seven lower working-class children are in schools which are overwhelmingly (> 70 per cent) lower working-class.

Table 9.4

Percentage Distribution of Children of Lower Working-class Background in Schools with Varying Lower Working-class Composition

Unskilled and Semi-skilled in Schools (%)	Unskilled and Semi-skilled Children (%)
≤10	1
10.1–20	3
20.1–30	9
30.1–40	18
40.1–50	22
50.1–60	20
60.1–70	13
>70	14
Number of Children	10 555

Immigrant Concentration

When we turn to examine the percentage distribution of immigrants, there appears to be more concentration than with either the middle-class or lower working-class.

Table 9.5

Percentage Distribution of all Children in Schools of Varying Immigrant Concentration

Immigrants in School (%)	Children (%)
≤10	47
10.1–20	24
20.1–30	13
30.1–40	8
40.1–50	3
50.1–60	4
60.1–70	1
Number of Children	27 154

In the survey population, immigrant children accounted for just under one-fifth (18 per cent). From Table 9.5 it can be seen that nearly half of all children are in schools with less than 10 per cent immigrants. Nevertheless, as with the indicators of social composition approximately two-fifths of all children are in schools with an immigrant composition comparable to that of the Authority as a whole.

As Table 9.6 shows, there is a different pattern of concentration for immigrants: only 16 per cent are in schools with less than 10 per cent immigrants. Three-fifths are in schools with under one-third immigrants but one in six are in schools which are predominantly immigrant, i.e. with more than 50 per cent immigrants.

In summary, then, when we consider the degree to which

Table 9.6

Percentage Distribution of Immigrant Children in Schools of Varying Immigrant Concentration

Immigrants in School (%)	Immigrants (%)
≤10	16
10.1–20	23
20.1–30	21
30.1–40	17
40.1–50	8
50.1–60	13
60.1–70	3
Number of Children	4293

London schools are socially and ethnically mixed, it is perhaps more useful to consider the three minority groups, the middle class, the lower working class and the immigrants. The indicator on which we have concentrated is the proportion of each minority group found in schools with a proportion of that minority group comparable to that in the ILEA as a whole. Table 9.7

Table 9.7

Percentage Distribution of Middle-class, Lower Working-class and Immigrants according to their Relative Proportions in the Authority as a Whole

School Composition	Middle Class (%)	Lower Working Class (%)	Immigrant (%)
Less than ILEA	15	13	16
ILEA average	40	40	44
Greater than ILEA	45	47	41
Number of Children	6231	10 555	4293

summarizes the position for each of the three groups (it is a summary of Tables 9.2, 9.4 and 9.6). The 'Authority' percentage is the percentage of the minority group found in the Authority as a whole ±10 per cent. Thus, for the middle-class it covers schools with a middle-class composition of 15–35 per cent, for the lower working-class it covers schools with a lower working-class composition of 30–50 per cent, and for the immigrants it covers the schools with an immigrant concentration of 10–30 per cent.

The most noteworthy point in Table 9.7 is the degree of similarity between the three groups; approximately two in five in each group are in schools approximating to the Authority average, while a further two in five are in schools with a greater than average proportion. Possibly, however, the lower working-class are slightly more polarized than the middle class who, in turn, are more polarized than the immigrants.

Relationship between 'Mix' of Neighbourhood and 'Mix' in Schools

Having examined the variation among London schools in social and immigrant composition, we turned to the question of the degree to which this variation is due to the variation in neighbourhood composition. Put another way, to what extent does the 'mix' of a school reflect the 'mix' of its surrounding neighbourhood? The argument in favour of socially (or ethnically) mixed neighbourhoods, in so far as it is related to education, seems to assume that socially mixed neighbourhoods will inevitably lead to socially mixed schools. This seems to us a doubtful assumption and one which needs testing if an important consideration in planning socially mixed neighbourhoods is the achievement of mixed schools. We have not been able to look at this relationship throughout London, but we have examined two boroughs in detail.

In one, in the north of the Authority, social composition in school and neighbourhood has been examined; in the other, south of the Thames, the ethnic composition. For the purpose of this exercise each borough was divided into small neighbourhoods containing at least two primary schools which were: (a) within a quarter of a mile of each other and (b) not separated by a large natural boundary, e.g. railway line. Thus, the neighbourhoods were, in geographical terms, very small and could be regarded as fairly homogeneous. The reason for considering only schools within a quarter of a mile of each other, apart from wishing to concentrate on very small, local areas, was that, as is explained in Appendix Two, an earlier study showed that with the exception of Roman Catholic schools, between two-thirds and four-fifths of a school's population lived within a quarter of a mile of the school, i.e. a neighbourhood of a quarter of a mile around a school should contain the vast majority of its children. However, as can be seen from the subsequent analysis, many primary school children in Inner London, certainly in the more densely populated areas, have a choice of schools within a quarter of a mile. Ideally, we would have liked to examine where the children living in a given neighbourhood went to school. In default of this we have compared the neighbourhood population with the intakes of schools within this quarter of a mile radius. From the analysis two sets of schools have been excluded. First, those schools which had no 'pair', i.e. another school within a quarter of a mile of it; in Borough 1 this accounted for the exclusion of seven schools, and in Borough 2 for 26 schools. (In the south of Borough 2 particularly densities are much lower and thus schools are further apart.) Secondly, all Roman Catholic Schools were excluded, primarily because from the earlier study mentioned it emerged that RC schools had much wider catchment areas than either County or Church of England schools, and it was thought unjustified to include them in these small neighbourhood comparisons.

Borough 1: Social Composition

Neighbourhood data for this were taken from the 1966 sample Census, and a school's neighbourhood was defined as all Census enumeration districts falling within a quarter of a mile radius of the school. The school population was defined by the population in the literacy survey which is used throughout this chapter. The measure of social mix used was crude and, as in the previous section, we have selected as an indicator the proportion of children whose parents were in semi- or unskilled manual occupations, i.e. the most underprivileged. The reasons for choosing this rather than, say, the proportion of non-manual were, first, that a stated reason for wanting social mix is to avoid the adverse effects of large concentrations of under-privileged. Secondly, we know from other evidence and would expect that middle-class parents would be more selective in their choice of schools. Thus it would not be particularly surprising to find marked differences in middle-class concentrations. However, the selected measure by focusing on the semi- and unskilled is, in effect, examining the choices of all except the underprivileged i.e. the skilled manual as well as the non-manual. Before examining the tables it is worth noting that in this Borough the proportion of children from non-manual homes was 22 per cent, that is slightly less than the Authority average while the proportion of semi- and unskilled was 42 per cent, i.e. exactly the same as in Inner London as a whole. In the tables below are given the percentages for each school, first, for the neighbourhood around the school—Census data—and, secondly, the school's actual population—literacy survey. Further, for ease of comparison an index has been constructed for each small area; the total area being given the value of 100 in each case. One last point on the tables; the schools have been numbered in order roughly from the south to the north of the Borough. As can be seen in areas C, D and E, for example, occasionally one school appears in more than one area.

Table 9.8 lists sixteen areas, half of them containing three schools, half with two schools; a total of thirty-two schools with thirty pairs of schools, each within a quarter of a mile of the other. There are a few points worth noting before considering the relationship between neighbourhood and school percentages. First there is the degree of variation *throughout the Borough* between neighbourhoods—not particularly great—and much more marked, the variation between schools. The range of neighbourhood values is of 31 per cent to 42 per cent but of school percentages 17 to 71. Secondly, it should be noted that *within* small areas the differences between schools' neighbourhood populations is not great, never more than 5 per cent and usually only 1 or 2 per cent. This is not particularly surprising since there was, of course, a degree of overlap in each catchment area. Finally, and much more important, there is the degree of similarity for the small area percentages between the area figure derived from the Census and the total schools' figure from the survey; e.g. for area A the Census data give a figure of 36 per cent for the total area, while in all schools in that area the percentage is 34. In half of the areas the two figures are within 5 per cent; in only five areas are the differences greater than 10 per cent. This would suggest that in most areas the schools do in fact recruit from the local neighbourhood. The larger differences in areas E, J, L, M, N could be explained in a number of ways. First, we would expect slightly higher proportions of children from semi-skilled/unskilled backgrounds than adults in semi-skilled/unskilled jobs, since these socioeconomic groups have higher than average fertility rates. Secondly, it is possible that in certain schools some children were wrongly classified. Thirdly, it is possible that certain schools, i.e. those with very high percentages, either attract lower working-class from a wider area than the immediate neighbourhood, and/or some of the other social groups in the area attend schools outside the area. Finally, it is possible that for some areas, the 1966 Census figure was no longer correct for 1968/9.

In considering the results it is perhaps easier to look first at those areas with two schools only. Of these, in five areas (B, F, G, I, P,), the differences between the two schools' population, and thus between the schools and the neighbourhood they serve, are very marked. In each of these areas one of the two

Table 9.8

Borough 1: Social Mix in Neighbourhood and School

| | | Semi-skilled and Unskilled (%) | | Index value | |
		Area	School	Area	School
Area A					
School	1	34	26	95	76
	2	39	33	108	97
	3	39	43	108	126
Total area		36	34	100	100
Area B					
School	4	37	50	100	139
	5	40	25	108	69
Total area		37	36	100	100
Area C					
School	6	42	61	102	145
	7	41	24	100	57
	8	41	39	100	93
Total area		41	42	100	100
Area D					
School	7	41	24	100	50
	8	41	39	100	81
	9	42	63	102	132
Total area		41	48	100	100
Area E					
School	7	41	24	100	44
	9	42	63	102	115
	10	41	64	100	116
Total area		41	55	100	100
Area F					
School	11	35	71	103	162
	12	33	21	97	48
Total area		34	44	100	100
Area G					
School	12	33	21	103	54
	13	30	62	94	159
Total area		32	39	100	100
Area H					
School	14	33	62	97	182
	15	33	17	97	50
	16	35	43	106	126
Total area		34	34	100	100

Semi-skilled and Unskilled (%)			Index Value	
	Area	School	Area	School
Area I				
School 17	41	29	103	74
18	40	59	100	151
Total area	40	39	100	100
Area J				
School 18	40	59	100	98
19	42	71	105	118
20	39	51	98	85
Total area	40	60	100	100
Area K				
School 21	33	33	100	100
22	34	31	103	95
Total area	33	33	100	100
Area L				
School 23	32	57	103	136
24	30	25	97	60
25	32	39	103	93
Total area	31	42	100	100
Area M				
School 26	33	48	100	107
27	33	39	100	87
Total area	33	45	100	100
Area N				
School 28	30	48	97	121
29	32	38	103	88
Total area	31	43	100	100
Area O				
School 29	32	38	94	105
30	37	44	109	119
31	34	24	100	62
Total area	34	37	100	100
Area P				
School 31	34	24	106	65
32	30	48	94	130
Total area	32	37	100	100

schools has twice (in two areas three times) the proportion of unskilled and semi-skilled that the other has. Furthermore, in nearly all five areas there is a marked similarity between the Census and Survey figures for the area as a whole. Thus, for example, area B has in total just over one-third in this social group; 37 per cent according to the Census, 36 per cent according to the Survey. However, only one quarter of the population of school 5 is unskilled or semi-skilled, whereas half of the population of school 4 is. Of the three remaining two-school areas, one stands out because of the similarity in school populations. In area K both schools, 21 and 22, have approximately one-third of their intake in this social group; the same proportion as is derived from the Census for the area, so that all index figures are very close to 100. Areas M and N are interesting in that, although there is a difference in the schools' percentages (of not more than 10 per cent giving index differences of 20 and 30), both schools in each area have percentages above the neighbourhood figure from the Census. As pointed out above, it is difficult to account for this difference. However, it would seem safer to assume that, although the schools have higher proportions of underprivileged than their immediate neighbourhoods, there is no marked selective recruitment between schools in those areas. Thus, we conclude from the analysis above that in three areas the differences in social intake (given the indicator which has been used) are slight—in one area non-existent—but in the other five areas the differences are significant and large, such that in each of the five pairs one school has twice the proportion of underprivileged of its neighbour.

In the three-school areas, with the exception of area E, we see a pattern of diversity with one school well below the area figure, one about the same and one above. In three areas (A, J, O) the greatest difference between any two schools' populations never exceeds 20 per cent. However, in the other areas (C, D, H, L) the smallest difference between any pair is 14 per cent (area L), whereas the greatest difference (in area H) between two schools, 15 and 14, is of 45 per cent. As in the two-school areas, there are pairs of schools, each school within a quarter of a mile of the other, with one school with more than twice the proportion of children from unskilled and semi-skilled backgrounds than can be found in the neighbouring school. Thus, in area C, for example, for which both the Census and Survey figures agree on the overall proportion of semi-skilled/unskilled (41/42 per cent) the percentage of School 6 is two-and-a-half-times greater than School 7. There are three other pairs showing this pattern; Schools 9 and 7, 14 and 15, and 23 and 24. Area E is only an exception in that two of the schools, 9 and 10, have very similar proportions. But, both are two-and-a-half-times greater than the third school. Thus, in all the three-school areas there are differences in the social intake of the three schools (with the single exception of Schools 9 and 10 in area E). These differences are not particularly marked in three areas, but in the remaining five they are to such an extent that there is one school with a population of underprivileged which, in proportional terms, is twice as great as that of a neighbouring school. Furthermore, in these schools far from being a minority the semi-skilled/unskilled predominate.

We conclude from this analysis that, in this Borough at least, similarity between the social mix of the neighbourhood and the social mix of the schools in that neighbourhood is the exception rather than the rule. It would seem from the fact that, in most areas the Census and Survey figures are fairly similar for the *area as a whole*, most of the schools do recruit from the immediate neighbourhood. What seems to happen in many areas, however, is that there is selective recruitment by schools in the same small area. Of the sixteen areas considered, in ten, differences between schools were very marked such that in one school in each neighbourhood the semi-skilled and unskilled constituted a majority in the school. Of the thirty pairs of schools examined, only two had very similar intakes, i.e. within 5 per cent, eight had intakes differing by 10 per cent or less, of the remaining twenty-two, thirteen varied by 20 per cent or more. One further point of interest is that these areas containing schools with markedly different social intakes are not all either areas of relatively low or high concentrations of semi-skilled/unskilled; areas L and P for example, have neighbourhood proportions, according to the Census, of 31–32 per cent whereas areas C, D, E and I are 40–41 per cent. It would seem (if the measure used is a fair indicator of social mix) that in this Borough which is less privileged than many, parents of primary school children and/ or the schools themselves are operating their right of parental choice to ensure a degree of social segregation.

Borough 2: Ethnic Composition

In this section we have looked at the proportions of immigrants in schools in small areas. Unfortunately, in this analysis we were unable to compare the school information with area data. The chief reason for this was that the statutory D.E.S. definition of an immigrant used by the schools (see p. 277 for definition) is not comparable with the definition used in the Census. Furthermore, unlike the social class character of an area, areas have changed considerably in a few years in their immigrant concentrations, i.e. 1966 area data might not give an accurate picture of the neighbourhood in 1968–9. As in Borough 1 the areas run roughly from south to north and, again, some schools are in more than one area. The percentage of immigrants is not simply that of the survey age group but of the whole school. We decided that Church of England schools should be included in this analysis since the majority of immigrants in the Borough (as in all South London boroughs) were West Indians most of whom are practising Christians in the West Indies, although not necessarily Anglicans. However, although the majority of non-immigrants are nominally C. of E., few are practising members. Thus, we thought that it was just as likely or unlikely for an immigrant child as a non-immigrant to want to attend a C. of E. school.

In Table 9.9, eighteen separate areas are listed, fourteen containing two schools, four with three schools making a total of thirty-three schools and twenty-five pairs of schools. The variation throughout the Borough in the percentages of immigrants in areas is almost as great as the variation between schools. The range in areas is from 8 per cent (area Q) to 53 per cent (area E), while the range of school concentrations is 1 per cent (School 5) to 72 per cent (School 12).

First, in considering the two-school areas it is clear that they split into two distinct groups; those in which there is little difference in the schools' immigrant concentrations and those in which there is a large difference. First, in the areas with similar school populations, three areas (E, P, R) in fact have identical immigrant concentrations; in the other three areas (L, O, Q) they differ by not more than 5 per cent. It should be noted that these six areas are not areas of either all high or all low immigrant concentrations. Area E has the highest concentration

Table 9.9
Borough 2: Immigrant Concentration in Schools

		Immigrants (%)			Immigrants (%)
Area A			Area J		
School	1 *	7	School	18 *	35
	2	18		19 *	1
Total area		14	Total area		16
Area B			Area K		
School	2	18	School	20	24
	3	5		21	32
	4	17		22	22
Total area		14	Total area		26
Area C			Area L		
School	5 *	1	School	22	22
	6 *	16		23	27
Total area		10	Total area		24
Area D			Area M		
School	7	4	School	23	27
	8	35		24 *	13
Total area		22		25	5
			Total area		14
Area E			Area N		
School	9 *	53	School	24 *	13
	10	53		25	5
Total area		53		26 *	16
			Total area		10
Area F			Area O		
School	11	18	School	26 *	16
	12	72		27	18
Total area		51	Total area		17
Area G			Area P		
School	13 *	9	School	28	12
	14	40		29 *	12
Total area		29	Total area		12
Area H			Area Q		
School	14	40	School	30 *	5
	15 *	8		31	9
Total area		27	Total area		8
Area I			Area R		
School	16	29	School	32 *	14
	17	4		33	14
Total area		14	Total area		14

* Church of England School.

of any in the Borough but areas P, Q, R are below 15 per cent while areas L and O are 24 and 17 per cent respectively. In the other eight areas, however, differences between schools are marked. The smallest difference is of 11 per cent (area A) while the greatest is of 54 per cent (area F). It is clear that in these areas the great majority of immigrants attend one school only. In seven of the eight areas, the proportion of immigrants in the low concentration school is less than 10 per cent, and in one area, J, one school has 1 per cent while its neighbour has 35 per cent. This extreme polarisation does not seem to be associated with areas of either low or high immigrant concentration. Areas A, C, I, J have immigrant populations of under 20 per cent whereas areas D, G, H have proportions which are higher but under one-third, whereas in area F the immigrants account for just over one half. Thus, areas in which pairs of schools have very different immigrant intakes are spread throughout the Borough.

In the three-school areas there are differences but these are not so great as those of the two-school areas, partly because the immigrant concentrations in the areas as a whole are lower. The greatest difference between any two schools is in area M between Schools 23 and 25 (22 per cent). However, it appears that in areas B, M, N there is one school with a markedly lower immigrant proportion than the other two schools. In these areas there is one school with only 5 per cent, while its neighbours have proportions two or three times larger. Further, in area M there is also one school with a markedly higher percentage than the other two, 27 per cent as compared with 13 and 5 per cent In area K the differences are not large. Of the eleven pairs of schools in these four areas, six are markedly different (i.e. differ by more than 15 per cent) and five are fairly similar.

As was stated at the beginning of this section, Church of England schools were included in the analysis because we could see no particular reason why their immigrant intake should differ from that of county schools. In fact, the tables would seem to bear this out. C. of E. schools, of which there are twelve, are found in twelve of the eighteen areas. In three areas (A, G and H), the C. of E. school has a markedly lower immigrant proportion than its neighbouring county school. In five areas, however, the county and C. of E. schools have either the same or very similar proportions (areas E, O, P, Q, R), and these range from areas of low immigrant concentration, e.g. area Q, to very high, area E. In areas M and N, the C. of E. school has an immigrant concentration mid-way between that of two county schools. Finally, in two areas, C and J, both schools are C. of E. and their immigrant intakes are markedly different. Thus, C. of E. schools, like county schools, vary in their immigrant concentrations from relatively low, to average to high. From this we conclude that whether a school is C. of E. is not an important factor in determining the size of its immigrant intake.

We conclude from this analysis of school data on immigrant concentrations that, once again, the 'mix' of an area is not necessarily found in all the schools in that area. However, unlike the analysis of social composition, what this analysis seems to show is that either both schools recruit equally or there is a marked difference. There are none of the finer shadings of difference which we saw in Borough 1; either both schools recruit equal proportions of immigrants or only one recruits them. Further, there are more pairs of schools with similar proportions than there were in Borough 1; eleven of the twenty-five pairs had immigrant concentrations which differed by not more than 10 per cent as compared with eight of the thirty pairs in Borough 1. One is tempted to conclude from this that those parents who make positive decisions about their choice of primary school are more concerned to avoid schools with lower working class than with immigrants.

The examination of these two Boroughs would suggest that there is no firm evidence to show that a mixed neighbourhood will provide mixed schools. We think from this examination and an earlier study that most primary school children travel only a short distance to school, that they will go to a very local school. However, given the densities in Inner London and the number of primary schools available, many children have a choice of two schools within a quarter of a mile, more if they are prepared to travel further. Thus it would seem that, within small areas, two neighbouring schools do not necessarily recruit equally from different social classes or ethnic groups. Two further points are worth considering. The size of the areas we have examined is very small, much smaller than planners would plan for. Secondly, given parental choice, it is difficult to see how this pattern of social/ethnic segregation within small areas could be changed. If, as seems probable, most children live very close to the school they attend, then any 'zoning' policy would have no effect. We would suggest that the only ways to ensure schools with a social/ethnic mix similar to that of the neighbourhood they serve would be either to adopt a policy of quotas or to find some way to make the 'unpopular' school as popular as its neighbour with those parents who make positive choices about schools.

Social and Ethnic Mix and Attainment

In this section we examine the effect on reading attainment of children of different social/ethnic backgrounds in schools of varying social and immigrant composition. We have not in this chapter considered both factors at the same time. As in the previous section we have not considered the *whole* social distribution but focused on two groups within it: the non-manual and the semi-skilled and unskilled manual. The attainment data used in this chapter are derived from the literacy survey of eight year olds and the measure of attainment used is the mean reading quotient (RQ) for groups and sub-groups. The test was standardized on a national sample with a mean of 100, standard deviation of 15 and range of 70 to 140. The mean RQ for the London survey was 94.4. Mean scores can be very roughly converted into reading ages. A mean score of 90, for example, is equivalent to a reading age of about one year below chronological age: a mean score of 80 is equivalent to a reading age roughly two years below chronological age. Overall, London children had a reading age roughly six months behind their chronological age.

Social Mix

We have concentrated initially on the social background of children in schools of differing middle-class and lower working-class composition. It seemed to us that the most important groups on whom to focus examination were the working-class since the argument in favour of socially mixed schools hypothesises that the attainment of working-class children will be improved if they are in such schools.

First, Table 9.10 examines attainment related to the middle-class composition in the school. It should be remembered that

Table 9.10

Mean Reading Score of Children of Different Socio-economic Background in Schools of Varying Middle-class Composition

Non-manual (%)	Non-manual Professional	Other	Skilled	Manual Semi-skilled	Unskilled
≤10	100.0 (44)*	99.6 (208)	94.4 (1481)	91.6 (1302)	88.8 (1276)
10.1–25	102.8 (541)	97.7 (1463)	95.2 (4101)	92.1 (2813)	88.8 (2434)
25.1–50	107.5 (852)	100.5 (1601)	93.3 (2153)	94.5 (1323)	91.8 (1066)
>50	108.8 (811)	103.3 (679)	100.0 (503)	94.9 (210)	91.6 (109)

* Figures in parenthesis in this and subsequent tables denote number of children in sub-group. Sub-groups with five or less children have been excluded.

non-manual children account for exactly one-quarter of all the survey children, and further that the modal London child is in a school whose non-manual composition is between 10 and 25 per cent.

The first point to note is that there is a clear trend in all (except possibly the other non-manual) of improved attainment with increasing middle-class composition. However, it should be noted that the differences are much greater among the non-manual and especially the professional groups. The range among the professional children is of nearly nine points which compares with a three point range among the semi- or unskilled. Further, it should be pointed out that the only manual group which has a mean score of 100, i.e. reading age equivalent to chronological age, is the skilled manual in schools which have a predominantly middle-class composition (i.e. more than half).

The relationship between class composition and attainment has been taken a stage further in Table 9.11 by relating them to

Table 9.11

Mean Reading Score of Children of Different Socio-economic Background in Schools of Varying Education Priority and Middle-class Composition

Non-manual in School (%)	Education Priority Rank			
	1	2	3	4
	(a) Professional			
<10	92.9 (10)	101.1 (10)	104.1 (15)	99.7 (9)
10.1–25	100.8 (41)	101.5 (115)	102.6 (216)	104.6 (169)
25.1–50	97.5 (34)	106.1 (61)	105.4 (175)	108.8 (582)
>50	—	—	102.1 (60)	109.3 (749)
	(b) Other non-manual			
<10	93.1 (29)	97.3 (64)	100.8 (79)	106.6 (36)
10.1–25	92.4 (133)	94.7 (351)	98.9 (626)	100.5 (353)
25.1–50	95.5 (39)	97.6 (201)	98.3 (469)	102.5 (892)
>50	76.6 (8)	—	100.3 (81)	104.0 (590)
	(c) Skilled manual			
<10	90.2 (255)	91.6 (381)	96.6 (581)	97.7 (264)
10.1–25	90.4 (334)	92.6 (977)	96.1 (1639)	97.4 (1151)
25.1–50	93.0 (48)	95.5 (187)	96.4 (558)	99.7 (1360)
>50	—	—	98.9 (57)	100.2 (444)
	(d) Semi-skilled manual			
<10	89.0 (204)	89.2 (395)	93.1 (491)	95.3 (212)
10.1–25	88.4 (254)	90.7 (747)	92.8 (1135)	93.9 (677)
25.1–50	91.3 (46)	94.9 (185)	92.9 (384)	95.6 (708)
>50	—	—	96.2 (19)	94.6 (189)
	(e) Unskilled manual			
<10	85.5 (266)	86.7 (355)	89.3 (474)	96.6 (181)
10.1–25	84.7 (302)	86.7 (562)	90.1 (977)	90.9 (593)
25.1–50	87.0 (61)	88.0 (174)	89.3 (306)	95.0 (525)
>50	—	—	91.7 (13)	91.8 (95)

the index of multiple deprivation (E.P.A. index). For the purposes of this analysis, schools have been grouped according to their E.P.A. rank: group (1) contains schools of very high priority, group (2) contains schools of high priority, group (3) contains average schools, and group (4) contains schools of low priority.

In testing the hypothesis outlined earlier the key groups for examination are the unskilled and semi-skilled and, to a lesser extent, the skilled manual. This and similar tables can be considered in three ways: reading across the rows, i.e. controlling for social composition but varying the priority grouping, reading down the columns, i.e. within each priority group but varying the middle-class composition, or reading diagonally across the table, i.e. varying both factors. If we read diagonally across Table 9.11 we find that for children from an unskilled background there is an overall range of six points; that is comparing children in schools in the highest priority group and with a low middle-class proportion (mean 85.5) with those in schools of low priority and with a high middle-class proportion (mean 91.8). The range is similar for the semi-skilled: six points. For children from other backgrounds, however, the range is much greater, ten points, or a year's reading age, for the skilled; eleven points for the other non-manual; and 16 points, or over eighteen months' reading age for professional children. When we concentrate on the factor of social composition (i.e. reading down the table) we find that for children from unskilled backgrounds there seems to be a trend in all except schools of low priority of higher attainment with higher middle-class concentration. However, none of the differences is significant and they are all slight—of one or two points only. In low priority schools, however, there appears, if anything, a reverse trend: attainment is highest in schools of under 10 per cent middle class. As far as the semi-skilled are concerned there is no clear trend discernible in any except the second priority group, which is the only group in which the differences are statistically significant. Further it should be noted that the highest mean score, in the third priority group in predominantly middle-class schools, is 96.2, i.e. an average reading age about four months behind chronological age. Perhaps, in all this analysis the most interesting group is the lowest priority group, that is those schools with few educational or social problems. In this group the attainment is almost identical regardless of the social composition. Among the skilled manual a much clearer pattern emerges in all priority groups. Within all groups higher attainment is associated with greater middle-class concentration and, in particular, attainment rises when the proportion of middle class is more than half. Nevertheless, it should be noted that although there is a clear trend the differences themselves are slight—only two to three points. Turning to the non-manual groups, it is not possible to discern any trend among the other non-manual; the factor of middle-class composition, when account is taken of education priority, would seem to be relatively unimportant. Similarly, among the professional group there is not a clear trend in all priority groups and only in low priority schools is there a trend which is clear with marked differences; the overall range is of nearly ten points, i.e. a year's difference in reading age. In summary, then, if account is taken of the general social and educational problems of a school, it would seem that children of lower working-class background (semi-skilled and unskilled manual) attain on average very much the same level regardless of the proportion of middle-class children in the school. The average working-class child (skilled manual background) will probably attain a slightly higher level if he is in a predominantly middle-class school. The performance of non-manual children is not likely to be markedly adversely affected by being in schools with very few other non-manual children. Finally, it should be noted in passing that the index of multiple deprivation or education priority would seem to be more important than the degree of middle-class concentration of the school.

In Table 9.12, the second index of social composition shows

Table 9.12

Mean Reading Score of Children of Different Socio-economic Background in Schools of Varying Lower Working-class Composition

Semi-skilled and Unskilled in School (%)	Non-manual		Skilled	Manual	
	Professional	Other		Semi-skilled	Unskilled
≤20	108.9 (889)	102.9 (845)	99.3 (948)	95.2 (274)	93.9 (143)
20.1–30	107.7 (445)	100.1 (696)	96.0 (1559)	93.7 (550)	90.0 (403)
30.1–50	104.1 (692)	99.3 (1640)	96.3 (3926)	92.9 (2401)	91.4 (1854)
>50	103.7 (222)	97.6 (770)	94.4 (1805)	91.9 (2423)	87.8 (2085)

the overall differences in attainment of different occupation groups. In considering this second indicator it should be remembered that the unskilled and semi-skilled account for two-fifths of all the children and that the average London child is in a school in which two-fifths of the children are from unskilled and semi-skilled backgrounds.

In all socio-economic groups there is a trend of declining attainment with increasing lower working-class concentration. The overall range is greatest among the unskilled, six points, and least among the semi-skilled, three points, with the other three groups having a range almost as great as the unskilled: five points. The trend is not smooth; among the unskilled there is a sharp fall-off in predominantly lower working-class schools. In nearly all groups, except the professional, there is a more marked decline when the proportion of lower working class becomes greater than one-fifth, and, then, later when the proportion is greater than half.

As for the first indicator examination was also focused on the measure of multiple deprivation and this is shown in Table 9.13.

Once again the important groups to examine are the semi-skilled and unskilled, and to a lesser extent the skilled manual, and we have concentrated our attention on the variation (for each occupational group) within each priority group, of social composition. Among the unskilled it is difficult to discern any clear pattern, certainly attainment does not regularly decline with increased lower working-class composition, nor, in most priority groups, is the attainment of children in low lower working-class schools higher than that of children in predominantly lower working-class schools. Among the semi-skilled, however, there would seem to be a pattern in all except schools of the lowest priority. Among that group, attainment is very similar regardless of the social composition. In the other groups, however, attainment falls when the proportion of lower working class rises above one-fifth (thereafter, however, little difference occurs). Among the skilled manual in the third priority group, the variation (with social composition) of mean scores is not very great, nor is it consistently in the same direction, although the mean scores of children in predominantly lower working-class schools are lower than those of children in schools with few lower working-class. Among the skilled manual in very high priority schools there is no clear pattern, although attainment is in fact highest in predominantly lower working-class schools. In the next highest priority group there is again no clear trend although there is a marked decline in attainment in schools of over one-fifth lower working class. Among the other non-manual in all except very high priority schools there appears to be a trend of decreasing attainment with increasing lower working-class concentration, but the differences are slight—of only one

Table 9.13

Mean Reading Score of Children of Different Socio-economic Background in Schools of Varying Education Priority and Lower Working-class Composition

Lower Working-Class in School (%)	Education Priority Rank			
	1	*2*	*3*	*4*
	(a) Professional			
≤20	—	112.7 (7)	103.1 (81)	109.5 (799)
20.1–30	103.3 (7)	99.0 (21)	103.8 (73)	109.1 (344)
30.1–50	96.9 (46)	103.7 (104)	102.9 (227)	106.1 (315)
>50	99.9 (32)	101.9 (54)	105.8 (85)	104.3 (51)
	(b) Other non-manual			
≤20	83.1 (13)	98.9 (17)	100.5 (115)	103.8 (700)
20.1–30	87.4 (13)	96.7 (52)	98.7 (167)	101.4 (464)
30.1–50	92.7 (83)	96.7 (292)	98.3 (671)	102.5 (594)
>50	94.1 (100)	94.6 (255)	99.7 (302)	102.1 (113)
	(c) Skilled manual			
≤20	89.8 (39)	99.9 (34)	97.5 (139)	100.1 (736)
20.1–30	87.8 (57)	89.7 (169)	95.2 (459)	98.3 (874)
30.1–50	90.3 (304)	93.6 (763)	96.7 (1539)	98.6 (1320)
>50	91.7 (239)	91.9 (579)	95.8 (698)	98.0 (289)
	(d) Unskilled manual			
≤20	94.9 (8)	97.0 (7)	96.2 (39)	94.9 (220)
20.1–30	80.5 (8)	89.5 (47)	91.4 (142)	95.5 (353)
30.1–50	89.3 (178)	90.8 (495)	93.3 (911)	94.5 (817)
>50	88.8 (312)	90.3 (778)	92.6 (937)	94.7 (396)
	(e) Unskilled manual			
≤20	—	—	89.4 (14)	94.9 (121)
20.1–30	89.1 (19)	85.5 (39)	89.4 (114)	91.7 (231)
30.1–50	84.4 (113)	88.4 (343)	91.0 (739)	94.5 (659)
>50	85.3 (493)	86.3 (706)	88.9 (903)	91.4 (383)

or two points. In high priority schools, however, there is a clear trend in the opposite direction, and the overall range is of eleven points. Finally, among the professional it is not possible to discern any pattern except in schools of very low priority where attainment is lower in schools of high lower working-class concentration; the overall range being five points. In general, then, this table does not show any general pattern.

Furthermore, such differences as exist are not large. The differences shown in Tables 9.11 and 9.13, and 9.18 and 9.19 are summarized in Appendix Two.

In this section we have examined two different indicators of social composition in an attempt to test the hypothesis that working-class children will perform better in socially mixed schools. We have not defined a 'socially mixed' school, but merely examined attainment in schools of varying middle- and working-class composition. In this examination we have also taken into account priority ranking on the index of multiple deprivation—that is, the general measure of social and educational problems. In conclusion, it would seem that, when account is taken of this factor, the average working-class child does not always or significantly perform at a higher level of attainment if he is in a school of either high middle-class or low working-class composition; when the mean attainment is higher it is only marginally so. When attention is focused on the average middle-class child it does not seem that his attainment is always or significantly lower if he is taught in a school with a high proportion of working-class children. In brief, this factor of social composition when compared with the more general factor of education priority would seem to be of little importance. However, it can be argued that the correlation is so high between the general factor of deprivation and these two indicators of social composition that it is incorrect to examine the effect of the latter in this way. If this is a valid argument, then there are two important points to be made. First, if one examines the first indicator (ignoring the deprivation factor), it can be seen that a variation in middle-class composition affects the lower working-class child hardly at all but the middle-class significantly. Secondly, the only schools in which the attainment of working-class children is markedly higher are schools with a social composition markedly different from that of the Authority overall. Average attainment changes markedly when the proportion of lower working-class is less than one-fifth or the proportion of middle class is over half; in the Authority as a whole the proportion of lower working-class is two-fifths and that of the middle-class is one-quarter. This means that, in general, attainment is only markedly affected by class composition when the social composition of a school is highly atypical of the London population.

Immigrant Concentration

In turning to the effect on children's attainment of immigrant concentration, we decided to look at the impact of high concentration immigrant schools on the performance of both immigrants and non-immigrants. Once again we have not defined a 'high' concentration, we have simply looked at variation in attainment in schools with varying immigrant proportions. In order to simplify presentation, we have dealt separately with non-immigrants and immigrants. Furthermore for the non-immigrants we have excluded the Irish and concentrated on children born in the United Kingdom.

Table 9.14

Mean Reading Score of UK Children in Schools with Varying Proportions of Immigrants

Immigrants (%)	Mean Score
0	99.0 (1104)
1–10	97.7 (10 578)
10.1–20	95.3 (5267)
20.1–30	95.6 (2348)
30.1–40	94.4 (1440)
40.1–50	96.5 (397)
50.1–60	93.7 (429)
60.1–70	88.9 (73)

Table 9.14 would suggest that there is a fairly marked relationship between attainment and immigrant concentration. The total range in attainment is ten points, i.e. approximately one year's reading age. There is a marked fall in attainment of children in schools with more than 60 per cent immigrants; excluding this last group the range is six points, which is, equivalent to six months' reading age; and the progression is not a smooth one. There is very little difference, for example, in the mean scores of children in schools of between 10 and 50 per cent immigrant concentration and, in fact, the mean of the 40–50 per cent group is marginally higher than those of the three previous groups.

In the following analysis in which we look at other factors, the distribution of immigrant concentration was grouped in what seemed the most meaningful way.

There are three important points which emerge from Table 9.15. First, for nearly all occupation groups there seems to be a trend of lower performance with higher immigrant concentration. For most occupation groups a marked fall in performance seems to occur when the immigrant concentration is greater than 10 per cent, and, in schools which have 50 per cent or more immigrants (although this latter is not true of the professional or the semi-skilled groups). Secondly, it should be noted that *within* each occupation group the differences in mean score are

Table 9.15

Mean Reading Score of UK Children Classified by Guardian's Occupation and School's Immigrant Concentration

Immigrants (%)	Non-manual			Manual	
	Professional	Other	Skilled	Semi-skilled	Unskilled
≤10	109.0 (1159)	102.0 (1973)	98.1 (3800)	94.5 (2335)	91.9 (2109)
10.1–30	106.6 (617)	100.1 (1054)	96.1 (2579)	92.9 (1745)	89.8 (1348)
30.1–50	105.5 (124)	99.4 (288)	95.6 (660)	92.8 (383)	89.7 (308)
>50	104.9 (22)	97.3 (81)	93.7 (159)	93.1 (112)	87.6 (98)

not so great as those shown in Table 9.14 (even allowing for the merging of the 60–70 per cent and 50–60 per cent immigrant groups). In most groups the range is of about four and a half points except among the semi-skilled where the range is of one and a half points only. Further, it is worth noting that parental occupation appears to be more important than the immigrant concentration of the school. This can be seen from the fact that in most cases a child whose parent is in a high status occupation but is himself in a school of high immigrant concentration attains a higher level than the child whose parent has a lower (occupational) status but is in a school with few immigrants. One example of this is that the mean score of children of professional parents in schools with more than 50 per cent immigrants is 104.9 as compared with a mean score of 102.0 for the children of other non-manual parents who are in schools with under 10 per cent immigrants. Finally, the figures in Table 9.15 are virtually identical with those in Table 9.12; in the latter it was lower working-class concentration, in the present analysis immigrant concentration. However, the differential impact on pupils from various socio-economic groups appears to be identical in direction and scale. As above in the examination of the social composition we include here the index of multiple deprivation. Once again it must be emphasized that, although this index included measures of immigrant concentration and social composition, these were only two of ten factors; Table 9.16 examines the variation in performance when schools are grouped by this factor. Because of the small numbers in some sub-groups, the analysis is presented for non-manual and manual groups and not for each occupation group separately.

Table 9.16

Mean Reading Score of Non-immigrant Children in Schools of Varying Education Priority and Immigrant Concentration

Immigrants (%)	1	2	3	4
		Education priority rank		
		(a) Non-manual		
⩽10	97.5 (67)	96.1 (174)	100.2 (613)	106.2 (2429)
10.1–30	96.6 (77)	99.4 (317)	101.7 (679)	104.8 (737)
30.1–50	94.2 (36)	101.3 (138)	101.2 (224)	103.9 (58)
>50	96.1 (35)	99.1 (47)	104.1 (17)	—
		(b) Manual		
⩽10	89.3 (371)	90.2 (712)	93.8 (2821)	97.0 (4881)
10.1–30	88.3 (730)	91.2 (1732)	93.2 (2615)	96.0 (1248)
30.1–50	92.6 (128)	91.8 (698)	94.1 (617)	94.5 (83)
>50	89.5 (203)	91.8 (178)	98.5 (26)	—

Among the non-manual group, none of the differences shown is significant, and, more important, there is no clear trend such as has emerged in previous tables, except possibly in the lowest priority group (4). However, it should be noted that in average schools (group (3)) there is a trend but it is in the *opposite direction*, i.e. performance appears to improve with increasing immigrant concentration. For the high priority groups there is no clear pattern. Further, it can be seen from Table 9.16 that the general indicator of social and educational problems is a more important factor than simply that of immigrant concentration. This can be deduced from the fact that in nearly all sub-groups the mean scores of children in a low priority group are higher than those of children in a higher priority group whatever the immigrant concentration. For example, the mean score of children in priority group (2) in predominantly immigrant schools is 99.1 as compared with the mean of 97.5 in those in schools of less than 10 per cent immigrants but in priority group (1). Among the manual children such trends as there are would seem to point towards high performance being related to high immigrant concentration. However, once again no differences are statistically significant and, furthermore, they are slight. In summary, it would seem from this analysis that when account is taken of other factors, in particular, parental occupation and the school's educational priority rank, the factor of immigrant concentration is of negligible importance in determining non-immigrants' performance.

A problem arose in the more detailed analysis of immigrants' performance. This was that the nationality distribution of immigrants varied considerably between schools of different immigrant concentration. The most important difference was that West Indians, who account for half of the immigrants in the survey population, are under-represented in schools of low immigrant concentration and over-represented in schools of high concentration. The reverse is true of the 'other' immigrants. This is important since West Indians perform on average much less well than the 'other' immigrants. For this reason it was decided to carry out the analysis for each nationality group separately. However, the resulting numbers in some sub-groups were so small that in most of the tables presented only the West Indians and 'other' immigrants have been included.

Table 9.17 shows that, among West Indians, attainment is very similar regardless of immigrant concentration, with the exception that there is a lower attainment in schools with over 60 per cent immigrants. The same appears to be true of Greek Cypriots and Indians, that is, that attainment is very similar regardless of the immigrant concentration. Among the Pakistanis and Turkish Cypriots, there is no clear pattern but the differences between sub-groups are much larger. However, the numbers of children involved are small and there is no clear trend discernible. Among the 'other' immigrants there appears to be a trend similar to that shown for the non-immigrants, i.e. declining attainment with increasing immigrant concentration. However, this trend appears to be reversed in the group of 50–60 per cent immigrants.

The most noteworthy point in Table 9.18 is the smallness in differences in mean scores within the sub-groups, whether one reads across or down the table, i.e. varying priority rank or immigrant concentration. The largest difference is of only six points. None of the differences is in fact statistically significant.

Table 9.17

Mean Reading score of Immigrant Children Classified by Nationality in Schools of Varying Immigrant Concentration

Immigrants (%)	W. Ind.	Ind.	Pak.
⩽10	88.1 (228)	90.5 (48)	90.7 (26)
10.1–20	89.1 (401)	90.2 (70)	92.1 (43)
20.1–30	87.3 (364)	89.8 (48)	94.3 (33)
30.1–40	87.4 (343)	89.6 (33)	87.3 (15)
40.1–50	88.0 (203)	89.9 (15)	83.1 (7)
50.1–60	87.6 (330)	87.9 (14)	88.3 (9)
60.1–70	84.7 (57)	75.4 (8)	78.7 (6)

Immigrants (%)	Gr. Cyp.	Tk. Cyp.	Other
⩽10	86.8 (63)	87.1 (32)	96.0 (230)
10.1–20	86.4 (81)	85.5 (48)	93.1 (256)
20.1–30	88.7 (100)	82.2 (39)	94.1 (173)
30.1–40	85.6 (51)	84.3 (73)	91.3 (120)
40.1–50	86.1 (22)	79.2 (25)	86.5 (43)
50.1–60	85.6 (50)	81.5 (30)	93.3 (54)
60.1–70	88.5 (14)	81.3 (17)	85.1 (14)

Table 9.18

Mean Reading Score of West Indian Children in Schools of Varying Immigrant Concentration and Education Priority

Immigrants (%)	Educational Priority Rank			
	1	2	3	4
⩽10	85.1 (19)	85.6 (52)	87.5 (81)	89.9 (107)
10.1–30	86.5 (110)	86.1 (279)	87.7 (370)	90.7 (172)
30.1–50	84.5 (72)	86.2 (271)	88.2 (273)	88.7 (27)
>50	84.3 (197)	87.8 (214)	90.9 (34)	—

Furthermore, it is not possible to discern any clear trend; in schools of very high and low priority, there is no trend, and in schools in high and average priority groups there is a *slight* trend of increased attainment with increased concentration.

If anything the pattern appears to be less clear among the 'other' immigrants, as Table 9.19 shows. The differences shown are, in fact, greater than those among West Indians, being in some cases as much as ten points. However, the only difference which is significant is that in the highest priority group between children in schools of 10–30 per cent immigrants and those in

Table 9.19

Mean Reading Score of 'Other' Immigrants in Schools of Varying Immigrant Concentration and Education Priority

| Immigrants (%) | Education Priority Rank | | | |
	1	2	3	4
≤10	—	89.8 (19)	90.8 (53)	97.6 (174)
10.1–30	92.1 (34)	90.7 (93)	92.9 (182)	95.2 (162)
30.1–50	82.6 (30)	88.2 (53)	89.4 (75)	104.6 (19)
>50	88.3 (27)	92.0 (38)	94.0 (7)	—

schools of 30–50 per cent immigrants; 92.1 as compared with 82.6. Furthermore, in no priority group is a clear trend discernible. Finally, for the 'other' immigrants (unlike the West Indians), education priority rank would seem to be an important factor. The differences between some sub-groups are large, for example, there is a range of twelve points between children in schools of 30–50 per cent immigrant concentration as between the lowest and highest priority schools.

In conclusion it would seem that as far as the analysis undertaken has gone there is no evidence to support the hypothesis that non-immigrant (or immigrant) children are adversely affected in their reading attainment by being taught in a school of high immigrant concentration, nor conversely is the attainment of immigrant children higher if they are taught in a school of low immigrant concentration. Compared with parental occupation and the index of multiple deprivation (education priority rank), the factor of immigrant concentration would appear to be of small and inconsistent importance. Children in high concentration immigrant schools are likely, however, to attain a lower level than their peers because they are more likely also to come from a less advantaged home background and—regardless of immigrant concentration—the school is more likely to be a disadvantaged school.

Conclusions

1 ILEA junior schools present considerable variety in the degree of both social and ethnic mix. Something like 40 per cent of ILEA pupils are in schools with a social or immigrant concentration comparable (within 10 per cent limits) to the Authority as a whole. About one-quarter of middle-class children are

in predominantly middle-class schools (i.e. 50 per cent or more middle class), nearly a half of all lower working-class children are in schools which are predominantly lower working-class (50 per cent+), while one-sixth of the immigrant children are in predominantly immigrant schools (50 per cent+).

2 In considering the desirability of social/ethnic mix in schools we have to make a reservation about our analysis. We have only considered educational benefit in terms of academic performance and that on one measure of attainment, and at one point in time. Examination of attainment at an older age or of different skills might have shown a different pattern. Further, there may be more important social benefits in terms, for example, of social relationships which are derived from socially and ethnically mixed schools, particularly for older children; on this we have no information.

3 An examination in two Boroughs suggests that whatever the social or ethnic composition of an area, schools in that area do not necessarily have a similar social or ethnic population, i.e. social mix in the neighbourhood does not automatically produce social mix in the schools in that neighbourhood. Further, there would appear to be a large degree of discrimination or choice exercised by parents within a very small local area, so that neighbouring schools within a quarter of a mile of each other may have very different populations. We would suggest that as it seems that most children attend a local school the only ways to ensure schools with a social/ethnic mix similar to that of the neighbourhood they serve, if that end were thought desirable, would be either to adopt a policy of quotas or to find some way to make the 'unpopular' school as popular as its neighbour with those parents who make positive choices about schools.

4 The relationship between social class composition and educational performance is confused, slight and certainly of less importance than the extent to which the school population is experiencing a multiplicity of depriving factors. In general, attainment of all children is higher if they are in schools with a high middle-class or low working-class composition. However, the attainment of working-class children is much less affected by the social composition of the school than is the attainment of middle-class children.

5 The effect of immigrant concentration on educational performance is similarly less important than the degree to which

schools are experiencing multiple deprivation. As far as immigrant children are concerned, their performance is only marginally affected by the immigrant concentration in the school. Non-immigrant children appear to be affected at the extremes of concentration: children in schools with less than 10 per cent immigrants have a reading age approximately one year in advance of those children in schools with over 60 per cent immigrants. However, the variation between these extremes is slight: children in schools of between 10 and 50 per cent immigrants attain very much the same level. Furthermore, the relationship between immigrant concentration and performance is not straightforward. Children in schools of low immigrant concentration come from predominantly higher status occupational backgrounds and the schools are furthermore low on the index of multiple deprivation. On the other hand, children in high concentration schools are predominantly working class and the schools are high on the index of multiple deprivation.

6 When social and ethnic mix appear to be closely related to performance, it is at a level which an explicit policy directed towards encouraging and supporting such social and ethnic mix could not achieve—at least not throughout the ILEA. For example, immigrant proportions of less than 10 per cent cannot be achieved in an Authority in which the overall percentage of immigrants is nearly twice that. The performance of lower working-class children appears to be higher when they are in schools which are predominantly middle class (50 per cent or more); this demands a social structure for the schools beyond the Authority's power since the overall proportion of middle class is only half the 'desired' one.

7 We are confronted, then, by a situation in which no matter how desirable for other social and educational reasons social and ethnic mix may be, it cannot be justified in terms of the performance measures used in this chapter. Either the gains are too small to warrant the policy effort or the objectives are unrealistic in terms of the characteristics of the population. Improved educational performance of working-class children might be achieved if appropriate action was taken based on an examination of the social and psychological dynamics which underpin the index of multiple deprivation used in this paper and the mobilization of suitable resources to alleviate the situation. This conclusion should not be allowed to deflect attention from the

minority of children in highly atypical school situations, especially when such extreme concentrations are deviant not simply from the Authority or Borough population, but from smaller, more local areas. Again whether larger gains could be achieved by a policy directed towards greater social and ethnic mix, or by national, regional and local policies of positive discrimination in educational resources towards the disadvantaged schools, is at least debatable. The pay-off in terms of educational attainment of greater mix is perhaps indicated in this chapter and may be small. Dramatic redistribution and proper utilisation of scarce educational resources might well have a more significant impact and is possibly consistent with the strong influence of 'multiple deprivation' on attainment.

References

1. COLEMAN, J. S., *Equality of Educational Opportunity*, U.S. Department fo Education and Welfare and the Office of Education, U.S. Government Printing Office, Washington D.C., 1966.

2. LITTLE, A. N. and MABEY, C., 'An Index for Designation of Educational Priority Areas' in *Social Indicators and Social Policy*, ed. Shonfield, A. and Shaw, S. (London: Heinemann Educational Books, 1972).

Chapter Ten

The Organizational Context of Housing Policy in Inner London: The Lambeth Experience

MICHAEL HARLOE, RUTH ISSACHAROFF
AND RICHARD MINNS

Summary

The chapter examines the roles played by six agencies in the housing market; local authorities, housing associations, private landlords, estate agents, building societies and private developers. These agencies play a crucial intervening role in translating housing (and other policies) into practice.

In inner city areas the local authorities have a key role to play in the housing situation and have been granted wide powers to intervene, both directly and by trying to influence the actions of other housing agencies. Lambeth Borough Council has been trying to mount a comprehensive attack on its housing problems by increasing its own efforts and by trying to enlist the help and co-operation of other agencies. The chapter discusses how differing ideologies, and resource and organizational problems, prevent co-operation.

The chapter concludes that private enterprise, whether it be producing housing for rent or sale, is unlikely to respond in a major way to Lambeth's initiatives. Housing associations will make a small contribution, but the main burden will continue to fall on public authorities so long as other agencies operate as they do. Certain conflicts exist within the local authority, for instance between the goals of the development plan and the exigencies of the current housing situation. Far more serious are a set of factors beyond Lambeth's control particularly the problem of land availability and land assembly.

The chapter concludes that one of the most important aspects of Lambeth's initiative has not been in concrete housing achievements in the Borough, but rather in its role as a pressure group for change in central government policies affecting inner city housing. Many of Lambeth's current problems can only be solved by further central government action.

Introduction

There has been a good deal of controversy in recent years, particularly in the context of the Greater London Development Plan Enquiry, concerning the nature and implications of trends in population and employment in Inner London. To some extent at least, the debate has been made more confused by a lack of basic evidence with which to support the various assertions that have been made. However, the existence of major and unmet need in the housing area is beyond doubt and, although the extent of need is a matter for detailed argument, it is equally certain that there will be no dramatic reduction or removal of the backlog of housing need in the near future [1]. In this situation a number of different solutions to the problem have been canvassed. Some place their major hopes in a rapid increase in public housing in the Outer Boroughs, others see the housing associations beginning to play a major role in the provision of accommodation, others would like to see an increase in the new and expanding towns programme. Of course, none of these policies are mutually exclusive and all of them are likely to play some part in meeting housing needs in the future. In fact, local authorities in Inner London and the Greater London Council will continue to spend much of their resources on housing. Accordingly, it is important to understand something of the ways in which local government can significantly affect the housing situation in its areas. In more general terms there is a need to investigate the crucial intervening role that bureaucratic structures play in the process of translating housing, planning, and other social policies into practice.

For the purposes of this discussion of Inner London we have concentrated on six of the housing agencies. They are local authorities, housing associations, private landlords, estate agents, building societies and developers. By the term 'housing agencies' we mean agents who provide, or facilitate the provision of, housing. These may vary from large formal organizations such as local authorities through to individuals, such as some private landlords. However our list excludes a number of important agencies. For example, insurance companies play a significant role in the provision of housing, particularly for the higher income groups, but we have not been able to study the operations of these agencies owing to lack of time and resources.

The 1960s saw an increasing concentration by central government, of whatever political persuasion, on the problems of inner areas. By a succession of acts and measures, attempts were made to increase and extend the efforts of the local housing authorities in these areas. A major effort was made to increase new building by improving the subsidy system and more resources were put into the improvement of older houses and the encouragement of housing associations. Local government was encouraged to intervene to a far greater extent than before in the running of the privately rented sector. Local authorities and the building societies, through the option mortgage and guarantee scheme, were encouraged to extend home ownership to poorer families and at the same time there was a growing concern about the need to restrict housing subsidies to the neediest families. However, while there may have been a broad growing measure of agreement on policy at the national level, implementation of the bulk of this policy depended on an agency's initiative and willingness.

Local authorities have been used as the main agencies of central government intervention in the housing situation in inner city areas. Any co-ordinated attack on the housing problem in these areas must therefore involve the local authority to a very great extent. Two questions about this situation now arise. The first (which we shall not discuss in detail in this chapter) asks why local authorities choose to play a more or less active role in the housing system. The second asks what the problems are when an authority *does* choose to mount a co-ordinated comprehensive approach to its housing problems. Lambeth is such a local authority, and in this chapter we concentrate on analysing this effort. The various housing agencies also have goals and operate under differing sets of constraints. Resources, ideologies and organizational factors have affected their reactions to Lambeth's initiative—as they will also affect the nature of the local authority's own operations which include this attempt to influence the workings of the other agencies. This chapter will sketch out the nature of these constraints and attempt to evaluate this example of local authority initiative.

Lambeth: Population, Housing and Social Structure

In common with the other Inner London Boroughs, Lambeth's population has been falling during the sixties. Preliminary results for the 1971 Census suggest that its population is now some 303 000, a drop of almost 40 000 since 1961. The fall in population in Lambeth, as in other areas of London, has not had a dramatic effect in reducing the demand for housing due to rising headship rates. As Greve has shown, in common with the rest of Inner London, the number of small households has been rising, and this is likely to continue due to migration and continuing changes in the employment structure [2]. In 1966 52.7 per cent of the households in the Borough were one or two person units. At the same time, in common with other Inner London Boroughs with high proportions of furnished tenancies, the ratio of households to dwellings appears to be rising, so that from 1961 to 1966 the average number of persons per household fell from 2.81 to 2.75 but the ratio of households to dwellings increased from 1.19 to 1.28.

Lambeth is one of the nine Inner London Boroughs which in 1966 had more than 30 per cent of its households occupying shared dwellings. The proportion of households living in shared dwellings increased from 28.2 to 38.1 per cent from 1961 to 1966. This appears to be a product of two movements, firstly the decline in the stock of dwellings in the Borough, and secondly, the growth in the number of households, particularly smaller ones.

Sharing is heavily concentrated in the private rented sector. According to the 1966 Census, about half the tenants renting private unfurnished dwellings and nine-tenths of the tenants renting private furnished dwellings, were sharing. Less than a tenth of local authority tenants, and three-tenths of owner occupiers did so.

As can be seen from Table 10.1 the major growth in tenure

Table 10.1

Household Tenure in Lambeth

	1961	1966
Owner occupiers	18.2	19.5
Local authority tenants	21.5	27.9
Tenants renting privately (unfurnished)	44.9	37.6
Tenants renting privately (furnished)	12.6	12.0

Source: 1961 and 1966 Census.

between 1961 and 1966 was in the local authority sector and the major decline in the privately rented, unfurnished sector. It is likely that the 1971 Census will show that the operations of the local authority will have continued to be the major influence in changing the composition of the housing tenure. There will have been a continued decline in the unfurnished rented sector as a result of local authority demolitions, but also as a result of the conversion of unfurnished to furnished tenancies. In furnished tenancies higher rents can be charged and tenants evicted more easily [3].

Owner-occupation is concentrated in the outer, southern part of the Borough, which has a lower than average percentage of local authority housing. Privately rented unfurnished accommodation is very evenly distributed throughout the Borough but furnished tenants are more concentrated in the central area. The fact that unfurnished privately rented accommodation is fairly evenly scattered throughout the Borough means that the changeover to furnished accommodation could occur in most wards. Multi-occupation could increase significantly in the southern wards where there have been previously far fewer signs of housing stress than in the northern and central wards.

Evidence available to the Council in connexion with their scheme for the registration of houses in multi-occupation suggests that this development is occurring.

As far as the condition of the housing stock is concerned, the GLC's 1967 Housing Survey showed that only three other London Boroughs, Southwark, Newham and Tower Hamlets, had a higher percentage of dwellings with a life of up to only seven years. Only two other London Boroughs, Newham and the City of London, had a higher percentage of dwellings with a life of eight to fifteen years [4]. Over 27 per cent of Lambeth's dwellings had a predicted life of up to fifteen years, and almost 10 per cent only had a life of up to seven years. In addition, according to a cumulative index produced by the GLC, in 1966 practically 50 per cent of Lambeth's households lacked basic amenities [5].

The social structure of Lambeth is that of a typical Inner London Borough, having fewer professional and managerial workers and more service and unskilled manual workers than Greater London as a whole. But the distribution of various socio-economic groups varies widely between boroughs in Inner London. Boroughs such as Kensington and Chelsea and the City of Westminster have as much as 30 per cent of their male residents in managerial and professional groups and less than the Greater London average (i.e. 22 per cent) in service, semi-skilled manual and unskilled manual groups. In Boroughs such as Newham, Tower Hamlets and Islington, there are far fewer managers and professional workers and relatively more service, semi-skilled manual and unskilled manual workers. Lambeth falls somewhere between these two extremes, having 11.6 per cent of its males in the managerial and professional groups, and 26.3 per cent in the other service and semi-skilled and unskilled groups. Its proportion of skilled manual workers, foremen, self-employed workers, supervisory and junior non-manual workers, is almost identical at 58.1 per cent with that of Greater London as a whole. The pattern of social class distribution within Lambeth corresponds closely to the picture already provided of the distribution of housing conditions throughout the Borough. Thus there is an above average concentration of manual and service workers in the housing stress areas and an above average concentration of the upper echelons of the white collar gradations in the southern wards.

Examination of Census data suggests that there are two sorts of movement taking place in the Borough. First, there are the middle class who move into London when young and single in order to be near their work but who move out a few years later when married to found a family in the suburbs. Secondly, there is a very high rate of movement among people in stress areas. This movement tends to be frequent and of a short distance, involving moves within the Borough, or between the Borough and the surrounding areas of Inner London. This sort of movement is probably involuntary. It is likely to be a response by service, semi-skilled and unskilled manual workers to a situation of high housing stress.

Most of the longer distance movement is highly directional. Very few people during 1961 to 1966 moved north to areas of Outer London or the South East. The net losses of any substantial size were all to London Boroughs in the south and south-east of Greater London. Analysis of Census data over the period 1961 to 1966 tends to confirm the popular contention that the middle class is moving out of the Borough and being replaced by an ever increasing proportion of unskilled and semi-skilled workers. However, an analysis of the one year migration data, 1965 to 1966, contained in the 1966 Sample Census suggests that this trend was not so sharp over the one-year period as it had been over the five-year period 1961 to 1966.

The picture derived from Census migration data is a familiar one of a high concentration of newly or recently arrived coloured population living in markedly worse housing conditions than their white working-class equivalents. Their main hope for decent housing in the future must be found in the local authority sector where a low but rising proportion of them are finding accommodation. This low figure is undoubtedly due to the operation of the local authority allocation system and possibly to a general lack of understanding of bureaucratic procedures rather than any overt discrimination. By comparing wholly moving families in 1965 with the whole period 1961 to 1966, it is significant to note that by 1965–66 a decreasing proportion of all migrants were able to envisage owner-occupation, and an increasing proportion of migrants within the area and from elsewhere in Great Britain were compelled to resort to privately rented furnished accommodation. This reflects the decline in the availability of houses for sale and the conversion of substantial numbers of unfurnished tenancies to furnished lettings on vacation. It is one indication of how in Lambeth, as in other areas of Inner London, increasing costs and a dwindling supply have led to a worsening of housing opportunities for families who earn less than average wages.

In fact the GLC 1967 Survey showed that 69 per cent of households in the Inner Boroughs had head of household incomes of less than £20 per week. The corresponding percentage for Outer Borough households was 57 per cent [6]. Similarly the proportion earning over £40 per week was double for households in Outer Boroughs compared with those in Inner Boroughs. Household incomes follow a similar pattern. However, although occupying fewer rooms at a higher occupancy rate, households in the Inner Boroughs paid a similar amount for their accommodation within each type of tenure as those in Outer Boroughs, an average of £310 per annum for owner-occupiers in both areas and £170 and £190 for tenants renting privately in Inner and Outer Boroughs respectively.

Between March and May 1970 the Francis Committee's research team surveyed three stress areas, one in Hackney, Stepney in Tower Hamlets and Clapham in Lambeth [7]. Unfortunately the data for the Lambeth stress area are not available separately. In the three stress areas as a whole, about 15 per cent of households in unfurnished tenancies (registered and unregistered) paid less than 10 per cent of the take-home pay of the head of the household in rent, about a similar proportion paid more than 30 per cent and the rest paid between these percentages. The median rent as a percentage of median take-home pay of the head of household was around 16 or 17 per cent for registered and unregistered tenants in the stress areas. The median take-home pay of heads of households in stress areas was less than that in the conurbation as a whole. The figures are £923 for registered tenants in the conurbation and £881 in the stress areas. The figures for unregistered tenants are £906 and £840 respectively. In comparison with the unfurnished sector, the furnished sector paid higher rents for inferior accommodation particularly in the stress areas. It is clear that there is more cheap accommodation in the stress areas but that the quality and conditions are very much worse. The same survey also shows that 48 per cent of the households in furnished accommodation in stress areas had a net income of under £20 per week, compared with 30 per cent of such households in the conurbation as a whole, and about 35 per cent of unregistered unfurnished households in the conurbation and stress areas alike.

The Political Background to Lambeth's Housing Strategy

Lambeth had a Labour administration from its foundation in 1965, but in 1968, at the height of the Labour government's unpopularity, the Conservatives were returned to power in the Borough. Before 1965, the Labour administration had the traditional Labour attitude towards housing issues, concentrating almost entirely on the production of a moderate programme of public housing. But after the election Labour's attitudes changed. We can only surmise that this change of attitude was a product of a number of factors including the evidence contained in work being done for the Greater London Development Plan, and the generally observable rise in housing problems, e.g. homelessness. An additional factor in Lambeth is likely to have been the presence of an activist housing manager, Harry Simpson,[1] who had arrived from Hackney in 1962. This and the stimulus which was presented by the Labour government's White Paper, *The Housing Programme 1965 to 1970* led the Labour administration to decide on a building programme of 1000 completions a year, subsequently amended to 1500. On the other hand the rising burden of interest repayments on loans meant that, in common with many other housing authorities in the mid-sixties, Lambeth was forced to consider the question of rent increases to help stem a growing rate fund contribution. Labour were on the point of putting through further rent increases when the election was declared, and they were also considering the possibility of setting up a housing advice service.

The new Conservative administration was, according to their Leader of that time, Bernard Perkins,[2] probably committed in

---

[1] In 1972 he became Director General, Northern Ireland Housing Executive.
[2] In 1972 he became Chairman of the GLC Housing Committee.

the majority to reducing local authority housing rather than increasing it. The fact that they actually increased the target for local authority building and the amount of the Council's resources devoted to housing can probably be explained, not so much in terms of a fundamental change of heart by the majority of councillors, but more in terms of the influence of a few policy makers among them. The key figures were the Leader and Councillor Peter Cary, who was at first Chairman of the Housing Committee and latterly Chairman of the Finance Committee. Few of the councillors had had any previous experience of local authority work, and the Conservatives organized themselves so as to give the Leader the power to appoint committee chairmen. The chairmen were directly accountable to the Leader and managed to dominate the committees.

Cary and Perkins decided that housing should be the new Council's number one priority. Although they were firm believers in private enterprise, they recognized that it could only make a very limited contribution in the Lambeth situation. As a result they took the line very strongly that the local authority must of necessity take an active housing role. They found an enthusiastic collaborator in Harry Simpson.[1] The publication of the 1967 GLC Housing Condition and Household Surveys, which were produced for the Greater London Development Plan, gave Cary the factual basis which he required to get his committee and the Council to accept an expanded local authority role in housing. Those who objected were simply presented with the facts and asked to suggest viable alternatives. On the basis of a powerful coalition of Housing Manager, Council Leader and Housing Committee Chairman, Lambeth launched an effort which was to make it a leading name in the world of housing.

The basic policy was laid out in a document entitled, 'Into the Seventies—Lambeth's Housing, A Review of the Demand, Supply and Costs'. It was published in 1969 but it incorporated

---

[1] Harry Simpson must take credit for helping them to arrive at this conclusion by swiftly ensuring that the new Housing Committee Chairman, Peter Cary, had first hand knowledge of some of the worst housing conditions in the Borough by taking him on a visit to the Geneva/Somerleyton area in Brixton and to the area community association.

policy decisions taken over the preceding twelve months. The document contains an analysis of the GLC Surveys and concludes 'the interpretation of these figures indicates a major problem in urban renewal and improvement which requires the marshalling of every available resource'. The plan aimed at a target of 2000 new completions a year, utilising all possible agencies, 1000 completed units a year from the conversion of larger houses into self-contained flats, and 1000 dwellings per year improved by the provision of modern amenities.

In the pre-election period, the Conservatives had attempted to formulate an approach to the housing problems of Lambeth and their manifesto had included a number of ideological imperatives. In particular they promised to encourage private enterprise development in the Borough, and to continue to extend the Labour Party's support for housing associations and societies. Other aims of the Conservatives included the sale of council houses to sitting tenants, encouragement to owner occupiers to maintain and improve their houses, the limitation of compulsory purchase powers, and 'fair rents' for all council tenancies with adequate rent rebates for those in need. Many elements of this programme could be found, in at least muted form, in the new policy. Thus it was envisaged that 25 per cent of the 2000 new completions a year 'should be provided by means of private sector participation'. Of the 1000 dwelling units from the conversion of larger houses 'it was anticipated that at least half would be provided by housing associations or similar agencies'. Two compulsory purchase orders were either modified or rescinded, although in retrospect this proved to be a rather token gesture, as did the sale of council houses to sitting tenants.

A serious constraint on the policy makers was that of finance and the level of rates. The new council was committed to keeping the rates down. The deficit on the housing account was already £1.4m. when the Conservatives took office, and they soon realized that, with housing given top priority, it would be impossible to reduce this deficit. Apart from other costs Lambeth needs forty acres of housing land a year for redevelopment which means that about 120 acres have to be in the pipeline at any one time. The debt charges on this alone produce a large deficit. In any event the Chairman of the Housing Committee had to pledge that rates would increase by no more than 12½p

within a five year period. In fact the rate was only increased by
½p until the Conservative's last year in office when the increase
was 11p. A corollary of this pledge was that rents had to be
increased and a series of rent increases, limited by prices and
incomes legislation, has increased rent levels to between 1.5 and
2.1 times the gross value, depending on the age of the property
concerned, from previous levels which varied between 0.8 and
1.5 times gross value. At the same time the Council introduced a
rent rebate scheme, broadly in line with the Ministry of Housing
and Local Government's model scheme [8] but more generous
in certain respects.

Another element in the housing policy which developed,
particularly after the 1969 Housing Act in which Lambeth had
a direct interest and influence, was the improvement of
conditions in the privately rented sector, especially the furnished sector, by the use of public health powers to control
multiple occupation and improve amenities.

In summary then, the Lambeth policy consisted of a number
of elements:

1   a greatly increased public housing programme;
2   encouragement and assistance for housing associations;
3   a vigorous policy of regulation, control and improvement
of the privately rented sector via public health and housing
powers;
4   attempts to encourage private enterprise building and
owner occupation in the Borough.

To this list should be added what is probably the most publicized of Lambeth's innovations, the Housing Aid and Advice
Centre. This co-ordinates under one roof most of the traditional
local government housing activities at the point of contact
between the authority and the client. It provides the basis for
Lambeth's comprehensive approach. The Advice Centre acts
as the frontline medium for contact between the authority and
the owners, managers and the tenants of the other various
agencies that the Council wants to involve in the concerted
attack on the Borough's housing problems. The emergence of
this policy is directly reflected in the subsequent reorganization
of the housing functions of the Borough, bringing together a
wide range of these services (although excluding physical
planning and building) under the Director of Housing and

Property Services. Figure 10.1 shows how the various functions have been combined in the new department.

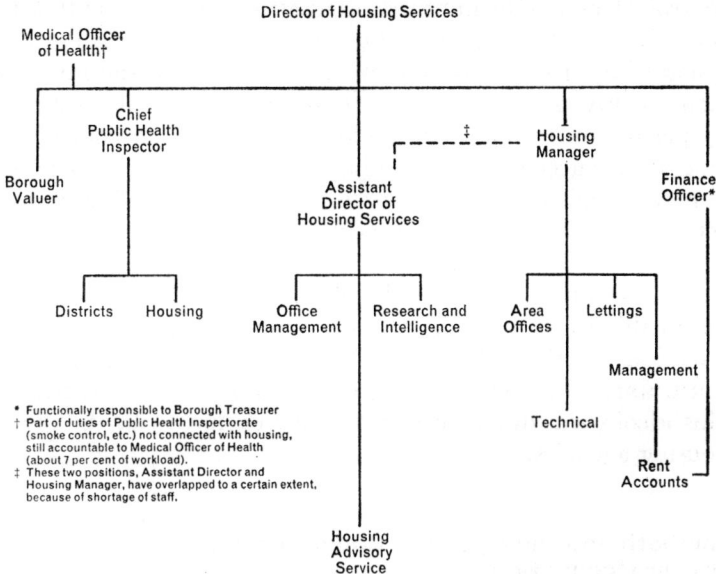

FIGURE 10.1 Lambeth's Directorate of housing and property services

Thus, the Conservatives decided that housing should be their number one priority and that for reasons dictated by ideology and the need for additional resources, a wide variety of agencies must be encouraged to combine in a joint effort to tackle the problem. Given the absence of any unified central government policy which would achieve this co-ordinated effort, Lambeth has tried to create its own system of control and accountability relying mainly on exploiting existing legislation, distributing resources, and the use of verbal persuasion and propaganda aligned to an increased public housing effort. At the same time no effort has been spared to use the results of this experience to bring pressure to bear on central government to alter the legislative and financial framework within which the authority operates, and this is as important a part of the Lambeth experience as its actual and immediate achievements in housing terms.

The powers of local authorities in the housing field can be

described under four general headings. First there is the power to provide, second to regulate, third the power to exhort and fourth the power to subsidize. In some areas, for example the control of houses in multiple occupation, the local authority can rely on coercive powers, but for other aspects, such as the general improvement of houses by landlords and the involvement of private developers and building societies, it must rely on persuasion through bargaining rather than on control by sanctions. Success in bargaining relies on the exchange of attractive offers. But a resource constrained local authority acting in isolation against markedly different ideologies will have limited success in contriving exchanges. The following sections examine in more detail the nature and success of Lambeth's efforts over the past few years, in particular paying attention to the influence of resource and organizational constraints on its own housing efforts and of these constraints plus ideological differences on its relationships with the other housing agencies.

Lambeth and the Agencies Concerned with Owner Occupation

According to Peter Cary, the reason why 500 of the target of 2000 new dwellings per year contained in 'Into the Seventies' was planned to come from private developers for sale was that 24 per cent of people in redevelopment areas were owner occupiers. This rather tenuous justification for a policy which was basically ideologically determined has not stood the test of reality for, unless central government or the Borough are prepared to subsidize heavily new private enterprise development, there is virtually no chance that new building for owner-occupation will make a significant impact in Lambeth in the foreseeable future. The percentage of Greater London's private housing which is located in Lambeth is minute—under 1 per cent in 1970 and the first six months of 1971 [10]. Even within the group A Boroughs—which themselves provided less than one-fifth of the metropolitan total—Lambeth only contained 3 per cent of the output in 1970 and 8 per cent in the first half of 1971. Of course there is little land available for such housing in Inner London but the Council was anxious to help private enterprise find sites—why then did their effort fail?

According to a survey conducted by the Department of the Environment (DoE) in 1970, almost 60 per cent of new housing was built by small firms constructing 150 houses per annum or less [9]. Furthermore there are only seventy builders who produce more than 250 houses per annum and the largest firm, Wimpeys, is the only one which builds over 3000 houses per annum. So there would seem to be two strategies open to Lambeth, either to interest one or two large developers or a number of smaller ones which between them would produce a reasonably sized output. The necessity for repeated negotiation with small firms with its attendant use of scarce staff time makes the possibility of getting the bigger builders involved an attractive one. In addition the larger firms are likely to have sufficient capital to carry the cost of development in an expensive area.

All builders, be they large or small are actuated by the profit motive rather than social considerations. If the two objectives can be combined, and the firm given a distinct image so much the better, but profits must be maintained to retain investors' confidence. The way in which this profit motive is expressed in the style of operation of the firm differs according to the character of top management, the company structure and the consequent financial objectives of the house building operation. In the last analysis a 'public good' ideology has no essential place in this frame of reference.

Building in Lambeth—not traditionally an area of new owner occupation—is thought to be a very risky venture. The main concentration of new private housing in Inner London is in parts of Camden, Kensington and Chelsea, Westminster and Lewisham, areas with a good environment and already existing concentration of middle-class housing. By contrast Lambeth has little open space and, except to the south, few areas of substantial middle-class housing. The small sites that are available are often in areas which estate agents would be stretched to label 'desirable'. The Borough found that a gap of up to £50,000 per acre existed between the price that developers were prepared to pay for cleared land and the cost of the authority providing this land (including relocation costs).

All firms, in a more or less sophisticated way, build to a section of the market they think will buy their product and work backwards from the price the house will sell for, deducting building and marketing costs, and finish with a residual sum which represents the amount they will pay for land. In Lambeth the gap—as we have seen—is simply too great.

Even if the calculations indicated reasonable profits, additional financial and organizational constraints might prevent the large firms going ahead. These firms want reasonably large sites which will provide space for at least twenty to thirty units as their building machine cannot cope efficiently with smaller areas. But, in a Borough with no free land, sites which provide the sort of quality services and environment necessary to sell the product are small and scattered. Because land costs are so high in Lambeth, developers are more likely to build flats, but these are not favoured by firms who aim to turn over capital at a rapid rate. Wimpeys told us that to develop a block of flats might take fifteen months with no one in occupation until all were complete, whereas the first people move into a new estate of houses in twenty weeks.

Small builders are ideal customers for small sites—and in Outer London they operate in precisely this way. But the smaller firms we interviewed expressed disinclination to experiment by building in Inner London. The demand for new housing in the London area outstrips the supply and the small builders can make a good living carving out a section of the market in the areas of Outer London where they are guaranteed buyers for their products. They do not need to take unnecessary risks in Lambeth. Some small firms set up by surveyors and architects are doing conversion work but, as of now, the larger firms only operate in the more desirable areas where most Inner London new building occurs (e.g. Camden and Westminster) and this is in the upper price ranges (e.g. £12 000 per unit was quoted by one large firm in this business).

One experiment that does offer some possibilities is a pilot scheme of seventeen houses built by the Council but for sale. The price was £8000–9000 but private developers would have charged £11 000. During the Labour Government restrictions were put on the extension of this form of municipal enterprise and it remains to be seen whether larger scale schemes are initiated. Another possibility, for new building by cost rent or co-ownership housing societies, seems to be almost entirely ruled out by the problem of costs.

To conclude, the chances of more private housing in Lambeth are bleak. New housing in the inner city is expensive anyway and being mainly in the form of flats is therefore unsuitable for families with children. The price of this housing is prohibitive given the type of people in housing need and in council housing which Lambeth wanted to see buying their own houses. Even increased densities, which might anyway be socially unacceptable, will only affect the price which developers will pay for land and will not necessarily reduce the selling price of the housing that they build on it.

The main opportunity for owner occupation in Lambeth must therefore be in second-hand housing. Here the clash between Lambeth's objective of encouraging owner-occupation and their commitment to increased public housing provision must be noted. The Directorate of Development estimates that the Council needs over sixty acres of land per annum to meet all their development requirements. This land can only be obtained by clearance and the removal of large numbers of houses already in owner occupation. Once again land availability emerges as possibly the major resource constraint.

The Council has attempted to stimulate increased owner occupation by trying to persuade the building societies to allocate a proportion of their funds to mortgages in the Borough, especially to support owner occupation in General Improvement Areas (GIAs). The Council, using their power under the 1969 Act, would improve the environment and thus raise values, and would encourage people coming into the Housing Advice Centre to deposit money in the co-operating societies. The bargain would seem to be a more attractive one to the societies than the sort of deal that the Council could offer the private developers.

The number of building society mortgages granted in Inner London is small. Special tabulations from the 1970 DoE 5 per cent mortgage sample survey showed that five times as many were granted in Outer London (1539) as in the inner area (325). The price of the houses granted mortgages and the age of the buyers suggests that such an option would be well beyond the means of the bulk of the Borough's population anyway. It may well be that there is nonetheless an unsatisfied potential demand for mortgages in Lambeth. But the disinclination of the building societies to stimulate this market is a product of ideologies which are institutionalized in the lending rules of the societies. The ideologies are reinforced by a Chief Registrar of Friendly Societies whose job is to ensure that building societies comply with legislative requirements.

In a recent study [11], an attempt was made to distinguish between three different sorts of ideological viewpoint that businessmen might hold. They are (1) The *laissez-faire* attitude —all that mattered was to maximize profits. (2) The long term company interest attitude—which claimed that in the end the best profit could be maintained by the firm behaving in a socially responsible way and (3) The social responsibility attitude—which saw the main purpose of the firm as being to serve society. In practice most businessmen rejected (1) and could not distinguish between (2) and (3) rejecting the more instrumental attitude in the LTCI ideology and the more idealistic in the SR one. Our interviews with building societies confirm this picture. The connexion between their social claims and the claims of business is a close one, the 'promotion of thrift and home ownership was good in itself' we were told. At the same time this social attitude is clearly constrained by what the Chief Registrar calls the requirements of 'good business'. It is this concern which puts serious limits on conclusions which academics and policy makers can draw concerning the possible expansion of the building societies' role to operate in a more 'social' or public policy oriented way in areas such as Lambeth.

What are these 'good business' requirements? The societies borrow short and lend long. Consequently they would theoretically be vulnerable to panic withdrawals in the face of a lack of confidence. In practice this rarely occurs, since it can be inhibited by rules which can be invoked to prevent hasty withdrawals and since there is a strong history of security. However this structure of operation is historically the reason why great emphasis is put by the societies on taking minimal risks. Like the developers, they are, in the words of the General Manager of the Bristol and West Building Society, 'run as a commercial enterprise and not as extensions of the Welfare State'.

The Building Societies Act 1962—the major statute governing the societies' operations—and the Chief Registrar who enforces it, make it clear that the major accountability of the societies is to their investors. The Registrar does not feel that the social or economic significance of the societies is his concern. If anyone is responsible for these it is the DoE and the Treasury respectively, but their lack of effective intervention is more evident than their presence. However, the vast majority of societies fully share the Registrar's concern, and their methods of recruitment and training—most people enter their employ from school and stay with the same society—ensure that this attitude is strongly held by most of their employees from the directors downwards.

In practical terms the result of such attitudes can be seen in the process of selection of new mortgagors. The two concepts of 'security' and 'status' dominate this procedure. The simplest way to illustrate what security means is to say that the ideally secure property is one which is new or recently built, is a house rather than a flat or maisonette and not more than two storeys high. Societies are consequently keen to stimulate new building and are unlikely to be really enthusiastic about a switch in national policy which emphasizes rehabilitation. Indeed we were flatly told by one executive that the 1969 Housing Act was the wrong approach and none of the societies we interviewed would consider taking the lead in a General Improvement Area. Their low level of involvement in housing finance in Inner London becomes understandable. Furthermore even if the societies were to lend on older property in GIAs, for example, a 75 per cent advance for a fifteen- or twenty-year period would be the usual limit, thus effectively excluding the marginal owner occupiers (unless the government was prepared to loan the remainder).

The second criterion for eligibility, 'status', is an ill-defined term, but we were assured that it is not a value loaded term but rather some measure of a person's capacity to pay. In our experience this is also related to the person's age and likely stability of future earnings. The ideal type here is the young professional with a secure job and guaranteed annual increments. Blue collar workers are at a disadvantage not only for the obvious reason that their earnings may be low—as Barbolet showed they may be comparable to those of some white collar workers [12]—but because the future level and stability of their earnings is, or is thought to be, in doubt. It is not clear how much purely subjective factors affect societies' decisions but one manager said that he was impressed by people who had 'worked things out in advance'. This suggests that the prospective buyer who did not have this ability might be at a disadvantage. It seems to us that managers build up an image in their minds of what qualities an applicant should have, some part of which may be purely objective, income level for instance, and some part of which seems purely subjective; for example, societies do not like 100 per cent mortgages because they suspect that people without savings may be incapable of paying regularly, but the fact that these people may be regularly paying high rents seems to be ignored. The problem for marginal house-buyers in Lambeth, moving between jobs with little spare capacity for saving, with high rents and transport costs, is obvious.

Above all the selection process is dominated by the fact that there is no shortage of applicants. Our interviews show that this is a major barrier in the way of any alteration of the societies' conception of suitability for a loan. If the traditional tried and tested market provides more than enough business, there can be no commercial rationale behind any direction of resources away from this field.

In summary it looks as if the bargain Lambeth hoped to make with the building societies will not produce major benefits. The promise of increased investment is not enough to upset or modify 'good business practice' and anyway we were told by one executive that they had a lot of investors in the area already anyway—it was just that they then *lent* to people in other areas.

But as we saw in Table 10.1, owner occupation in Lambeth *is* increasing, though only slightly. Data from the Lambeth register of multi-occupation suggest that a substantial proportion of loans in stress areas may be finance company or private mort-gages. Many of these are for inferior property which the building societies would not consider and there is evidence to suggest that exorbitant real rates of interest—in excess of 20 or even 30 per cent—are paid. Clearly there would be very little common ground between such companies and individuals and the Borough's housing policy, and no attempt has been made to enlist the co-operation of such sources of entry into the owner-occupied sector. But their importance—especially as the costs they impose on the mortgagor encourage subletting and conse-quent multi-occupation—as an element of the situation which is beyond Lambeth's control or influence is significant.

Another important source of finance for owner occupation is local authority mortgages. In Lambeth there are two options

available—GLC and Borough schemes. The amount of resources available via these schemes has fluctuated widely in
recent years, depending on central government restrictions.
The GLC has been the most important source of finance for
housing loans. The categories of people who are eligible for a
GLC mortgage and the fact that loans are generally restricted
to older houses and limited to £7500, shows that the scheme is
aimed at the marginal home buyer. Further discussion of the
GLC scheme will be found elsewhere.[1]

It is surprising that the Borough's own scheme does not appear
to have a considered part to play in Lambeth's attempt at a
comprehensive approach to its housing problems. The scheme,
unlike many others, enables Lambethians to buy outside the
Borough, thus aiding dispersal, but our examination of mortgage data suggests that few 100 per cent mortgages are given,
especially on older property. Many of the loans are on older
property but it is not clear that any *conscious* attempt is made to
act as a lender of last resort for the marginal housebuyer and so
perform a strategic role (unlike the GLC). It is not certain why
the possible role of Lambeth's mortgage scheme has been a
matter for so little attention by the Borough, but an insufficient
supply of suitable housing, low incomes and the frequently
large gap between price and valuation probably explain why
many applications are subsequently withdrawn. In addition,
staff shortages led to a reliance on the service of outside valuers
who often applied over-stringent criteria in judging property.
In many cases they even allowed considerations of the applicants' status to affect their recommendations, thus exceeding
their normal concern solely with the property. Furthermore,
there was resistance from the officials when the Conservatives,
having liberalized the scheme already by taking into account
some part of the wife's income, wished to make further amend-
ments. According to the Conservative former Chairman of the
Housing Committee, Lambeth has far more money available
for mortgages than it spends. Only about 60 per cent of the
available money was spent in 1970–1.

---

[1] This chapter is a small part of a study of the London housing market
conducted by the authors with the help of a grant from the Social Science
Research Council. The study was supervised by Professor D. V. Donnison.

Lambeth and the Housing Associations

Different ideologies provide the basis for different associations' efforts. Some began out of social work and charitable endeavour and others, which include many formed over the past few years, are linked with businesses, property and the associated professional interests. Although the associations are virtually non-profit making, the opportunities for using them to further business interests or to create professional work are many and are sometimes exploited. Associations also suffer from a lack of available resources. The shortage and cost of land in Inner London results in little new building by associations (or housing societies for cost rent or co-ownership) in this area, and the shortage of suitable houses for conversion puts severe limits on their rate of expansion. Apart from the obvious desire to expand, associations need growth in order to break through the organizational constraints imposed by a small-scale operation. Just as serious is the inability to employ full-time professional staff to manage properties and do development work, both of which are essential if the associations are to become a major force in the housing market. They also suffer from a further disability. Unless they have additional charitable funds, few of them can afford to house families with social or psychological problems. Nor do they have the same ease of access to local authority social services that the housing department has. Also distortions in the subsidy system encourage associations to convert to small units, despite the fact that this does not always match the demand as shown by analysis of their waiting lists.

The movement tends to criticize local authorities for being bureaucratic agencies unable to recognize needs speedily enough. In practical terms this often results in an attitude of disdain for local authority allocation procedures, including points systems and waiting lists. There is a lack of realization that there are procedures of discrimination which for reasons of equity and justice, organizations providing housing are forced to employ once they get beyond a certain size, especially when there are more people competing for their goods than they can satisfy. Very often associations end up with waiting lists compiled in a rather haphazard manner through a grapevine of references from various agencies. Or the associations work on a 'first come first served' basis which does not necessarily mean that the neediest cases are housed.

Although the associations have a status defined in legislation, they are only controlled by the government in a very general way. Councils have permissive powers to support associations and, if they choose, can exert considerable control over the scope and nature of their activities. It is in the field of housing association activity more than any other we have examined that Lambeth seems to have most power to bargain for co-operation in a co-ordinated strategy. By offering resources—especially money and expertise—in exchange for accountability the Borough has managed to eliminate or reduce many of the more apparent disadvantages besetting housing associations outlined above.

In March 1967 Lambeth Borough Council decided to support housing associations actively. Since then, the Council has instituted a streamlined procedure to expedite the processing of applications for valuation and planning clearance so that delays which might otherwise result in sales to other parties are minimized. A joint working party representing all the Council departments concerned was set up to co-ordinate negotiations, and block loan sanctions were obtained from the Ministry for the biggest housing associations. In addition the Council makes a rate fund contribution of up to £100 per dwelling to bridge the deficiency between the cost rent on the one hand and the fair rent which is fixed for association units on the other. The Borough Council nominates tenants to 50 per cent of the lettings produced by associations and these tenants have their fair rents rebated in accordance with the Council's rebate scheme for its own tenants. Furthermore an experiment was undertaken by the London Housing Trust whereby Lambeth agreed to rebate the rents of all the tenants of the L.H.T. in the Borough where necessary, not just the rents of the Borough's own nominees. In fact an informal agreement along these lines also existed with the other of the two largest associations working within the Borough—the Metropolitan Housing Trust.

The Council expects associations to be providing 500 dwellings per year by conversion by 1972. New building by housing associations has not yet been undertaken and it would only be feasible in a situation where there was little or no rehousing commitment. The Council has actually stated that, if its own commitments allowed, it was prepared to rehouse existing tenants to enable an association to convert premises or to clear a site, provided that an equivalent number of nominations are given to the Council in the dwellings provided.

The Council also attempts to verify the *bona fides* of any association before making a loan and to ensure that their activities are not to the detriment of any section of the local population. Various problems and anomalies still persist in the relationship between the Borough and associations, though to a lesser extent than in other London Boroughs. Lambeth has had to yield to the Ministry's directive about the ceiling on the allowable cost on which subsidy is payable and it has had to amend the technical brief with which it requires associations to comply when doing conversions. The net result is that they actually convert to a lower standard than the Council itself.

It became apparent to the Director of Housing that there were too many associations bidding for too few properties (seventeen have agreements with the Council, and in the last three years several others have been turned away). Moreover, the Council's officers expressed apprehension at 'the proliferation of housing associations with limited ability, limited experience and limited objectives'. So the Council decided to rationalize the activities of the associations by allocating an individual zone to each. Suitable zones were found for the London Housing Trust and the Metropolitan, and the remaining associations had to be allowed to purchase anywhere in the Borough apart from the two designated areas.

But these zones were insufficient to keep the two housing associations fully occupied. The London Housing Trust in particular was disappointed at its slow rate of expansion. In fact Lambeth has had no powers to prevent housing associations with GLC funds intruding into the two zones but has insisted that housing associations which borrow from it must not obtain funds from the GLC to operate in the Borough as well, and the South London Family Housing Association, which has obtained money from both sources, conceded that it would only borrow from the Borough in future. Nevertheless, the Family Housing Association (the parent, a completely separate body) has bought about 130 units in Lambeth, all with GLC money, including some in the area zoned to the London Housing Trust, much to the latter's chagrin.

Attempts by the Town Clerk of Lambeth in September 1969, and by the Director of Housing in July 1970 to persuade the GLC not to finance additional housing associations operating in the Borough proved fruitless. Housing associations acting with Lambeth money are obliged to house Lambeth residents, those such as the F.H.A. supported with GLC funds have no such obligation. It is alleged that the housing associations working in Lambeth with GLC funds have an additional advantage in that the GLC values local houses at about £200 to £300 higher than the Borough. The result was that GLC backed associations so that they could often buy a house when the London Housing Trust, for example, could not, because the vendor's price would exceed the Borough Council's valuation. The GLC have seemed to be unconcerned by the chaos caused by competition since it appears that their main concern is to distribute £25m per annum.

In its evidence to the Cohen Committee [13], the Council expressed concern that the total cost of staff and other resources taken up by the processing of applications from housing associations was quite high. The number of valuations carried out by the Council Valuer to assist housing associations was several times the number of houses eventually purchased. The Council insists in its conditions for assistance to associations that they must not pay more for a property than the Council valuation. By doing this the Council hopes to prevent the price of houses rising as a result of competition between housing associations. Nevertheless, the fact that the GLC Valuer is valuing above the Borough Valuer has had an inflationary effect on house prices.

In terms of encouraging owner occupation, private buyers of marginal eligibility, or those who are simply held up by the amount of time it takes building societies to process their applications, are once again at a distinct disadvantage in competing with housing associations.

Lambeth has clearly used the powers and resources it has to try to integrate the work of selected housing associations into its attack on the Borough's housing problems. It has probably succeeded in using the associations in a more purposeful way than many other London Boroughs. The result is that the associations have worked as a supplement rather than a substitute for the Borough's own efforts. It has recognized many of the associations' limitations, e.g. it does not expect that the associations it backs can or should house 'problem families' and will offer assistance including rehousing if problems do arise.

However, apart from general arguments regarding the strategic value of a large housing association movement, particular problems remain in Lambeth. The Council does not have control over certain aspects of the associations' activity and it is dependent on action by external agencies to achieve some changes it desires. The prime examples are, firstly the disruptive effect of GLC backed activity (which may be reduced or stopped when zoning arrangements are finally agreed), and secondly the bias that the subsidy system introduces into the size of units that the association provides [14]. Resource constraints, especially the shortage of available housing for conversion, limit the role of the associations unless they can move on to do more new building. This seems unlikely to happen as the familiar problems of land availability and cost, lack of expertise and loss of economies of scale consequent on several small scale association projects, would make most association schemes unfavourable in comparison with the alternative of more public housing. Support for such schemes is likely to be based on anti-public housing prejudice or on the view that diversity of ownership brings benefits to tenants. At present we have no evidence that this latter proposition is substantially true.

Lambeth and the Private Landlords

The most intensive use of both its coercive and persuasive powers is seen in the relations that the Borough has with private landlords and, to a lesser extent, owner occupiers. As we have seen, the Borough suffers from two general problems, first dilapidation and the lack of amenities, and second overcrowding and sharing. Although elements of this situation are present in a wide range of the Borough's housing stock, the problems tend to be most intense in multi-occupied housing, where houses originally designed for one family are now being occupied by several. This leads to a lack of adequate amenities, serious fire risk and a decline in the general standard of cleanliness and repair.

Apart from work to repair and improve these houses, which is often a short-term matter, there is also the question of long-term improvement of other property. Here the property is more likely to be in single family occupation and may be owner occupied or belong to a landlord. In the latter case, especially where small landlords with no expertise are involved, the properties may well be managed by estate agents who are crucial intermediaries in the exchanges between the landlord and the local authority. As far as the Borough is concerned the public health inspectorate—now integrated into the Directorate of Housing and Property Services—bears the major responsibility for implementing this part of the housing policy.

Many aspects of this work, such as the prevention of over-crowding, which were previously dealt with by rather punitive and hence negative, public health legislation now form the substance of a housing strategy which aims at a more co-operative and constructive relationship between the owner and the authority. At the same time the attempt is being made to bring a wider range of phenomena, such as multi-occupation, under control.

Two important ideological considerations often inhibit these developments. The first is belief in the freedom of the individual to do what he likes with his own possessions within limits. This is inevitably circumscribed by the extension of regulatory powers, but it may inhibit the use of such powers when available. (Thus Harry Simpson said that he was waiting for some local authority to use section 72 of the 1969 Housing Act to enforce repair on an unfit owner-occupied house remarking that some would see this as an attack on individual liberty.) [15] The second is the belief that the public authority has a duty to ensure that families at least have a roof over their heads (hence Part III accommodation for the homeless). [16] Thus any action by local government which is clearly creating homeless-ness is likely to incur opprobrium and to be politically impos-sible. As a result some powers are unlikely to be used, and others not sought when they would cause homelessness. Some earlier legislation had a draconic quality—for example the legislation on overcrowding in the 1957 Act—and as a result is rarely used in areas such as Greater London where it would cause more problems than it would solve.

The clash of goals between the public authority, committed to the maintenance of adequate standards, and the landlord and agent, concerned with profit, is evident. Some landlords, typically the larger ones holding better quality property, often unfurnished, share the view expressed in the fusion of the LTCI/SR ideologies [11] and wish, within limits, to maintain their property in good condition, prevent overcrowding and maintain a reputation as good landlords. To this end they will use grants available under legislation—especially as these usually result in their being allowed to increase rents—and are generally fairly co-operative with the local authority. They may well dislike legislation and seek to change it (see the Freshwater Company's evidence to the Francis Committee), or they will operate it to the very limits of legality, but they will only rarely act illegally. Lambeth's relationships with such landlords are generally cordial and the Borough provides services, especially grants, which the landlord wishes to use.

It is a different matter with smaller landlords. Lambeth is conscious for its part that a large proportion of the Borough's population will continue to find accommodation in the privately rented sector, but the council is constrained by lack of resources from pursuing a policy of wholesale public ownership even when party ideology does not dictate that public acquisition should be limited. Therefore the Council needs to employ a judicious mixture of the stick and the carrot to gain their objective of improved housing conditions in the private sector. This in turn requires, in Harry Simpson's view, a new public health philosophy in which the landlord is not chased out but invited into the Housing Advice Centre, given both financial and technical help, and encouraged to co-operate [15]. Lambeth's inspectors have to be skilled persuaders and tireless and persistent workers, and these skills, being in short supply, place very real limits on the expansion of the Council's housing policy in this area. The landlord for his part should receive increased rents and a more valuable property but the picture is often not such a rosy one. Apart from the fact that the total rent flow from a multi-occupied property may actually fall when occupancy is reduced, even with increased individual rents, the landlord may simply not be interested in taking the time and trouble to improve his property.

A further problem from Lambeth's point of view, and one that can only be solved by central government, is the gap between the standard of fitness and unfitness into which much property falls. The standard of unfitness at which a building qualifies to be cleared is a minimal one, even excluding the absence of a hot water supply, whereas the standard which enables a building to receive grants to improve it to either the '5 point' or '12 point' standard [17] is far higher and includes a provision regarding the likely future life of the building. This means that very often all that can be done is to try to persuade landlords to patch up their property and then wait until it sinks low enough to be condemnable. This being so a considerable proportion of the Borough's housing stock is bound to remain in poor condition for years to come. An examination of the workings of the scheme for the registration of multi-occupied buildings highlights a number of other difficulties.

The 1964 Housing Act contained provision for such a registration scheme, and it was initially used by the Borough in six central wards with limited success. The powers were strengthened in the 1969 Housing Act, and in July 1970 Lambeth introduced a scheme covering the whole Borough. This was thought necessary by councillors and officials because of the spread of multi-occupation into Streatham and other southern areas of the Borough. The scheme was designed to:

1 give the Council information about houses in multiple occupation;

2 prevent any increase in multiple occupation except under conditions specifically approved by the Council;

3 enable action to be taken in relation to multi-occupation in accordance with the 1961 and 1964 Acts to improve conditions inside the houses, but on a Borough wide basis.

This complements and greatly extends the traditional individual referral system of properties requiring action which the Public Health Inspectors have been involved in. The use of this legislation to improve conditions has great potential but there are serious limitations. Firstly, Parliament's concern with ensuring that owners' rights are respected means that the authority has to trace and notify anyone with an interest in a property before making a management order to specify the duties of a manager/owner/agent (Section 12, 1961 Housing Act). The lengthy delays incurred before a council may act blunt the effectiveness of this measure. Secondly, the attempt to limit occupation under Section 19 of the 1961 Housing Act often means that tenants must testify as to who lives in the property. They may be harassed by the landlord or completely dependent on him for accommodation—particularly in view of the decline in the privately rented sector in Inner London— and therefore be unwilling to testify. Thirdly, orders under Section 15 of the 1961 Act and Sections 73–94 of the 1964 Housing Act to require improvements or to take over and do work on a property are slow to apply and may involve the local authority in considerable costs.

The problem of staff shortage means that the sections which require actual provision of amenities, or for default work to be arranged and supervised, may have received less than equal emphasis (see Table 10.2). These sections (14 and 15), which

Table 10.2

Action in Relation to Multiple Occupation in Inner London and Group A Boroughs 1969

	Section 12	Section 14	Section 15	Section 19
Camden			238	3
Greenwich			12	
Hackney	28	7		227
Hammersmith			84	35
Haringey	2	179	219	4
Islington	7		28	62
Kensington	10	68	105	
Lambeth	126	2	23	161
Newham		3	1	
Southwark	37		34	67
Tower Hamlets	35	32		28
Wandsworth	6	1	36	4
Westminster	8	2	34	51

Source: *Annual Abstract of Greater London Statistics (GLC, 1969)* Table 7.5.

are used less by Lambeth than some other Boroughs, are the main powers for ensuring anything gets done. The heavy investment in staff time on registration schemes and collecting information about the extent of multiple occupation may well have detracted resources and staff from the application of the other sections.

Another problem is the high proportion of owner occupier or small landlords in the multi-occupied sector (see Table 10.3). Here the problem of finding finance for improvements and the loss of income caused by the reduction of occupants is quite significant. Often the properties are managed by agents who may have a positive attitude to improvement and may attempt to persuade their clients to co-operate. Others however will not be so reputable and the persuasion of the public health inspector may well have to be backed up by statutory action. Either way the process is a time consuming one. We have been told that it may take two or three years continuous work to get one house into satisfactory shape. So far as finance is concerned Lambeth has often done works in default but the difficulty of recovering the money means that there are limits to the extent to which this can be done.

Table 10.3

Action on Houses in Multiple Occupation in Lambeth, and Type of Landlord of Properties

	Section 12	Section 14	Section 15	Section 19	Total
Small landlord:*					
(a) landlord at same address as property	17	1	9	30	57
(b) landlord elsewhere in Lambeth	18	10	1	25	54
Small or unrecorded large landlord:	9	6	5	14	34
Large Landlord:	10			21	31

* We based our assessments of size on an analysis of Lambeth's Rating List. Agents or landlords who did not appear on the list as managing or owning ten or more properties are recorded as small, or as a small/unrecorded large landlord if they appeared on public health officer records as living outside Lambeth and did not appear on the Rating List as owning ten or more. They could thereby be small, or large, with ten properties elsewhere in London.

Perhaps the reliance on a strategy of co-operation between local authority and landlords/owner occupiers is seen most clearly in legislation in the 1969 Housing Act dealing with General Improvements Areas. The measure assumes that landlords and owner occupiers are in a financial position to co-operate, and that they share the same views as to the need to improve older property. Lambeth is trying to strengthen its bargaining position with landlords and property owners, as described earlier, by encouraging building societies to lend for improvements. It is also offering to rehouse tenants (in exchange for a return nomination to the improved property) so that the landlord can claim an immediate, not a phased, rent

increase.[1] But the only sanction it can use is the strongest—
compulsory purchase—which the local party in power may be
averse to using, and which central government may be unwilling to approve. Two c.p.o.s were revoked when the Conservatives came to power in Lambeth in 1968 and, although as
we have mentioned above, this may have been a symbolic
gesture, none of these subsequently approved were for improvement. Central government has recently refused c.p.o.s
for some clearance schemes (e.g. in Southwark) and referred
them back for (voluntary) general improvement. It remains to
be seen whether compulsory purchase for improvement will be
allowed.

In conclusion, Lambeth's efforts to improve the condition
of existing private rented and owner occupied housing are on a
scale which few other authorities appear to match. There are,
however, serious limits to the extent of this activity. Apart from
lack of financial resources and suitably trained staff, which
both affect the scale and effectiveness of what can be done,
differences of ideology mean that bargains have to be struck
which benefit both sides. Once again this can be extremely
difficult. Additional problems are created by the difficulties
central government faces when limiting individual freedom.
Central government may also fail to realize the problems
encountered in the intensive application of such legislation.

One further aspect of Lambeth's policy in this area must be
mentioned. The registration scheme is a conscious effort to
attack the housing problem in Lambeth on two fronts, by improvement of the stock and by the *permanent reduction of the
resident population*. This latter aim raises serious planning
questions. Firstly it seems to clash directly with the Planning
Department's wish (as expressed in evidence to the Greater
London Development Plan) to maintain population and employment. Secondly if Lambeth reduces opportunities for
settlement, will this not lead to increased pressure on surrounding areas? On the first issue there is undoubtedly an

---

[1] Under the 1969 Housing Act a landlord can decontrol any of his rent
controlled property by improving it. The Rent Officer would then set a
'fair rent'. This increased rent could only be claimed from the tenant in
increments phased over a period varying according to circumstances, of
two to four years.

unresolved conflict between different departments of the Council and the respective committees. So far as the second issue is concerned, Lambeth hopes that the pressure it creates will lead other Inner Boroughs to introduce schemes and there are signs that this is occurring.

This in turn raises the question of whether the GLC strategy of attempting to stem the decline in population is a correct one. It also suggests that, if this policy persists, before long housing conditions may begin to deteriorate in Outer London regardless of the reluctance of these Boroughs to help with present problems. If this is so, the present political controversy on the issue may begin to be seen in a different light.

Lambeth and Public Housing

The limitations of the attempt by Lambeth to extract the maximum contribution to their housing policy from other agencies reinforced the need for a growing supply of public housing. The Council needs accommodation for families from the waiting list and for decanting families from cleared areas. It also needs accommodation for the growing number of people from Part III (homeless) accommodation and from other departments (i.e. medical, children's and welfare cases). Finally, the Council needs to offer rehousing as an essential support element in its strategy of reducing multi-occupation and improving the stock of privately rented housing. To some extent the Council may benefit by obtaining in turn nominations to the improved properties, but where a reduction in occupation is the outcome this will not be so.

The supply of dwellings comes from a number of sources, mainly relets of Lambeth property and nominations to GLC property (or via the GLC to Outer Borough housing) and from the Borough's own programme of new building. In addition, via the Industrial Selection Scheme, suitably qualified applicants may move to new and expanded towns. The problems concerning the latter scheme are well known. Normally it is the young skilled worker who is in demand in these new communities. Lambeth has only sent about 200 people per year out of the Borough in this way but recently they have (in conjunction with the Peterborough Development Corporation) carried out a major publicity campaign. There is some hope that more people will in future go to this and other new and expanding towns as well as to places such as Leeds which still have job vacancies and also have Council housing which is surplus to their own needs. It is interesting to note that, despite the formal position, which is that the GLC is responsible for overspill, these arrangements were settled as a result of the Borough's initiative.

The GLC itself has made available some 2000 nominations to Lambeth over the past five years. Most nominees are housed in the Lambeth area, but a significant number also move to GLC housing in the Sutton/Merton/Croydon area where there are cottage properties. These are in demand because many people like them and Lambeth has few such properties in its own stock.

As well as GLC buildings in Lambeth, the Borough has its own target, as laid down in 'Lambeth into the Seventies', to produce 1500 new Council houses per annum. The attempt to achieve this goal has met with several problems.

Two constraints, finance and land, appeared until recently to dominate the mounting of a large scale programme. The financial problem was not so much the capital cost of the programme but its revenue effect, i.e. the rising rate burden. The Conservatives displayed their priorities by allowing housing expenditure in 1971–2 to rise at an annual rate of 20 per cent, whereas other services were restricted to 7½ per cent. The cost of debt servicing is largely responsible for the rapidly increasing deficit on the Housing Revenue Account which went up from £1.2m to £2.4m in three municipal years. Such a growth could not be maintained, but the increase was allowed on the assumption that changes in housing finance were imminent. The new legislation will in fact greatly, if temporarily, reduce Lambeth's deficit.[1]

Land assembly is a far more intractable problem. The core of redevelopment until now has been the existence of substantial areas of slums which—with the addition of added 'grey' land— is presented at a public enquiry for compulsory purchase.

---

[1] In 1972 the Borough estimated that the new subsidy system in the Housing Finance Act, 1972, would cut the then current annual deficit on the Housing Revenue Account by 50 per cent. By 1974 it was expected to be up to £2m again.

However, the amount of slum clearance which remains to be done is falling and so, to enable reasonable sites to be obtained, the proportion of grey land in c.p.o.s has risen accordingly. These are areas of housing which are not unfit; their inclusion is justified if they help to make a more logical clearance site. There is a limit to permissible grey land, and the Council has had to rely more and more on clearing sites under Part V of the 1957 Housing Act. This involves the demolition of fit houses if there is an overwhelming housing need to do so, and if a 'housing gain' would result. However, with the increased emphasis nationally on rehabilitation the DoE is becoming more stringent in allowing compulsory purchase of properties under Part V of the Act. They have even, as we have seen above, referred back a Part III (i.e. slum) order in neighbouring Southwark for rehabilitation rather than clearance. The conflict at national level between, on the one hand, the policies of encouraging inner city councils to increase output (which is a major justification for the new Housing Finance Act), and on the other hand, the emphasis on rehabilitation, means that there is now real doubt whether sufficient land can be made available to sustain 1500 new Council houses per annum in Lambeth.

The scale at which land becomes available for housing also depends on the speed at which a number of council departments and the DoE can process it. We have not investigated the working of the DoE, but we have been told that they do sometimes cause considerable delays. So far as the Borough organization is concerned, pressure of work, shortage of skilled staff in the public health inspectorate and the lack of the sort of organization in the Planning Department appropriate to the acquisition of over sixty acres of land per year seem to be the major constraints. Standing up to hostile cross examination on an order at a public enquiry requires a highly skilled and experienced public health inspector and such people are in short supply. The new housing policy places great additional burdens on the inspectorate anyway. This has resulted in delays, especially at the start of Lambeth's expansion.

Until recently there were plenty of slums and the land which should be redeveloped was fairly obvious. But the link between overall development and planning was weak. Sites tended to be selected in a rather arbitrary way with the final process of selection often determined by a brief external examination from a passing car. Now it is felt that a much more scientific attempt to survey the needs of the area as a whole is required. The previous piecemeal approach has in some cases created significant problems for the future. In one area in Stockwell which needs comprehensive redevelopment, there is now a council block built in the last decade in the middle of the area. This cannot of course be demolished.

Rehousing and legal problems also cause delays. Lambeth, like many other authorities, built far too many three bedroom dwellings for its current needs. Many of the families from clearance areas are small and there is a shortage of available alternative accommodation. Of course the current programme aims to correct these deficiencies, but it will take several years to do so. The detailed referencing of property interests in redevelopment areas is a skilled and time consuming job and the increase in the programme revealed that there were insufficient staff in the administrative and legal departments of the Council.

Furthermore, it is increasingly doubtful whether redevelopment is leading to any net housing gain. Indeed there may actually be a loss in the future. The Council has begun to redevelop areas of heavy multi-occupation which they have previously tried to avoid by opting for areas where there would be a housing gain. In these new areas there is an overspill of people requiring public housing, which tends to outweigh the gain created by owner occupiers and others who find their own solutions. Since there are also competing demands for land for open space, it seems likely that the already high proportion of people housed by Lambeth from clearance areas will increase and the proportion housed from the waiting list falls still further.

Conclusion

We have shown how the complex interplay of organizational, resource and ideological constraints places severe limits on the likely outcome of Lambeth's attempts to involve a wide range of agencies in a comprehensive attack on its housing problem.

Two limitations on the progress of the housing programme emerge from such an analysis. First, despite the fact that additional resources have been allocated and a new department created to carry out the policy, we must question whether the increased demands it placed on other departments of the Council were foreseen by its initiators. Factors such as the ability of planners to expand and modify their organization to cope with increased demand create problems. Also there has been difficulty in persuading the Directorate of Management Services to increase the departmental establishment or to raise the salary range for a post in order to attract a man with the right qualifications.

Of course other departments will not fully share the Housing Directorate's commitment to its programme. The personal qualities which infuse the Lambeth housing effort may not be matched in other departments on which this effort to some extent relies. The discretion given to officials and committee chairmen also means that it is difficult for leading politicians to interfere in other departmental and committee level decisions. Furthermore, conflict also seems to exist between planning goals in Lambeth and what the housing policy appears to be achieving in practice. To the extent that the Housing Directorate accepts these planning goals, there is also a conflict between different aspects of that policy itself.

The aims of the Borough's Development Plan which affect the field of housing include:

1 the stemming of the rate of decline of population;
2 a better age structure;
3 a better spread of tenure, i.e. more owner occupation;
4 a socially balanced community (linked to category 3 as this is seen to require more owner occupation) [18].

As we have seen, the control of multi-occupation aims to reduce population and the increased public housing programme is probably a major factor leading to a decline in owner occupation. The help the Borough is giving the housing associations also reduces the ability of the (presumed) middle-class owner occupier to compete effectively for available housing. As a result he will increasingly be forced to seek housing elsewhere. Furthermore, according to the I.M.T.A., [19] Lambeth charged more than all but two other London authorities for a post-1964 3-bedroom flat in 1970–1. These factors mean that an increasing number of Council tenants who can pay the full rent move out of Lambeth and buy. Yet these are likely to be the skilled and white collar workers that the Borough's Plan (and the G.L.D.P.) aims to retain. Harry Simpson himself has pointed to this conflict between goals and performance.

Much of the difficulty stems from the fact that the Borough can only fill the gap between the current housing situation and the desired future situation by relying on agencies which will not co-operate. The present housing problems are too intense for the Council to sit back and wait for agencies to help it achieve its long-term goals. Our analysis of what is being done to deal with the present housing situation strongly leads us to conclude that increased public housing or public supported housing is inevitable.

In general we would argue that an assessment of the possibilities for change in Inner London must contain within it the sort of organizational analysis contained in this chapter. But is it possible to suggest changes in the structure of agencies which would achieve the required goals? Here we must return to a consideration of the people involved. In this chapter we have been unable to discuss the characteristics of the groups of clients served by various agencies. Our final report to the Social Science Research Council shows that in Lambeth there are significant differences between the characteristics of these groups. Any major change in the proportionate contribution of the various agencies in the provision of housing in the Borough is likely to affect the housing life chances of these groups differentially. In particular we conclude that a majority of these who form the core of the housing problem which Lambeth hopes to eliminate are and will remain, effectively excluded on financial grounds from any form of housing which is not either public or quasi-public housing (such as local authority subsidized housing associations). Even if furnished accommodation were eligible for rent allowances, along with privately rented unfurnished accommodation, the Secretary of State himself admits that the 1972 Housing Finance Act is unlikely to call forth new building in the privately rented sector. Yet the stock in this sector is increasingly inadequate and even Lambeth's efforts to obtain improvements and better maintenance will do no more than ensure a slower decline for a very large proportion of the dwellings involved.

To summarize: our examination of the Lambeth experience leads us to believe that the strategy of involving the widest possible range of agencies in an attack on the housing problem only bring forth a very limited and inadequate response to that problem. The gains are doubtless welcome but the reality for Lambeth, as for other areas in Inner London, must be an increasing public authority effort or a further decline in the housing situation, so long as the other agencies continue to operate in the way they do. The severe shortage of land, the increased emphasis on rehabilitation and the difficulties of involving profit motivated agencies in socially oriented activity, lead us to suggest that a large scale takeover of existing housing by public authorities in Inner London is a likely development in the next decade. Ideological objections to this may result in actual ownership and management being vested in a number of quasi-public agencies such as housing associations. Whether the old paternalistic system of local authority management will survive in this situation, or whether new forms which give tenants more effective control over their environment will arise is an open question. The public acquisition of privately rented housing will not create more housing, indeed it will probably reduce occupancy, but it will lead to a reduced population enjoying better physical conditions and greater security of tenure than at present. Even a determined Inner Borough such as Lambeth cannot house all the people who want to live there in decent conditions.

Finally the Lambeth experience may be seen as having great importance in a political and legislative sense. There is no doubt that, aided by the close links between the Lambeth Conservatives and those in their national party concerned with housing, innovations such as the Housing Advice Centre have been incorporated into the policy of central government. Pressure from Lambeth was exerted on Labour and Conservative governments over measures such as the 1969 Housing Act and the 1972 Housing Finance Act and Lambeth's advice was sought on various matters. The Director of Housing has been an influential member of the DoE's Standing Working Party on London Housing. The extent to which Lambeth's housing effort brought the Borough and its officials and politicians to the forefront may be judged by the appointment of Harry Simpson as the first Director General of the Northern Ireland Housing Authority in late 1971 and Bernard Perkins to the chairmanship of the GLC Housing Committee early in 1972. Invitations to see conditions in Lambeth were used to arouse the interest and engender the commitment of Ministers in the present and previous governments to help inner urban areas. Lambeth has been one of the most important pressure groups in the last few years working for changes in the attitudes of central government to inner city housing problems and for consequent new legislation. It is not clear that this was their original intention, but as it became clearer that many of their problems were beyond their control, they turned to influencing central government. Many problems, such as the need for more housing in the Outer Boroughs, still await decisive government action.

By showing the scope and limitations of an attempt by a vigorous local authority to solve its problems with the resources and agencies to which it has access, Lambeth has highlighted the need for further public intervention by central government in the housing problems of Inner London.

References

1. See for example, *London's Housing Needs up to 1974*, Standing Working Party on London Housing, Report no. 3 (M.H.L.G., 1970).
Report of the Committee on Housing in Greater London, Cmnd. 2605, (London: H.M.S.O., 1965).
GREVE, J., PAGE, D. and GREVE, S., *Homelessness in London* (Edinburgh: Scottish Academic Press, 1971).
Report of the Committee on the Rent Acts, Cmnd. 4609 (London: H.M.S.O., 1971).
The Greater London Development Plan: Report of Studies (GLC, 1969), ch. 2.
2. GREVE, J., *et al.*, *op. cit.*, ch. 1.
3. *Ibid.*, pp. 63–4, 85–6.
4. *The Condition of London's Housing* (GLC, 1970), Appendix Table 4.21, p. 137.
5. Unpublished GLC data. The GLC constructed a cumulative index showing the percentage of households without the three basic amenities as a percentage of all households. Households lacking more than one facility were included more than once.
6. *The Characteristics of London's Households* (GLC, 1970), Table 7.2.
7. Report of the Committee on the Rent Acts. Cmnd. 4609 (London: H.M.S.O., 1971), Appendix II, pp. 317–440.
8. *Rent Rebate Schemes*, Circular No. 46/67 (M.H.L.G., 1967), see the appendix for the model scheme.
9. *Housing Statistics*, No. 24 (London: H.M.S.O., 1972), Table 6 (b).
10. *Local Housing Statistics*. Nos. 17 and 19 (London: H.M.S.O., 1971), Table 4.
11. NICHOLS, T., *Ownership, Control and Ideology* (London: Allen and Unwin, 1969).

12. BARBOLET, R. H., *Housing Classes and the Socio-ecological System*, University Working Paper 4 (Centre for Environmental Studies, 1969).

13. Sub-Committee of the Central Housing Advisory Committee, *Housing Associations* (London: H.M.S.O., 1971).

14. 'A particular problem which arises with conversions is that the present subsidy structure tends to encourage the creation of small units unsuitable for family occupation'. *Ibid.*, para. 2.31, p. 25.

15. *Housing Review*, **20**, no. 2, p. 51.

16. National Assistance Act, Part III, Section 21 (i) (b).

17. For definitions of these two standards see *Improvement and Conversion Grants—Practice Notes*, Circular 29/62 (M.H.L.G., 1962).

18. As quoted in Lambeth's *Community Plan 1972–3*, the Council's corporate planning, programming and budgeting exercise.

19. *Housing Statistics Part 1* (Institute of Municipal Treasurers and Accountants, 1971).

Chapter Eleven

Furnished Lettings in Stress Areas

BARBARA ADAMS

Summary

This chapter reviews recent evidence on furnished lettings in Inner London, drawing particularly on data collected for the Committee on the Rent Acts (the Francis Committee) in 1970.

In the conditions of continuing housing shortage in Inner London, furnished lettings in stress areas are on virtually all counts the worst accommodation, the majority consisting of only one or two rooms with shared domestic facilities. Evidence about landlords in stress areas is slender, but they seem to be predominantly young or middle-aged working immigrants, many in skilled occupations and many letting parts of their own homes. The stereotype of the furnished tenant as a young single person is not applicable: only a quarter of tenants are single persons, and the dominant age group is twenty-five to thirty-four. Half are families with children, and one in three of these are fatherless families. Nearly half of the tenants in stress areas are thought to live in furnished accommodation only because they are unable to obtain an unfurnished home, their low incomes preventing them from obtaining the amount of living space they need.

Hardship is particularly evident among the families with children. Lack of security of tenure remains the greatest worry though tenants also pay high rents for inferior accommodation, and harassment and illegal eviction persist.

The evidence suggests that as the privately rented sector diminishes and the proportion of unfurnished lettings within it

declines, families will find it increasingly difficult to get a foot
on the housing ladder leading out of the furnished sector. The
recent rise in house prices puts house purchase beyond the reach
of the overwhelming majority.

Measures to improve the lot of the furnished tenant in stress
areas, including the proposals of the Francis Committee, are
considered. It is concluded that the only prospect for substantial
improvement to their situation lies in more direct intervention
by local authorities. Several measures are reviewed, ranging
from wider control of multi-occupation, and piecemeal acquisition in advance of redevelopment, to compulsory acquisition
of considerable acreages in stress areas as originally proposed by
the Milner Holland Committee. It is suggested that it is also
essential that the Outer London Boroughs make greatly increased housing provision for inner areas and that since their
objections have not yielded to persuasion, a measure of direction
from the Minister may now be needed.

Within the broad picture of improvement, albeit slow, in the
housing situation in Inner London, certain groups of people and
certain areas still exhibit housing conditions of considerable
deprivation. While the Housing Problem areas[1] have the worst
physical conditions and are steadily redeveloped, within them
Housing Stress areas[1] demonstrate some of the worst social conditions—multiple occupation of large old houses, the sharing of
domestic facilities and overcrowding. Furnished lettings in these
stress areas provide some of the worst homes in the country and
house some of the most socially handicapped people. (The
recent Greve [1] study of homelessness in London found that
most of the homeless had always lived in furnished accommodation.) This chapter considers furnished lettings in stress areas
and possible measures to improve the lot of those who live,
many involuntarily, in this type of property.

Furnished dwellings rented from private landlords are primarily a London phenomenon, about half of the 600 000
in England and Wales being in the metropolis; and within
London they are highly concentrated in Inner Boroughs,
notably Kensington and Chelsea, Westminster, Camden,

---

[1] Greater London Development Plan classification.

Hammersmith, and Islington. While the number of privately rented unfurnished dwellings in Inner London is rapidly declining, the number of furnished lettings seems to be static. They thus constitute an increasing proportion of private lettings, now about one quarter.

First, however, it is important to view furnished lettings in the broader housing context.

The Housing Shortage

Perhaps the most widely accepted quantitative assessment of shortage and future change is the report produced in 1970 by the Standing Working Party on London Housing (consisting of representatives of the Ministry of Housing and Local Government, the Greater London Council and the London Boroughs Association) under the title 'London's Housing Needs up to 1974'.

Briefly, the report demonstrated that the shortage of dwellings in Greater London was reduced from 12 per cent of potential households to 9 per cent between 1966 and 1969, leaving a deficit of 233 000 dwellings. Of these, 162 000 were in Inner London, and the deficit was greatest in the north-east sector. It was estimated that by 1974 the shortage of dwellings would be reduced to 106 000 or 4 per cent of potential households. The shortage was expected to have disappeared in many Outer London Boroughs, which taken together show an estimated surplus of 4000 dwellings; but in Inner London the anticipated deficit was still 110 000 or 10 per cent. The area of worst shortage was expected to be the north-east (12 per cent). The highest Borough deficits were expected in Kensington and Chelsea, and Islington (19 per cent), Lambeth (18 per cent), Camden (14 per cent), Tower Hamlets (12 per cent) and Southwark (11 per cent), though great reliance should not be placed on the estimates for particular Boroughs.

These figures made no allowance for the quality of dwellings. If unsatisfactory dwellings were added to the shortage, the Committee estimated that the shortage of *satisfactory* dwellings in Greater London was 553 000 in 1969 (21 per cent of households) and would fall to 336 000 in 1974 (13 per cent of households). In Inner London the proportion of unsatisfactory stock still would be 23 per cent in 1974 but only 6 per cent in outer areas. Thus the evenly spread improvement is worsening the relative position of Inner London. Within Inner London the 1974 projections showed the north-east sector having a continuing deficit of satisfactory dwellings of as much as 29 per cent, mainly the result of deficits in Islington (37 per cent), Newham (37 per cent) and Tower Hamlets (33 per cent). Thus in these areas one family in three was still expected to be unsatisfactorily housed in 1974.

The Committee warned that it had adopted favourable assumptions, and events have proved some of these projections over-optimistic. Neither local authority nor private building reached the assumed level: both have been falling. The assumed gains from conversion have also not been achieved. In addition, the anticipated increase in the rate of slum clearance has not taken place, and obsolescence is accelerating. On the other hand, losses from such causes as demolition for schools, roads, etc., have not been as high as estimated and the population decline revealed by the 1971 Census suggests that demand may be less than anticipated. The alternative less optimistic projection made by the Committee for 1974 gives a 1974 dwelling deficit of 156 000 (compared with 106 000 in the standard estimate). The Department of the Environment's current updating of the Committee's standard estimate of the dwelling deficiency in 1974 is 75 000–100 000 dwellings. It seems clear that, though current trends may alter the size of the deficit, there will be a very considerable housing deficit in 1974 and for many years thereafter.

On the Committee's most pessimistic estimates, the deficit of *satisfactory* dwellings was being reduced by only about 10 000 per annum. At this rate, nearly fifty years would be required to get rid of all of them. During that period more dwellings would become obsolete, and it is known that the rate of obsolescence will be increasing rapidly: the GLC Report of Studies suggests that after 1974 the number of dwellings becoming obsolete will double and from 1983 will double again. Although more recent figures suggest that the 10 000 per annum reduction in the deficit of satisfactory dwellings quoted above was pessimistic, there can be little doubt that the situation improves only slowly. Unless the crude shortage can be eliminated, it is clear that woefully inadequate resources will be available to tackle the accelerating obsolescence.

Recent Research on Furnished Lettings

Against this broad picture of continuing shortage, the furnished sector in stress areas is considered in more detail, since it is arguably here that living conditions in London are at their worst and most intractable.

Recent research[1] for the Committee on the Rent Act, Chairman Mr. Hugh Francis, QC, provides the most up-to-date

---

[1] Three surveys were undertaken by the Department of the Environment in 1970 on behalf of the Committee on the Rent Acts (The Francis Committee) and reports on them are published as Appendices to the Report of the Committee on Rent Acts, Cmnd. 4609 (London: H.M.S.O., March 1971).

The first two surveys were directed and supervised by the statistical staff of the Department (B. C. Brown, H. S. Phillips and D. Vatcher).

The Tenants Survey (Appendix I) covered representative samples of tenants in each of four areas, the Greater London, West Midlands and Central Clydeside conurbations, and the South Wales Coastal Belt (including Cardiff), and separate samples in a few small areas of housing stress within the three conurbations. The survey was designed to reveal the particular characteristics of tenancies in stress areas and to indicate why a very large proportion of regulated tenants had not taken advantage of the Rent Officer and Rent Tribunal systems. It provided a great deal of information about the tenants and their households (by age, income, social grade, family type, etc.) and their attitudes to their landlords, the tenancies, and the Rent Act procedures, as well as about their rents and the nature and condition of their accommodation.

The Landlord Survey (Appendix II) had a more limited coverage and for various reasons it is difficult to draw quantitative conclusions from it. It covered the landlords (or agents) owning (or managing) the dwellings visited in the tenants survey in Greater London and the West Midlands conurbation. The report analyses the sample of landlords interviewed by age, origin, social grade, and number and type of tenancies, their familiarity with Rent Act procedures and their views about their relations with their tenants and the rent regulation machinery.

Appendix III is the report of a study of Rent Tribunal cases in Greater London carried out by the Sociological Research Section of the Department (Barbara Adams, Jenny Griffin, Sylvia Proudman) in collaboration with the Centre for Environmental Studies. This study looked at the outcome of one hundred applications to Rent Tribunals in London made between 1 February and 30 April 1969. Information was collected on the furnished accommodation forming the subject of the application and on changes in the lettings about a year after the Tribunal case. Both landlord and tenant were interviewed. A separate sample of tenants who made applications but withdrew them before the Tribunal hearing was interviewed to find out why they had not continued with the case.

evidence available on the privately rented sector, and the situation in 1970 as revealed in these surveys can be briefly summarized. The figures quoted relate primarily to stress areas, three areas of acute housing pressure in Tower Hamlets, Lambeth and Hackney, selected 'for their substantial concentrations of older houses inhabited by families living in poor social conditions'. These areas were selected on the basis of advice provided by Senior Rent Officers and Secretaries of Rent Assessment Committees as areas of housing stress which had not been surveyed recently and were intended to represent different types of area (some with more multi-occupied premises than others). These areas cannot be taken as representative of Inner London 'but only as illustrative of some types of areas of housing stress, not necessarily the worst'. 262 tenants in furnished accommodation in these areas and 792 in unfurnished were interviewed. The three areas are located within or immediately adjacent to the housing stress areas defined in the Greater London Development Plan, which house in all about 300 000 households. Furnished tenancies are those stated as so described by the landlord at the commencement of the tenancy, plus those where the tenant shared a kitchen with the landlord. Tenancies described as partly furnished were excluded.

The Accommodation: Size and Domestic Facilities

During the 1960s[1] domestic facilities in furnished accommodation in the conurbation improved steadily, and the sharing of domestic facilities was steadily reduced (though the position in stress areas at the end of the decade was still worse than that of the conurbation in the beginning). Perhaps contrary to expectations, the proportion of very small (one and two room) furnished dwellings in the conurbation seems to have fallen slowly (though we must await the results of the 1971 Census to be sure). By 1970, however, furnished lettings in the conurbation were still relatively small, over half being of only one or two rooms, and over half still involved sharing a W.C.

---

[1] Reliable trends are singularly difficult to ascertain because of deficiencies in, and non-compatability between, the Censuses of 1961 and 1966 and the Ministry's housing surveys of 1964, 1967 and 1970. Whenever trends are suggested in this chapter, the figures are more than usually suspect.

In stress areas virtually all furnished lettings in the 1970 sample were built before the First World War. There were no whole houses among them, two-thirds consisting of 'rooms' only. This figure would have been even higher if premises necessitating the crossing of landings, halls, etc., to get from one room to another had been included. A third of these furnished lettings in stress areas consisted of only one room and only a third had more than two. Two-fifths either shared a sink or had none, and more than three-quarters shared a W.C. In two cases in five the landlord lived in the same building, but unfortunately we do not know to what extent landlord and tenant shared domestic facilities. The structural condition of furnished lettings was slightly better than that of unfurnished: *on all other counts* furnished accommodation in stress areas was appreciably inferior to unfurnished.

Landlords of Low-standard Furnished Lettings

Separate information for landlords of furnished accommodation is not available from the Landlords' Survey carried out for the Francis Committee but only from the Study of Rent Tribunal cases. A random sample of tribunal cases arising throughout the conurbation in 1969 revealed a great similarity between both the tenants and the dwellings referred to the tribunals and those in stress areas, and probably provides the best evidence we have, albeit slender, of landlords of low-standard furnished dwellings in London. They cannot, however, be taken as representative of landlords of all furnished accommodation in the conurbation, for in higher-standard lettings company landlords and non-resident landlords are more common.

Almost all these landlords of furnished dwellings referred to the Rent Tribunal were private individuals holding only one house and having occupations other than managing their property. Skilled workers were the largest social class and half were under forty; the great majority had been born abroad, the largest group in the West Indies. The spoken English of one in seven was rated by interviewers as difficult to understand, and over half lived on the same premises as the dwelling referred to the tribunal, and most of these shared some amenities with tenants.

Almost all landlords in tribunal cases said that they let only furnished accommodation because it was easier to get tenants out, they liked their own furniture in the dwellings and could charge higher rents. A very small minority were found to charge more than the rent fixed by the Rent Tribunal. In stress areas two tenants out of five had no rent book, although the law requires the landlord to provide one.

Tenants

Three groups of tenants are normally distinguished within furnished lettings. First, single people, living either separately or sharing, who are traditionally among the main customers for furnished lettings and who are said to be increasing in numbers and increasingly moving to London. Second, newly married couples who prefer to start married life in furnished accommodation but who have income sufficient to enable them ultimately to become owner-occupiers. Lastly, those living in furnished accommodation only because they cannot get the unfurnished tenancy that is their aim and who cannot afford to buy a house. Unfortunately, none of the data enables us accurately to estimate the numbers falling into these three groups, but the Francis Committee considered that the third group, the involuntary furnished tenants, was about 30 per cent of the total in the conurbation and nearly half in stress areas. It is with this third group that this chapter is mainly concerned.

Furnished tenants are generally younger than unfurnished ones, but those in stress areas were not as young as those in the conurbation as a whole: only 19 per cent were under twenty-five, compared with 43 per cent in the conurbation as a whole. As many as two-thirds in stress areas were in semi-skilled and unskilled occupations compared with less than a quarter in the conurbation and a third in unfurnished. More than half were coloured compared with only a fifth in unfurnished accommodation in stress areas or in furnished accommodation in the whole conurbation. Nearly half came from the West Indies, Africa or South America, and spoken English was rated as slightly or very difficult to understand in two cases out of five. In stress areas they had lived in their present homes for rather longer than furnished tenants in the conurbation. Unfortunately, we do not know how long these households had lived in the furnished sector generally, i.e. moving from one furnished

letting to another. Two-fifths of tenants said that they had difficulty in coping with everyday problems. One in five lacked all
knowledge of Rent Tribunal machinery, and only half said they
would turn to official bodies for assistance if they were trying to
get their rent reduced.

Furnished tenants in stress areas did not partake of the
superior incomes enjoyed by furnished tenants in the conurbation. Just over half of all household incomes were under £20
per week in 1970. Two in five in furnished lettings in stress areas
were dissatisfied with both their rent and their accommodation,
a higher proportion than in unfurnished in stress areas or than
in either sector in the conurbation as a whole.

Half of the households in the furnished accommodation in
stress areas had children, again a higher proportion than in unfurnished accommodation, and to be compared with only 17
per cent in all furnished accommodation in the conurbation.
A third of these families with children in furnished accommodation in stress areas were fatherless families compared with
only one-tenth in unfurnished. Overcrowding was at its worst,
26 per cent living at more than $1\frac{1}{2}$ persons per room (p.p.r.) and
11 per cent at more than 2 persons per room. (Among Rent
Tribunal cases, comparable figures reached 55 and 37 per cent
respectively, and in all the cases of severe overcrowding (2+
p.p.r.) there were children present. Of the children in this
sample of Rent Tribunal cases for whom we have data, only 13
per cent lived at or below 1.5 p.p.r., 8 per cent lived between
1.5 and 2.0 p.p.r. and as many as 79 per cent lived at more than
2 p.p.r.) The National Child Development Study has recently
demonstrated that seven-year-olds in overcrowded homes are
retarded, on average, by about nine months in reading age. (It
is known that some local authorities turn a blind eye to over-
crowning in order to avoid making families homeless.) Children
from families not having sole use of any of three basic amenities
were also a *further* nine months behind in reading attainment.
This remains true when allowance is made for social class, type
of accommodation and tenure.

Thus on practically all counts the furnished tenant in stress
areas was more handicapped than the unfurnished tenant. The
stereotype of the furnished tenant as a young single person is not
applicable to London's stress areas. The dominant age group
was twenty-five–thirty-four, an age when most people want a

home of their own, and only 25 per cent of households consisted of one person only. Half were families with children. These figures lend support to the Francis Committee's view that nearly half of furnished tenants in stress areas were living in furnished accommodation only because they were unable to obtain an unfurnished home.

Hardship

Fieldworkers visiting furnished lettings for the Francis Committee were struck by their remarkable similarity to furnished homes of twenty-five years ago: it is clear that at the bottom of the housing ladder conditions have changed little, despite marked improvements elsewhere. The descriptions of home conditions given below, taken from the fieldworkers' reports, are unfortunately less than adequate to bring home to the reader the equally unsatisfactory surrounding environment, obsolescent and ill-equipped with community facilities, in which these dwellings are situated.

Case 91

'From the outside the whole house appears to be in very poor repair. The front door is located in an alley way off a busy East End street. The interior is also in bad repair and in need of substantial redecoration. The house is tall and narrow, four floors, with two rooms on each floor and a gas stove on each landing. There is no bathroom, one kitchen, and the only W.C. is in the yard. A large number of children clustered in and around the front door and on the first floor landing. The landlord said that he had already paid over £200.00 in a fine for over-crowding and was in constant fear of the same thing happening again.

'The tenant occupied one single room on the third (attic) floor. There were seven in the family, which included four young children. The attic room was low ceilinged, small, damp and in very bad repair. The tenants had brought in a couple of bunk beds to ease the sleeping arrangements. They were dissatisfied with their accommodation and angry at the landlord for not making improvements. Both parents were working full time and explained that they could afford to pay more rent but with four children had found it impossible to find an alternative place to live.'

Case 94

'This young couple in their early twenties live with two small children in a "flat" above a small shop. Their flat consists of one front room and a back kitchen. Originally they shared the bathroom and toilet with the landlords (two partners who at this time were using the shop and living on the premises). All the parties to this case are British.

'At this point events began to change, the two "landlords" "doing a bunk" and the real landlord turning up to collect the rent for the property from his two "tenants".

'Electricity and gas were disconnected. The true landlord later refused to accept rent from the tenants and a court action was started, but later, after discussions between solicitors, it was dropped. The tenants remain in the flat virtually as squatters. They have no electricity, and the gas, which has been reconnected, is for cooking only. They have no bath or hot water for themselves and their two children, one of whom was born since moving in, and their only lighting consists of two paraffin lamps. For heating they have an oil stove. According to the tenants, the toilet is blocked and useless; the ceiling in the kitchen is collapsing and there are mice in the building, which is now completely empty except for themselves. The stairs have no natural light and in the absence of electricity are dangerous for the children. The whole family sleeps in one room.'

Case 27

'An Irish couple were living with their two young children in one room of a Victorian semi-detached house. The room was adequately furnished although several articles were in need of repair. It was notable, however, for one or two omissions, namely a window pane, for which a piece of polythene had been the longstanding "temporary" repair and two areas of wall. Plaster had fallen away to reveal one hole of 12 inches by 9 inches immediately adjacent to the bed, which had to be blocked each night by a child's drawing board. Additions to the room included several layers of dirt and an overwhelming smell of confined humanity. There was no bathroom for the tenant's use and no running water in the room. Water had to be fetched from a sink on the floor above but there was no light on the landing or stairs.

'The tenant's wife reported that the landlord had refused to make any alterations or repairs to the room although he had decorated and rewired the remainder of the house. The children were not allowed in the garden and the landlady complained that they made too much noise but sometimes they couldn't sleep because of the landlady decorating the rooms above. Their mother said she hated the place because of its condition and said they would get out if they had the chance but that it was difficult to find accommodation with two children.

'The Greek owner of the house had purchased it in January 1969 with three sets of tenants in residence, but wanted it for the sole use of his own family. He had moved in by the summer, when two of the tenants had moved out. At this time he offered the remaining family £200.00 to leave, but to no avail. Since that time the landlord had carried out some of the badly needed repairs and decorated much of the house, with the exception of the tenant's room.

'The landlord's wife, interviewed in the spotlessly clean living room, described the problems of having the couple living there: "much trouble is tenants". She said that they were dirty and that the tenant "drinks 7 days a week" and had urinated in the passage.'

Only limited data are available to explain why these families find themselves in such conditions. We have seen that the overall housing shortage inevitably condemns *some* people to such homes, but it is arguable that these homes would cause considerably less hardship to young single people such as students and to childless couples than they do to families with children. It is clear that these furnished tenants were mainly unskilled or semi-skilled workers in the service trades of the metropolis, their relatively low incomes preventing them from affording better housing in the centre or better housing in cheaper outer areas involving travelling expenses. They were thus forced to compete for the diminishing stock of inadequate privately rented dwellings, where their low wages prevented them from obtaining the amount of living space they needed. (There is some evidence to suggest that these trades are also receiving wage increases below the average, so that these families may well become relatively more deprived and even less able to compete successfully for better housing.)

Lack of Choice

Many were trying to move at the time of the interviews. Throughout the 1960s between a quarter and a third of furnished tenants in the conurbation seem to have been trying to move. In 1970 the figure for stress areas was 40 per cent. The proportion of would-be movers in the furnished accommodation trying to rent rather than to buy may be rising: in 1970 the proportions were 83 per cent in the conurbation and 89 per cent in stress areas. The great majority were looking to the local authority rather than the private landlord. The recent steep rise in house prices is likely to make it increasingly difficult for furnished tenants to buy their way out of the rented sector.

44 per cent of furnished tenants in stress areas said that they would have preferred unfurnished accommodation when first they moved in, and it is reasonable to assume that some who initially preferred a furnished place would, as time went by, want an unfurnished place. Among Rent Tribunal cases too, all of which related to furnished accommodation, the proportion who had wanted unfurnished accommodation when first they moved in was over half and only a quarter had particularly wanted furnished accommodation. So it seems likely that at least half of those in furnished accommodation in stress areas were forced into furnished lettings and prevented from building up 'a home of their own'. Among the half of furnished tenants in stress areas who had children, no doubt the proportion preferring unfurnished accommodation would have been higher still.

Lack of choice again operated in the case of the families in Rent Tribunal cases who had to move out. Over half had originally wanted unfurnished accommodation when they moved into furnished and more than four-fifths of those trying to move after the tribunal case so desired, but it is estimated that two-thirds again had to take a furnished place. And this despite the fact that tribunal tenants having to move were generously assisted into unfurnished accommodation by local authorities and Housing Associations—particularly tenants with children. Nevertheless it is estimated that two-thirds of the families with children moved again into a furnished dwelling.

An examination of the changing distribution of the families in furnished accommodation in inner areas of the conurbation since 1961 suggests that large households (4+ p.) may be becoming more common: they rose from 12 per cent in 1961 to 22 per cent in 1967 in Inner areas. In stress areas in 1970 they constituted 25 per cent of all households.

It is difficult to estimate the ratio of furnished to unfurnished vacancies on offer in the private sector in London at present. The ratio of lettings is about 1:4. In 1964 an enquiry for the Milner Holland Committee found that accommodation on offer from estate agents and on notice boards in four selected Inner London Boroughs occurred in the ratio of 15:1 furnished to unfurnished. An enquiry for the Francis Committee involving an analysis of lettings advertised in the *London Weekly Advertiser* in 1963 and 1970 produced ratios of 25:1 and 100:1 respectively. These figures doubtless disguise the true situation since more unfurnished than furnished lettings are let without advertisement. Nevertheless there is little doubt that the great majority of vacancies on offer in private housing in both stress areas and in the conurbation are furnished.

Lack of Security

The furnished tenant has no long-term security of tenure: if given notice to quit by his landlord, he may seek security from the Rent Tribunal within the next four weeks. If he does not take such action, and many tenants are ignorant of this right, there is no way in which his security can be extended. The fear of landlord reprisals prevents some applications. If he does apply to the Tribunal, he is unlikely to gain security for longer than eighteen months at the most.

In 1963, research for the Milner Holland Committee showed that mobility in furnished lettings in the conurbation was 45 per cent per annum and that about 10 per cent of households in furnished lettings found themselves obliged to move against their will.

The urge for security was also the main motivation for Rent Tribunal applications (rather than a rent reduction), and half of the applicants in the Study of Rent Tribunal cases outstayed the period of security granted. The tribunal application provided most applicants with a breathing space, but for nine cases out of ten this was six months or less. Of a random sample of applicants studied, 80 per cent had moved within a year, 10 per cent were under notice to quit and only 5 per cent were not trying to move. Having been forced into furnished accommodation when they would have preferred unfurnished, many tribunal applicants were forced out when they would have preferred to stay. The Francis Committee explained:

> The general approach of Rent Tribunals on questions of security is that prima facie, the landlord of a periodic furnished letting is entitled to terminate it by notice to quit and that the purpose of the security provisions . . . is to ensure that the tenant is given adequate time to find other accommodation.

Evidence from the Study of Rent Tribunal cases shows that this objective was not always achieved: from the eighty tenants who had moved among the one-hundred tribunal cases, six families went into accommodation for the homeless.

The households in furnished accommodation in stress areas show a marked similarity to the applicant families in the latest homelessness survey [1]. Over three-quarters of the furnished tenants applying for homeless accommodation in Greater London were in difficulties because of their landlord taking action against them, or in a minority of cases because of the landlord himself being in difficulties through mortgage default or through having notices served on him by the local authority, sometimes for overcrowding but more often for essential repairs to be carried out. The landlords were evicting tenants mainly because they wanted the accommodation for themselves or in order to sell with vacant possession. Court action for possession was often precipitated by tenants approaching the Rent Tribunal or the Public Health Department. Court actions by landlords for the recovery of residential premises are increasing.

The lack of a rent book must also contribute to the furnished tenant's feeling of insecurity; in 1970 only six out of ten furnished tenants in stress areas had a rent book. Since the survey carried out for the Milner Holland Committee, the proportion of furnished tenants in Greater London without a rent book has appreciably increased.

From the viewpoint of the furnished tenant, the greatest single improvement in his position would be achieved by granting him security of tenure, thus reducing the worry and uncertainty about his home and enabling him to exercise his rights in relation to the level of rent and to repairs without fear of losing the roof over his head.

The Francis Committee was not moved by this argument. The

committee considered it of overriding importance to preserve the existing stock of privately rented accommodation—'to give positive encouragement to the private landlord to *let* accommodation, whether furnished or unfurnished, rather than to sell'. The granting of full security to furnished tenants had been urged upon the committee in evidence, but the committee felt that this would act as a deterrent to landlords and lead to a substantial overall reduction in privately rented furnished accommodation. The committee therefore issued a solemn warning against the extension of security to furnished tenants. The Secretary of State for the Environment has accepted this proposal.

Miss Lyndal Evans in her Minority Report disagreed and estimated that most furnished accommodation was unsaleable for owner-occupation and that, if full security were granted, the vast majority would continue to be let furnished, while some might revert to unfurnished lettings. There is no evidence that the security granted to unfurnished tenants in 1956 accelerated the decline in such lettings. Miss Lyndal Evans argued that security was a basic fundamental right and that hardship arose from the lack of security for those forced to take furnished accommodation, particularly young couples starting a family, immigrants to the cities, and families least able to manage their affairs. She proposed the extension of full security to furnished tenants, with the same exemption as the Race Relations Act provides for resident landlords sharing some accommodation with not more than two households. Certainly it would be necessary to ensure that landlords letting part of their own homes were not forced to keep indefinitely tenants they wished to get rid of.

The Minority Report proposed that Rent Assessment Committees should notify the Social Services Department of the local authority whenever a family with children is given a limited period of security, so that the family can be given support and help in finding alternative accommodation.

Rents

Insecurity of tenure inhibits tenant complaints about such matters as lack of maintenance or overcrowding or exorbitant rents because of the fear of eviction, and thus helps to perpetuate those conditions. Only 15 per cent of furnished tenants in stress areas reported that their rent had been fixed by a tribunal. Yet only 37 per cent of all furnished tenants in stress areas said they were satisfied with the rent, and a third of those dissatisfied with their rents gave as their reason for not applying to the Rent Tribunal the fear that the landlord would attempt to evict them.

The Tenants Survey findings suggest that the furnished sector pays higher rents for inferior accommodation (as measured by gross annual value), particularly in stress areas. Average weekly rent for 'rooms' in stress areas was £3.62 compared with £4.90 in the conurbation as a whole. The median annual rent of furnished tenancies in stress areas was £200 and constituted 24 per cent of median take-home pay of the head of household compared with £144 and only 17 per cent among unfurnished tenancies.

Concerning rents, the Francis Committee recommended that the Rent Tribunals should be merged with the organization of Rent Officers and Rent Assessment Committees, and the Secretary of State for the Environment has accepted this proposal. The committee proposed that Rent Officers would, on application, fix furnished rents, provided security was not involved, and subject to appeal to the R.A.C. Where security was involved, all cases would be dealt with by the R.A.C. The furnished tenant would thus continue to have to take the initiative to obtain security, or rather to delay eviction. But he would be able to apply for security alone without raising the matter of the rent, which is not at present possible.

The proposal that fair rents should become mandatory, either in stress areas and/or tenancies generally, was rejected as likely to reduce the supply of dwellings and put an undue burden on Rent Officers. The committee proposed that there should be power to increase the rent of furnished dwellings not only on a landlord's reference for reconsideration but also when an extension of security is granted. And landlord, tenant or local authority should have the right to apply for re-registration of the rent after three years without proof of change of circumstances.

Furnished tenants were originally excluded from the proposed rent allowances to be paid to the private sector, but the Secretary of State is currently considering how best to include some or all of them. It is difficult to see how the tenant is to benefit, for without security of tenure he is liable to lose his tenancy if he applies for a fair rent, and without a fair rent he will presumably be ineligible for a rent allowance. However, if this problem could be overcome and a high level of take-up achieved, rent allowances could go a long way to alleviate the hardship caused by high furnished rents in stress areas.

The Francis Committee proposed that the provision of a rent book should be obligatory where rent is paid at intervals of up to two months, that the tenant rather than the landlord should hold the rent book, and that it should contain an inventory of the furniture provided. Notice to quit would have to be given in writing, and the notice would tell the tenant of his rights in relation to eviction.

Repairs

Furnished tenants in stress areas were more satisfied than unfurnished tenants with the condition of their accommodation, and a smaller proportion (13 per cent) thought that outside repairs were needed. A quarter thought inside repairs were needed in both furnished and unfurnished dwellings.

The Study of Rent Tribunal cases, however, showed that an appreciable proportion of applicants approached the tribunal not for security or for a rent reduction, but in an attempt to bring pressure on the landlord to carry out repairs or to restore or improve services or to cease harassment. Some local authorities refrain from taking action in such cases in order to avoid the risk of homelessness for the tenant. These are, of course, matters falling outside the jurisdiction of the Rent Tribunal, but the applicants felt unable to act to secure the repairs or reinstatement or improvement of services they needed without the security offered by the tribunal, limited in duration though that is. It is not clear that they understood that, having obtained security and perhaps then managed to get repairs, etc., carried out, they were unlikely to enjoy the improvement for more than a few months before losing the tenancy.

Harassment

Studies for the Milner Holland Committee suggested that there were more than 3000 cases of tenant 'abuse' per annum at that time (1963) in both unfurnished and furnished accommodation in Greater London. The great majority were cases of illegal eviction, unorthodox attempts to gain vacant possession, withholding of rent books and exorbitant rents demanded as an alternative to eviction. The abuses were disproportionately concentrated in furnished accommodation in the inner areas, and landlords were predominantly individuals rather than companies and mainly living on the premises.

Under the Protection from Eviction Act 1964, the offence of harassment was created for 'acts calculated to interfere with the peace and comfort of the residential occupier . . .', and for withdrawing services. Eviction without a court order was also made an offence. Fines of up to £100 for the first offence and £500 or imprisonment for up to six months or both can be imposed. From the passing of the Act to March 1970 there were 302 convictions for unlawful eviction in the Metropolitan Police District, and 267 convictions for harassment, three-quarters of all such convictions in the country. The average fine imposed for these offences during the first half of 1970 was approximately £16. Like the Milner Holland 'abuses', these offences were concentrated in areas of overcrowding and multi-occupation in inner areas and among resident landlords.

Research for the Francis Committee estimated that some 20 000 private renters in Greater London would claim some disturbance of their peace and comfort by the landlord, and among furnished tenants in stress areas the figure was 5 per cent. We do not know how far such disturbance would count as illegal harassment or how far the landlords' evidence would refute these claims. The Francis Committee concluded that cases of harassment and unlawful eviction were probably of significant proportions in stress areas only and among furnished tenants. The committee also concluded from evidence that individual landlords are sometimes harassed by tenants.

The Study of the Rent Tribunal cases in London revealed that in at least a quarter and possibly over half of the cases studied, the tenant's complaints about his landlord could constitute harassment. In more than one case in six, physical violence was reported. Grossed up, these figures for physical violence would involve more than 1100 furnished tenants in the year 1970. It is not known how far such complaints would count as illegal harassment or how far landlords' evidence would refute these claims.

Two out of five of the furnished tenants applying for homeless accommodation in the latest Greve study reported harassment or illegal eviction. The persistence of harassment in the furnished sector can probably be taken as proved.

The Francis Committee proposed that fines for harassment and unlawful eviction be raised to £400 for a first conviction and £750 for others, with maximum imprisonment of twelve months. For stress areas a harassment officer was proposed to ensure that the 1965 Act's provisions on harassment and eviction are observed and enforced. And a summary procedure was proposed to enable the harassment officer to give temporary protection (e.g. seventy-two hours) to tenants threatened with eviction. A new offence of harassment of the landlord was recommended.

Stress Areas: Management Powers

In areas of housing stress in conurbations, to be designated by the Secretary of State, the Francis Committee recommended that the local authorities be under a statutory duty:

1 to advise both landlord and tenant on the Rent Act;
2 to ensure that rents of multi-occupied privately rented dwellings in the lower r.v. bands are not unduly excessive compared with registered rents;
3 to enforce the 1965 Act provision concerning harassment and unlawful eviction.

In order to carry out these functions, the authority would have power to require particulars of tenancies, to require the landlord to register the rent, to call for the rent book and to take over management of the house in cases of persistent excessive rents, harassment or threats of unlawful eviction.

Most areas of housing stress in conurbations contain both furnished and unfurnished dwellings. The effect of the Committee's proposal on furnished dwellings is not entirely clear, but they themselves say that such a scheme 'may be less effective in relation to furnished tenants', presumably because furnished tenants would still lack security. But they thought it was worth considering giving the local authority management powers where the landlord was trying to evict a furnished tenant without reasonable cause, and where the tenant would have difficulty in finding suitable accommodation.

The Committee also recommended that Housing Aid Centres and centres giving legal aid and assistance should be set up in stress areas, and the Secretary of State has already issued advice to local authorities on setting up such centres.

Future Prospects

It will be clear from the foregoing that the furnished tenant in stress areas is in dire need of help. Maurice Ash has suggested [2] that the whole weight of the forces at work in the London housing market is concentrated on the furnished sector, since other types of tenure are insulated by their legal status: 'It is upon furnished accommodation rented from private landlords that the full force of the storm has broken, diverted thereto by the storm-barriers put up by other tenures . . .'

While some of the proposals of the Francis Committee would benefit the furnished tenant, it seems unlikely that the lot of the deprived families in furnished accommodation in stress areas would be greatly or speedily improved if the recommendations of the committee were implemented. Indeed the unacceptable living conditions in stress areas seem likely to persist.

Insecurity of tenure in particular seems likely to persist, despite the acknowledged injustice of the distinction between furnished and unfurnished tenancies. In addition, if the committee's recommendations are accepted, it will be possible for a tenancy to be defined as furnished when furniture meets the tenants' essential domestic needs, even if it is of little monetary value; and because of the advantages to landlords of the absence of security, there may be a tendency for more unfurnished lettings to be changed to furnished. The proposal to lay a statutory duty on authorities with areas of housing stress to play a more active role in giving advice to landlords and tenants, and in preventing excessive rents in low rented, multi-occupied dwellings, harassment and unlawful eviction, could be of help to unfurnished tenants; but without security of tenure this seems likely to be of only limited value to the tenant of furnished accommodation. Nor can we be certain that all local authorities would provide sufficient resources effectively to carry out these duties. If rent allowances are provided, some financial hardship may be reduced, but only if the problem of security can be solved.

Tenant Self-help

The characteristics outlined earlier of the tenants in London stress areas suggest that the families with children, now half of all furnished tenants, increasingly occupying sub-standard but expensive furnished lettings because they cannot get unfurnished accommodation, are unlikely without special help to be able to improve the standard of their accommodation—handicapped as they are in the private rental market by children, poverty, lack of a male wage earner, colour, lack of knowledge of housing opportunities and inability to cope with everyday problems. Unfortunately we have no data to show how long such families stay in the furnished sector generally, but only how long they stay in one particular furnished dwelling. It seems possible that they are increasingly staying for longer periods.

Few of these families can be expected to buy houses at London prices: a family income of about £42 per week is currently needed to finance a GLC 100 per cent loan on an old house. In stress areas, 34 per cent of household incomes in furnished tenancies were over £25 per week in 1970, but we do not know how many were over £42 per week. Among Rent Tribunal applicants only 2 per cent had household incomes of more than £35 per week.

There is evidence to suggest that where such low income families do manage to buy a house, they do not always manage to improve their living standards as much as the owner-occupation image suggests. A study of old housing areas in north-east Islington by Anne Holmes [3] showed that households buying their homes commonly paid as much as 30 per cent of their household income in mortgage payments, having had to take out an expensive second mortgage to cover that part of the cost on which the building society would not lend. Sub-letting was necessitated by these high outgoings and commonly both the owner-occupier and the sub-tenant were overcrowded. Nor does owner-occupation necessarily bring the standard amenities to every family: the building society may require the installation of one bathroom, but not two. Improvement grants are known to benefit primarily the middle rather than the lower income groups: many small landlords in areas such as these have hardly heard of the grants, they could not afford to bring the property up to the standard required to qualify for grant; or they prefer not to reveal a state of multiple occupation to the local authority. Others prefer not to create a second self-contained unit in the house which they hope ultimately to occupy themselves as a single-family dwelling. For all these reasons a low-income family in Inner London may fail to achieve an acceptable standard of living, even by buying.

Because unfurnished vacancies are insufficient and the stock of private unfurnished lettings is declining rapidly, the chance for furnished tenants to move quickly to a satisfactory private letting (the most common route out of furnished accommodation in the past) is not good. Only about half of landlords letting unfurnished accommodation intend to relet if it becomes vacant: many of the remaining lettings will be sold for owner-occupation and some of the rest will be changed to furnished lettings. The furnished tenant in fit property can look for little assistance from new local authority building since so much of this is required for residents from slum clearance areas, areas demolished for roads, etc. Only a small percentage of new local authority dwellings are available for the waiting list.

Nor can those in housing need in Inner London expect much help from other areas. Clearly it will be an uphill task to maintain the target figure of 10 000 families a year (from the GLC area) to go to new and expanded towns. Outer London Boroughs are still not prepared to make as a big a contribution as needed for families in housing need from inner areas either by making tenancies available or by welcoming Inner London Boroughs to build.

Landlord Activity

It is not clear how far the private landlords providing for furnished tenants in stress areas, being mainly young or middle-aged working immigrants, are competent to manage a significant part of Inner London's private lettings, or willing and financially able to bring them up to an acceptable standard, particularly for family occupation.

The improvement of this multioccupied property is not mandatory and the rate of improvement is slow. There are many reasons for this. Firstly, the furnished stock is itself constantly changing. Unfortunately we do not know the rate at which furnished dwellings are brought onto, or withdrawn from, the market or how long they remain as furnished lettings. In the Study of Rent Tribunal cases, within a year of the tribunal hearing one-third had been withdrawn from the market, half of them being occupied by the landlord. This rate of withdrawal from the market among tribunal cases is, of course, likely to be higher than among furnished properties in general. But it seems certain that furnished lettings in owner-occupied houses are less permanent than other types of tenure and therefore possibly liable to less landlord improvement.

Some resident landlords are only temporarily letting parts of their own homes and may be reluctant to install additional domestic facilities for which they will have no continuing use. Half the landlords in Rent Tribunal cases said that they viewed the house containing the accommodation referred to the tribunal as a place to live, and only a third viewed it as an investment. A significant number were letting in order to help pay off the mortgage. These figures are available only for Rent Tribunal cases in 1970 but a comparable question among all furnished landlords in the conurbation in 1963 (Milner Holland) revealed 62 per cent of furnished lettings regarded as an investment and only 8 per cent regarded as a place to live. The marked difference between these figures is probably due to the fact that the first set refer only to Rent Tribunal cases, at the bottom end of the market, while the second set refer to all furnished lettings in the conurbation. On the other hand, it is possible that furnished lettings may be increasingly of an impermanent nature.

We cannot assume that all landlords in stress areas wish to improve their property. The Francis Committee said of stress areas: 'These are without doubt the areas where most of the small minority of greedy and unscrupulous landlords thrive.' And many of those landlords who are not greedy or unscrupulous naturally take advantage of the high rents that the general shortage of private lettings enables them to charge for unimproved property.

Nor is it likely that these generally low-income tenants would be able to afford the market rent of improved dwellings of adequate size for their needs. It has been estimated that in

Islington the market rent of an unfurnished family dwelling would have to be £10–12 per week (1971 prices), assuming a 10 per cent return on the landlord's investment. The rent of a furnished dwelling would clearly be higher, and it is not yet clear what help will become available in rent allowances to tenants of furnished dwellings.

The Francis Committee suggested that the preservation of the existing stock of private lettings was critical, and to this end proposed that no further security be given to furnished tenants. But it is unlikely that this measure alone will preserve the privately rented stock for letting, though it may slow down sales of furnished lettings. All the evidence suggests that the market forces are unlikely to be resuscitated. John Willis has put the Shelter view: 'The housing market has become a residual investment for owners who have held property for a long time: opportunist investors and owners: and finally, people who have become beneficial owners through bequests. None of these groups represents any foundation for long-term housing.'

What Can be Done?

Since neither tenant self-help nor landlord activity seems likely quickly to improve furnished living conditions in stress areas, what can be done? In the short term, direct intervention by local authorities and housing associations seems to offer the only prospect of substantial improvement. For families with children in stress areas, they offer virtually the only route out of inadequate furnished accommodation. It is to be hoped that the local authorities in particular will give higher priority to furnished tenants in the future as they come to realize that many live in such accommodation not from a feckless refusal to furnish their own home but rather because they cannot get unfurnished accommodation. Increased local authority allocations are the major hope of keeping furnished tenants on the move up the housing ladder. The current rise in house prices could quickly cause a human log-jam in furnished accommodation in stress areas as those few who might otherwise have bought their way out fail to do so.

However, several palliative measures could help. Overcrowding is triply bad: bad for the families living under these conditions; bad for the houses, which deteriorate more rapidly;

and bad financially, by giving landlords a financial inducement not to improve, and by driving up the market price of property. Regulation schemes under the 1969 Housing Act can bring down the degree of multi-occupation, though this may lead to a wider geographical spread of less serious multi-occupation. To date, local authority response has been disappointing. Figures are difficult to obtain but only five London Boroughs— Lambeth, Tower Hamlets, Hackney, Greenwich and Newham —are operating full schemes. The essential thing is that schemes of regulation should be applied now to all the Inner Boroughs and to all the areas to which multiple occupation is likely to spread.

The landlord is not always able to avoid exploiting his house: in many cases, particularly among immigrants, the landlord has borrowed money for a short period at an exorbitant rate of interest in order to provide himself with a home, and has to sub-let part of the house, possibly crowding it, and possibly charging exorbitant rents. Now that the 'ceiling' on local authority mortgage lending has been removed, local authorities could help by making mortgage advances on reasonable terms to such owner-occupier landlords to enable them to pay off their present mortgages. Using their powers as mortgagors, local authorities could lay down conditions about maintenance, management, rents, etc.

Then there is the most direct intervention of all: acquisition. Housing associations are already buying houses for improvement at a growing rate in Inner Boroughs. Report No. 4 of the Standing Working Party on London Housing has suggested, *inter alia*, that they should increasingly purchase for conversion property that is occupied rather than vacant, as it comes onto the market. (Unfortunately for tenants, the vacant possession price is an incentive to landlords to harass and evict.) Further control of multi-occupation could bring more of this property onto the market. Moreover, housing associations might be encouraged to concentrate first in stress areas. This line of action could have great potential where the property merits conversion and grants will be available for both conversion and acquisition. Even for short-life property not meriting conversion, acquisition would still be worth while simply to secure more efficient and humane management.

But the probability is that the local authority will themselves in the end be purchasing the property in stress areas for re-development. It is suggested that they announce *now* their readiness to buy in advance in order to secure better management and maintenance. It would be immaterial whether they managed the property themselves or leased it to housing associations: either way could be expected to ensure responsible management.

Compulsory Aquisition in Stress Areas

Such a policy of piecemeal acquisition might not, however, prove sufficient. In stress areas with the worst property, conditions and management, it may be that only substantial compulsory purchase will enable the area to be tackled adequately in an organized way. There would be serious difficulties for the authority—market prices would presumably have to be paid, costly repairs and improvements would have to be undertaken, rents might not come down and the authority would probably not be able to abate overcrowding straight away, which might result in much criticism. Moreover, such a policy would require a greater redistribution of housing resources from the better-off areas.

From the tenants' viewpoint, the advantages of public acquisition are obvious. Public acquisition would not only ensure preservation of this stock but would presumably also ensure more equitable allocation, security of tenure, fair rents, prompt repair and maintenance, and perhaps even environmental improvement. Dwellings could be furnished or unfurnished according to need. (It is not always realized that housing authorities have the power to let furnished dwellings.) When local authorities have acquired large numbers of furnished dwellings, they may be expected to show less discrimination against furnished tenants on redevelopment. In particular, they may be expected to be sympathetic towards families with children.

The longer some form of public acquisition is delayed, the smaller will be the remaining stock of privately rented dwellings and the larger the proportion of furnished dwellings (occupied but some not wanted furnished). We know that between 1975 and 1983 the number of dwellings becoming obsolete will double and between 1983 and 1993 will double *again* because of the period of construction. Clearly conditions in stress areas will show accelerating deterioration, and more stress areas will develop unless accelerating preventive measures are taken quickly.

It is suggested that a beginning be made in stress areas of Inner London where hardship is greatest. This is not a novel proposal: in 1965 the Milner Holland Committee urged further consideration of the proposal to designate 'areas of special control' for which 'some authority might be set up, with responsibility for the whole area and armed with powers to control sales and lettings, to acquire property by agreement or compulsorily over the whole area or parts of it, to demolish and rebuild as necessary, to require improvements to be carried out or to undertake such improvements themselves, and to make grants on a more generous and flexible basis than under the existing law'. One of the main purposes was the need to preserve an adequate pool of rented accommodation. Today the need is greater still. The local authorities are already well equipped for such an activity and probably best fitted to carry it out effectively. Alternatively, the government should investigate forthwith the advantages of setting up a Joint Metropolitan Housing Agency with powers to act over the whole of Greater London. Another measure that might help would be an organization akin to a New Town Corporation for such tracts of Inner London as Dockland, where there is potential for large-scale housing development with little housing loss.

But neither the improvement of the existing stock nor the improvement of the building programmes of the Inner London local authorities and housing associations is likely to be sufficient to eliminate in the foreseeable future the appalling living conditions in furnished lettings in stress areas.

It is essential that the Outer London Boroughs make greatly increased housing provision for families from the inner areas. Their objections have not yielded to persuasion and it seems that nothing short of direction will ensure that they make the necessary contribution to the housing of the Inner London poor. The Inner London Boroughs have the power to apply for compulsory purchase orders on land in the outer areas but are reluctant to use these powers. The Minister should consider requiring the Outer London Boroughs to accept X nominations from the GLC every year. This would be unpopular with the Outer Boroughs but perhaps less so than one alternative that has been suggested—giving complete house building powers to the GLC, leaving only management powers with the Boroughs.

References

1. GREVE, J., PAGE, D. and GREVE, S., *Homelessness in London* (Edinburgh: Scottish Academic Press, 1971).

2. ASH, MAURICE, *A Guide to the Structure of London* (Bath: Adams and Dart, 1972).

3. HOLMES, ANNE, *Better Than No Place* (London: Shelter, 1971).

Chapter Twelve

Micro-politics of the City

DAVID DONNISON[1]

Summary

Almost unnoticed amidst recent reforms of borough and metropolitan government, new kinds of small-scale administrative and political organization have been developing in many quarters. Initiatives of this sort, to be seen in many fields, have come from government and from independent groups of various kinds, prompted by the desire to improve and co-ordinate public services, to promote public participation in local affairs (neither of which present insoluble difficulties) and to bring help to deprived neighbourhoods. This third and more difficult task has been attempted both by professional staff and by political activists. Each has run into difficulties if it is not complemented by the other. Central and local government too must be effectively engaged in such programmes if they are to succeed. The second half of this chapter suggests how that might be achieved. These proposals do not offer a solution to inner city problems, nor will they eliminate poverty, but they could help to make more sense of the unco-ordinated and expensive initiatives already taking shape at the 'micropolitical' level of city government.

---

[1] I am grateful to many people for help in preparing this paper—particularly to some of those who in London, Coventry and Liverpool do the kind of work it describes.

After years of debate, the local government of London and the central departments responsible for planning and urban development have all been reorganized. There is still plenty to be said about these levels of government and their unresolved problems. But it is time we considered smaller scales of government which have had less systematic attention: the 'micro-politics' of the city.

Because most of these smaller-scale activities are not recognized by the law, they take place in what might be called an 'unofficial' arena of administration and politics, beneath the accredited decision-making procedures of central and local government. They may be none the less effective for that. It is often in local area offices that innovations in the social services begin [1]. Meanwhile in the world of local community action and politics we have not exhausted the capacity for innovation which created trade unions, political parties and other institutions, once regarded as subversive, that are now recognized by the law and incorporated in statutory decision-making procedures.

This chapter is about two different but related things: administrative organizations which operate at a scale smaller than the smallest units of local government—in London the Boroughs—and the penumbra of independent, small-scale, 'unofficial' political processes which surround the accredited institutions of government. The chapter begins with a brief survey of recent administrative and political developments at this scale of operations which shows that a good deal is already happening—but for diverse and conflicting purposes which I attempt to disentangle in the discussion that follows. This analysis poses problems which call for action. The concluding section of the chapter presents practical proposals, not as a cut-and-dried programme, but as a way of formulating and exploring some of our political and professional dilemmas.

Recent Initiatives by Government

Because some of the oldest bits of British government, such as the parish councils, operate on a miniature scale, while the newest, from the London Boroughs to the Department of the Environment, operate on an increasingly large scale, we often assume the trend of government is always towards larger organizations.

Yet government itself has in recent years shown a growing interest in units working at the smallest scales. Some of these initiatives, taken by government and by bodies appointed to advise government, can be briefly listed. Most of them have reached a point lying somewhere between purposeful talk and established tradition.

The Plowden Committee, reporting in 1967 [2], called for the identification of 'educational priority areas' where the schools need special help and many education authorities are now beginning to follow these policies of 'positive discrimination' in favour of deprived neighbourhoods. The following year, a new Planning Act [3] introduced the term 'action area' to describe patches of the map chosen for intensive development or redevelopment. The year after, the Skeffington Committee's report [4] on public participation in planning proposed 'community fora', served by 'community development officers', which would become local arenas for the formulation and testing of ideas about planning. These proposals drew on earlier discussions of community work and the training of community workers—notably a report from a study group set up by the Gulbenkian Foundation [5]. In 1969 a new Housing Act gave planning and housing departments extra powers and subsidies to bring to bear within 'general improvement areas', chosen for comprehensive renewal that would demand the support and collaboration of local residents. The following year action was taken on the report of the Seebohm Committee [6] which had concluded that most of the work of the more comprehensive social service departments it recommended should be done through multi-disciplinary 'area teams', concentrating resources particularly heavily in the sort of areas the Plowden Committee had in mind for its E.P.As. Proposals for the reform of the health services made in successive reports and green papers seem likely to lead to a reorganization which will bring services now managed by different agencies into larger and more comprehensive teams serving areas much smaller than those administered by local authorities. One of the most carefully prepared of these proposals, presented in the Plan for Milton Keynes new town [7], would create teams of a dozen general practitioners with associated laboratory, nursing, dental, pharmaceutical and hospital services for areas of 30 000 people. Building on the initiative of the educational priority areas and the American poverty programme, the Home Office in 1969 launched 'community development projects' in deprived or disorganized districts, staffed by people whose job was to enable local residents to identify needs and to demand (and sometimes themselves provide) new resources for meeting them. Meanwhile funds were offered through the 'urban programme' to promote new or additional work by statutory and voluntary bodies in deprived areas—the provision of day care and nursery schooling in neighbourhoods with many working mothers is a typical example of the sort of project which has been supported.

Scarcely noticed amidst these developments, the parish councils have been growing steadily more active, taking on more work and pushing up their expenditure at a faster rate than the rest of local government [8]. In Scotland, where parish councils were abolished in 1929, the government appears to have accepted the Wheatley Commission's proposal that a similar body, to be called a community council, should be revived [9]. In Wales the government promises 'community councils' with the powers of parish councils for rural areas and any urban area that wants them [10].

Independent Initiatives

Meanwhile people have been creating their own micropolitics without waiting for government. 'Community action groups' of various kinds have been formed to conduct surveys of deprived urban neighbourhoods, to mobilize opinion, and to agitate for more housing, access to open space, stronger action against landlords, better public services and grants from urban programme funds [11]. Associations representing claimants to welfare services, racial and religious minorities, opponents of motorways, users of state education and others making demands on government often speak for particular areas, or consist of loose national federations of local groups. Civic and amenity societies, seeking to conserve, improve and enliven local communities have also been growing fast.

The number and variety of such groups which can be mobilized within a few wards of one London Borough can be illustrated from the experience of the Islington Borough Council whose Policy Committee proposed in 1969 to close a set of public baths. Meetings were called, petitions were circulated and within a few days the Council was being lobbied by the Islington Society, the Canonbury Society, the Barnsbury Association, and local groups and branches of the Consumer's Association, the Association for the Advancement of State Education, the Fabian Society, the Swimming Teachers, the primary school heads, the Sub-Aqua Club, old-age pensioners (users of the hot baths), orthodox Jewry (users of the bath for men only) and others. While there was some overlap in their membership—between the Fabians, the Consumer's Association and the Association for the Advancement of State Education, for example—most of these groups represented different, independent, local interests. (The Council decided to keep the baths open.)

To stimulate these energies and focus them more effectively upon the affairs of the small communities which the Redcliffe-Maud Commission and others have identified as the neighbourhoods which mean most to people, an Association for Neighbourhood Councils was formed in 1970 to press for the creation of a nationwide system of elected councils [12]. In 1971, with support from charitable sources, a local council of this sort was elected for the Golborne ward in North Kensington.

This boom in the activities of associations representing groups drawn from fairly small areas which built up towards the end of the 1960s had diverse origins and motives. Increasing affluence and the acquisition of a growing range of consumer goods turned people's attention to 'public goods', like clean air, peace and quiet and safety on the roads, which they could not readily buy for themselves. They found, moreover, that other people's private goods (cars and radios, for example) threatened these public goods. The community had to act together to improve or defend the quality of its environment—and to start with, a 'community' often had to be created for the purpose.

Some people were more concerned with poverty than affluence, and with the needs of the oppressed or ill-organized, and of vulnerable groups such as immigrants. But they, too, believed it might be easier to extend opportunities and improve attainments if the services required were directed not to individuals, but to communities 'as a whole'. Hence the Plowden, Skeffington and Seebohm Committees called for 'community schools', 'community development officers' and 'community workers' and wider participation by the public in the services discussed in their reports.

Services hitherto wielding clearly specified powers, such as development control, and offering clearly specified rights, such as standard improvement grants, are gaining broader powers to promote more comprehensive programmes of social development—through housing aid centres and the new structure plans, for example. The Seebohm area teams likewise have a more comprehensive, open-ended task than the old child-care officers. To succeed, these services must secure legitimizing public support; to focus their efforts, they need a better understanding of what people want. Even those officials whose interpretation of 'participation' amounts to no more than the manipulation of public opinion need a forum of some kind in which to manipulate.

Growing investment in slum clearance, road building, urban renewal and central redevelopment schemes has brought the planners and engineers into the dense social fabric of long-established cities—sometimes with dramatic effects. Peripheral building in green fields on the fringes of urban areas was conducted by anonymous developers and bureaucrats for anonymous clients: when they are being planned no one knows exactly who will live in the new houses and attend the new schools. But when thousands of people have their houses pulled down in slum clearance schemes, or to make way for urban motorways or new polytechnics, the power of government is (literally) brought home to them and those who wield it and those who gain or lose in the process are more clearly visible.

There are signs, too, that the British are growing less deferential to public officials and authority in general: thanks partly to television, planners, teachers, bureaucrats and politicians are more often expected to justify their decisions to a more critical public. This change in manners, which emerged on the national scene through the mass media with *Braden's Week*, *Private Eye* and *That Was The Week That Was*, is now percolating to neighbourhood level—as every headmaster knows.

Discussion

The motives underlying the micro-political developments I have briefly surveyed are mixed in diverse ways. Two reasonably straightforward extremes can be distinguished: from the bureaucrats' side of the counter, the attempt to provide more effective public services; and from the citizen's side, the demand to be heard, to secure rights and benefits and to participate in public affairs. Both motives entail conflict—among bureaucrats, among citizens and between both—but within the context of a particular set of values each can be pursued consistently, effectively and honestly.

The main (though not the only) purposes of the planners' action areas and the Seebohm area teams are to concentrate resources and co-ordinate decisions more efficiently, to find out what people want and gain their help in providing it—to produce, in fact, a more effective public service. The population to be served must therefore be *big* enough (50 000 to 100 000, the Seebohm Committee suggested) to justify the employment of a sufficient array of resources—human, technical and financial—to be effective. The staff providing the service must be employed by, and accountable to, the larger system of government which gives them these resources and the authority to use them. Decision-making procedures and the allocation of responsibilities will change from time to time, but they must at each stage be defined as clearly and authoritatively as possible. Although any team of people work better if they enjoy doing things together, this 'expressive' side of their job must not imperil their 'instrumental' task of delivering an efficient service to the public.

On the other hand, the main (though again not the only) purposes of community action groups and neighbourhood councils are to enable local people to clarify common problems, formulate their own demands, bring pressure on government and organize themselves to provide services of their own—in fact, to promote participation in public affairs. The population to be served must therefore be *small* enough (5000 to 15 000, the advocates of neighbourhood councils have suggested) to retain or develop a sense of community. Leaders will adopt a charismatic or a bargaining style, rather than appealing to administrative rank or professional loyalties. Whether they are paid or unpaid, those who work for them must be accountable to local groups, not to higher levels of government. Differences in personality and allegiance and the changing political opportunities of the moment will throw up competing movements which may prove fruitful, despite their apparent confusion, for competition may give more people an opportunity to participate, and enable the community to alternate successfully between moderate and militant tactics when dealing with authority—in ways that a more disciplined and consistent organization would find impossible. The expressive aspects of local politics (the comradeship generated by tramping the streets together with a petition, for example) may prove more important than the instrumental aspects (getting the completed petition delivered at the right time and place).

Somewhat caricatured though they are, these contrasting accounts of the aims, style and values of bureaucratic and political organizations will be widely recognizable. Each in its own way can be consistent and effective. But each has limitations which become obvious when we consider a third type of organization that is designed for redistribution.

Many of the micro-political innovations noted at the start of this chapter—such as educational priority areas, local projects of the urban programme and planners' action areas in neighbourhoods due for redevelopment—are intended mainly (not only) to focus resources and attention on deprived groups and areas and to attune public services more closely to their needs in order to improve their living conditions and extend their opportunities and attainments. If these programmes are intended to enable poor people to catch up with richer people—to 'bring in the rearguard'—they must redistribute resources, power and status from rich to poor. New political institutions would not be required for this purpose if those who control the conventional machinery of government were wholeheartedly in favour of it, for redistribution would then present merely technical problems which government could solve in time without such innovations. But because a major and sustained redistribution cannot be achieved *without* using the powers and resources of government—the law, the courts, taxation and the social services—initiatives which are confined to voluntary institutions and never win the support of the bureaucracy cannot succeed. Redistribution therefore demands a combination of bureaucratic and political organization. The rest of this chapter explores the dilemmas facing those who try to fashion that combination at a micro-political scale. (Since these are among the classic dilemmas of politics the world over, there are many other scales at which they arise. Moreover I am not suggesting that the best way of helping the poor is to operate only at a small spatial scale.) I shall explore the frontier between these worlds first from the bureaucratic and then from the political side.

A wholly bureaucratic or professional style of organization can go a long way to improve conditions and extend opportunities for deprived people, if it does not alarm the public and its representatives. But it tends to run into difficulties sooner or later. The needs of the most deprived groups may be extreme or bizarre by the standards of more conventional neighbourhoods. The people of one educational priority area expressed no interest in Plowden policies, asking instead that the police should each night clear drunken derelicts, more deprived than themselves, from their tenement stairs. In Londonderry the Bogsiders asked not for police protection but for protection *from* the police. Many meetings called to discuss local plans and renewal schemes have broken up in recrimination about unemptied dustbins, leaking roofs and broken toilets [13].

There are unavoidable conflicts, never far beneath the surface, between those who allocate the benefits of public services and impose the social controls which go with these benefits and those who seek the benefits and experience the controls. Public officials who learn to deal more responsively and humanely with the needs of deprived groups do not conjure these conflicts away: they simply shift some of them 'up the line' towards the town hall where their bosses grow increasingly critical of the lax standards and unpredictable behaviour of subordinates who appear to be 'going native', if not outright subversive. To succeed in their redistributive job, these subordinates must develop a loyalty to their area and do battle with their bosses from time to time on behalf of its people. But their bosses are accountable to a council elected to represent a larger area, not only its more impoverished minorities. Unless the council is prepared to give clear redistributive directives and stick to them, any professional team working in a really deprived neighbourhood will be compelled either to assume an increasingly subversive role, or to act increasingly as the ruling majority's agents—controlling, comforting and monitoring the deprived, rather than bringing them justice. Neither is an easy or wholly honourable course.[1]

That is why many egalitarian reformers would reject this bureaucratic or professional model of action altogether and adopt a frankly political one, seeking a power base within the deprived community rather than within the bureaucracy, demanding help for that community and deliberately leaving it to others to work out how that help can be delivered and paid for. This approach can take us a long way and for some purposes it is the only effective strategy. But it soon runs into difficulties too.

Political pressures generated within small local communities are most effective in vetoing action proposed at higher levels by one department of government. 'Save our swimming bath!' 'We'll have no mental hospital/motorway/rent increase . . . (you name it) here!' Where civil disobedience such as rent strikes, squatting in empty houses or obstruction of the highway can be readily organized and publicized, such protests have often been dramatically effective. But it is easier to squat in the unoccupied house or private park you want to capture for the people than in the school or the jobs which do not yet exist. Thus more positive and comprehensive programmes of reform (bringing, perhaps, new opportunities for work, better policing and refuse collection, rerouting of traffic and improvement of rented housing) are harder to achieve because they call for a costly, co-ordinated and sustained redirection of policies and resources in many departments of government accountable to much wider areas of society.

If the spokesmen of deprived communities have failed to get

---

[1] The problem is illustrated by a recent conflict in the Social Services Department of a London Borough. 'About 50 demonstrators, most of them social workers, paraded with placards on the steps of the town hall . . . in support of a senior social worker . . . who, they claimed, has wrongly been moved from his post as a team leader in the department. The demonstrators alleged that [he] had been victimised because of his efforts to achieve greater community involvement in the work of the social services department . . . Conflict had arisen because of his efforts to involve members of his team in decision-taking and over contact with voluntary groups—some of them militant—which were helping some of the social workers' clients.' *Guardian*, 9 February 1972.

what they want from the conventional machinery of government, they must bring some new influence to bear. All the militants can do is to draw attention to needs which might otherwise be forgotten (mobile, non-voting people like the gypsies will *normally* be neglected by conventional democratic procedures) and bring the influence of a broader public opinion and higher levels of government to bear on local affairs. (The Bogsiders—one of the most deprived urban communities in the United Kingdom—have played a part in abolishing first their town council and then the Stormont Government by compelling Westminster, Dublin, Washington and the United Nations to pay attention to them.)

To achieve such things, all sorts of tactics may be effective: advocacy and the aggressive use of legal rights and processes, petitions, demonstrations, strikes, civil disobedience and guerilla warfare have each had their successes. But in the short run each can only veto action. In the longer run—and it takes a long run to bring about a sustained redistribution of resources—micro-political groups succeed by gaining the support of larger populations and higher levels of government. However roundabout the route, their pressures must eventually lead to action taken through conventional administrative machinery. The success of those who fail to win this support is short-lived at best. If advocates gain more help from the laws than public opinion will sanction, the laws will be changed. (The welfare rights lawyers who in 1970 got a judgement from the Supreme Court compelling New York to raise its 'standard of need' to take account of changes in the cost of living, as the Social Security Act required, ultimately succeeded only in establishing that States all across the country were entitled to pay whatever percentage of the 'standard of need' they chose [14]. What at first seemed a triumph proved to be a disaster.) Even guerilla warfare is no exception to this rule, for the gunmen very rarely defeat the police and the army in a military sense. They do not need to if they can deprive them of the support of public opinion. (That is why the French army had to be withdrawn from Algeria, after virtually destroying armed resistance there.) The public may be alienated from the forces of law and order in all sorts of ways—by distaste for brutality, by reluctance to accept the sufferings imposed on soldiers and their families, or by the financial cost of military operations [15].

Those who would rely wholly on political action to batter the government into redistributing resources in favour of deprived communities must demonstrate not only that this sort of micro-politics can succeed—we know it can—but that *they* will succeed more often than rival operators working for more privileged people. If the competition is conducted through petitions, demonstrations and advocacy, it is not obvious why deprived neighbourhoods will do better than those in which more people have lawyers, journalist-friends, cars, telephones, typewriters and organizing skills [16]. If the game is to be played with guns and bombs, past experience shows that the Right is more likely to win than the Left. Revolts by the oppressed seldom succeed unless directed against colonial governments, or regimes already defeated in war, or powerfully supported by foreign arms—although thousands more will doubtless be misled by the apparent exception of Cuba into disregarding these elementary historical facts. (Many would argue that Cuba, where the defeated regime was a discredited client of a semi-colonial power, was no exception to this rule.)

Even those who are convinced they can beat the odds by militant action, whether of a violent or non-violent kind, should carefully reckon the price their country may pay for the destruction of conventional political processes. Britain is not yet a country in which these processes are wholly corrupt, or which discriminates wholly against the deprived.

Those who would on principle reject collaboration with government and administrative and professional innovation in favour of purely political strategies of action are putting their faith in (political) free enterprise in a (political) market place. And in Britain those who do best in the economic market place will generally come out on top in a political free-for-all too.

The conclusion to which this discussion leads is that if we want to help deprived groups and areas, professional and political strategies are complementary, not conflicting. Neither can succeed without the other. A professional team set up to improve living conditions and extend opportunities for a deprived community must discover what local people want and enable them to participate in preparing a programme of action. Otherwise, a plan prepared, at best, with the help of a few door-to-door surveys will eventually have to be 'sold' to public

meetings at a stage when it is too late to make major amend-
ments without intolerable delays. Later, when they set about
implementing the programme, officials will have to persuade
their superiors to furnish the resources they need without the
support of the people they want to help—often, indeed, in face
of their opposition. The story is only too familiar. Bureaucrats
need politicians.

Too familiar, too, are the local community action groups
which demand from public authorities a response that no one is
prepared or empowered to give. As frustration mounts, leaders
bid against each other for followers by making increasingly
militant demands. Eventually their following may disintegrate
altogether as people grow disillusioned by meetings, marches
and petitions which achieve nothing. Just as the bureaucracy
needs effective local representative institutions to do business
with, so local leaders need an official institution of some sort
which provides services, information, a target for complaints
and the occasional concessions which enable them to retain a
following.

Tender-minded liberals and tough-minded militants are often
equally reluctant to recognize the complementary contributions
of political action and professional service in any serious
programme for reform. One side clings to the idea that men of
goodwill can set the world to rights if they will only take counsel
together. Hence we have local councils of social service and
community relations committees which provide meeting places
for leaders of the community but have neither the resources to
do anything for the deprived, nor the political 'clout' to secure
effective intervention from government [17].

The other side is apt to mistake noise for action, forgetting
that it is easier to hold up the traffic and get on to the television
screens than to create administrative structures and professional
procedures with the staying power to bring about a continuing
improvement in the living conditions and life chances of poor
people.

These confusions also help to explain why workers in the fields
of community development and race relations are often riven
by such embittered feuds. Expecting to join a band of brothers
labouring to make the world a better place, they soon find themselves in the thick of an imperfectly comprehended battle
between the exponents of bureaucratic and political strategies

for reform. Since these strategies express entirely different values, not merely a disagreement about methods, each side finds the other's behaviour devious, if not outright treacherous. Too often they end up doing more damage to each other than to the pervasive and complex fabric of social injustice.

A Proposal

What should we do? The proposals that follow are not a cut-and-dried programme; and they are certainly *not* a solution to the problems of the inner city, most of which call for action on a national and regional scale. They are an attempt to explore practical ways of resolving the dilemmas I have discussed.

If it is the more deprived areas that concern us most, any programme of action must *first* provide more and better services of conventional kinds for them—otherwise it will be mere rhetoric, soon viewed with cynical hostility by all concerned. New kinds of service and the help of indigenous local people may also be needed, but they will make little difference by themselves: we must also have more or better houses, more or better jobs, better schools and social services, higher rates of take-up for rent and rate rebates and other benefits, and whatever else can be offered by conventional services to meet people's needs and give them their rights. These things cannot be achieved unless the public services are adequately staffed by people ultimately accountable to the conventional machinery of government.

Secondly there must be better opportunities for local people to seek their rights and make their demands heard; and that means conflict. We are dealing with the allocation of resources and power and therefore with problems that are essentially political, not technical. It is the politicians' task to manage conflict constructively, not to eliminate it.

Thirdly the political leaders of the deprived and those in the bureaucracy who are prepared to respond to their demands must be given some access to a broader public opinion. There would be no call for new procedures at all if those already in power locally were determined and able to help the deprived, without prompting or pressure from outside. Thus to succeed, any programme for redistribution must provide opportunities for appeal to a wider audience. We can now turn to more specific proposals for creating and articulating these three elements of a micro-political system.

To improve public services in deprived areas, to co-ordinate them more effectively at ground level and to make them more responsive to local needs, we should set up decentralized local service centres, combining the functions of a citizens advice bureau and the local offices of housing, social services, education and other departments. They would do as much work as can be devolved to this smaller scale of administration from town or county hall. Included among these services might be a public library, a planning office doing much of that department's design work for the area, and a housing aid service. Other statutory or voluntary services not provided by the local authority, such as the rent officer, the probation officers or a Family Service Unit, together with maternity and child welfare services (which are likely to be hived off soon to an area health authority) could also be based at these centres. Each service should be more readily available to the public, more alert to local needs and aspirations and better able to collaborate with each other than is normal in the town hall and its divisional offices and out-stations. The range of services to be included will vary from place to place, but it should in principle be as wide as possible. If people are to seek help, to participate more effectively in government, and to question its actions, no one can confine their participation to particular services or predict to which their questions will be addressed. Considerable responsibility should be delegated to the officers in charge of each local service, under the leadership of an area officer who would have a general responsibility for all local authority services in his neighbourhood, and some scope for deploying funds between different projects or services. He would be a 'company commander', generally responsible for this bit of the 'front', to adopt a military analogy. But the staff of such service centres must be employed by and ultimately accountable to, the local or national services to which they belong: the volume of resources and the quality of staff required could be secured in no other way. They should seek opportunities, however, for recruiting and paying local people to help them whenever the skills needed can be found in the neighbourhood they serve.

For these reasons, the population served by such a local centre must be fairly large. The lower limit of the range

proposed by the Seebohm Committee for its area teams was
50 000 but, for the richer mix of services needed in the more deprived areas where these centres would be most needed, a smaller
population would be sufficient. There are 360 children in public
care for every 50 000 people in Tower Hamlets—and that is
more than the totals in care in seventeen of the twenty Outer
London Boroughs. The demands for many other services—
dealing with slum clearance, public health inspection, old
people's welfare and probation, for example—are also heavily
concentrated in Inner Boroughs. If public services in the Outer
Boroughs can operate effectively and economically (and they
generally can) then Inner Boroughs like Tower Hamlets could
maintain effective local service centres of the sort I have proposed for areas of about 25 000 people.

The second, political, half of these proposals cannot be spelt
out so clearly because people must be enabled to develop their
own political action independently—and therefore unpredict-
ably. Space, in every sense of the word, must be left for that.
Local people and their (often conflicting) organizations must
be encouraged to take responsibility and to nominate their
spokesmen to consultative groups attached to statutory services;
they must be given information when they want it and offered
space in the local centre for their own meetings and activities.
They should be helped whenever possible to set up their own
services—particularly services which the bureaucracy finds it
hard to provide: providing legal advice about racial discrimination, social security rights or the mutual obligations of landlord and tenant, for example, should come before the provision
of youth clubs and day nurseries.

If a nationwide system of neighbourhood councils is established in urban areas, there would probably be several in the
territory of one local service centre. They could strengthen the
organization I have proposed, becoming the most important
element in the array of indigenous groups operating in the area.
Tenants' associations, political parties, claimants' unions, old
people's clubs and recreational clubs would be among the
others active there.

If they are to survive, these developments must be recognized by the conventional system of local government and
incorporated in it. Councillors will inevitably be anxious, if not
openly hostile, about proposals that threaten to challenge their

own authority and communications. At the moment they are organized to represent their party and direct their authority's services. Chairmanship of the party group and of committees responsible for education, housing and other major spending services give them more power than any other local post: these are the routes to O.B.E.s and a seat on the bench. There is no local government committee for the Isle of Dogs, Liverpool 8, St. Ann's, Easterhouse or Sparkbrook. In future there should be committees of elected members entitled to speak for priority areas and their local services. Local councillors and aldermen— together, perhaps with the local MP and a few co-opted members—might together act as the management committee for a local service centre. The elected representatives might hold their own party meetings and 'surgeries' there.

Many of the most deprived areas (partly for lack of this sort of political structure) are poorly represented on their Councils. Since the Conservatives are unlikely to win these seats they do not get the attention of that party's ablest members, and for the same reason they are not thought to need the attention of the best Labour party members either. Their councillors may have been chosen by a poll in which no more than a fifth of the electorate turned out to vote. Some deprived areas are more fortunate, but there will have to be changes in the representation of others before their political leadership can bear heavier burdens. As a livelier indigenous politics develops in these areas, members of the Council will have to listen to local leaders or co-opt them if they are not to be replaced by them. Neighbourhood councils could provide a forum for this sort of politics.

The central government must also play a part in these developments if they are to be effective. Grants to local authorities for service centres in deprived areas would convey public recognition of the programme and ensure that its costs are not imposed wholly on authorities whose rate payers may already be poorer and more heavily taxed than those of more fortunate areas. Without such grants, nothing much will happen.

The area officer in charge of each local centre must be firmly established in the local government service. (The excellent people chosen to run community development projects are mostly too young, too underpaid and too inexperienced for this purpose.) He should be a professional, equivalent in rank to a chief officer's deputy; an office manager, of lower status will not do. Even then he may need some protection from the pressures to which he will be exposed if he does his job properly. The central government could take power to veto or confirm appointments and dismissals of such officers, as it already does for Medical Officers, Directors of Social Services and other key officials.

People in deprived areas are not necessarily inarticulate; through established organizations (such as miners' or transport workers, unions) they can defeat national governments. But they are often poorly equipped for local community action. Indigenous groups will thus need financial support if they are to thrive. That is already available through urban programme grants, but, since these have to be approved by the local authority, any group suspected of being too truculently independent cannot get help. The central government has often paid money directly to bodies which may get into conflicts with local authorities—Direct Grant Schools and New Town Development Corporations, for example. But if such precedents are to be avoided, funds could instead be distributed through a central commission, rather like the Research Councils or the University Grants Committee, which would include representatives of local government but would be less exposed to local political pressures. Its opponents would object to such a commission (as they did to the Land Commission) because it might intrude in local affairs. That, of course, would occasionally be its purpose.

Conclusion

These proposals, I must stress again, are not presented as a 'solution' to the problems of deprived urban areas, many of which call for action on regional and national scales. Nor am I suggesting that they would eliminate social conflict and the threat of urban guerilla warfare: on the contrary, their aim is to promote more productive conflict and furnish procedures for successive, temporary arbitrations and agreements. When people conflict over housing, play-space, jobs, welfare services and other things which can in time be extended, subdivided and redistributed almost indefinitely, such arbitration is feasible because everyone can gain something from it. Thus the class

conflicts common in urban society are in the longer run relatively benign, unlike the conflicts that arise between religious
or ethnic groups, where the contenders are apt to find themselves playing 'zero sum games' in which every gain is someone
else's loss [18].

We must also beware of assuming that all forms of deprivation are sufficiently concentrated spatially to be effectively
reached by a programme that discriminates in favour of particular areas. They are not. Some needs (and in some Boroughs
most needs) are scattered fairly randomly across the map;
and even when needs are concentrated it will sometimes be best
to help people disperse to other places where the opportunities
are better.

What I have offered is no more than a discussion of dilemmas
posed by administrative and political developments which are
already taking place at micro-political or neighbourhood scale,
followed by proposals for better ways of handling these developments. If they are worth experimenting with, these proposals
should be tried out in a few places carefully chosen to ensure
that staff, capital investment and local enterprise can be concentrated sufficiently heavily to make an impact worth studying.
(We already know what will be revealed if we 'monitor' the
effects of an extra teacher, half an inspector and some trips to
the country upon very deprived primary schools—nothing.)

These proposals are not intended to displace or denigrate
other administrative or political developments whose purposes
fit the simpler professional or political models with which my
analysis began. There is everything to be said for the establishment of area teams up and down the country to administer the
personal social services or to prepare plans for action areas and
for many other initiatives designed to co-ordinate and deploy
public services more effectively. Likewise, in areas of all kinds,
there are important jobs to be done by amenity societies, parish
councils and other bodies that enable people to participate in
public affairs and improve their neighbourhoods and the local
public services.

But when our main purpose is to raise the living conditions
and opportunities of the most deprived people nearer to those of
the more fortunate, then neither the purely professional nor the
purely political models of action will serve. We need a more
sophisticated combination that 'meshes' each with the other,

recognizes the inevitable conflicts between them, and provides more effective means for arbitration between government and the governed to make these conflicts more productive. To do that we must also bring on to the local scene the mediating influence of national government, without which the oppressed and deprived seldom make lasting progress.

Clearly these proposals present daunting problems. They challenge the whole tradition of local government departmentalism—a tradition rooted in professional *esprit de corps*, and reinforced by the departmentalism of central government. They challenge political traditions such as the principle that 'fair shares' are equal shares—traditions unfriendly to 'positive discrimination' in favour of deprived groups within the local population. Before surrendering to these traditions, however, we should recognize that the alternative to action is not benign neglect.

Micro-political developments of all sorts are already on foot: in London, as in other cities, community development projects and local action groups of various kinds are at work—many supported by public funds—in Southwark, Islington, Lambeth, Kensington, Camden, New Ham and elsewhere. Community relations committees are to be found in twenty-two Boroughs. Most of them are inadequately staffed, have attracted no matching investment of enterprise from local government and have unsatisfactory communications with authority and an ambiguous role. Similar things are going on all over the country. In Liverpool alone a community development project, an educational priority area and SNAP—the Shelter Neighbourhood Action Project—have been set up to serve different areas in an unco-ordinated way. Not surprisingly, the response of local government has been halting. In London, as elsewhere, various departments of central and local government set up geographical divisions, area offices and out-stations for the administration of their services which reinforce departmental and professional barriers. These units serve different areas from different buildings when the same investment in buildings and administrative organization could have produced a more effective system, more accessible and comprehensible to the public. At the time of writing yet another ministry—the Department of the Environment—appears to be entering the field with a scheme for centrally funded development projects in deprived neighbourhoods without joining forces with community development projects, educational priority areas and all the other initiatives already in play. In these projects, indigenous community action has at best a precarious role. It could be a powerful co-ordinating influence if properly meshed with the bureaucracy's initiatives. Once they start talking, people cannot be confined to the agenda of the service which called the meeting. Officials who are prepared to listen to them must soon start talking to their colleagues in other departments.

The outcome of present good intentions, backed by much public expenditure, is likely to be disappointing if we cannot devise an approach which is politically more realistic, administratively more effective and more likely to help deprived people and the neighbourhoods in which many of them live.

References

1. See DONNISON, D. V., CHAPMAN, VALERIE, et al., *Social Policy and Administration* (London: Allen and Unwin, 1965), for case studies and a discussion of such locally originated innovations.

2. *Children and their Primary Schools*, Report of the Central Advisory Council for Education (England) (London: H.M.S.O., 1967).

3. Town and Country Planning Act, 1968.

4. *People and Planning*, Report of the Committee on Public Participation in Planning (London: H.M.S.O., 1969).

5. *Community Work and Social Change. A Report on Training* (London: Longman, 1968).

6. *Report of the Committee on Local Authority and Allied Personal Social Services*, Cmnd. 3707 (London: H.M.S.O., 1968).

7. *The Plan for Milton Keynes* (Milton Keynes Development Corporation, Wavendon, Bletchley, Bucks.), Vol. II, 1970; p. 222.

8. *Report of the Royal Commission on Local Government in England*, 1969; Cmnd. 4040, Vol. III, Research Appendices, Appendix 8.

9. *Report of the Royal Commission on Local Government in Scotland*. Cmnd. 4150, 1969. See also PROPHET, JOHN, 'A case for parish councils in Scotland', *Public Administration*, Winter 1971.

10. *The Reform of Local Government in Wales. Consultative document* (London: H.M.S.O., 1971) p. 13.

11. See, for example, *People, Participation and Government*, Fabian Research Series 293, and LAPPING, ANNE (ed.), *Community Action*, Fabian Tract 400, 1970.

12. See BAKER, JOHN and YOUNG, MICHAEL, *The Hornsey Plan. A role for neighbourhood councils in the new local government*. The Association for Neighbourhood Councils (18 Victoria Park Square, London E2), 1971.

13. For examples of the unforeseen demands thrown up when government tries to discuss its plans and programmes with the public see UNGERSON,

CLARE, *Moving Home* (Occasional Papers on Social Administration, no. 44 (London: Bell, 1971)), p. 54.

14. The case is *Rosado v. Wyman*, mentioned in a forthcoming book by Peter Marris, who quotes Edward V. Sparer, 'The right to welfare', in DORSEN, NORMAN (ed.), *The Rights of Americans: What They Are—What They Should Be* (London: Pantheon, 1971).

15. See KITSON, FRANK, *Low Intensity Operations. Subversion, Insurgency and Peacekeeping* (London: Faber, 1971), for a thoughtful analysis of these problems.

16. DENNIS, NORMAN, *People and Planning* (London: Faber, 1970). The author discusses the handicaps of working-class people in participating in decision making, e.g. p. 348 ff.

17. See HILL, MICHAEL J. and ISSACHAROFF, RUTH M., *Community Action and Race Relations* (Oxford University Press, 1971), for a crictical analysis of these problems in the race relations field.

18. Richard Rose's exploration of these problems in Northern Ireland *Governing Without Consensus* (London: Faber, 1971), also throws light on conflicts nearer home.

Chapter Thirteen

The Mood of London

RUTH GLASS

It is an awkward period to talk about 'planning' in London—or rather to make plans for planning. The more reason, perhaps, to talk about it. In the context of our society and political system planning is based on the assumption that three prerequisites exist: first, a considerable measure of consensus on major decisions affecting land-use and the economic and social organization involved; second, a widely accepted definition of the 'public interest', in terms of which these decisions are supposed to be made; third, the conceptual, institutional and technical equipment which would enable us to apply such a definition in practice to plan-making and development control. In short, planning as an institution, and as a process, is supposed to be essentially 'rational' (in terms of a collective rationality) and also seen to be rational; and such rationality, in turn, rests upon a demonstrable 'objectivity'. But are these attributes actually in evidence in the current London planning scene—on paper or on the ground? There can be little doubt that the answer to that question would be generally negative. Indeed, this is one of the very few observations which would nowadays be regarded as an objective one.

What then is wrong? Why is it now, and will be, for some time to come, so exceptionally difficult to make sense of planning; to develop an agreed definition of the 'public interest'— or even to agree to differ?

What is the Public Interest?

First, though the basic notions—consensus, public interest, objectivity—have a ringing sound, they are in fact rather hollow. (There is a sort of conceptual sloppiness about them.) Of what exactly is the 'public interest' thought to be made up? Is it the sum total of individual, discrete, unambiguous interests, or of socially involved interests, taken with regard to the context in which they arise? Is it 'the greatest good of the greatest number'? What does the 'collective rationality' consist of? Each of these questions leads to a series of others which are not merely a matter of theoretical speculation, but of direct practical importance. For instance, if we use a Benthamite formulation, we can easily get stuck: is the 'greatest good' a fixed entity, at a fixed point of time? Which 'greatest number'? It cannot possibly include the young and unborn generations for the sake of whom planning is primarily intended. But even if we were to forget them (that is, expect them to be exact duplicates of the existing population) and assume that every man here and now is fully aware of his and his children's 'own good', the planning profession would be in a dilemma: they would either have to take lessons in telepathy, or become mail order clerks who collect votes on every planning issue—or declare themselves redundant altogether.

However, questions of this kind were not spelt out when our planning machinery was established after the Second World War, nor did they need to be spelt out at that stage. Rather vague notions of welfarism seemed quite sufficient, and had then actually a fairly solid social basis—in line with the old common law tradition of neighbourliness. It was a period of exceptional 'socialization'. (When the bombs fall, individual and public interests do indeed become synonymous.) Several factors were therefore taken for granted: that there was a stable and indeed growing sense of social interdependence; that as the alternative choices of urban development in a densely built-up island society such as ours were so severely limited, there would not be much cause for political controversy; moreover that, although planning does involve a considerable discretionary element, the appropriate authorities could be relied upon to play the game fairly and squarely. (In fact there was then a good deal of bipartisan agreement both in the acceptance of planning legislation at the national level, and in major planning decisions at the local level, not least in London. Incipient conflicts were papered over, and did not come to the surface until the mid- and late-fifties.) The post-war planning system was thus built essentially on two articles of faith: the expectation of increasing social harmony and of continued trust in public authorities.[1]

Although such beliefs provided a rather slender basis, they did support the elaborate planning machinery for some time. Good will, enthusiasm, talent, intuition—coupled with various object lessons of imaginative redevelopment and innovation—proved to be quite an effective substitute for a rigorous analysis (or for 'planning theory' as it would be called nowadays). There was an urgent job of reconstruction to be done, and not much time or money for tortuous introspection. (The term 'urban renewal', with all its unpalatable connotations, had not yet been imported from the United States.) There was no need to search for 'social goals'—they were quite self-evident—or to devise 'planning strategy'. (No one then had much taste for martial verbiage.) There was a new sense, indeed a glow, of civic pride—at its peak in 1951 during the Festival of Britain: 'good old London' had become 'our beautiful London' in the common parlance (long before it became swinging London in the travel brochures). And not all this has vanished; if you look around London, you will see the distinction between the architectural styles of the 'positive' planning period and those of more recent years. It is a clear contrast between rather modest plain-speaking and massive ambiguity.

But of course the circumstances of that period were also far less ambiguous than ours are at present. Resources and expectations were still rationed, so to speak; differences in incomes and standards of living were less striking than they are now; private cars were still a luxury; technology in transport, industries and homes was changing too slowly to cause major disruption; plans were made on the assumption of a fairly stable population; competition between various land-uses caused by rising living and space standards was still comparatively mild, and still (it seems in retrospect) conducted in a spirit of give and take. Altogether, the tense interlocking of problems of affluence and poverty, and their consequent mutual accentuation, were much less evident than at present.

---

[1] It should be remembered that utopian ideas of 'social harmony', 'social balance', and the like were recurrent themes in the development of British planning doctrine and institutions, not least in the post-war period, as shown especially in the plans for the first generation of New Towns.

It was then, moreover, the avowed purpose of land-use planning to serve the public interest by promoting a more equal and 'balanced' distribution of resources and living conditions. And however imperfect the planning system was in this respect, it did have an elementary integrity: it did at least practise to some extent what it preached. The concept of the 'public interest' was incorporated in a concrete form—in terms of the public ownership of development rights and values.[1] The basic idea was that the benefits of development belonged to the people: development should not, and in fact then could not, be used to make the rich richer and the poor poorer. Property prices were stabilized; real estate speculation was largely ruled out. Local authorities were enabled to proceed with, or to encourage, development schemes in a fairly systematic manner, and they were not penalized for doing so. (For instance, development of site A did not then, as it did before, and does again now in a 'free' market situation, convey a floating unearned value on the surrounding sites B, C and D, thus making the costs of further public schemes on these sites prohibitive.)

The Town and Country Planning Act of 1959, by which development rights and values were de-nationalized, changed all that. Henceforth, land-use (or non-use) was determined not by socio-locational criteria but by 'free' market forces—indeed by *laissez-faire* with a vengeance.[2] And so the plague of spiralling

---

[1] The term 'development' is here used in the statutory sense, as first defined in the Town and Country Planning Act, 1947.

[2] This is far too cursory a reference to a key subject that should have a prominent position in any current book on British urban policy and planning matters—especially since, not surprisingly, the earlier relevant bluebooks, statutes and experience have almost been forgotten. But as the question of the nationalization or municipalization of urban land is becoming topical once again, it would certainly be advisable for all those who are concerned with it to take the Uthwatt report (the report of the *Expert Committee on Compensation and Betterment*, Cmnd. 6386, 1942) off the shelves. It is worth while to remember, too, that the denationalization of development rights and values was introduced in the 1959 Act by the back door, through the apparently innocuous device of changing the basis of compensation for compulsory acquisition from existing use value to current market value. Moreover, this innovation was hardly noticed or debated at the time, apart from some strong opposition expressed in professional journals as, for instance, in a symposium in the *Architects'*

property values has descended upon Britain: it has distorted the society of London, and disfigured its townscape. The full impact has only now begun to be recognized. 'Planning' has suffered from diminished responsibility, and has become largely a misnomer. As it has been deprived of a plausible definition of the public interest, and of tangible means of serving it, it has lost its sense of direction and reputation.

Arbitrariness

In the circumstances, the arbitrary aspects of planning operations are liable to become more obtrusive. Land-use planning— whatever its administrative and ideological apparatus—is in any case heavily dependent on value judgements for which no 'objective' criteria (on any test of objectivity) can be offered. Aesthetic taste in civic design and architecture is bound to play a considerable role. Beauty or ugliness are in the eyes of the beholder (in this case, the planning committees, their officers, civil servants, the Minister, the Royal Fine Arts Commission, etc.). And as solid citizens make such decisions—whether or not, for instance, a particular building is 'contrary to the amenities of the area'—and as there is anyhow a culture lag in the perception of our habitat, conservative tastes tend to prevail.[1]

Journal, 13 November 1958 (in which I am glad to have been on record in criticizing the new 'Anti-Planning Bill'). Most important, the Labour Party, then in opposition, under whose aegis the 1947 legislation had been introduced, bore equal responsibility with the Conservative Government for opening the floodgates of real estate inflation: the Labour Party did not oppose this crucial Bill. And yet the Bill ran contrary to the previous bi-partisan agreement to maintain the principle of the nationalization of development values (and the appropriate basis of compensation), the necessity of which was repeatedly stressed by Mr Harold Macmillan, then the Minister of Housing, a few years earlier. For instance, the 1952 White Paper (Cmnd. 8699) which introduced the 1952 and '54 Planning Acts warned: 'If this principle is not maintained, effective control of land-use would again become impracticable, as it was before the war.' And so it has become. None of this is dead history.

[1] However, this culture lag in the perception of the environment is not confined to the older age groups. It cannot be assumed that there is a clear-cut generation difference in this respect. Many young people, too, are conservative in matters of visual taste.

(Hence there is a much higher common denominator in favour of the preservation of existing buildings and of out-dated fashions, low rise or high rise, than for experimentation with new forms of design.) Moreover, every routine step in plan-making and development control involves some kind of a discretionary judgement—about the location of different kinds of land-uses, about space quotas for homes, schools, public services, recreation, hotels, office or industrial workers. And in the *causes célèbres*, which have emotive, far-reaching implications (such as Piccadilly Circus, Covent Garden, a new airport, a ringway system), the ultimate decisions can often be no more than a gamble, not a choice between the greater and the greatest good, but between two kinds of a lesser evil.

Planning Technique

But have not the advances in planning technique narrowed the area of arbitrariness? Certainly, developments in spatial measurements, in the definition of environmental standards, and in moving towards a broader approach (including demographic and socio-economic factors) in land-use considerations —all these have been useful. In some respects, there is now a better chance of more precise, more factual argument about planning issues than there was two or three decades ago. Even so, it is no more than a chance: it is bound to be quite often ignored by new capricious elements in the current 'free' market situation. We can see this, too, all around us. London has sufficient examples of recent prominent buildings and blueprints to show how little attention is paid to technical criteria in schemes which are essentially determined by real estate speculation and political compromises. Indeed, there cannot be much impetus for functionalism, and thus for an appropriate care in design and construction, when the activities of developers are non-functional, except in terms of their private financial gains— when in fact such activities are highly profitable to them, regardless of the actual use of their sites, and irrespective of whether their buildings remain empty or not.[1]

---

[1] Centre Point is one of the best known, most notorious examples. This high-rise office block has produced so much irritation because it represents

Yet even where the functional approach is in principle still alive—in public schemes which are designed for specific uses—the limited role of technical expertise is evident. There are many tall reminders that techniques do not make a plan: they cannot, by themselves, generate and enforce decisions.[1] There is no supreme technique (or master-mind) that can collect *all* relevant technical criteria; that can adjudicate between those which frequently lead to incompatible conclusions; and that can persuade committees and officials to accept instantly the results of the whole complex exercise—long before it is out of date. In addition, there are humdrum difficulties: designers or technicians cannot rely on an appropriate utilization of their skills. The team which designs a high-rise residential block, for example, in accordance with specified terms of reference, not only has to take these terms for granted, but it also has no say when they are changed *ex post facto*—when a group of people unsuitable for such a building are selected as occupiers; or when an estate, visualized (on unrealistic assumptions) as a text book 'community', becomes a fortress, a colony or a ghetto.[2] (It is not the architects, for instance, who allocate the top floors of

the non-functional, truly 'vacant' intention of a building scheme, concerned solely with private financial profits, in such a monumental, unpleasing form. It is an eyesore precisely because it could be left empty for so long. The architectural idiom of such buildings is bound to differ from that of other speculative development schemes which were (or are) built for use, and the financial returns on which are dependent upon their use.

[1] Indeed, technical criteria are more likely to be used as handmaidens of political decisions. It is increasingly difficult to isolate the contribution of technical expertise to major planning schemes or policies. On what technical grounds, in terms of economic and environmental considerations, for example, is the policy of selling council houses based?

[2] The social fate of a new estate—whether or not it becomes integrated into, or segregated from, the society of the surrounding area—depends of course no less on the conditions and population of that area than upon the design and inhabitants of the estate itself. (If a magic carpet would lift a working-class estate from a fraternal area into a stand-offish or hostile one, its own social posture and designation would change: in this way, a 'neighbourhood' might well appear to become a 'colony' or a 'fortress'.) But this important 'social location' aspect is one over which the designers of a particular scheme have no control, and which can often not even be anticipated—especially when the new schemes are rather piecemeal and slow.

multi-storey blocks to families with young children. That is done by another department.) Moreover, the architect's brief is invariably restricted: it does not allow sufficient elasticity to make his scheme workable on alternative assumptions so that it could accommodate groups of occupiers who may need special compensatory facilities—such as play space and supervision of small children—in the new habitat. Quite often, the very efficiency of the technical design of such buildings shows up the inefficiency of its use. ('If the planners could do it that well, why could they not do it a little better?' 'Why did they not think of *us*, who live here?' These are familiar questions.) Through no fault of the designer, his skills and good intentions can lead to a rather mean reality, and to one from which he and his manuals seem very remote. The trouble is that we have gone further in planning techniques than in planning objectives. (Hence the uncertain or ineffective application of techniques.) It is that which explains why we hear so much talk about the lack of 'a human scale' in recent public housing schemes.

The New Empiricism

In some ways, this may seem surprising. Surely, the 'human' element and scale have not been forgotten? Are there not more studies now of the 'clients' of planning—of their distribution, characteristics and conditions, of population and employment trends and many ancillary matters—than there ever were before? Yes—that is so. The empirical apparatus for London planning, in particular (maintained by the Greater London Council, the Boroughs, by other official and academic bodies) has been greatly expanded in the past ten years. On the face of it, social research for planning has become established, in terms of its organizational basis and professional representation. But that does not mean, of course, that social research has been successful, or can be relied upon to become successful, in 'humanizing' the planning process and its results.[1]

The same constraints which limit the role of technical exper-

---

[1] The term social 'research' is used here rather broadly, including activities which would, more strictly, be referred to as social surveys, documentation, information services.

tise in physical planning matters also affect the role of social research and related activities—even more so. The various professions which contribute to planning technique 'on the ground' are concerned with tangible entities: their work is based on verifiable observations from which predictable cause and effect sequences can be deduced. They can therefore evolve and defend, fairly unequivocal standards of professional practice; and they are, by and large, subject to definite tests of performance. Not so in the social sciences. (There is an acknowledged expertise in calculating stress factors in engineering, for example, but not in assessing stress factors in social relations.) Social scientists, hard or soft, do not predict but at best project; their observations and conclusions are rarely unambiguous; and even more rarely regarded as such by their professional colleagues. (A mere change of terms and taxonomy applied to any one observation, however apparently clear-cut, can usually produce a notable change of interpretation.)[1] Moreover, while the terms of reference given to practitioners of physical planning techniques are often inadequate or misleading, these people have at least a job to do (even if it is later spoiled or undone). Social scientists, and their kinsmen, have no such brief: in the official set-up, they are supposed to be informants rather than doers, prompters rather than actors or producers. Occasionally, they are allowed to write their own brief—preferably a cautious one, in line with their backroom functions. So they are in a rather

---

[1] One example, relevant in this context, of the radical change in interpretation which a re-shuffling of categories can produce is provided by the varying views on London's population changes. Has London grown, declined or remained stable? The answer will differ according to the area (which London?), and the measurements, that are considered. The population of Inner London has declined steadily since 1901. The population of Greater London has started to decline, in absolute terms, during the last decade. But in relative terms, London has remained stationary: London's share of the national population has remained virtually unchanged during the past one hundred years. In 1871, the old London (Inner London) contained just over 14 per cent of the population of England and Wales; in 1971, the new London (Greater London) contained almost the same proportion—just over 15 per cent (and this was only a very slight drop since 1961, when the figure was 16 per cent). In other words, alarms about London's population growth or decline respectively are based on partial observations (see also footnote 1 on p. 416).

awkward position, hardly able as yet to exercise an appreciable influence (whether or not they actually wish to do so) on the direction and execution of planning policies.

And there are other factors against them, not least the very novelty of a substantial social science presence in official planning institutions. Indeed, the new empiricism is grafted on to a non-empirical, or even anti-empirical, tradition in British town planning—which has been influenced more by the nineteenth-century utopians than by the sanitary, social and political reformers of that period. The latter, in their various ways, accepted the reality of the industrial and urban 'revolution'. Because they wanted to improve it, or change it, they needed facts—a monumental array of facts, cogently presented—to make their case. Their contemporaries, the utopians, could not come to terms with this reality, and therefore did not wish to look at it closely.[1] Somehow or other, they hoped to be able to turn the clock back to an idealized past—through schemes for industrial villages, Christian colonies, model settlements, garden cities— through a firm belief that they, like a *deus ex machina*, could create an environment that would remould society, rather than the other way round. (For them, the ideal society was one without modern industry, subsisting on a rural and crafts economy, broken up into a series of small-scale, self-contained, self-disciplined communities, where everyone stayed in his allotted place.)[2] A similar imagery has inspired most of the pioneers of British town planning: carried along by their assurance and by their fervour (an elegant fervour, strong but never strident) they managed to be quite successful without the benefit of empirical

---

[1] The label 'utopians' is applied here to a rather diverse series of nineteenth-century writers and reformers—including, for example, Robert Owen, J. Minter Morgan, William Morris, Ebenezer Howard—some of whom actually tried to implement their schemes. (One of the outstanding, most versatile, but almost forgotten reformers of this type, from whom Howard derived most of his ideas for his model garden city, was James Silk Buckingham.) Their common theme was the dislike, if not fear, of industrialization and urbanization.

[2] Very similar, though more obtuse, prescriptions have cropped up again very recently in the Doomsday literature, particularly in *A Blueprint for Survival*, by the editors of *The Ecologist*, (Harmondsworth: Penguin, 1972) see e.g., pp. 50–8.

ceremony.[1] And this vogue continued, with some variations, until well into the forties. (The Abercrombie plans for London, however distinguished in many respects by comparison with recent efforts, still had a very slender factual basis, and got by without bothering with elementary demographic and socio-economic data about which planning students are nowadays supposed to be informed.)[2]

Gradually, of course, as the planning profession and administration expanded rapidly, and as the daily chores mounted up, the optimism conveyed by the old gentlemen prophets became rather wobbly; their *élan* and style was diluted. (The 'Master Plan', once confidently expected to be fulfilled on the stroke of midnight twenty years hence, did not seem quite so masterly

---

[1] HOWARD, EBENEZER, *Tomorrow: a peaceful path to real reform*, 1898 (later re-published as *Garden Cities of Tomorrow*, 1902, with subsequent editions) provides one of the clearest, remarkably cavalier, and much copied examples of this deliberately non-empirical approach, particularly in relation to the crucial issues of urban growth. For instance (first edition, pp. 5, 6): 'It may perhaps be thought that the first step to be taken towards the solution of this question—how to restore the people to the land—would involve a careful consideration of the very numerous causes which have hitherto led to their aggregation in large cities. Were this the case, a very prolonged enquiry would be necessary at the outset. Fortunately, alike for writer and reader, such an analysis is not, however, here requisite, and for a very simple reason, which may be stated thus: whatever may have been the causes which have operated in the past, and are operating now, to draw the people into the cities, those causes may all be summed up as "attractions"; and it is obvious, therefore, that no remedy can possibly be effective which will not present to the people, or at least to considerable portions of them, greater "attractions" than our cities now possess, so that the force of the old "attractions" shall be overcome by the force of new "attractions" which are to be created.'

[2] It is still well worth while to compare the Abercrombie and similar reports of the forties (written during or just after the war) with their successors—not as a nostalgic pastime, but so as to see whether, and in which respects, planning literature has progressed. The earlier reports are superior in terms of the directness of their approach, the clarity, felicity and not least the economy, of their style. While they contained, mercifully, far less verbiage and jargon than their current counterparts, they were, however, more restricted in their scope. For instance, the County of London and Greater London Plans of 1943 and 1944 did not include estimates of natural increase; 'industry' was still thought of as being almost synonymous with manufacturing industry; the decline of the latter in Greater London, and the growth of office employment, were hardly

any more. The passage of time began to look like a fearful variable in its own right.) But just because the certainties wore thin, there was, and is still, a strong desire to hang on to some of them—to stick to standard prescriptions and formulae. Hence the persistence of *idées fixes*, such as the 'magnet' notion —that of London's continued population growth—which was maintained right up to 1971, despite the plain evidence to the contrary in successive censuses since the beginning of the century.[1] Hence also the crude remnants of utopianism—the dislike of cities, of concentrations of people (the fewer, the better); the dislike of industry (it's dirty, smelly, vulgar, not an amenity, it should go somewhere else); the cult of orderliness in civic design; indeed the cult of emptiness—a William Morris vision of sheep grazing in the pasture that was once Parliament Square.[2] The most stubborn survival of the old ideology, however, is the non-empirical approach to matters of planning policy and practice. Factual evidence, historical or contemporary, is inconvenient for the use of planning cook books with simple rigid recipes. An

---

anticipated; and highly relevant data, such as those in the journeys to work report of the 1921 Census (subsequently repeated in the 1951 Census) were not taken into account. See, e.g., FORESHAW, J. H. and ABERCROMBIE, SIR PATRICK, *County of London Plan, 1943*) (H.M.S.O., 1945); and ABERCROMBIE, *Greater London Plan 1944* (H.M.S.O., 1945).

[1] The stubborness with which this evidence has been ignored is indeed remarkable. Even in the Greater London Development Plan of 1969, the trend of London's population changes was still underestimated, and has, predictably, since then already been overtaken by the actual changes, as shown in the 1971 Census. It was not until the preliminary results of the last Census were publicized—which showed (as could be expected) an accelerated absolute population decline, and redistribution over a wider area, in all the British conurbations—that these facts of life began to be recognized, gradually, though often still half-heartedly. So the old alarm —'London's population is becoming too large'—is now being replaced in some quarters by a new one: 'London is becoming too small'. (In fact, London's share of the national population has remained rather stable. See footnote on page 413.) Ever since the start of this century, the real problem has been, and still is, the expansion of London's area, a quite disproportionate expansion in relation to the absolute population changes (first growth, then decline) which have occurred.

[2] MORRIS, WILLIAM, *News from Nowhere, or, An Epoch of Rest, being some chapters from a utopian romance*, London, 1891. This included Morris's vision of London, or rather a non-existing London, around the year 2003,

anti-social, anti-urban doctrine is indifferent to social data, especially in quantitative form. Thus until recently the planning profession was, on the whole, oddly non-numerate—preoccupied with misleading averages, such as the average occupancy ratio, average population density, the average family—a weakness which has had unfortunate, long-lasting results.[1]

Altogether, it is not a promising background for the installation of the new research apparatus, nor is it a matter of bygones. Weak and pretentious numeracy, the old non-empirical habits and the new empirical zeal, exist side by side. And one cannot expect instant reason to emerge from the latter. A surfeit of data can be as enervating as a paucity of data—particularly to those who are not used to the diet. Monitoring systems, mathematical models, cost-benefit analyses (in which inevitably the assumptions on both the quantifiable costs and benefits are partial and hypothetical), a barrage of research papers and computer print-out, data banks and the like—all these cannot by themselves enrich planning policies unless there is the intention and capacity to utilize such material. But it is precisely these preconditions which are so weak at present, while at the same time the new research technology is becoming more ornate. (Of course, 'planning' in the genuine sense needs information far more than *laissez-faire*, and is also, in principle, better able to plan the learning process itself—to judge what information is

---

when the metropolis and centralized government had disappeared, and the Houses of Parliament were 'used for a sort of subsidiary market, and a storage place for manure'. (Second edition, 1891, p. 34.) Naturally, the antithesis provoked by such anti-urban notions and hopes, and by the latter-day variants (such as the low-density and garden city gospels), has often been equally fierce—high rise with a vengeance.

[1] The effects of this lack of numeracy have been most serious, and most long term, in relation to housing provision. The vast predominance of dwellings for 'average' households (two- or three-bedroom dwellings), which was maintained until recently in most public and private housing schemes, has produced a sharp (by now well-known) discrepancy between the distributions of household and dwelling sizes—a functional maldistribution of the housing stock (quite apart from the locational and economic maldistribution). There are too many dwellings of the wrong kind and size, in the wrong places, at the wrong prices. It is this maldistribution which causes severe specific housing shortages—paradoxically just because there is an abundance of large dwellings, unsuitable for the

needed, when and where.) As matters stand now, the facts are
liable to remain silent: the present system is too opportunistic to
have much interest in them; and the research mill which grinds
them out is so ponderous that it can quite easily be used to
stifle comprehension.

Waiting for Facts?

Indeed, is this not perhaps a case where less might produce
more? 'Waiting for facts' can always be a scenario for an empty
stage. Yet it would be quite wrong to argue that planning was,
or is, held up because of a lack of essential information. Although an expanded empirical aid programme has only
recently been introduced into the planning establishment, it has
not sprung suddenly, fully formed, from the head of Zeus. It is
not a new device, nor does it cover entirely new ground. There
has been for many years a good deal of evidence on the conditions and main problems of London—on the interrelated problems of housing, employment, education, transport; on poverty,
minorities and the position of other vulnerable groups. The tendencies in population movements and distribution are well
documented. Official sources and committees, independent
surveys, newspaper enquiries have built up a substantial volume
of information. (It does not pass unnoticed: quite often, a new
instalment is heralded as yet another 'shock report' on the day
of publication. But the shocks are cast off quickly, and policy
reactions to even the most elementary 'neutral' facts—on
household size distribution and urban population shifts, for
example—are long delayed.) Though the existing evidence is
incomplete or out of date in some respects, it would be quite
sufficient, in theory, to get on with the priorities which have
been indicated, repeatedly, by diverse investigations; or at least
to avoid evident mistakes. Could it really be said, for instance,
that the housing market remains uncontrolled because too little
is known about the extent and effects of real estate inflation? Or

---

current household structure, and thus a considerable net surplus of
domestic space (as measured by the excess in the number of rooms over
that of persons in Greater London as a whole). Nor are matters helped by
recent policies which hinder redistribution—such as those for the extension of owner-occupation, in general, and the sale of council houses,
in particular.

can scant remedies against homelessness be explained by a scarcity of facts about it?[1]

Moreover, while the positive 'do's' which can be deduced from the available information might well be controversial, the 'don'ts' are usually quite straightforward. There is, for instance, not a single piece of evidence (right, left or centre) that justifies the predominance, or monopoly, of expensive luxury housing in major current development schemes—from the Barbican to Covent Garden and St. Katherine's Wharf. The official planning precepts, too, are against it. (Naturally so, since such predominance of luxury housing, with rentals of well over £1000 to almost £5000 per annum, could only be produced on wholly improbable assumptions—either that in London of the seventies and eighties all workers will be rich; or that they will have become an extinct species whose jobs will henceforth be done by robots.)[2] Nevertheless, the same tender concern for the wealthy is shown in every successive scheme, with a monotonous indifference to common sense.

Misuse or non-use of facts is a familiar feature in London's history (and a routine occupational hazard of research workers). Nowadays, there is bound to be more of it, despite the frequent social reportage produced by the media, and despite the diligent empirical homework that is being done in planning offices. Arbitrariness is still built into the system: it has become more rather than less evident. Anyhow, London is not in the mood to accept the authority, and to trust the objectivity, of planners who have failed to earn high marks on either score. This is the most important constraint in the current situation: London has become so split up that there is not much neutral ground left. Both the capacity to produce and to accept 'objective' policies or research ('objective' in the sense of non-partisanship) is severely restricted. There are several Londons with divergent interests.

---

[1] Homelessness is a case in point. Although there might well be disagreement about the precise definition, and the estimated extent, of homelessness, there is certainly sufficient information to make at least a determined start in tackling the problem.

[2] For example: exclusive rents (without rates) for municipal flats in the new Cromwell Tower in the Barbican are likely to range, to begin with, between £1275 and £4750 per annum (as reported by Judy Hillman in *The Guardian*, 28 July 1972).

A Disjointed Society

London society in the early seventies is too disparate to have much in common, not even an image of its own discrepancies.[1] Of course, London is not unusual in this respect: most large cities have a segmented pattern (though variously shaped) of socio-geographical divisions with an in-built inertia of their own. The very existence of such divisions helps to conceal them, and thus to perpetuate them. When social groups live in separate compartments, their perception is liable to be partial—their perception of other groups, of the whole universe to which they belong, and not least their awareness of their own position or enclosure. And in so far as the group boundaries are recognized by those who live behind them, there is often an added deliberate tendency to keep them—as a defensive (or aggressive) device; for the sake of establishing a refuge, a group identity, mutual aid, and an internal status system. (Every out-group is also, by definition, an in-group.) There are benefits in maintaining socio-geographical partitions of various kinds, strong or flimsy—not only in the extreme cases of racial, ethnic, caste or class ghettos.

London, like other large cities, has such partitions. But here—and that is the special feature in London's structure—they are camouflaged far more than in most other metropolitan areas of the Western world.[2] It is only in a few places in the inner sector (in and around parts of Kensington–Chelsea, Westminster, Camden, Islington) that social juxtaposition is visible within a fairly narrow range. And even in these places, there is usually

---

[1] The discussion of London's structure both in this and in the next section is based on some parts of an extensive analysis, presented in detail in my forthcoming *Third London Survey*, to be published by Weidenfeld and Nicolson in 1973. The survey is based mainly on data for 1961 and 1966, and covers area units at different levels (enumeration districts, wards, boroughs). It includes the full documentation of various aspects—such as the typology of London's areas, social class and ethnic distribution, mobility, the sociological implications of London's structure—which are very briefly referred to here.

[2] The relevant comparison is with cities of the 'Western' world (using the term as a synonym for 'developed' countries) since cities elsewhere, especially those in the 'Third World', have of course specific features of their own, and usually an even sharper pattern of socio-geographical differentiation.

a transition zone of bedsitter districts, interposed between affluent and poor quarters. Moreover, in these areas, too, the geographical class distances are becoming longer as the higher classes increasingly invade, and take over, adjacent working-class districts. (A 'mixed' street does not remain mixed for long.) Elsewhere in Greater London, the pattern of social differentiation is so widely stretched out, and usually so fuzzy at the edges, that it presents hardly any striking contrasts. Large chunks of territory with scarce visual variety are occupied by kindred social groups—mainly the working and lower middle classes in the eastern and western areas of outer London, the higher classes in the northern and southern suburban areas. And there is, contrary to popular belief, in fact very little criss-cross movement between the various metropolitan sectors—neither in the course of migration from one home to another, nor for daily journeys to work. (Working-class Barking in the east, for example, has hardly any contact with Lewisham, south-east; similarly, the distance between Barnet in the north and Hillingdon, north-west, is longer than the crow flies.) Most internal migration in Greater London is along short routes be-tween fraternal areas; and this applies also to the movements to, from and within the inner sector which has such a high turnover rate. Indeed, the high rate in parts of Inner London, particularly in the bedsitter zones, is not mainly due to long-distance migra-tion, but to the many unavoidable movements within a rather nar-row circle from one furnished or temporary lodging to another.

It is a rather strict, though non-codified, system of controls—resulting from historical and contemporary, planned and un-planned factors—that allocates the population of greater Lon-don to separate compartments, which have few connexions with one another. But the system does not seem as strict as it is be-cause the compartments are widely spaced out; because there is a sufficient volume of social and territorial mobility, though mainly short-distance, to give a semblance of flexibility; and—most important—because the lines of demarcation are, on the whole, fairly subtle.[1] The population is passed through a fine sieve, sorted out and 'slotted' into appropriate localities accord-ing to a combination of characteristics—social class, age, house-

---

[1] It is because the distinctions in the social geography of Greater London are truly multivariate, and thus apparently rather subtle, that there is

hold type and size, tenure, origin. It is this combination which distinguishes the profiles of various kinds of areas. There are therefore different types of higher-class and working-class quarters in Inner and Outer London; and they do not show a consistent correlation between social class and housing conditions, for example. The younger generation of the higher classes, single people and young couples, often live in rather shabby places in the inner sector (as in the bedsitter areas of Earls Court and Notting Hill). By comparison, working-class families, mainly in suburban council estates, often have superior housing conditions. Similarly, there are different kinds of hospitable and inhospitable areas with specific social and demographic features. The elite quarters of the West End (and their more recent outposts), which have been traditionally the most cosmopolitan places in London, still have the highest proportion of 'immigrants' (though they are not called this in Belgravia, Mayfair or Hampstead). And these localities also still have a surplus of young women. The classic poor reception areas (in the northwestern, eastern and south-eastern parts within, or just beyond, the previous county line) contain immigrants—old-timers and newcomers—of various shades, and various degrees of insecurity; and they still have, true to type, a surplus of men. Indeed minorities, old and new, like everyone else, have been 'integrated' into the social geography of London. Their location, too, is determined more by their social status, age and household type than by their colour or origin. London has a substantial coloured middle class who are dispersed among others (natives and foreigners) of comparable rank. It is the black working class, mainly the West Indians, who are concentrated in a few scattered clusters, which are, however, too widely apart to be likely to coalesce, and to form a massive black ghetto.[1]

---

so much controversy about the actual shape of the pattern (whether it is concentric, sectional, cross-wise, etc.). There are indeed different patterns if they are traced in terms of the distribution of any one set of variables only (such as social class *or* housing conditions). The picture is far more clear-cut and consistent, however, if it is seen in multivariate terms (that is, in terms of an area typology which takes the combinations and permutations of various factors of differentiation into account).

[1] As there is a wider occupational (social class) spread among the coloured, especially the Asian, population in London than in most provincial cities, their geographical dispersal is wider here, too.

London's pattern, though firmly and consistently delineated, is therefore not dominated by sharp dichotomies—East versus West; poor versus rich; foreigners versus natives; black versus white. London has many incongruities, but they are not as crude as in many other large cities. (We have no suburban shanty towns like Paris or Rome; we have no rat-infested Harlem next to the glitter of mid-town Manhattan.) London society is not, and is not likely to become, 'polarized'.[1] Any attempts to oversimplify or to overdramatize, the actual and emerging divisions within London can only help to underrate their quite remarkable tenacity. The metropolitan structure is so strong precisely because it contains elements of elasticity.

It has certainly been a resilient structure. In a sense, London has so far been very successful in adapting itself to all sorts of changes without either falling apart, or becoming a monotonous undifferentiated agglomeration. While the lines of demarcation have been lengthened, and the distinguishing features of areas have been altered, the distinctions as such have been maintained. There is still a pattern—modified, larger, but no less textured than before. Working-class areas have gone up or down in the world, but they have retained their identity as distinct localities even when they have got a new class label. While traditional reception areas, as those in the East End, have accommodated successive groups of immigrants (Huguenots, Irish, Jews, Asians) and changing sub-cultures, they have remained reception areas, though in some cases on a smaller scale. The East End itself has been expanded beyond the previous county boundary: it has a different look, but is still almost solid working-class territory. The old elite enclaves in the West End have acquired more young adults and different life styles; they no longer need (or want) their previous working-class underpinning. But they have thereby become more homogeneous; they have consolidated their position, and extended their

---

[1] The image conveyed by the term 'polarization' (alias 'the rout of the middle classes') is, first, that both the top and bottom groups in the society of London are becoming larger, at the expense of the middle strata; second, that the extreme groups are, or will be, located in sharp juxtaposition to one another—on either side of the 'tracks'. Both these images are false. In fact, the upper and middle strata are becoming stronger, numerically, in Greater London, and the skilled manual group has

domain. Altogether, the importance of social class as a key index in the demarcation of areas has been accentuated rather than diminished through its tie-up with other factors of differentiation. Indeed, recent changes in the habitat and society of London have not produced a radical transformation. London has not become more egalitarian, or more cohesive. On the contrary: it seems to be on the way of becoming more disjointed, and perhaps also more aware of this fact.

Dissension

There are several major indications of this trend. One of them—the lack of connexion between the various sectors of London (which has been mentioned)—has to some extent been planned. Though the location or decentralization of both homes and employment have been rather haphazard, these movements have been sufficiently matched to make parts of Outer London fairly self-contained. By contrast, another significant symptom—the increasing separation of social classes, especially in Inner London—is the product of non-planning (and contrary to early post-war planning doctrine). Superimposed upon an already highly stratified pattern, class separation and succession are now promoted by free market forces, no longer checked by factors that had previously blurred the lines. The intervention of the public housing sector has been steadily weakened. Traditional reasons for maintaining some social mixture—such as the need of the higher classes to keep 'servants' in the basement or nearby—have almost disappeared. And as the geographical solidarity of the higher classes is becoming stronger, the same applies of course to the working class too—even more than it did before.[1]

---

remained stable, while the proportion of non-skilled workers has decreased. Moreover, there are hardly any places where the top and bottom groups (the professional/managerial versus the non-skilled manual strata) confront one another, on their own, without the presence of intermediate groups (white-collar and skilled manual workers). Nor is there any reason to suppose that such a 'confrontation' will become more frequent. Indeed, the incidence of fairly extreme social juxtaposition within a rather narrow geographical range, which existed mainly in or around the elite precincts in the West End, is declining (see footnote on p. 424).

[1] The social class map on its own—that is, the class composition of areas in quantitative terms—provides only a one-sided picture of geographical

Moreover, the 'colonizing' drive of the higher classes in Inner London has been accelerated; and so the working-class quarters are becoming more constricted. Apart from the very rich, it is mainly the young members (or aspiring members) of the middle-upper strata, single people or couples without family responsibilities, who are prepared to pay the exorbitant housing prices of the inner sector, despite the fact that they rarely get value for money[1]. As these people live mainly in one- or two-person households, they have a disproportionately large number of households, and a disproportionately large housing demand, in relation to the total population size of their group.[2] By virtue of their social position, reinforced by their youth, they are therefore bound to have expansionist tendencies—the more so as

---

class distribution, seen from above, so to speak. The picture needs to be seen also 'from below'—from the vantage point of members of social classes. (To what extent are they concentrated? How are they located in relation to other classes, etc?) Thus a more detailed examination shows that London's class map is indeed spurious in some respects: in particular, the social mixture which seems to exist in some London areas, large or small (whether enumeration districts, wards or boroughs) is more apparent than real, and is likely to be transitory. For instance: traditionally the most elegant neighbourhoods with the best addresses (such as those in Mayfair) used to be socially mixed (or, as might be said nowadays, 'polarized'). While in such areas the upper class was socially predominant, it was statistically in a minority—frequently outnumbered, or at least matched, by manual, mainly non-skilled workers. This kind of mixture is beginning to be much slighter: in such places, the top class (the professional and managerial group) has already become, or is on the verge of becoming, the statistical majority. At the same time, a new kind of apparent class mixture is developing in inner areas which were previously almost wholly working class, and which have now acquired a quite substantial middle-upper class component. But this is likely to be quite often only the first stage of the gentrification process, whereby the working class will be reduced, before long, to the status of a statistical minority in such areas.

[1] A good deal of detailed evidence on population characteristics and conditions, and on the inverse relation between incomes and rents, in the private housing sector of Inner London, and especially in the furnished sector, is now available. See, for example, Centre for Urban Studies, *Housing in Camden*, published by the London Borough of Camden, 1968.

[2] For instance: already in 1966, there was a considerable difference in the number and size of households headed by non-manual and manual workers in the three 'West End' Boroughs (Kensington—Chelsea, Westminster, Camden). While in that area 70 per cent of all households

there are few hurdles in their path. The working-class population of Inner London, old-timers or recent recruits, are in every
respect 'less equal'—not only in terms of income, status, expectations, but also in terms of age and dependency ratios. They have
a higher share of old people, young children, large households.
They find it difficult to resist being displaced or hemmed in.
And neither the comprehensive development schemes nor the
real estate speculators are on their side. Yes—London is now
being 'renewed' at a rapid pace—but not on the model about
which we are so often warned. Inner London is not being
'Americanized': it is not on the way to becoming mainly a
working-class city, a 'polarized' city, or a vast ghetto for a black
proletariat. The real risk for Inner London is that it might well
be gentrified with a vengeance, and be almost exclusively reserved for selected higher-class strata.[1]

The very fact that Inner London, however defined, is set off
so clearly as the problem centre of the metropolitan area is an
important symptom of disjointedness. And it is one that has
become increasingly overt ever since the two Londons, Inner and
Outer, were formally linked in an administrative union—an
arranged marriage for which they are not well suited, and which

---

in the non-manual group consisted of one or two persons only, 58 per
cent of the households in the manual group were of that size. In the West
End Boroughs, there were thus 45 households per 100 persons in the non-
manual group, and 39 households per 100 persons in the manual group,
as compared with 34 households per 100 for all strata in the whole of
Greater London. Moreover, in the West End and nearby, the many small
households in the non-manual group (professional, managerial and white-
collar grades) consist predominantly of young people. One of the often
repeated laments—that it is the young, rather well-to-do people who are
leaving Inner London—is certainly not supported by the facts. On the
contrary. It is precisely this group of single or young married people for
whom Inner London is so powerful a 'magnet', and who are taking over
large chunks of the inner territory.

[1] It needs hardly to be explained why this is called a 'risk'. It is that (in my
view) not least because such a development would be a symptom of
patent social injustice. Moreover, if Inner London were largely the domain of selected higher class strata (mainly of those in the pre-parental
stage), it would be, not so paradoxically, seriously impoverished in many
respects. It would then be deprived of the vigorous working class culture;
its functions, its horizon, its population structure (with a very small
component of children and old people) would be severely restricted.
Inner London could then no longer claim to be the capital of Britain.

is bound to bring out the discrepancies between them. Greater London has certainly not become a more united London. Quite the reverse. It is in Inner London (which now extends beyond the territory of the previous county, including Brent and Haringey) where the uncertainties are unavoidable.[1] It is here where the contradictions of the metropolitan area are concentrated—wealth and poverty; power and insecurity. By contrast, Outer London is on the whole far more orderly, comfortable and placid. It is hardly surprising that the Outer Boroughs want to keep themselves to themselves. They are reluctant to be drawn into the orbit of inner urban pressures—especially as there are not many specific reasons for a reciprocal attachment. The catchment area of the metropolitan centre for employment, shopping, entertainment, education, for population transfers, extends well beyond the boundary of Greater London. By and large, the linkages between the two universes within that boundary are part of a wider network.

The divergence between the interests of Inner and Outer London will be a recurrent item on the political agenda. At the same time, other divisions on the London map have begun to be more clearly recognized. Latent dissensions have become acute—in the course of fierce competition for living space; higher-class take-over bids of working-class districts; misuse of key sites for conspicuous space consumption; worsening traffic snarls; rising rents and fares; general inflation; industrial disputes; anxieties about jobs, wages, pensions; immigration scares; and so on in a long catalogue of social strain. There has been a greater spread of social literacy, and with it a stronger self-assertion of

---

[1] The statistical differences, in terms of demographic, socio-economic and housing indices, between Inner and Outer London are so sharp that they are shown up with equal clarity irrespective of how exactly Inner London is defined—as the old County on its own (now the area of the Inner London Education Authority) or with the addition of Brent and Haringey, or with some other combination of parts of boroughs. (For instance: 17 per cent of all households in the 'old' Inner London were owner-occupiers in 1966, versus 53 per cent in Outer London. When the boundary of the inner area is revised to include Brent and Haringey, the gap is just as wide, and the respective percentages are virtually the same.) In fact, as our analysis of wards and boroughs, both in 1961 and 1966, for the Third London Survey showed, Brent and Haringey now belong to the inner urban universe (though they do not have the same kind of inner urban characteristics).

the identity of groups. Illusions of togetherness have been stripped off.

In London, this process has been assisted by the handiwork of developers who provoke a 'them and us' response. Almost every month, there are new causes of protest against yet another development or non-development scheme. And there is a growing irritation, too, with the mumbo-jumbo of official alibis for doing so little, so late, often in the wrong places—blowing alternately hot or cold; exaggerating or belittling London's problems; setting up phoney dilemmas (should we help the rich or the poor?); finding successive scapegoats (transients, the poor, immigrants, tourists). No doubt, London has a load of troubles. The most easily quantifiable, immediate problems alone—such as those of poverty and housing shortages—are severe, large scale, and in several respects disproportionately large even in relation to London's population size. For instance: in 1966, Greater London contained 15 per cent of *all* the dwellings in England and Wales, but 56 per cent of those which were shared. And London's 'primacy' in terms of various associated housing defects (overcrowding, lack of essential domestic facilities) was similarly marked. More important still, as our own Third London Survey has shown, in 1966, over a million people—one in seven of all Londoners—lived in poor wards (that is, in places with indubitably poor living and economic conditions).[1] The number of these people, which will hardly have been reduced in the last few years, represents a population greater than that of Birmingham, Britain's second largest city.

Even so, such deficits have to be seen in perspective. By comparison with conditions in some other parts of Britain, and in many cities of the world, London has still considerable assets—in its fabric, its standards and ways of life. Its problems are not insuperable. They are mainly caused by maldistribution and mis-allocation rather than by net shortages; they have piled up as a result of indifference, muddle, lethargy and lack of foresight. In principle, with the resources available, they would be quite manageable. Nevertheless hardships, old and new, are still left

---

[1] These are 'poor' wards as categorized in the multivariate classification of the Third London Survey (see footnote 2, page 419). Both the absolute number and proportion of the population in wards of this type had increased from 1961 to 1966.

to accumulate—just because they are tucked away; because they present, apparently, as yet no major threat to the society at large (like the fear of contagion from epidemics in our nineteenth-century cities); and because the deprived groups have so far been rather patient. Will that state of affairs continue? Nowadays, it would be rash to take the patience of Londoners for granted. The frustrations and frictions are mounting up.

But of course this does not mean that the many frictions can necessarily be expected to coalesce, and to form 'one impetuous and overwhelming surge against the reigning authority'.[1] Nor is it probable that before long all the diverse protesters will join one long march towards a massive battle. There is still too much fragmentation built into the social system, in general, and into London's structure, in particular. It is visible everywhere, not least among the protest campaigns or movements themselves. Images of instant revolt, of barricades around Whitehall, seem to be somewhat premature.[2]

On the Sidelines

'What should *we* do in this situation?' ask the young social scientists (of any biological age). 'What should be *our* function in the planning process?' Naturally, many of them, too, are affected by the climate of discontent, and are unwilling to play the role of bystanders which is usually assigned to them. However, it is in the nature of their discipline that each of them has to come to terms with his (or her) doubts in his own way. As the

---

[1] This is a quotation from CHALMERS, T., *The Christian and Civic Economy of Large Towns*, 3 vols., Glasgow, 1821–26, vol. II, p. 40. It is tempting to use it in this context since Chalmers put forward his 'principle of locality', a forerunner of the neighbourhood unit idea (that is, the splitting up of the city into separate parochial units) precisely for the purpose of preventing such an 'overwhelming surge', so as 'to divide and to weaken the force of popular violence'. It is not a deliberate application of his 'principle of locality', but a less explicit, pervasive 'principle of fragmentation' which still helps to serve the same purpose now.

[2] The accent here is on barricades around 'Whitehall'—that is, against the likelihood of a major confrontation with the central state power. It is this which seems improbable in the foreseeable future, especially in view of the persistent splintering (traditional in British history) of protest and reform movements. Separate *ad hoc* campaigns are started (against the Covent Garden and Piccadilly plans, for example). And within each

society (singular or plural) which is their subject, and which has conditioned them, is divided, they cannot possibly be unanimous, or non-partisan, in interpreting their professional responsibilities. There can be no common code of professional conduct that would set out the kind of involvement and alignment in social affairs to which social scientists would be obliged to adhere. While standards of craftsmanship in assembling and interpreting data, and objective tests for their verification, can be developed, all the preliminaries—the choice of professional location, of subjects for study, or the decision whether or not to accept the briefs given to us—all these are value-loaded, if they are not compulsive or matters of sheer chance.

But that is one view only—the view that partisanship, and thus disagreement, are inherent in the social sciences. It follows that this view itself is bound to be strongly contested. A substantial faction of our colleagues regard themselves, explicitly or implicitly, as independent neutral observers, somewhere on top of society—a sort of sociological book-keeping or peace-keeping force.[1] Others again call themselves 'social engineers', or wish to provide technical assistance for particular policy or planning schemes. (And some fulfil these various functions at different times.)

The doubtful young social scientists, however, who ask themselves what they should do next, are not concerned with theoretical discussions about objectivity or value neutrality. They feel that they are already involved: they want to know where and how they could become more involved. In particular, they have a strong desire to get their hands dirty; to leave their offices and to go into the streets; to belong to a place where one might help to produce some visible change (if only a playground, a shelter for squatters or drifters, a tenants' association)—instead of sitting behind a desk, adding up sums or writing reports. This new 'participant' approach is shown in various

---

locality, or in relation to any one issue, the 'grass-roots' groups are divided, if not at loggerheads with one another. But although (or just because) there are few signs of mass-based, concerted actions, sporadic militancy (sit-ins, no-go areas) can certainly be expected, and are liable to become more noticeable.

[1] The phrase 'sociological book-keeping' was used (in a derogatory sense) by C. Wright Mills, who said very firmly, in a similar context, 'I am not a sociological book-keeper'.

ways—in practice in a movement towards diverse action groups or grass-roots schemes; and also, more generally, in scepticism about empirical research. (Is it really worth while? Is it not merely another smoke screen?) A rather simplistic distinction between 'concrete' and 'abstract' forms of enquiry has therefore become popular. It is reflected, especially, in a growing distaste for statistical material, which is regarded as being 'too abstract', 'unreal', alienated from the lives around us. (True, in the style of scientism it is often just that. But then again quite simple statistics can seem 'unreal' when the beholder himself is alienated from the situations which they convey, and has not sufficient imagination, or sense of identification, to visualize the three-dimensional 'figures' behind them.)

Anyhow, one way or another, quite a number of people who come from, or are related to, the social sciences try to move away from the sidelines. It remains to see how far they will be successful in doing so.

A Mixed Mood

It will certainly be useful, however, if they take a cool look at the institutions, not least the planning institutions, in which they work, at the assumptions which they have been asked to take for granted, and at the history behind them. The premises on which the planning system was based no longer exist: a considerable measure of consensus, and trust in public authority. Nowadays, the 'public interest' is usually seen to be no more than an assertion of dominant private interests, or at best a tenuous compromise between conflicting interests. Planning has become a political instrument. And it is not surprising if the planners (or their assistants) feel uneasy. Whom do they serve? Are they not, however unwittingly, aiding property speculation, the public enemy Number One? Can they remain satisfied with small mercies? Can they go on totting up obtuse questions so as to evade the necessity of giving some clear answers? Not much longer. It is hardly possible for anyone who is involved in the development process, directly or indirectly, to claim to be non-partisan.

Moreover, dissensions are inherent in the metropolitan structure. So far, they have been rather subdued. Just because London's society is disjointed, one of its major problems is that of partial perception: its own divisions are thus obscured and maintained. But this need not, and probably will not, be a vicious circle. The growth of self-consciousness depends as much on external as on indigenous influences. Both have put London into her present mood—a mixed mood of inertia and restlessness. It is not a state of harmonious co-existence.

Social Class Comparison, 1951 to 1966

PETER WILLMOTT AND MICHAEL YOUNG

We wanted to find some way of making a comparison over time of Census data on social class in the London Region. We decided to try to compare the Census of 1966 with that of 1951, in the hope that the fifteen-year run would show the trends more clearly than a 1961–6 comparison. (We would, of course, have preferred to go back to 1931 or even earlier had that been possible.) This was not something we could do from existing data; the classification of occupations changed between the two Censuses, as did the local government areas, at least in Greater London.

A first decision was to use the five-fold social class analysis rather than some combination of socio-economic groups. One reason for this was that it would allow a simple three-fold comparison: 'top', 'middle' and 'bottom' (I and II; III; IV and V). A second and more compelling reason was that the system of classification of occupations into s.e.g.s changed even more dramatically after 1951 than that for social classes. We were able to get from the Census Branch of the Office of Population Censuses and Surveys the social class distributions for 1966 for occupied and retired men on the basis of the pre-1965 local authority areas inside Greater London: the distributions for the O.M.A., where the local authority boundaries had in general not changed since 1951, were available from Part III of the *Sample Census 1966 Economic Activity Tables*. Since we also had, in the appropriate *County Reports*, the 1951 figures, we had distributions for both dates.

The next task was somehow to convert the 1951 distributions into the same classification scheme as was used in 1966.[1] The key seemed to lie in the 1961 Census, which marked the change in the classification scheme from that of 1951. In analysing that Census, a sample of one in 200 'economically active' males in England and Wales was classified on the 1951 basis as well as the 1961. The two schemes could thus be compared, and the effects of the changes studied. The Census people themselves did this for England and Wales as a whole in the *General Report* of the 1961 Census (published in 1968), and at our request and expense they produced a set of figures for each of the pre-1965 local authority areas in Greater London, together with a set for the O.M.A. as a whole.[2] Since these sets of figures showed how the distribution in each area was affected by the changed classification, they offered a method of converting the 1951 distributions into comparable terms with those of 1966. With the advice of Dr J. A. Heady of the MRC Social Medicine Unit, we devised what seemed a suitable method of carrying out this conversion.

Some Limitations

Before we explain the conversion process, we have to explain some of the limitations and some of the assumptions that we had to make in proceeding with the analysis. The first difficulty was that the 1951 distributions were for occupied and retired males

---

[1] We thought that it was more sensible to convert from 1951 to 1966 rather than the other way round, since we would be publishing some other social class data on the more recent basis in the full report of our study.

[2] As we now see, it would have probably been more sensible to have asked for the O.M.A. data for each separate local authority area. We did not do this partly because we knew the numbers would be small in some areas, partly because of the extra expense and partly because at the time we did not realize that we would want to carry out the detailed comparisons that we have done for the O.M.A. There are disadvantages, as we remark below, in using a 'general' formula for all of the O.M.A.

and (though, if we had wanted to, we could have separated out the retired for 1966) the 1966 distributions had also to be in that form to compare with 1951. The 1961 distributions however were, as explained, for 'economically active' (i.e. 'occupied') males only. We had therefore to assume that the class distribution of retired men was broadly similar in 1961 to that for occupied men, which was doubtful, or that, since we were using 1961 only as a 'converter', any differences in these distributions would be unlikely to make a major difference to the conversion process or to its outcome.

The second difficulty was about the men who, though classified in 1961 on the 1961 basis, could not be classified on the 1951 basis. In England and Wales, these amounted to 3.5 per cent of the total one in 200 sample. We excluded such people in making our 'conversions' and we had to assume that they were distributed evenly enough across the social class scale not to upset our calculations radically.

The third problem was about the size of the sample. One in 200 was small and in some local authority areas amounted to only forty or fifty men. Partly because this was more likely to go wrong with the smallest classes, particularly Class I, we combined Classes I and II right from the beginning. We also combined Classes IV and V, so that throughout we were dealing with three 'classes'. Because of the small numbers, we decided, incidentally, not to try to include a 1961 distribution between those for 1951 and 1966: but we had to assume that, despite the small numbers and the fact that the 1961 sample distribution might be a poor guide to the actual distribution in 1961, it was a reasonably good guide to the changes in classification between the two Censuses.

Since we had the sets of 1961 figures only for the O.M.A. as a whole and not for local authority areas within it, we had to use one 'conversion formula' for all the O.M.A. local authorities, and this is likely to have introduced further errors with those areas.

All these difficulties have to be borne in mind, as too does the fact that the 1966 Census itself was only on a 10 per cent basis and that, as the Census reports point out, there were some deficiencies in the sample [1]. Because of these various limitations it would be unwise to regard the changes in any particular local authority area as more than an indication. As we have explained, this is particularly so with the areas in the O.M.A.

The Conversion Process

The procedure is illustrated below, with Westminster the example. The distribution into the three groups for 1961 on the

FIGURE A1.1

1951 actual	1961 Census 1951 basis	1961 Census 1961 basis
27.7% I + II	32.3%	27.6%
		3.1%
		3.9%
45.6% III	44.9%	33.9%
		3.9%
		0.8%
26.7% IV + V	22.8%	7.9%
		18.9%
100.0%	100.0%	100.0%

1951 basis is shown in Figure A1.1, together with the movements that took place in switching to the 1961 basis.

Figure A1.2 puts these into percentages of the total 127 and includes also the actual percentage distribution for 1951.

FIGURE A1.2

	1961 Census 1951 basis	1961 Census 1961 basis	
I + II	41	35	39
		4	
		5	
III	57	43	53
		5	
		1	
IV + V	29	10	35
		24	
Total number	127	127	

We next assumed that what we had to do was to rework the '1951 basis' percentages in terms of the '1951 actual' distribution and apply these to the percentages in the '1961 basis' column. We said, for example, '32.3 per cent on the 1951 basis was, under re-classification, re-distributed on the 1961 basis as 27.6 per cent to I + II, 3.9 per cent to III and 0.8 per cent to IV + V. What would those three percentages have been had the starting proportion been, not 32.3 per cent, but 27.7 per cent?' In this instance we then made the following three calculations:

(a) *Transfer from I + II to I + II*

$$\frac{27.3}{32.3} \times 27.6 = 23.7$$

(b) *Transfer from I + II to III*

$$\frac{27.7}{32.3} \times 3.9 = 3.3$$

(c) *Transfer from I + II to IV + V*

$$\frac{27.7}{32.3} \times 0.8 = 0.7$$

We did the same kind of calculations for transfers from III $\left(\frac{45.6}{44.9} \times 3.1, \text{etc.}\right)$ and from IV + V $\left(\frac{26.7}{22.8} \times 3.9, \text{etc.}\right)$. Figure A1.3 shows how the '1951 actual' distribution compared with the various '1961 basis' percentages from Figure A1.2, reworked:

FIGURE A1.3

	1951 actual per cent	1951 converted to 1961 basis per cent
1+II	27.7	26.8
III	45.6	42.4
IV+V	26.7	30.8
Total	100.0	100.0

The final stage is shown in Figure A1.4, which compares the 'converted' 1951 distribution with that for 1966.

FIGURE A1.4

	1951 (per cent)			1966 (per cent)		
	I+II	*III*	*IV+V*	*I+II*	*III*	*IV+V*
Westminster	27	42	31	36	34	30

The same sets of calculations were made for each pre-1965 local authority area in Greater London, using the two sets of 1961 figures for the area in question. With the O.M.A., similar calculations were made, but using the single conversion formula.

The Results

The findings are presented in full in Table A1.1, for Inner London, Outer Greater London and the Outer Metropolitan Area (parts (*a*), (*b*) and (*c*) respectively).

Table A1.1

Social Class of Occupied and Retired Men in 1951 and 1966, Extent of Deviance from Class Distribution of London Region, and Change in Deviance between 1951 and 1966.

(*a*) *Inner London*

	Census 1951 I+II III IV+V per cent			Degree of Deviance	Census 1966 I+II III IV+V per cent			Degree of Deviance	Change in Deviance 1951–1966
Battersea	9	58	33	18	14	52	34	20	+2
Bermondsey	4	42	54	48	9	47	44	38	−10
Bethnal Green	7	42	51	42	7	55	38	34	−8
Camberwell	11	53	36	14	14	53	33	20	+6
Chelsea	34	33	33	38	45	36	19	42	+4
City of London	26	23	51	58	36	29	35	44	−14
Deptford	9	44	47	34	10	51	39	28	−6
Finsbury	5	52	43	26	10	50	40	30	+4
Fulham	12	54	34	12	17	54	29	14	+2
Greenwich	12	51	37	14	18	48	34	18	+4
Hackney	11	58	31	14	10	56	34	28	+14
Hammersmith	12	50	38	16	12	53	35	24	+8
Hampstead	35	45	20	34	40	40	20	32	−2
Holborn	27	40	33	24	31	39	30	24	=
Islington	8	55	37	20	12	52	36	24	+4
Kensington	36	36	28	36	38	39	23	28	−8
Lambeth	10	53	37	16	13	53	34	22	+6
Lewisham	17	56	27	8	18	55	27	12	+4
Paddington	20	48	32	8	27	44	29	14	+6
Poplar	3	48	49	38	8	51	41	32	−6
St. Marylebone	34	37	29	32	45	36	19	42	+10
St. Pancras	13	48	39	18	17	49	34	18	=
Shoreditch	5	45	50	40	7	56	37	34	−6
Southwark	6	45	49	38	8	50	42	34	−4
Stepney	4	46	50	40	8	46	46	42	+2
Stoke Newington	12	58	30	12	11	57	32	26	+14
Wandsworth	16	57	27	10	20	54	26	8	−2
Westminster	27	42	31	20	36	34	30	34	+14
Woolwich	16	52	32	4	20	51	29	8	+4
	(*b*) *Outer Greater London*								
Acton	17	55	28	6	18	54	28	12	+6
Barking	8	54	38	20	11	53	36	26	+6
Barnes	32	47	21	26	36	45	19	24	−2
Barnet	29	52	19	22	35	48	17	22	=
East Barnet	29	55	16	28	34	51	15	20	−8
Beckenham	35	53	12	36	41	48	11	34	−2
Beddington & Wallington	21	67	12	36	35	51	14	22	−14

(b) Outer Greater London (contd.)

	Census 1951 I+II III IV+V per cent			Degree of Deviance	Census 1966 I+II III IV+V per cent			Degree of Deviance	Change in Deviance 1951–1966
Bexley	19	54	27	6	25	57	18	14	+8
Brentford & Chiswick	22	53	25	10	23	50	27	4	−6
Bromley	30	48	22	24	37	46	17	26	+2
Carshalton	15	59	26	14	26	51	23	4	−10
Chingford	21	53	26	8	25	56	19	12	+4
Chislehurst & Sidcup	22	48	30	8	27	52	21	8	=
Coulsdon & Purley	39	45	16	42	46	44	10	44	+2
Crayford	14	59	27	14	19	57	24	12	−2
Croydon	20	56	24	12	23	55	22	8	−4
Dagenham	6	53	41	24	9	54	37	30	+6
Ealing	21	57	22	16	24	55	21	8	−8
Edmonton	12	56	32	12	18	55	27	12	=
Enfield	15	52	33	6	22	54	24	6	=
Erith	15	48	37	14	17	52	31	14	=
Feltham	11	54	35	14	17	58	25	14	=
Finchley	28	49	23	20	36	46	18	24	+4
Friern Barnet	30	38	32	28	30	51	19	12	−16
East Ham	10	52	38	16	12	53	35	24	+8
West Ham	5	48	47	34	8	50	42	34	=
Harrow	25	56	19	22	33	50	17	18	−4
Hayes & Hardington	13	56	31	10	17	58	25	14	+4
Hendon	28	50	22	20	36	46	18	24	+4
Heston & Isleworth	19	58	23	14	22	54	24	6	−8
Hornchurch	17	59	24	14	24	55	21	8	−6
Hornsey	24	55	21	18	25	53	22	6	−12
Ilford	20	59	21	18	25	56	19	12	−6
Kingston-upon-Thames	16	59	25	14	28	51	21	8	−6
Leyton	10	56	34	16	13	59	28	22	+6
Malden & Coombe	30	52	18	24	40	44	16	32	+8
Merton & Morden	20	61	19	22	24	57	19	12	−10
Mitcham	16	57	27	10	16	58	26	16	+6
Orpington	27	54	19	22	38	47	15	28	+6
Penge	15	56	29	8	16	54	30	16	+8
Richmond-upon-Thames	25	50	25	14	35	44	21	22	+8
Romford	15	55	30	6	18	56	26	12	+6
Ruislip & Northwood	27	61	12	36	36	49	15	24	−12
Southall	10	57	33	16	13	55	32	22	+6
Southgate	37	48	15	38	37	50	13	26	−12
Surbiton	29	58	13	34	30	54	16	18	−16
Sutton & Cheam	23	54	23	14	34	51	15	20	+6
Tottenham	10	57	33	16	11	58	31	26	+10
Twickenham	25	52	23	14	33	49	18	18	+4
Uxbridge	16	59	25	14	23	54	23	6	−8
Walthamstow	13	55	32	10	15	57	28	18	+8
Wanstead & Woodford	34	53	13	34	38	47	15	28	−6
Wembley	25	54	21	18	29	53	18	14	+4
Willesden	13	60	27	16	14	54	32	20	+4
Wimbledon	26	52	22	16	33	48	19	18	+2
Wood Green	16	61	23	18	16	58	26	16	−2
Yiewsley & West Drayton	7	64	29	24	17	56	27	14	−10

(c) Outer Metropolitan Area

	Census 1951 I+II III IV+V per cent			Degree of Deviance	Census 1966 I+II III IV+V per cent			Degree of Deviance	Change in Deviance 1951–1966
Bedfordshire									
Leighton & Linslade U.D.	16	49	35	10	48	34	18	48	+38*
Luton C.B.	16	54	30	4	14	55	31	20	+16
Luton R.D.	16	47	37	18	21	48	31	12	−6
Dunstable M.B.	15	55	30	6	20	54	26	8	+2
Berkshire									
Reading C.B.	17	53	30	2	18	54	28	12	+10
Maidenhead M.B.	21	51	28	5	30	50	20	12	+7
New Windsor M.B.	17	56	27	8	27	48	25	6	−2

(c) Outer Metropolitan Area (contd.)

	Census 1951 I+II III IV+V per cent			Degree of Deviance	Census 1966 I+II III IV+V per cent			Degree of Deviance	Change in Deviance 1951–1966
Berkshire contd.									
Wokingham M.B.	22	47	31	10	37	44	19	26	+16
Bradfield R.D.	21	45	34	14	30	48	22	12	−2
Cookham R.D.	23	44	33	16	33	41	26	20	+4
Easthampstead R.D.	18	51	31	2	28	47	25	8	+6
Windsor R.D.	19	48	33	8	33	41	26	20	+12
Wokingham R.D.	20	55	25	10	33	48	19	18	+8
Buckinghamshire									
Aylesbury M.B.	17	52	31	2	17	56	27	14	+12
Beaconsfield U.D.	26	46	28	16	46	36	18	44	+28
Bletchley U.D.	13	56	31	10	15	63	22	24	+14
Chesham U.D.	18	55	27	6	27	54	19	12	+6
Eton U.D.	20	50	30	4	27	47	26	8	+4
High Wycombe M.B.	16	59	25	14	17	59	24	16	+2
Marlow U.D.	21	49	30	6	32	46	22	16	+10
Slough M.B.	16	54	30	4	16	52	32	16	+12
Amersham R.D.	27	45	28	18	40	42	18	32	+14
Aylesbury R.D.	17	52	31	2	29	42	29	18	+16
Eton R.D.	26	46	28	16	33	42	25	18	+2
Wing R.D.	16	39	45	30	28	41	31	20	−10
Wycombe R.D.	20	50	30	4	30	50	20	12	+8
Essex									
Southend-on-Sea C.B.	25	52	23	14	25	52	23	4	−10
Basildon U.D.	16	52	32	4	19	54	27	10	+6
Benfleet U.D.	20	54	26	8	23	56	21	10	+2
Brentwood U.D.	24	48	28	12	32	49	19	16	+4
Canvey Island U.D.	15	54	31	6	12	56	32	24	+18
Chelmsford M.B.	20	53	27	6	25	53	22	6	=
Chigwell U.D.	22	52	26	8	30	51	19	12	+4
Epping U.D.	18	49	33	6	33	47	20	18	+12
Harlow U.D.	19	48	33	8	22	55	23	8	=
Rayleigh U.D.	21	51	28	6	28	54	18	14	+8
Thurrock U.D.	12	49	39	18	13	51	36	22	+4
Waltham Holy X U.D.	14	46	40	20	22	51	27	4	−16
Chelmsford R.D.	19	46	35	12	30	44	26	14	+2
Epping & Ongar R.D.	21	44	35	16	32	42	26	18	+2
Rochford R.D.	17	48	35	10	21	56	23	10	=
Hampshire									
Aldershot M.B.	12	67	21	30	16	58	26	16	−14
Farnborough U.D.	17	65	18	26	30	50	20	12	−14
Fleet U.D.	24	53	23	14	35	51	14	22	+8
Hartley Wintney R.D.	16	57	27	10	30	48	22	12	+2
Hertfordshire									
Baldock	14	53	33	8	21	54	25	6	−2
Berkhamsted	25	49	26	14	35	48	17	22	+8
Bishop's Stortford	21	51	28	6	29	48	23	10	+4
Bushey	25	51	24	14	33	48	19	18	+4
Cheshunt	14	50	36	12	21	52	27	6	−6
Chorleywood	43	39	18	60	51	34	15	54	−6
Harpenden	31	49	20	26	47	41	12	46	+20
Hemel Hempstead	17	53	30	2	21	53	26	6	+4
Hertford M.B.	20	52	28	4	27	52	21	8	+4
Hitchin	20	53	27	6	24	54	22	6	=
Hoddesdon	19	47	34	10	28	45	27	12	+2

* This comparison is misleading, because there were major boundary changes between the two census dates.

(c) Outer Metropolitan Area (contd.)

	Census 1951 I+II III IV+V per cent			Degree of Deviance	Census 1966 I+II III IV+V per cent			Degree of Deviance	Change in Deviance 1951–1966
Letchworth	20	55	25	10	25	55	20	10	=
Potter's Bar	30	50	20	24	36	48	16	24	=
Rickmansworth	25	48	27	14	34	49	17	20	+6
Royston	27	55	18	24	23	57	20	12	−12
St. Albans M.B.	23	52	25	10	28	51	21	8	−2
Sawbridgeworth	23	49	28	10	36	43	21	24	+14
Stevenage	20	52	28	4	21	54	25	6	+2
Tring	20	49	31	6	25	48	27	6	=
Ware	15	48	37	14	24	49	27	4	−10
Watford	18	54	28	4	20	55	25	8	+4
Welwyn Garden City	23	50	27	10	30	49	21	12	+2
Berkhamstead R.D.	25	41	34	22	40	37	23	32	+10
Broughing R.D.	20	40	40	24	32	35	33	32	+8
Elstree R.D.	19	50	31	4	25	51	24	2	−2
Hatfield R.D.	22	50	28	8	28	51	21	8	=
Hemel Hempstead R.D.	20	51	29	4	32	45	23	16	+12
Hertford R.D.	20	42	38	20	35	39	26	24	+4
Hitchin R.D.	19	45	36	14	26	43	31	16	+2
St. Albans R.D.	18	50	32	4	30	49	21	12	+8
Ware R.D.	17	43	40	20	29	39	32	24	+4
Watford R.D.	22	51	27	8	24	53	23	4	−4
Welwyn R.D.	26	46	28	16	39	42	19	30	+14
Kent									
Chatham M.B.	13	52	35	10	15	53	32	18	+8
Dartford M.B.	16	53	31	4	19	57	24	12	+8
Gillingham M.B.	15	59	26	14	18	58	24	14	=
Gravesend M.B.	17	49	34	8	20	49	31	12	+4
Maidstone M.B.	17	53	30	2	21	53	26	6	+4
Northfleet U.D.	12	48	40	20	15	54	31	18	−2
Rochester M.B.	16	52	32	4	18	49	33	16	+12
Royal Tunbridge Wells M.B.	23	50	27	10	27	50	23	6	−4
Sevenoaks U.D.	29	48	23	22	42	39	19	36	+14
Southborough U.D.	21	50	29	6	22	58	20	14	+8
Swanscombe U.D.	10	46	44	28	10	57	33	28	=
Tonbridge U.D.	19	52	29	2	24	54	22	6	+4
Dartford R.D.	16	46	38	16	25	50	25	2	−14
Maidstone R.D.	20	39	41	26	29	44	27	14	−12
Malling R.D.	15	47	38	16	23	49	28	6	−10
Sevenoaks R.D.	23	43	34	18	35	40	25	22	+4
Strood R.D.	16	44	40	20	24	49	27	4	−16
Tonbridge R.D.	20	41	39	22	31	42	27	18	−4
Oxfordshire									
Henley-on-Thames M.B.	22	48	30	8	30	45	25	12	+4
Henley R.D.	21	43	36	18	34	41	25	20	+2
Surrey									
Banstead U.D.	36	44	20	36	43	42	15	38	+2
Caterham & Wallingham U.D.	25	52	23	14	41	43	16	34	+20
Chertsey U.D.	20	52	28	4	25	54	21	8	+4
Dorking U.D.	24	48	28	12	30	47	23	12	=
Egham U.D.	21	50	29	6	30	46	24	12	+6
Epsom & Ewell U.D.	31	48	21	26	43	42	15	38	+12
Esher U.D.	32	47	21	28	43	42	15	38	+10
Farnham U.D.	22	50	28	8	34	46	20	20	+12
Frimley & Camberley U.D.	20	59	21	18	34	46	20	20	+2
Godalming M.B.	19	53	28	4	27	49	24	6	+2
Guildford M.B.	22	52	26	8	28	50	22	8	=

(c) *Outer Metropolitan Area (contd.)*

	Census 1951 I+II III IV+V per cent			Degree of Deviance	Census 1966 I+II III IV+V per cent			Degree of Deviance	Change in Deviance 1951–1966
Surrey contd.									
Haslemere U.D.	27	46	27	18	38	45	17	28	+10
Leatherhead U.D.	30	46	24	24	41	41	18	34	+10
Reigate M.B.	22	51	27	8	29	49	22	10	+2
Walton & Weybridge U.D.	27	49	24	18	38	45	17	28	+10
Woking U.D.	22	52	26	8	35	45	20	22	+14
Bagshot R.D.	20	47	33	10	32	42	26	18	+8
Dorking & Horley R.D.	25	44	31	16	31	46	23	14	−2
Godstone R.D.	23	45	32	14	33	43	24	18	+4
Guildford R.D.	22	50	28	8	34	44	22	20	+12
Hambledon R.D.	22	43	35	18	35	39	26	24	+6
Staines U.D.	21	52	27	6	25	53	22	6	=
Sunbury on Thames U.D.	22	50	28	8	32	50	18	16	+8
Sussex East									
Burgess Hill U.D.	26	46	28	16	31	52	17	16	=
Cuckfield U.D.	22	53	25	10	40	43	17	32	+22
East Grinstead U.D.	20	49	31	6	35	43	22	22	+16
Cuckfield R.D.	23	43	34	18	35	38	27	26	+8
Uckfield R.D.	22	44	34	16	33	39	28	24	+8
Sussex West									
Horsham U.D.	20	52	28	4	29	51	20	10	+6
Horsham R.D.	21	43	36	18	31	40	29	22	+4
Crawley New Town	21	50	29	6	24	55	21	8	+2

Reference

1. See, e.g., *Sample Census 1966. Great Britain, Economic Activity Tables*, Part III, pp. xix–xxi.

Additional Tables for Chapter 9

ALAN LITTLE AND CHRISTINE MABEY

The following tables have been derived from Tables 9.11, 9.13, 9.17 and 9.19 and simply show the gain or loss in RQ of each group, when compared not with the ILEA mean score but with the appropriate mean for the group under discussion.

Children from professional backgrounds, partly because of their high mean scores, appear to do relatively badly unless in schools that are highly advantaged (group 4) and with a high percentage of middle-class pupils (25 per cent). Pupils from all other backgrounds do better in advantaged schools, although the relationship with middle-class concentration, say, is by no means consistent.

What is striking about these tables is the strong confirmation of the importance of E.P.A.: with the exception of the pupils from professional backgrounds, positive advantage, as far as RQ is concerned, appears to accrue from being in a school in group 4 (the least disadvantaged schools). It is not just that positive advantage compared with social class peers in other schools appears to accrue, but the size of the gains are fairly large.

Table A2.1 (From Table 9.11)

Divergence from Group Mean of Children of Different Socio-economic Backgrounds According to the Education Priority Ranking and Middle-class Composition of School Attended.

Non-manual in School (per cent)	Education Priority Rank			
	1	2	3	4
(a) Professional (106.7)				
≤10	−13.8	−5.6	−2.6	−7.0
10.1–25	−5.9	−5.2	−4.1	−2.1
25.1–50	−9.2	−0.6	−1.3	+2.1
>50	—	—	−4.6	+2.6
(b) Other non-manual (99.9)				
≤10	−6.8	−2.6	+0.9	+6.7
10.1–25	−7.5	−5.2	−1.0	+0.6
25.1–50	−4.4	−2.3	−2.6	+2.6
>50	−23.3	—	+0.4	+4.1
(c) Skilled manual (96.2)				
≤10	−6.0	−4.6	+0.4	+1.5
10.1–1.25	−5.8	−3.6	−0.1	+1.2
25.1–50	−3.2	−0.7	+0.2	+3.5
>50	—	—	+2 7	+4.0
(d) Semi-skilled manual (92.7)				
≤10	−3.7	−3.5	+0.4	+2.6
10.1–25	−4.3	−2.0	+0.1	+1.2
25.1–50	−1.4	+2.2	+0.2	+2.9
>50	—	—	+3.5	+1.9
(e) Unskilled manual (89.5)				
≤10	−4.0	−2.8	+0.2	+7.1
10.1–25	−4.8	−2.8	+0.6	+1.4
25.1–50	−2.5	−1.5	+0.2	+5.5
>50	—	—	+2.2	+2.3

Table A2.2 (From Table 9.13)

Divergence from Group Mean of Children of Different Socio-economic Backgrounds According to Education Priority Rank and Lower Working-class Composition of School Attended

Lower Working-Class in School (per cent)	Education Priority Rank 1	2	3	4
	(a) Professional (106.7)			
≤20	—	+6.0	−3.6	+2.8
20.1–30	−3.4	−7.7	−2.9	+2.4
30.1–50	−9.8	−3.0	−3.8	−0.6
>50	−6.8	−4.8	−0.9	−2.4
	(b) Other non-manual (99.9)			
≤20	−16.8	−1.0	+0.6	+3.9
20.1–30	−12.5	−3.2	−1.2	+1.5
30.1–50	−7.2	−3.2	−1.6	+2.6
>50	−5.8	−5.3	−0.2	+2.2
	(c) Skilled manual (96.2)			
≤20	−6.4	+3.7	+1.3	+3.9
20.1–30	−8.4	−6.5	−1.0	+2.1
30.1–50	−5.9	−2.6	+0.5	+2.4
>50	−4.5	−4.3	−0.4	+1.8
	(d) Semi-skilled manual (92.7)			
≤20	+2.2	+4.3	+3.5	+2.2
20.1–30	−12.2	−3.2	−1.3	+2.8
30.1–50	−3.4	−1.9	+0.6	+1.8
>50	−3.9	−2.4	−0.1	+2.0
	(e) Unskilled manual (89.5)			
≤20	—	—	−0.1	+5.4
20.1–30	−0.4	−4.0	−0.1	+2.2
30.1–50	−5.1	−1.1	+1.5	+5.0
>50	−4.2	−3.2	−0.6	+1.9

Table A2.3 (From Table 9.17)

Divergence from West Indian Mean Score of West Indians in Schools of Varying Immigrant Concentration and Education Priority Rank

Immigrants (per cent)	Education Priority Rank			
	1	2	3	4
West Indians (87.3)				
≤10	−2.2	−1.7	+0.2	+2.6
10.1–30	−0.8	−1.2	+0.4	+3.4
30.1–50	−2.8	−1.1	+0.9	+1.4
>50	−3.0	+0.5	+3.6	—

Table A2.4 (From Table 9.19)

Divergence From 'Other' Immigrants' Mean Score of 'Other' Immigrants in Schools of Varying Immigrant Concentration and Education Priority Rank

Immigrants (per cent)	Education Priority Rank			
	1	2	3	4
'Other' immigrants (92.9)				
<10	—	−3.1	−2.1	+4.7
10.1–30	−0.8	−2.2	—	+2.3
30.1–50	−10.3	+4.7	−3.5	+11.7
>50	−4.6	−0.9	+1.1	—

Index